STOP!

This is the back of the book.
You wouldn't want to spoil a great ending!

This book is printed "manga-style," in the authentic Japanese right-to-left format. Since none of the artwork has been flipped or altered, readers get to experience the story just as the creator intended. You've been asking for it, so TOKYOPOP® delivered: authentic, hot-off-the-press, and far more fun!

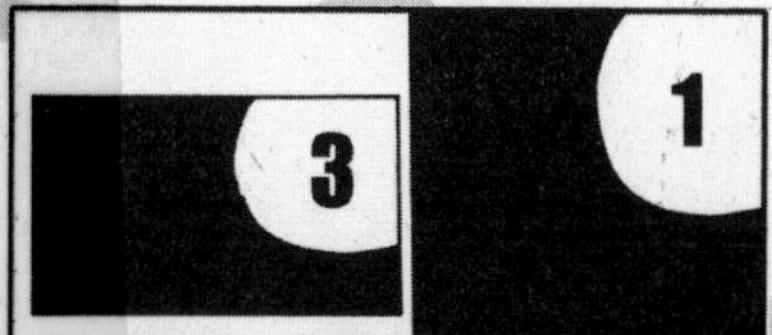
1
2
3
4
5
6
7
8
9
10

DIRECTIONS

If this is your first time reading manga-style, here's a quick guide to help you understand how it works.

It's easy... just start in the top right panel and follow the numbers. Have fun, and look for more 100% authentic manga from TOKYOPOP®!

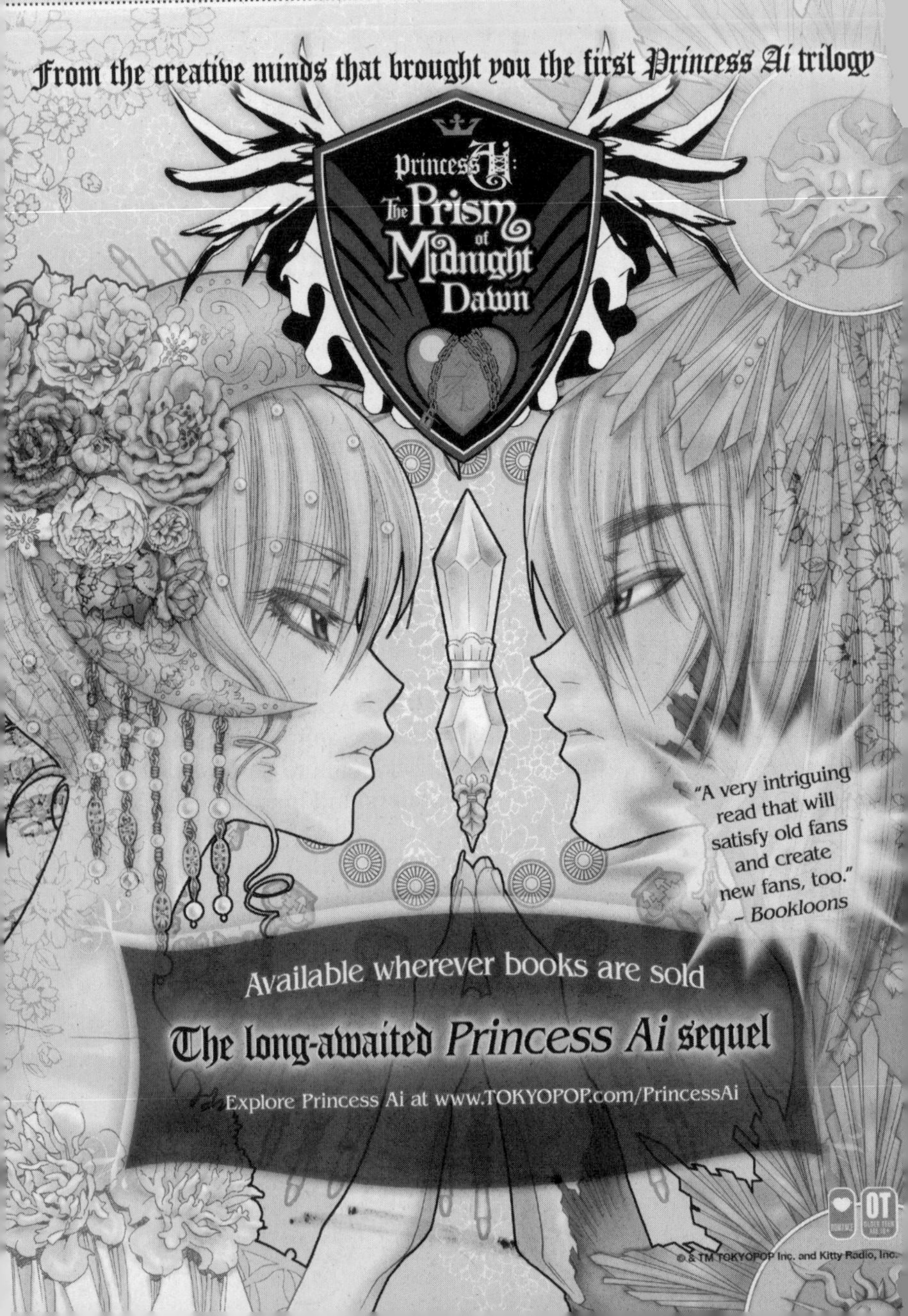
From the creative minds that brought you the first Princess Ai trilogy
Princess Ai: The Prism of Midnight Dawn
"A very intriguing read that will satisfy old fans and create new fans, too." – Bookloons
Available wherever books are sold
The long-awaited Princess Ai sequel
Explore Princess Ai at www.TOKYOPOP.com/PrincessAi
OT
© & TM TOKYOPOP Inc. and Kitty Radio, Inc.

NG LIFE™

FROM THE CREATOR OF *MUGEN SPIRAL* COMES A NEW LOOK AT ROMANCE—WITH A LITTLE GENDER-BENDING FROLIC AND FUN!

NG LIFE
FROM THE CREATOR OF MUGEN SPIRAL!
TOKYOPOP
Mizuho Kusanagi
1

Keidai Saeki is a high school student who remembers his past life... His friends around him are all also reincarnated—although they don't quite remember things the way he does. And Keidai's wife from the past? She's now a middle school boy—while his best male friend is now a cute girl?!

AVAILABLE NOW WHEREVER BOOKS ARE SOLD

ROMANCE

T TEEN AGE 13+

BE SURE TO VISIT WWW.TOKYOPOP.COM/SHOP FOR EVERYTHING YOU COULD EVER WANT!

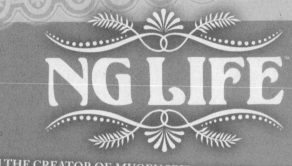

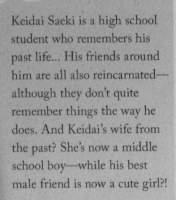

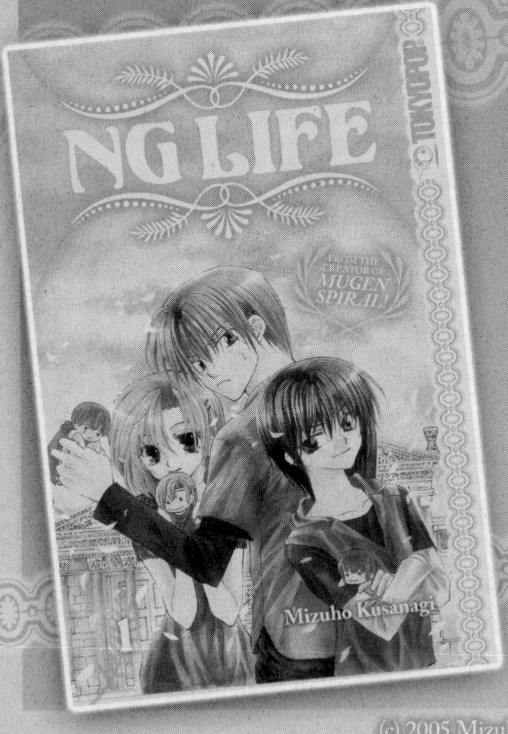

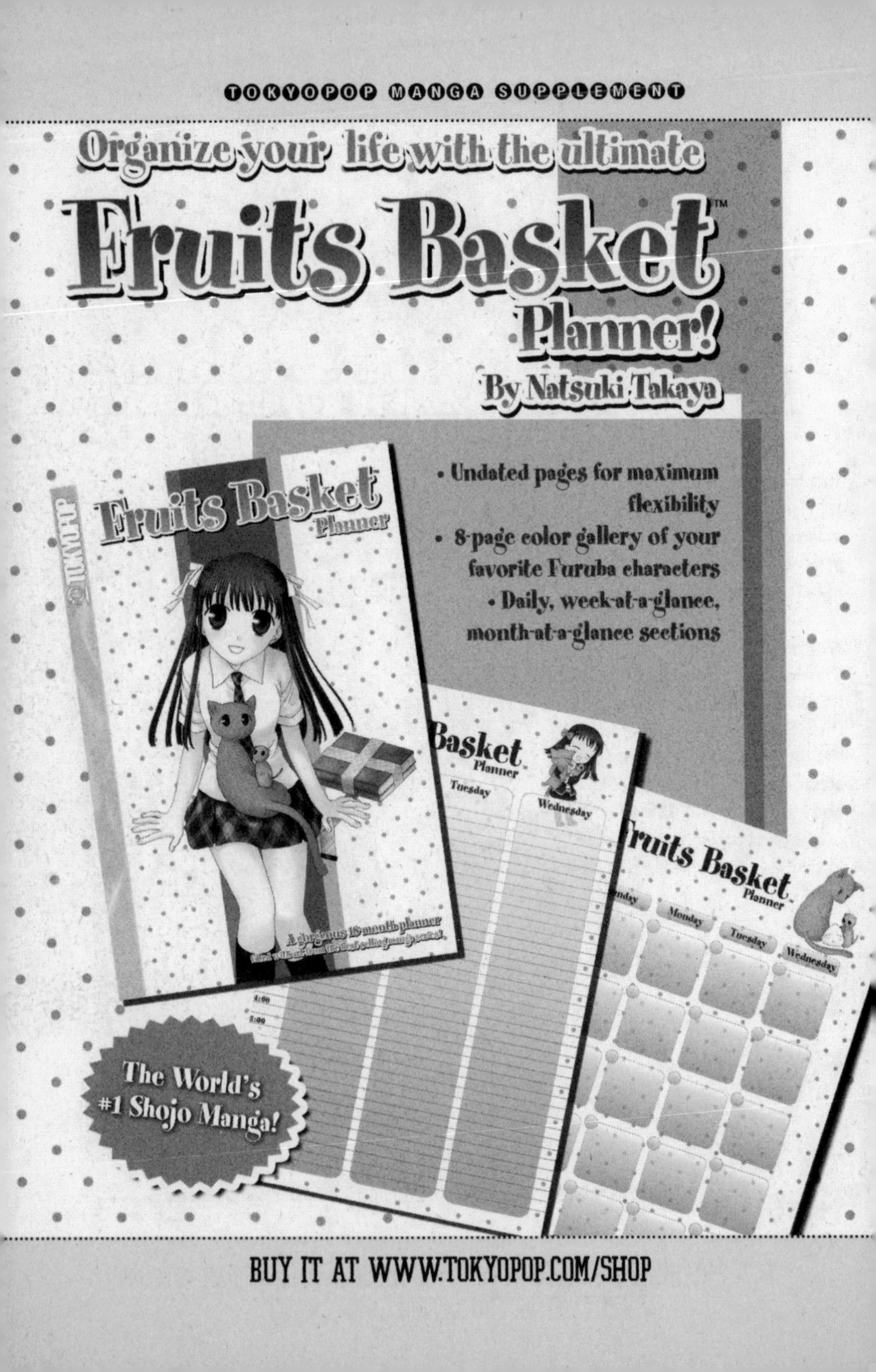

Organize your life with the ultimate
Fruits Basket™
Planner!
By Natsuki Takaya
• Undated pages for maximum flexibility
• 8-page color gallery of your favorite Furuba characters
• Daily, week-at-a-glance, month-at-a-glance sections
TOKYOPOP
Fruits Basket
Planner
A gorgeous 18-month planner
Basket
Planner
Tuesday
Wednesday
Fruits Basket
Planner
Monday
Tuesday
Wednesday
The World's #1 Shojo Manga!

BUY IT AT WWW.TOKYOPOP.COM/SHOP

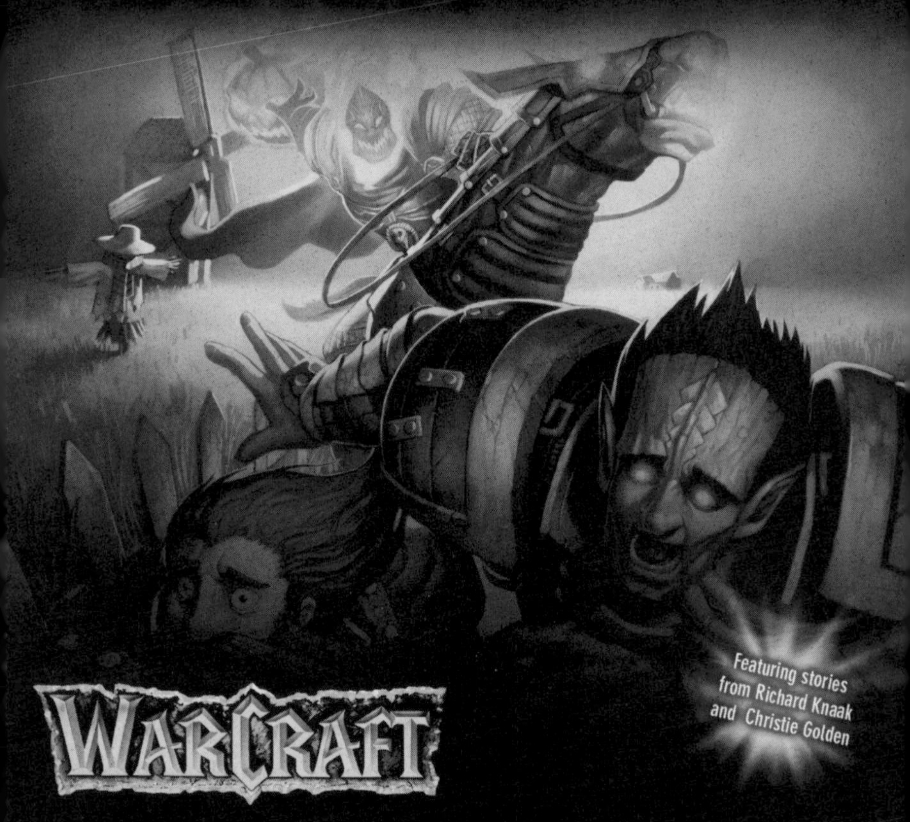
Featuring stories from Richard Knaak and Christie Golden
WARCRAFT

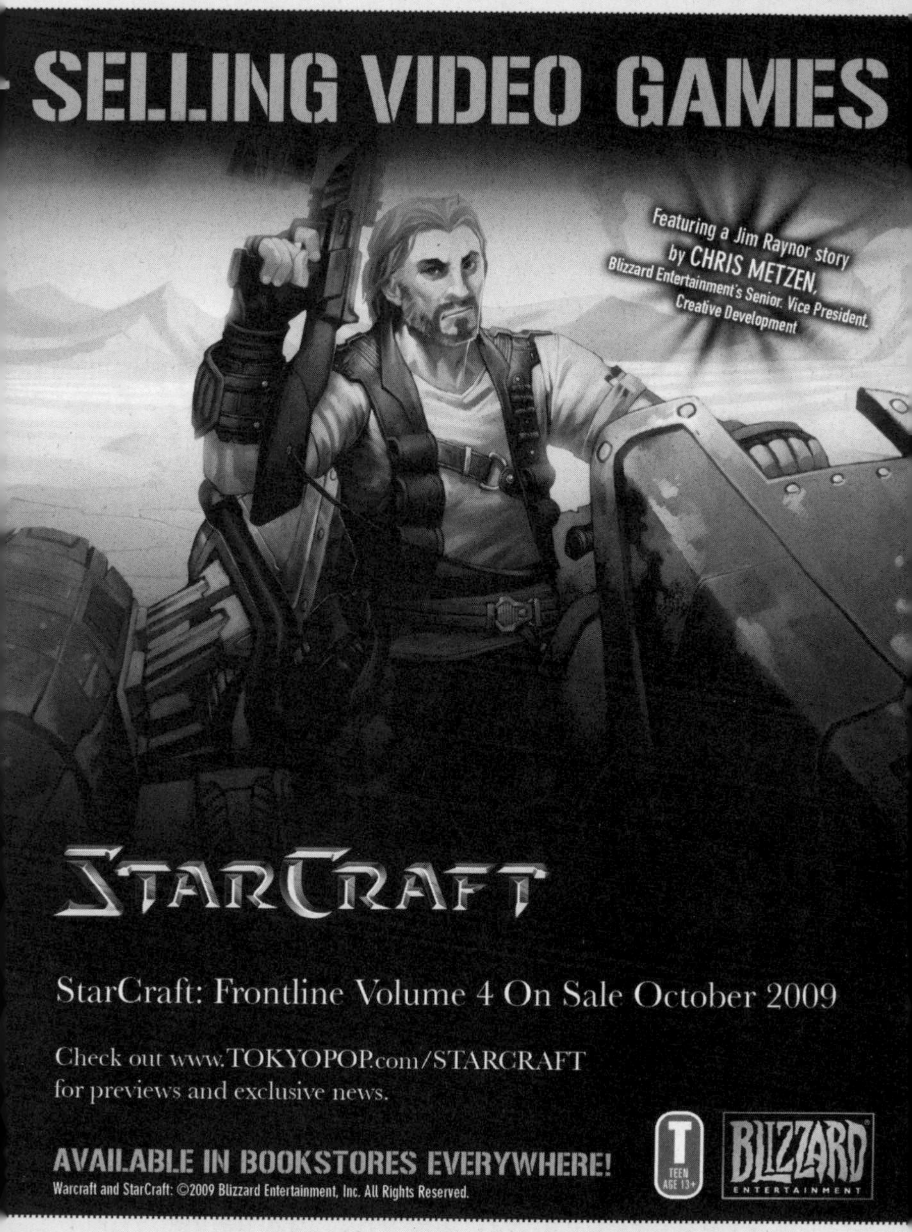
SELLING VIDEO GAMES
Featuring a Jim Raynor story
by CHRIS METZEN,
Blizzard Entertainment's Senior. Vice President,
Creative Development
STARCRAFT
StarCraft: Frontline Volume 4 On Sale October 2009
Check out www.TOKYOPOP.com/STARCRAFT
for previews and exclusive news.
AVAILABLE IN BOOKSTORES EVERYWHERE!
Warcraft and StarCraft: ©2009 Blizzard Entertainment, Inc. All Rights Reserved.
T
TEEN
AGE 13+
BLIZZARD
ENTERTAINMENT

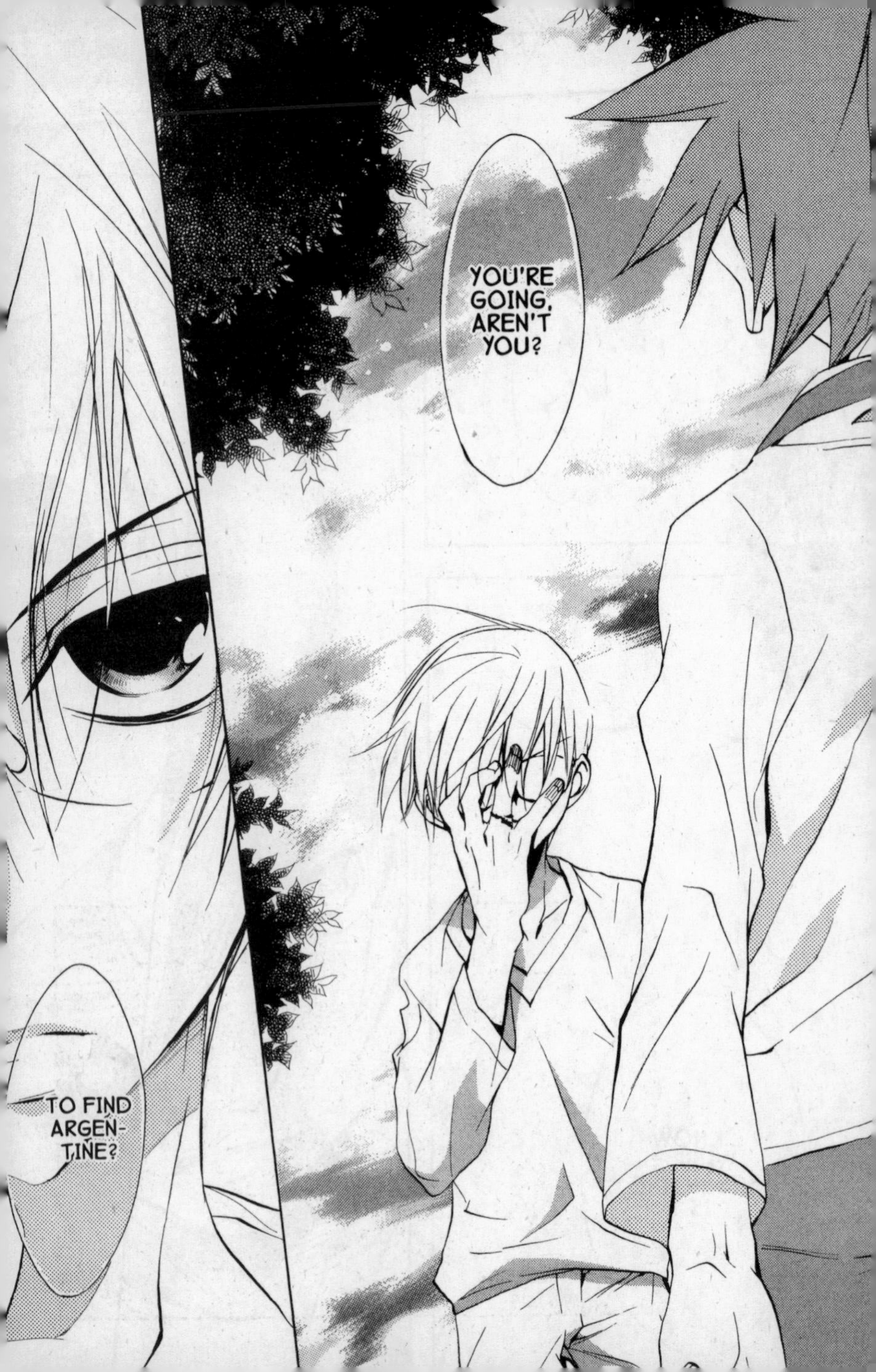
YOU'RE GOING, AREN'T YOU?
TO FIND ARGEN-TINE?

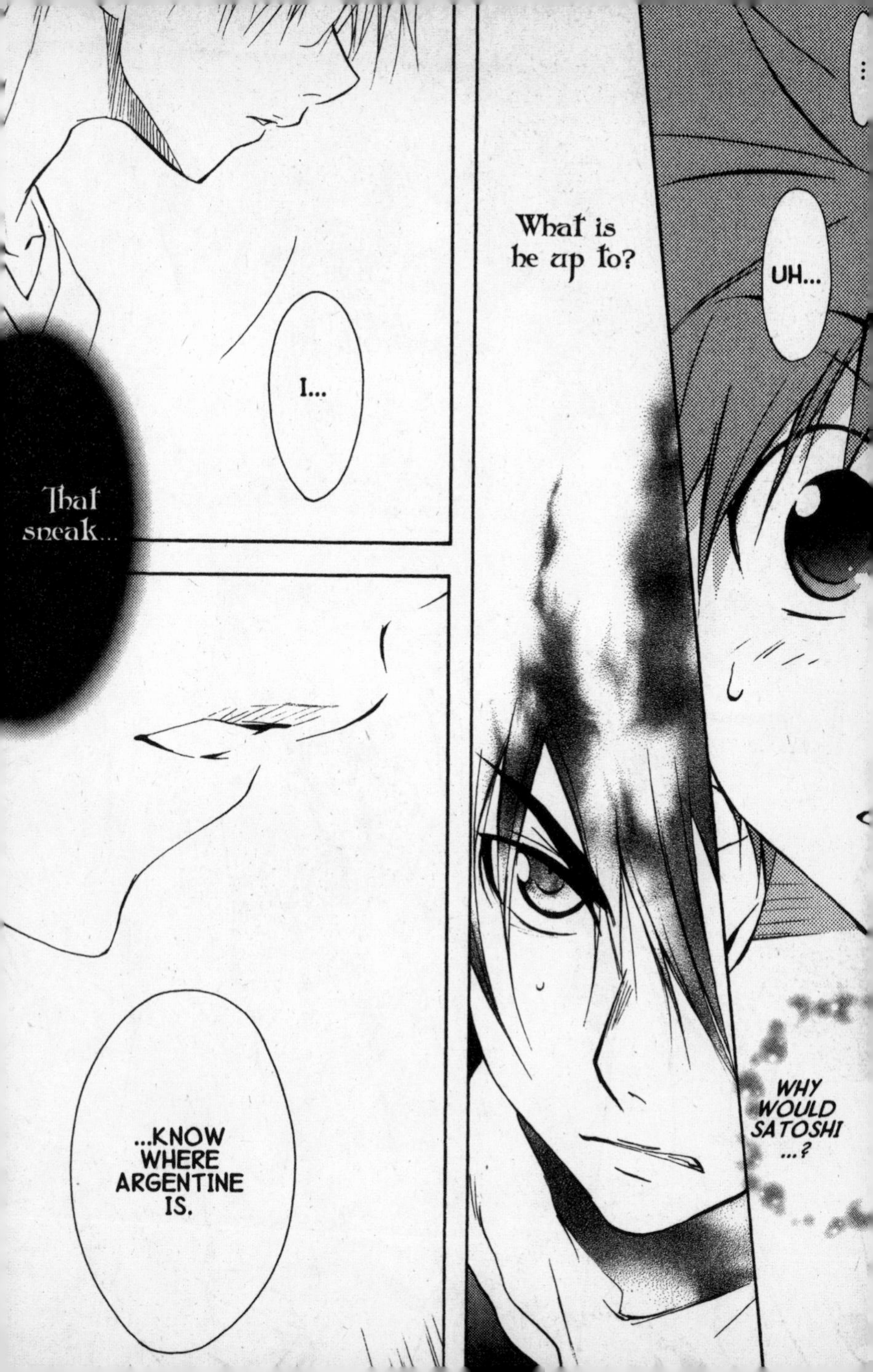
...
UH...
What is he up to?
WHY WOULD SATOSHI ...?
I...
That sneak...
...KNOW WHERE ARGENTINE IS.

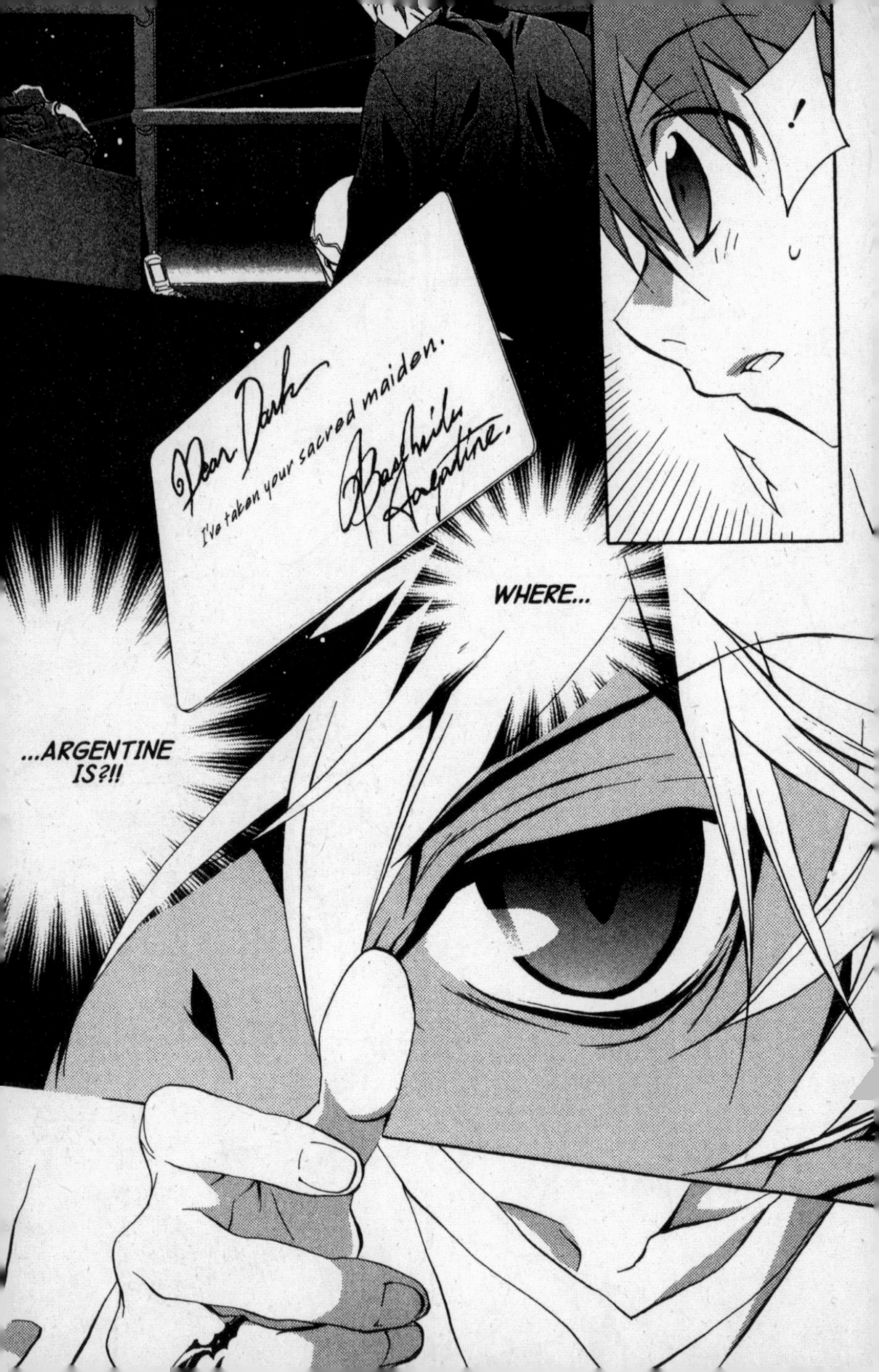
!
Dear Dark
I've taken your sacred maiden.
WHERE...
...ARGENTINE IS?!!

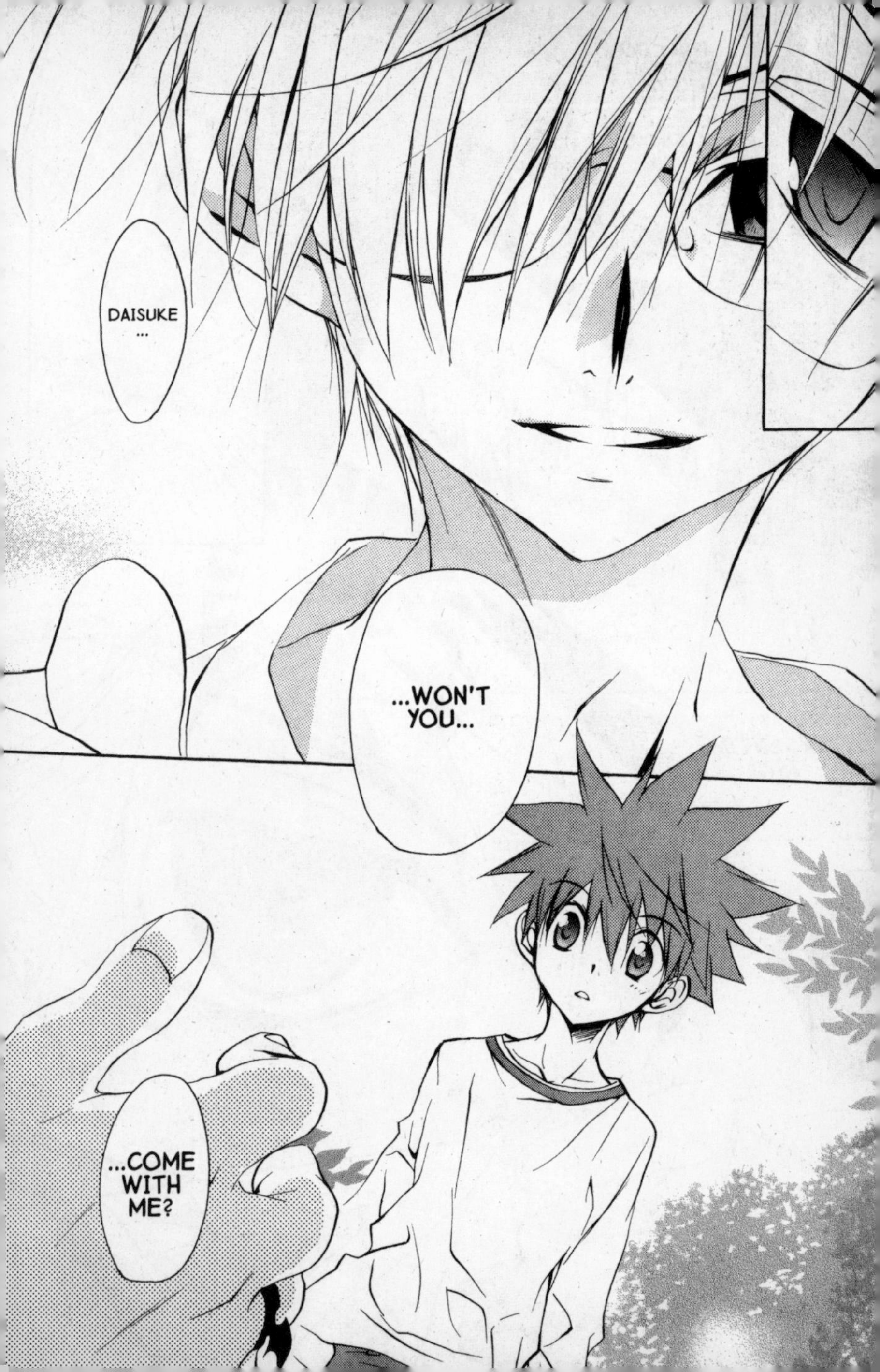
DAISUKE ...
...WON'T YOU...
...COME WITH ME?

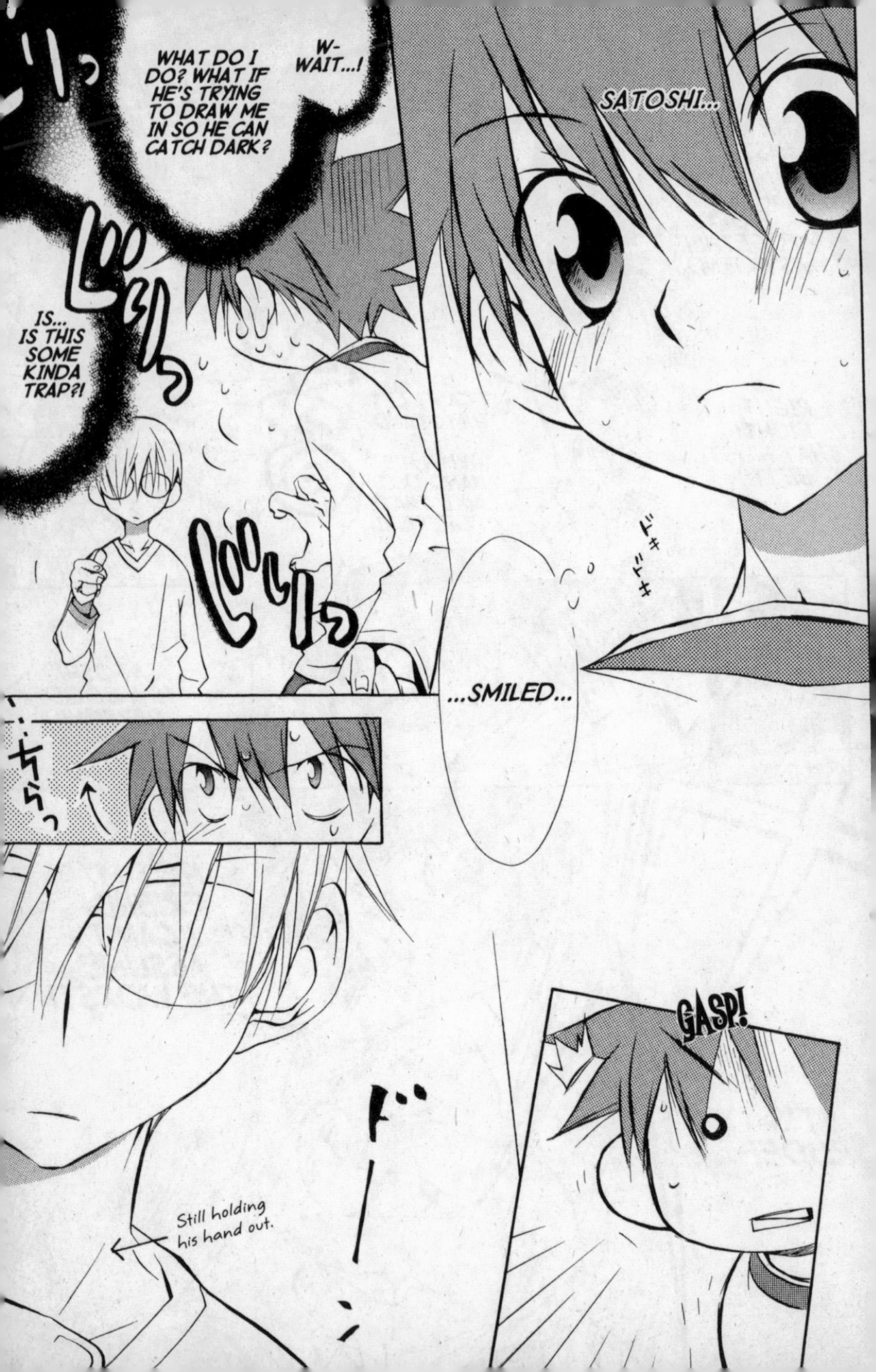
SATOSHI...
ドキドキ
...SMILED...
W-WAIT...!
WHAT DO I DO? WHAT IF HE'S TRYING TO DRAW ME IN SO HE CAN CATCH DARK?
IS... IS THIS SOME KINDA TRAP?!
GASP!
Still holding his hand out.

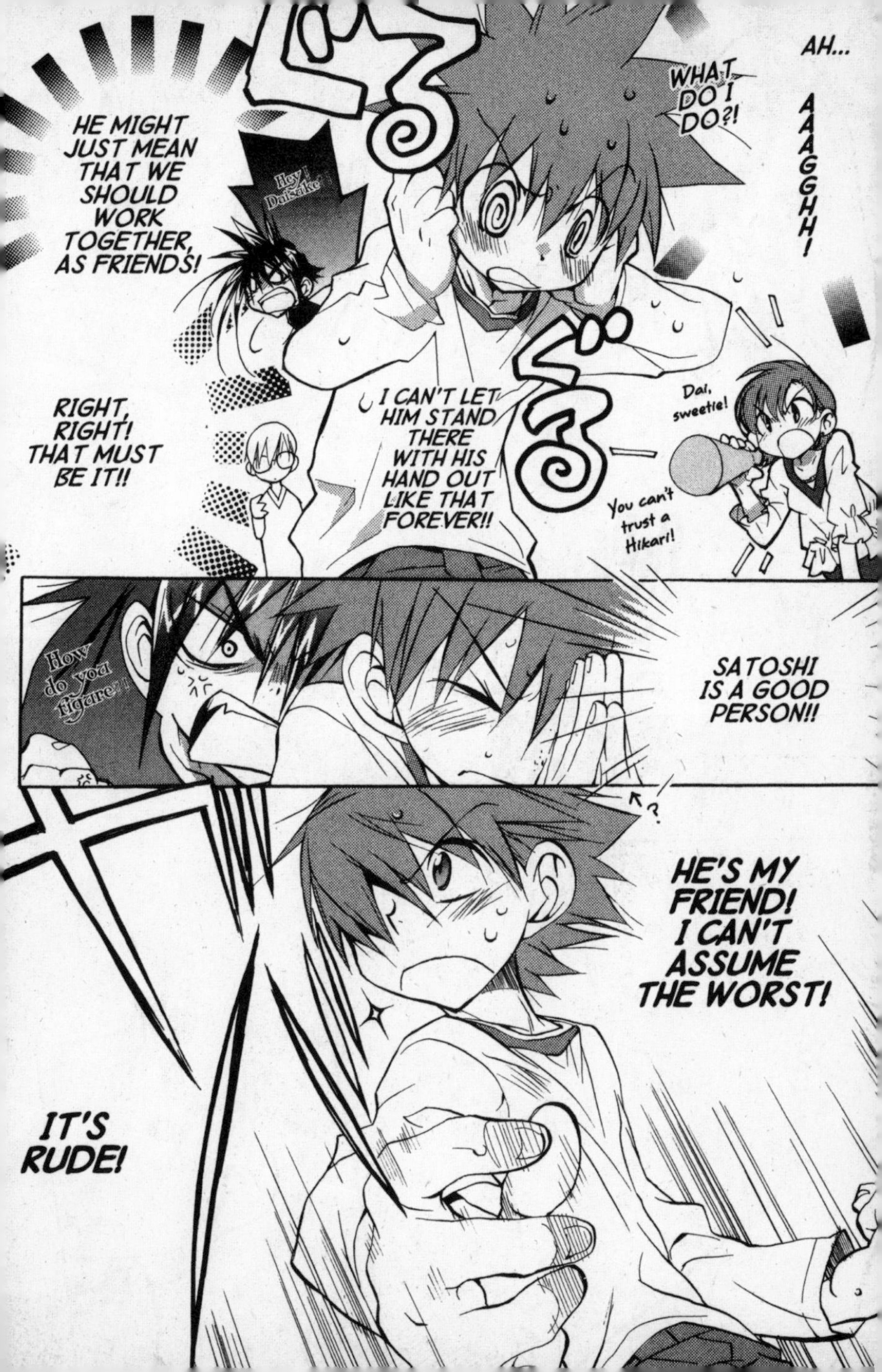

AH...
AAAAGGHH!
WHAT DO I DO?!
ぐる
ぐる
Dai, sweetie!
You can't trust a Hikari!
I CAN'T LET HIM STAND THERE WITH HIS HAND OUT LIKE THAT FOREVER!!
Hey! Daisuke!
HE MIGHT JUST MEAN THAT WE SHOULD WORK TOGETHER, AS FRIENDS!
RIGHT, RIGHT! THAT MUST BE IT!!
SATOSHI IS A GOOD PERSON!!
How do you figure?!
HE'S MY FRIEND! I CAN'T ASSUME THE WORST!
IT'S RUDE!

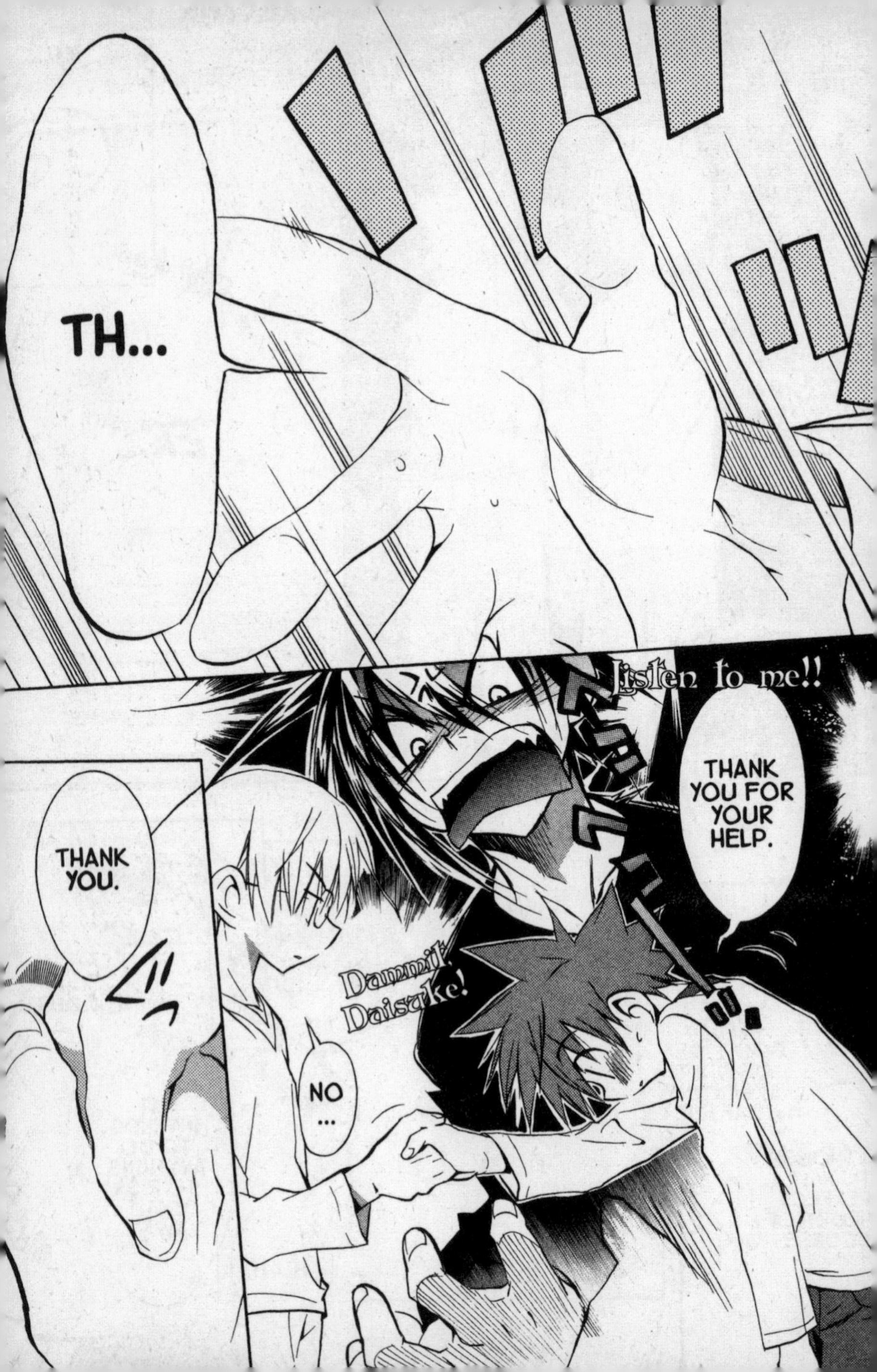
TH...
Listen to me!!
THANK YOU FOR YOUR HELP.
Dammit, Daisuke!
NO ...
THANK YOU.

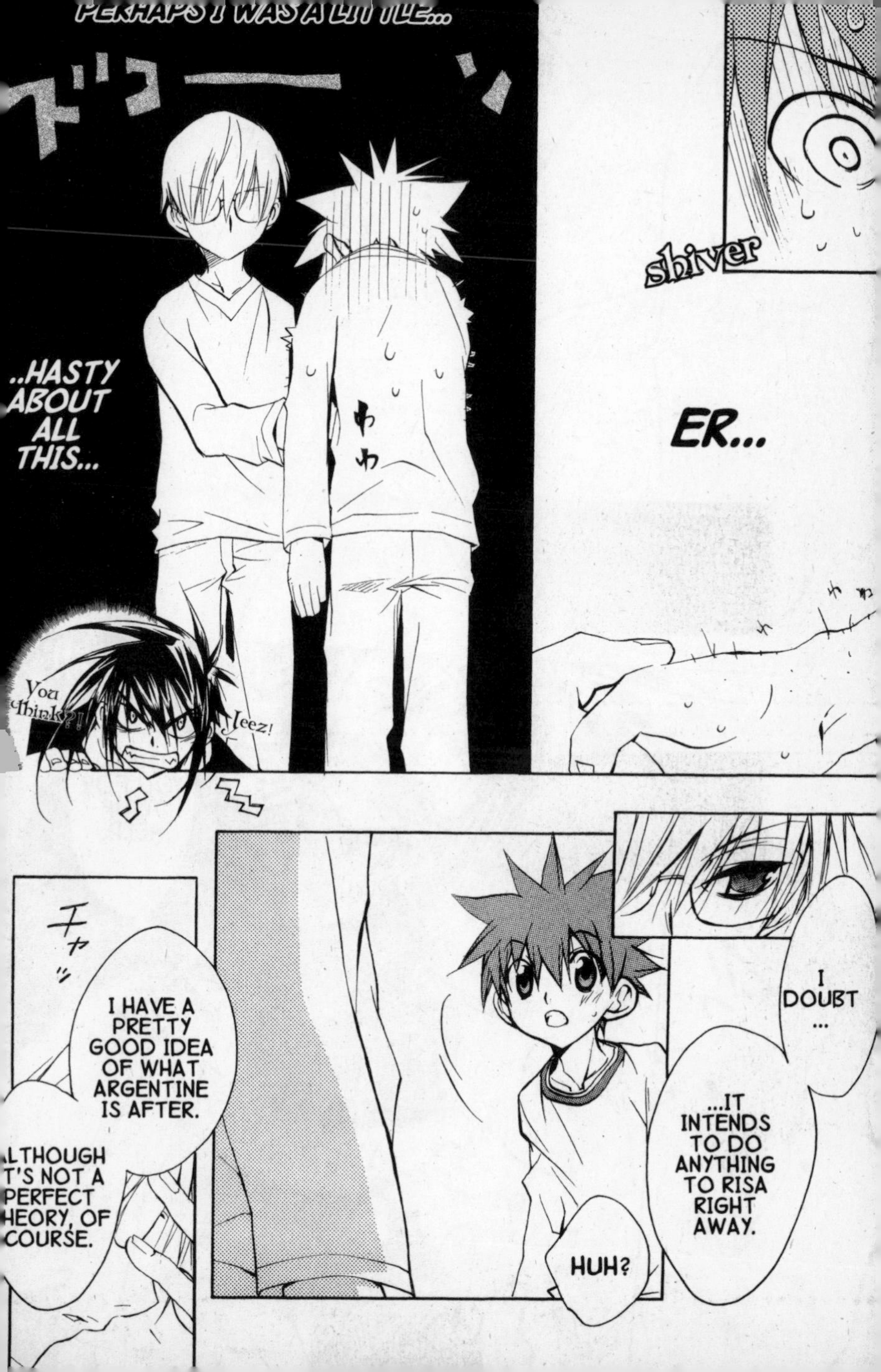

shiver
ER...
PERHAPS I WAS A LITTLE...
ズコーーン
..HASTY ABOUT ALL THIS...
わわ
You think?!
Jeez!
I DOUBT...
...IT INTENDS TO DO ANYTHING TO RISA RIGHT AWAY.
HUH?
チャッ
I HAVE A PRETTY GOOD IDEA OF WHAT ARGENTINE IS AFTER.
LTHOUGH T'S NOT A PERFECT HEORY, OF COURSE.

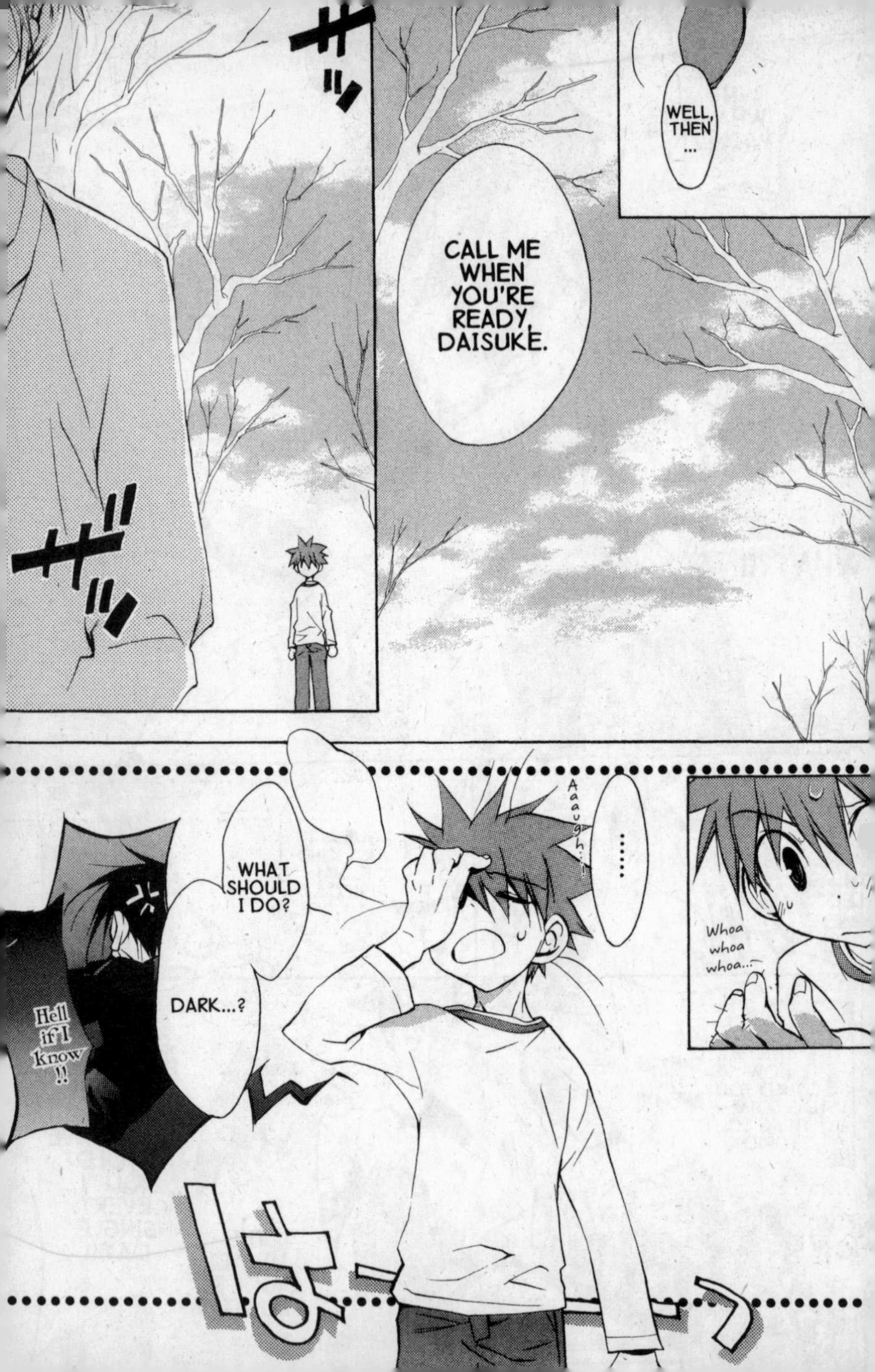
WELL, THEN...
CALL ME WHEN YOU'RE READY, DAISUKE.
ガッ
ザッ
Whoa whoa whoa...
......
Aaaugh...!
WHAT SHOULD I DO?
DARK...?
Hell if I know!!
はーっ

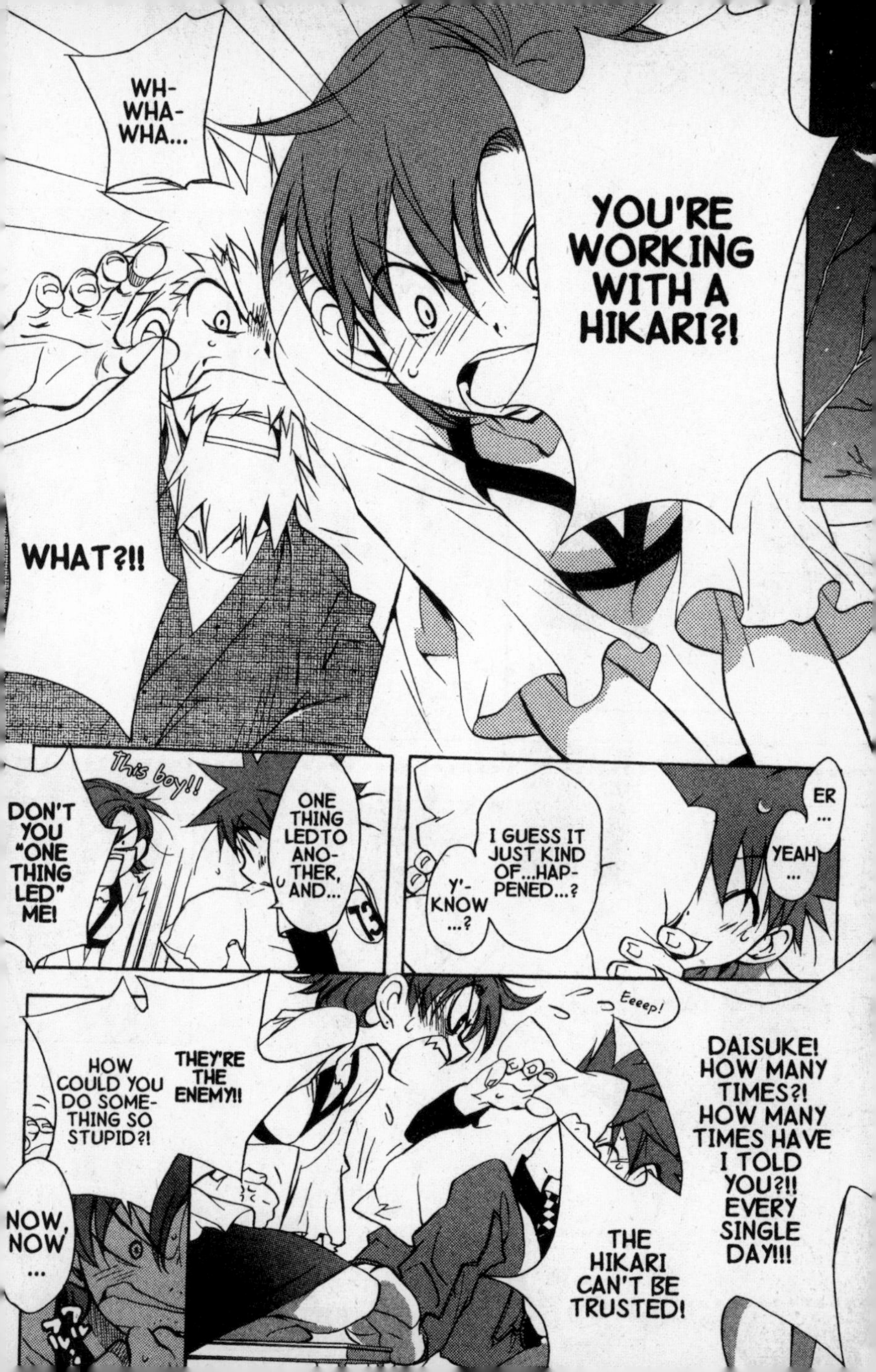
YOU'RE WORKING WITH A HIKARI?!
WH- WHA- WHA...
WHAT?!!
ER... YEAH...
I GUESS IT JUST KIND OF...HAP-PENED...?
Y'-KNOW...?
ONE THING LED TO ANO-THER, AND...
This boy!!
DON'T YOU "ONE THING LED" ME!
Eeeep!
DAISUKE! HOW MANY TIMES?! HOW MANY TIMES HAVE I TOLD YOU?!! EVERY SINGLE DAY!!!
THEY'RE THE ENEMY!!
HOW COULD YOU DO SOME-THING SO STUPID?!
THE HIKARI CAN'T BE TRUSTED!
NOW, NOW...

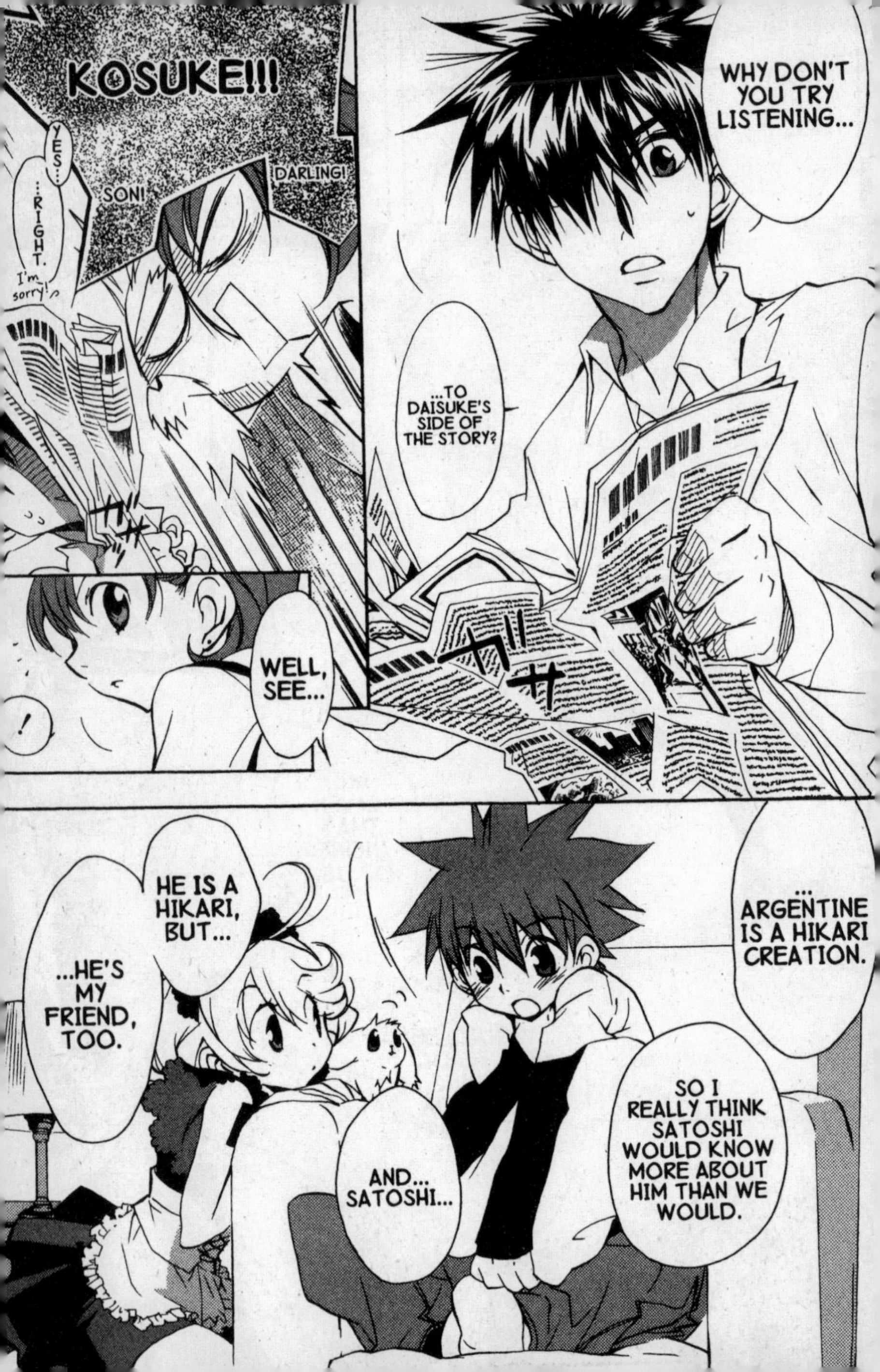
WHY DON'T YOU TRY LISTENING...
...TO DAISUKE'S SIDE OF THE STORY?
KOSUKE!!!
DARLING!
SON!
YES...
...RIGHT.
I'm sorry!
WELL, SEE...
...ARGENTINE IS A HIKARI CREATION.
SO I REALLY THINK SATOSHI WOULD KNOW MORE ABOUT HIM THAN WE WOULD.
AND... SATOSHI...
HE IS A HIKARI, BUT...
...HE'S MY FRIEND, TOO.

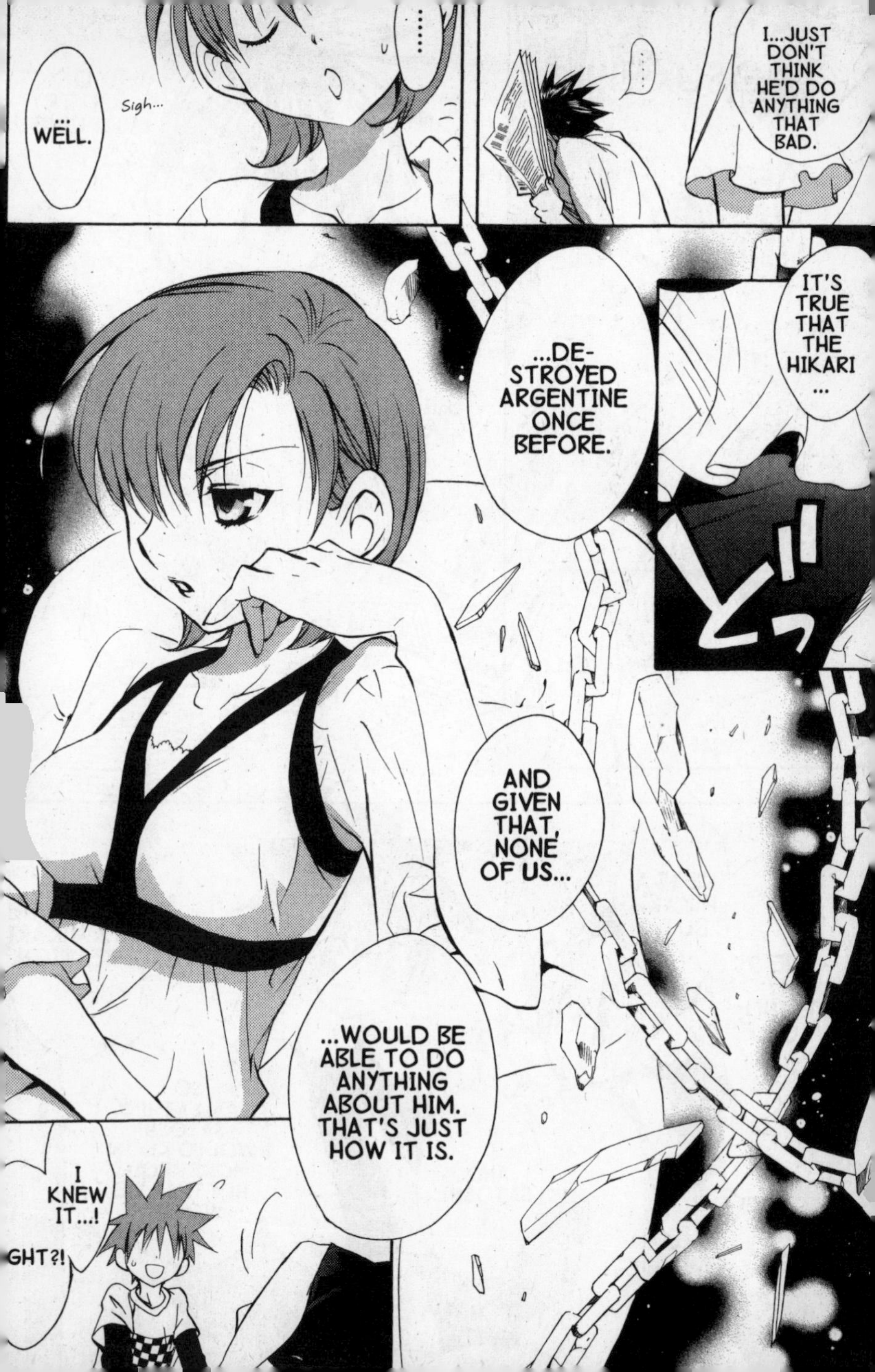
I...JUST DON'T THINK HE'D DO ANYTHING THAT BAD.
...
......
Sigh...
...WELL.
IT'S TRUE THAT THE HIKARI ...
どっ
...DE-STROYED ARGENTINE ONCE BEFORE.
AND GIVEN THAT, NONE OF US...
...WOULD BE ABLE TO DO ANYTHING ABOUT HIM. THAT'S JUST HOW IT IS.
I KNEW IT...!
GHT?!

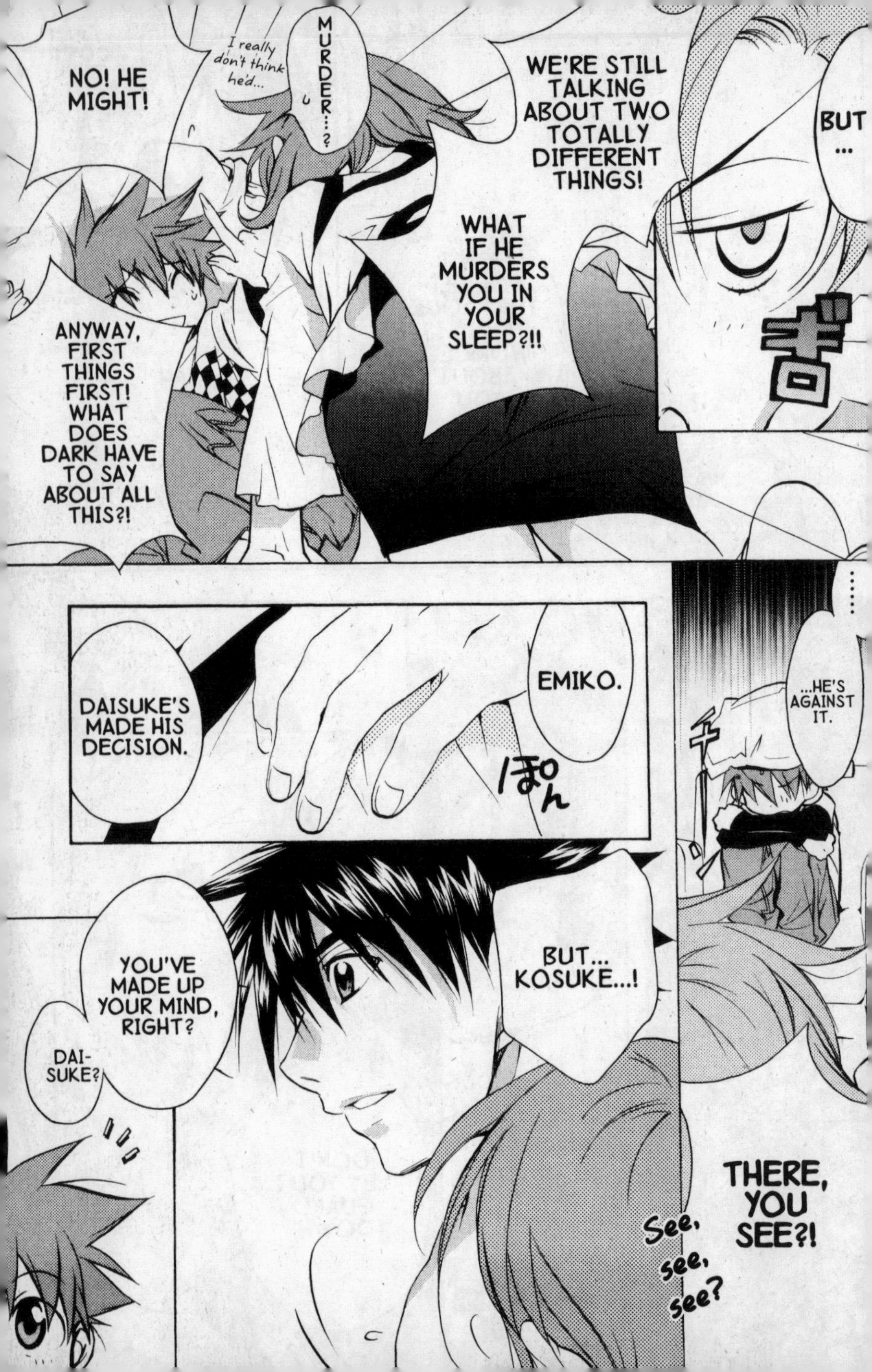
BUT ...
WE'RE STILL TALKING ABOUT TWO TOTALLY DIFFERENT THINGS!
MURDER...?
I really don't think he'd...
NO! HE MIGHT!
WHAT IF HE MURDERS YOU IN YOUR SLEEP?!!
ANYWAY, FIRST THINGS FIRST! WHAT DOES DARK HAVE TO SAY ABOUT ALL THIS?!
......
...HE'S AGAINST IT.
THERE, YOU SEE?!
See, see, see?
EMIKO.
ぽん
DAISUKE'S MADE HIS DECISION.
BUT... KOSUKE...!
YOU'VE MADE UP YOUR MIND, RIGHT?
DAI-SUKE?

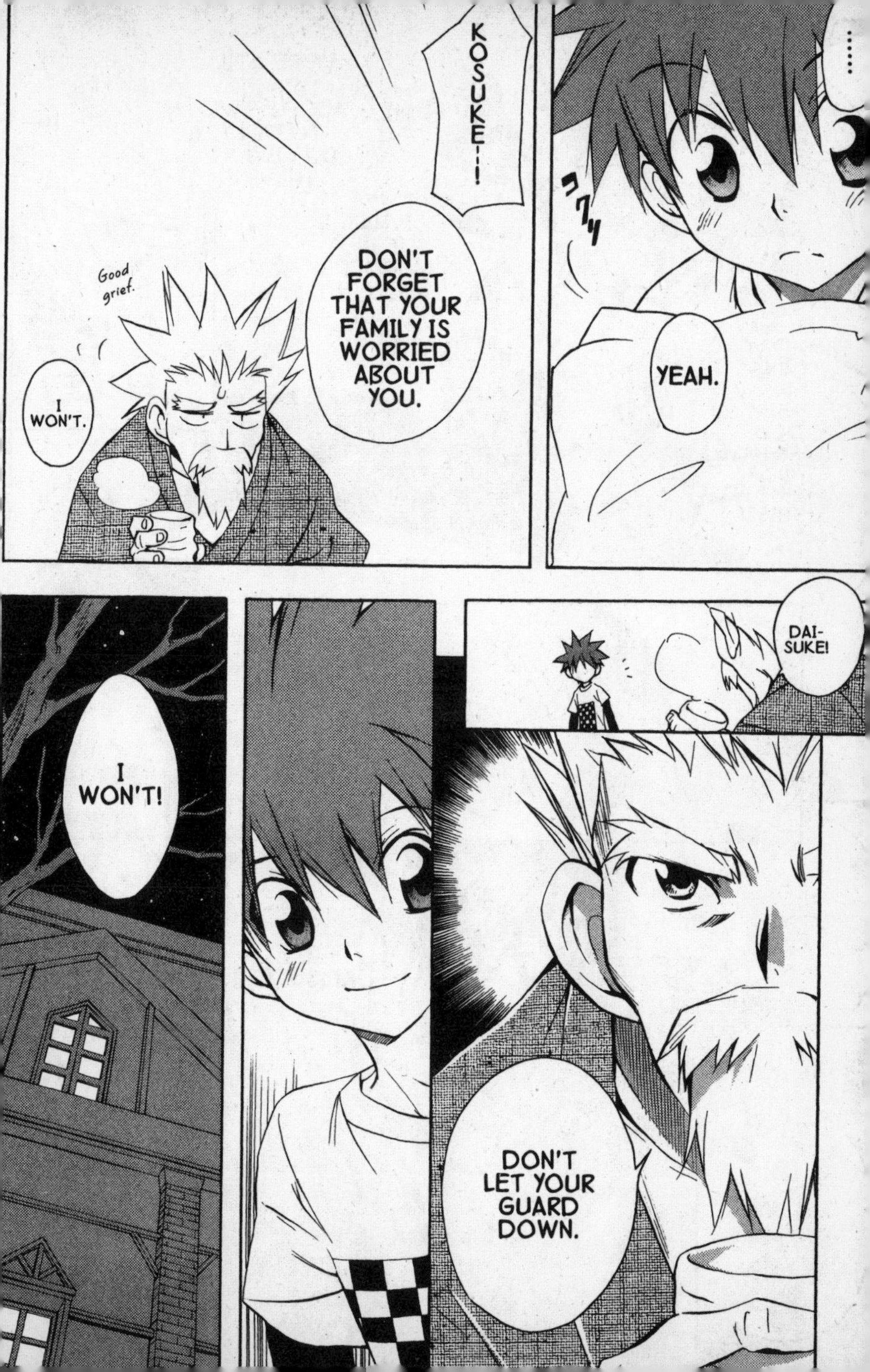
......
YEAH.
KOSUKE!!
DON'T FORGET THAT YOUR FAMILY IS WORRIED ABOUT YOU.
Good grief.
I WON'T.
DAI-SUKE!
DON'T LET YOUR GUARD DOWN.
I WON'T!

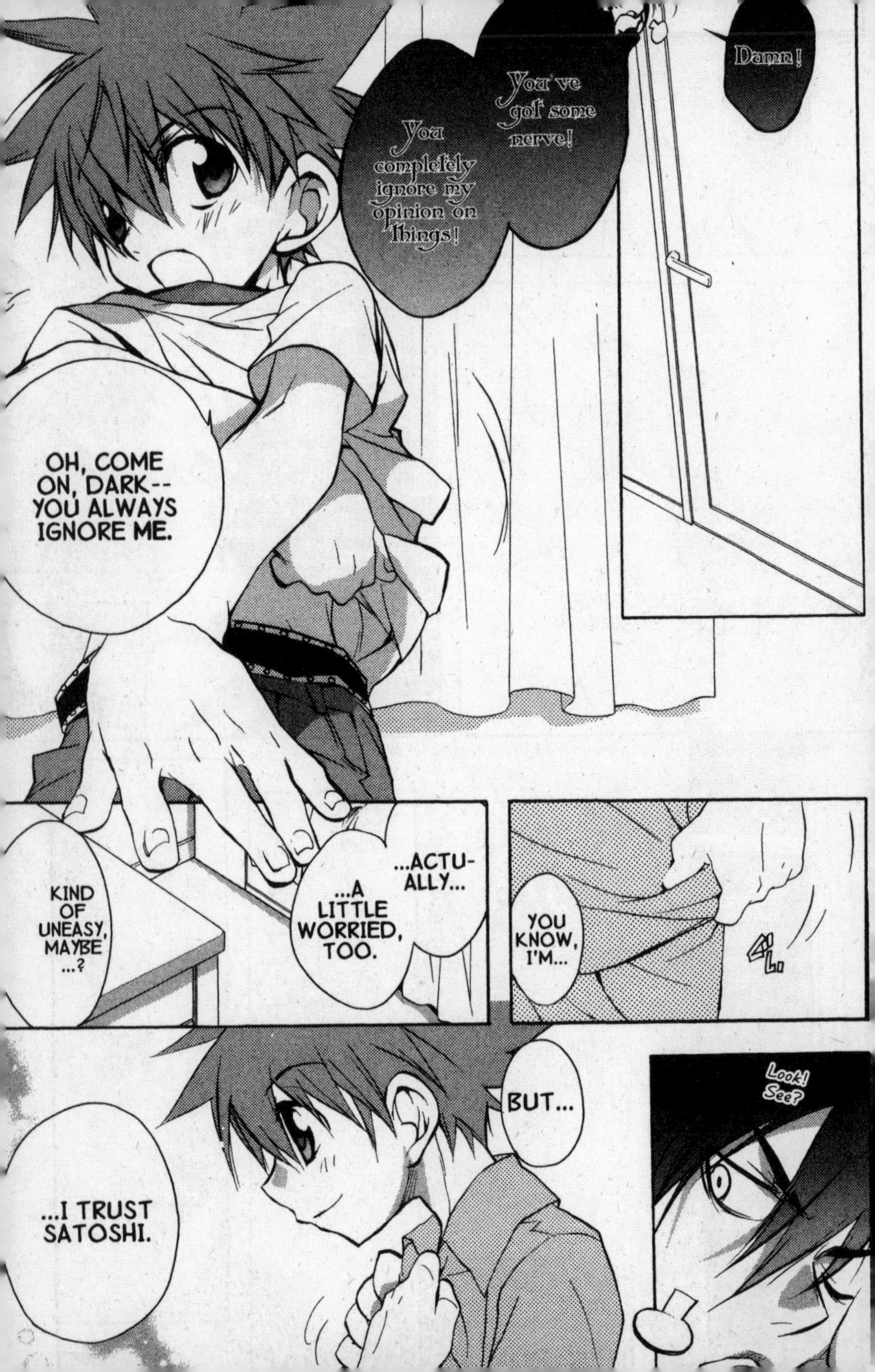
Damn!
You've got some nerve!
You completely ignore my opinion on things!
OH, COME ON, DARK-- YOU ALWAYS IGNORE ME.
YOU KNOW, I'M...
...ACTU- ALLY...
...A LITTLE WORRIED, TOO.
KIND OF UNEASY, MAYBE ...?
Look! See?
BUT...
...I TRUST SATOSHI.

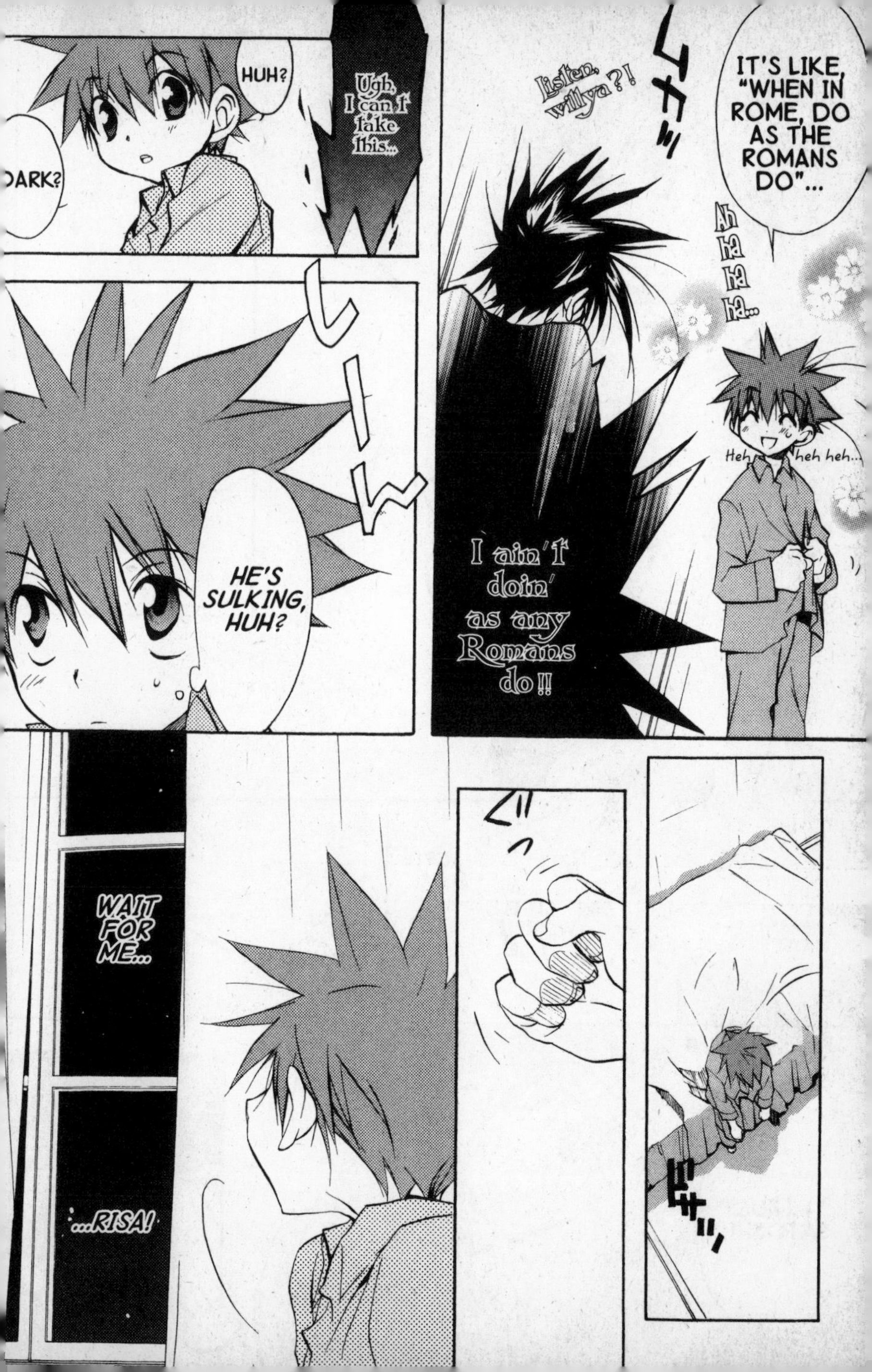
IT'S LIKE, "WHEN IN ROME, DO AS THE ROMANS DO"...
Ah ha ha ha...
Heh heh heh...
Listen, willya?!
I ain't doin' as any Romans do!!
HUH?
DARK?
Ugh, I can't take this...
HE'S SULKING, HUH?
WAIT FOR ME...
...RISA!

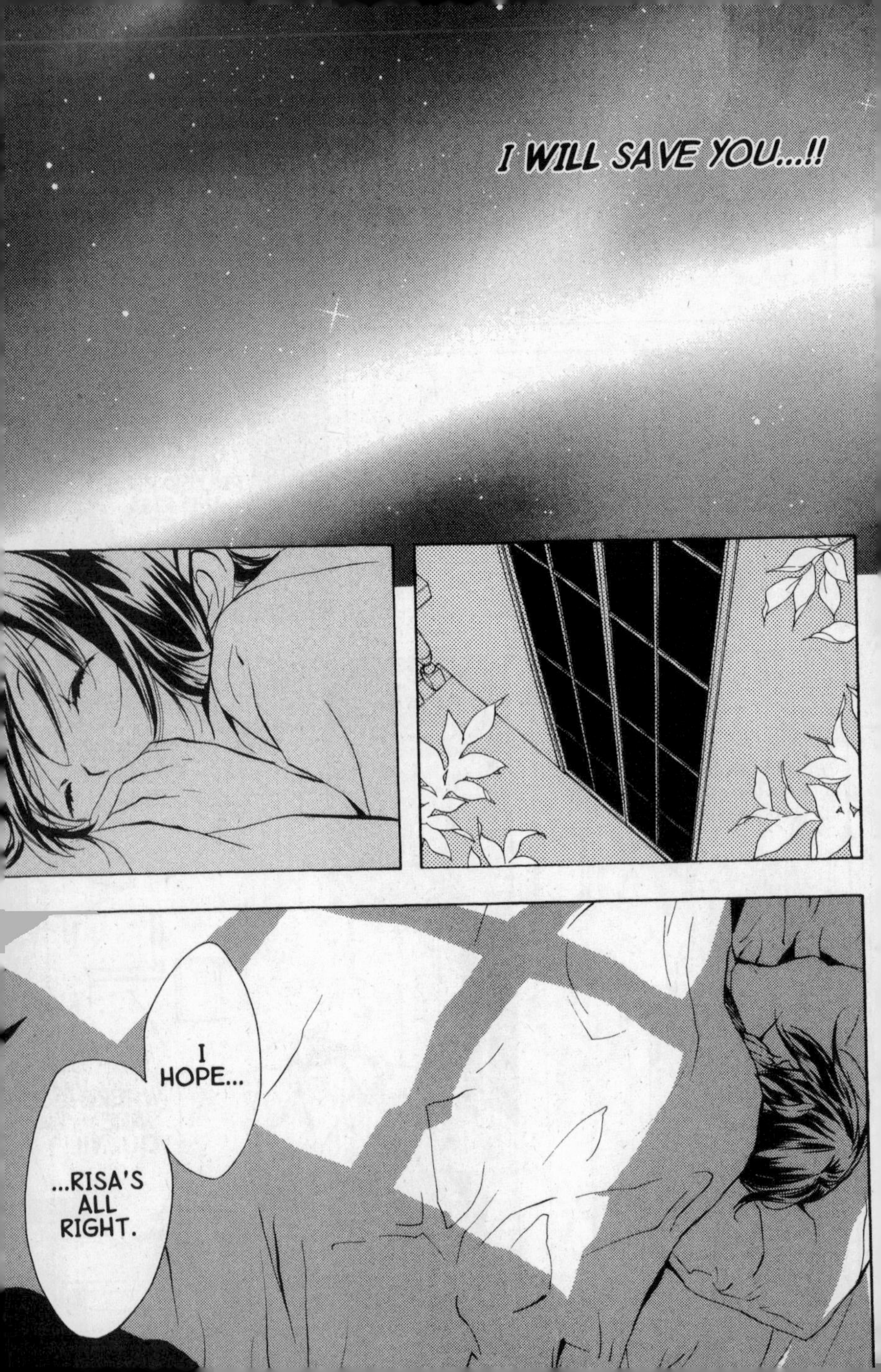
I WILL SAVE YOU...!!
I HOPE...
...RISA'S ALL RIGHT.

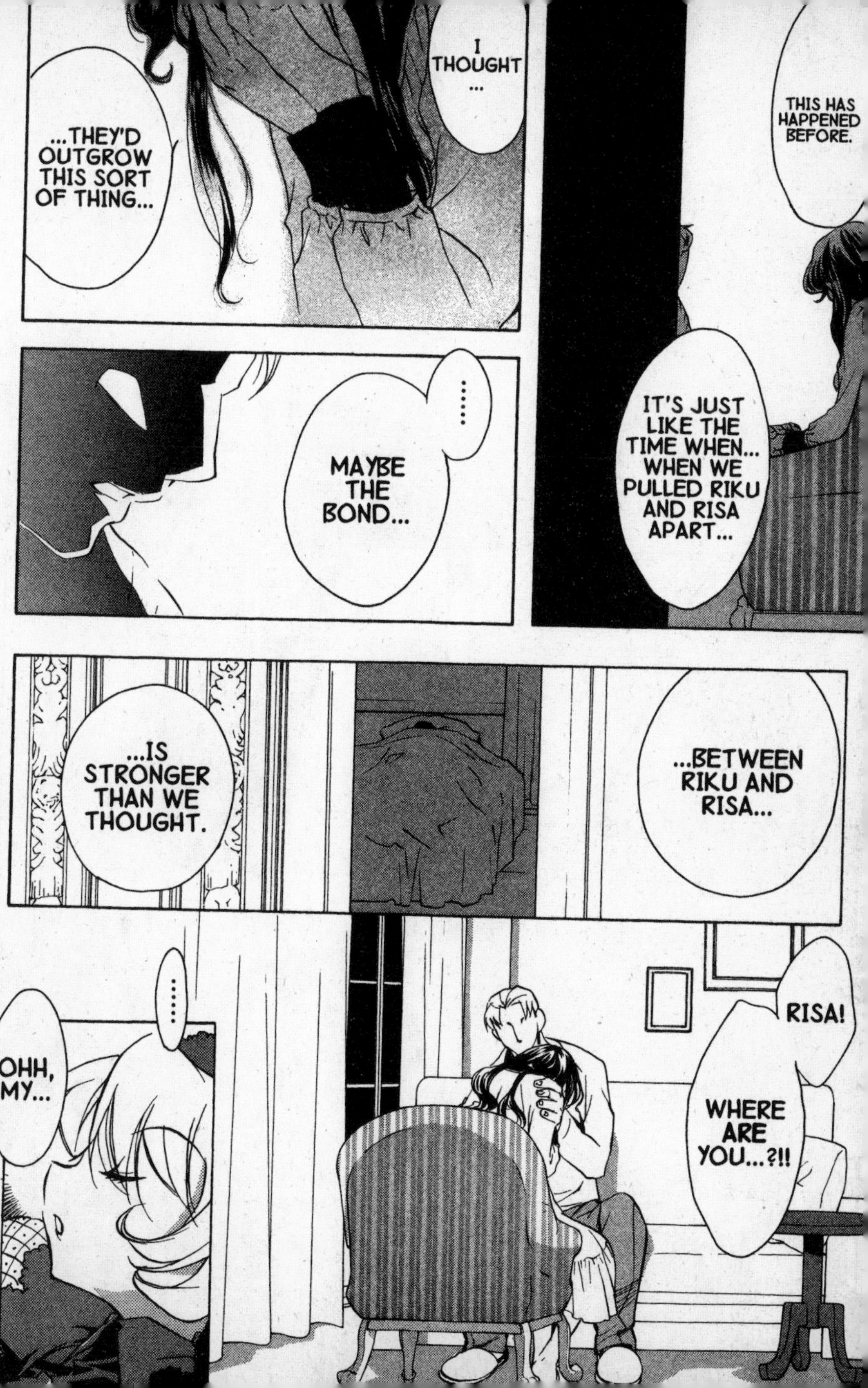
THIS HAS HAPPENED BEFORE.
IT'S JUST LIKE THE TIME WHEN... WHEN WE PULLED RIKU AND RISA APART...
I THOUGHT ...
...THEY'D OUTGROW THIS SORT OF THING...
......
MAYBE THE BOND...
...BETWEEN RIKU AND RISA...
...IS STRONGER THAN WE THOUGHT.
RISA!
WHERE ARE YOU...?!!
......
OHH, MY...

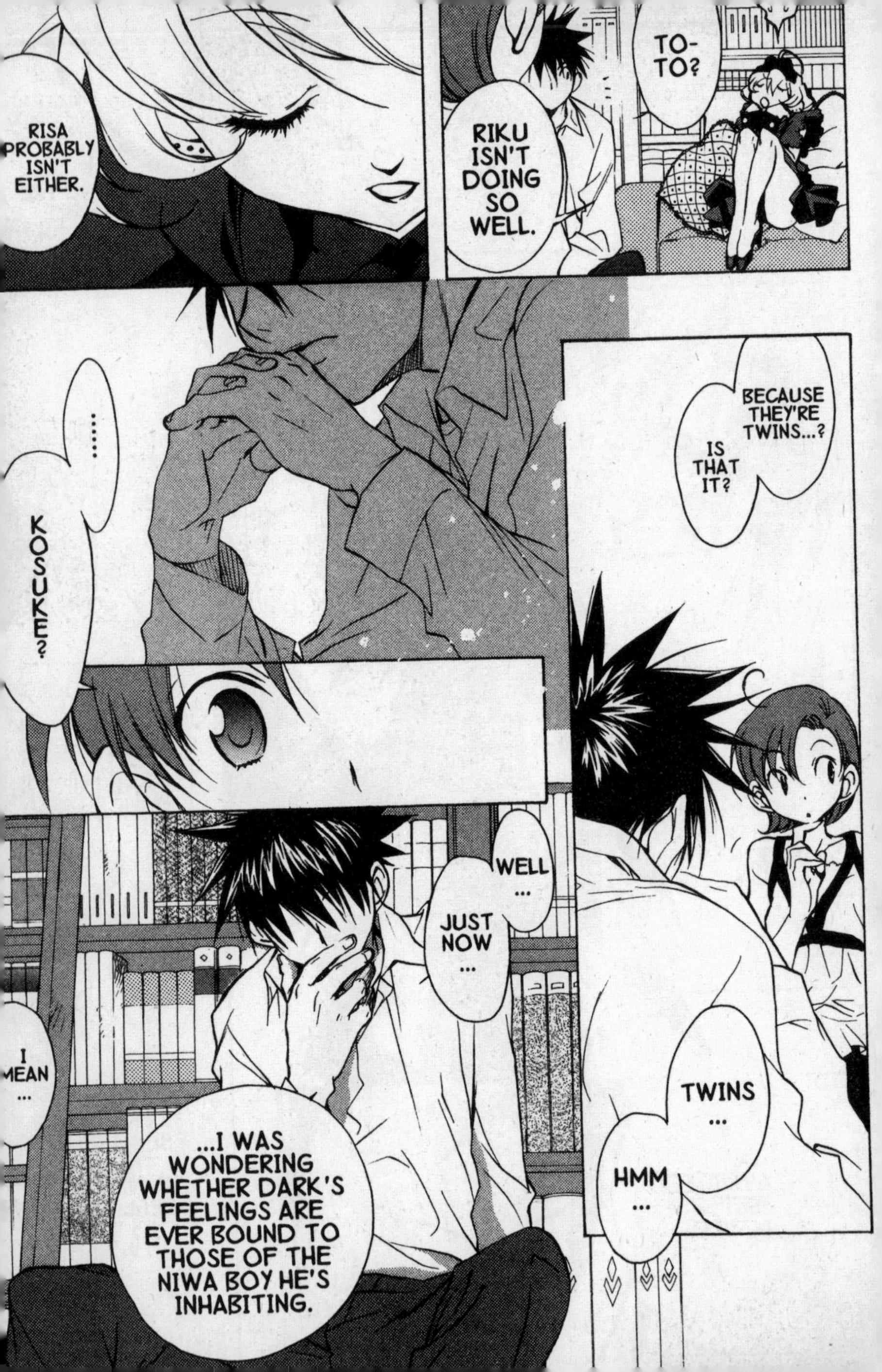
TO-TO?
RIKU ISN'T DOING SO WELL.
RISA PROBABLY ISN'T EITHER.
BECAUSE THEY'RE TWINS...?
IS THAT IT?
TWINS ...
HMM ...
......
KOSUKE?
WELL ...
JUST NOW ...
I MEAN ...
...I WAS WONDERING WHETHER DARK'S FEELINGS ARE EVER BOUND TO THOSE OF THE NIWA BOY HE'S INHABITING.

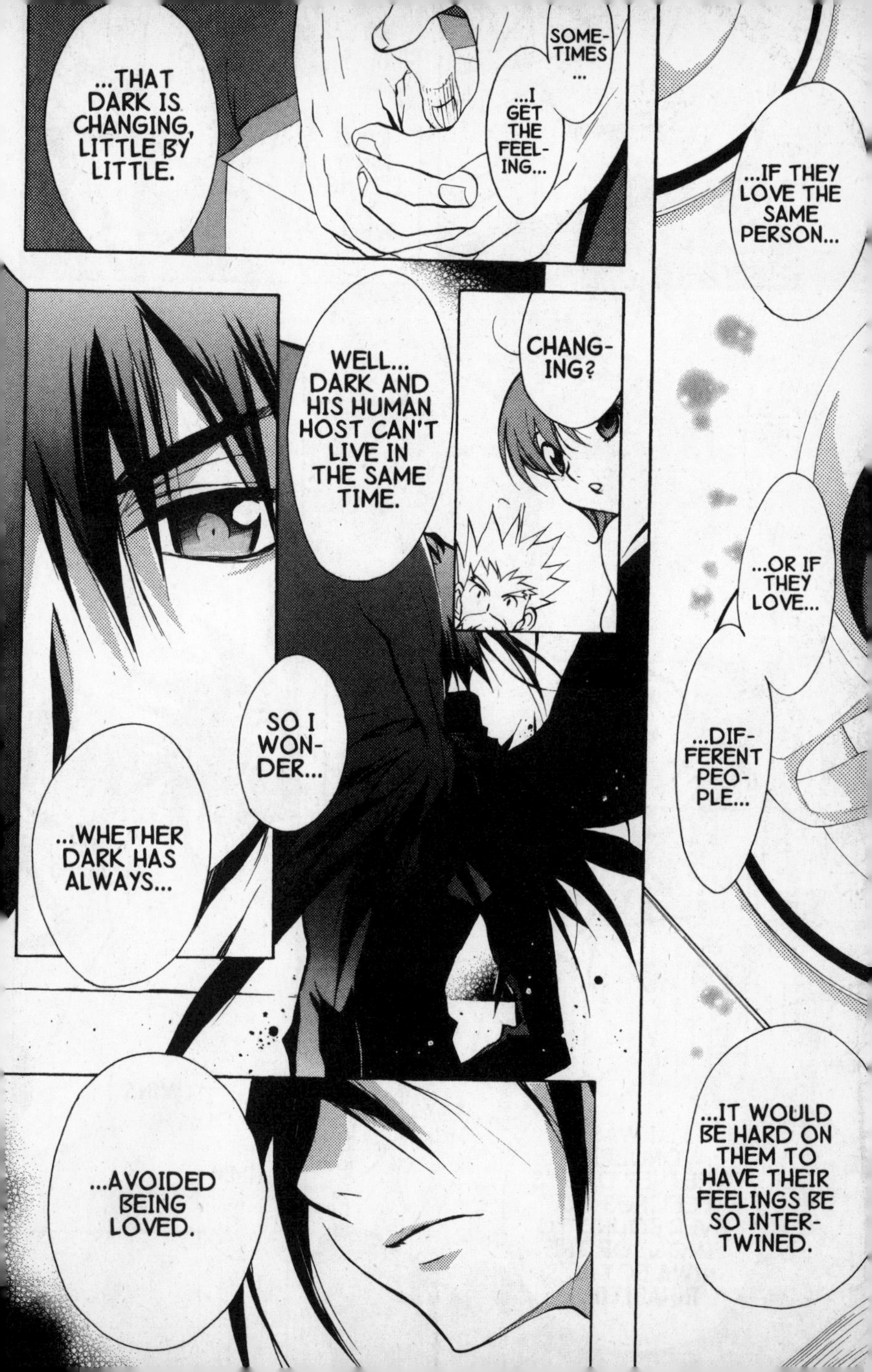
...IF THEY LOVE THE SAME PERSON...
...OR IF THEY LOVE...
...DIF-FERENT PEO-PLE...
...IT WOULD BE HARD ON THEM TO HAVE THEIR FEELINGS BE SO INTER-TWINED.
SOME-TIMES ...
...I GET THE FEEL-ING...
...THAT DARK IS CHANGING, LITTLE BY LITTLE.
CHANG-ING?
WELL... DARK AND HIS HUMAN HOST CAN'T LIVE IN THE SAME TIME.
SO I WON-DER...
...WHETHER DARK HAS ALWAYS...
...AVOIDED BEING LOVED.

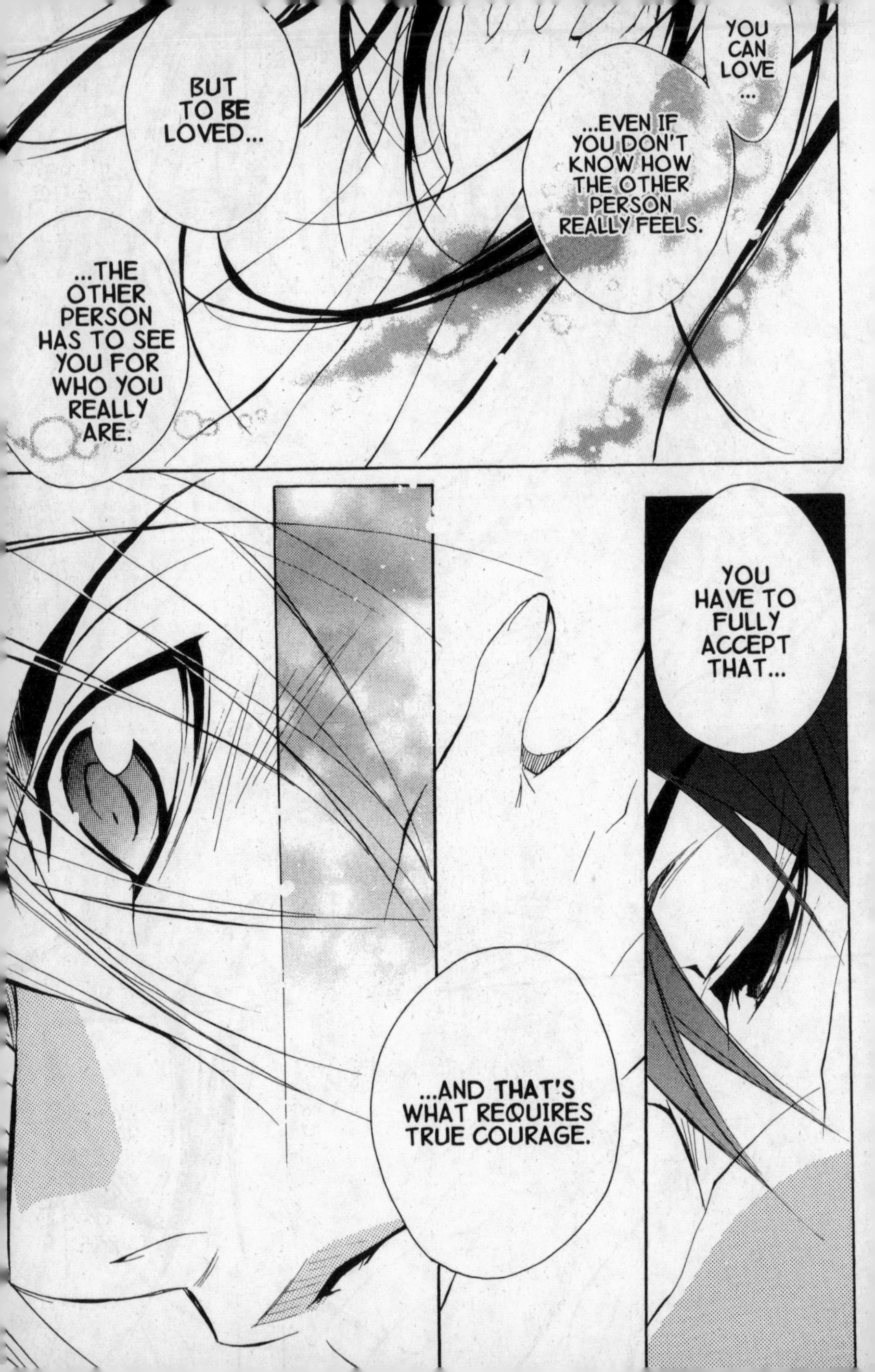
YOU CAN LOVE...
...EVEN IF YOU DON'T KNOW HOW THE OTHER PERSON REALLY FEELS.
BUT TO BE LOVED...
...THE OTHER PERSON HAS TO SEE YOU FOR WHO YOU REALLY ARE.
YOU HAVE TO FULLY ACCEPT THAT...
...AND THAT'S WHAT REQUIRES TRUE COURAGE.

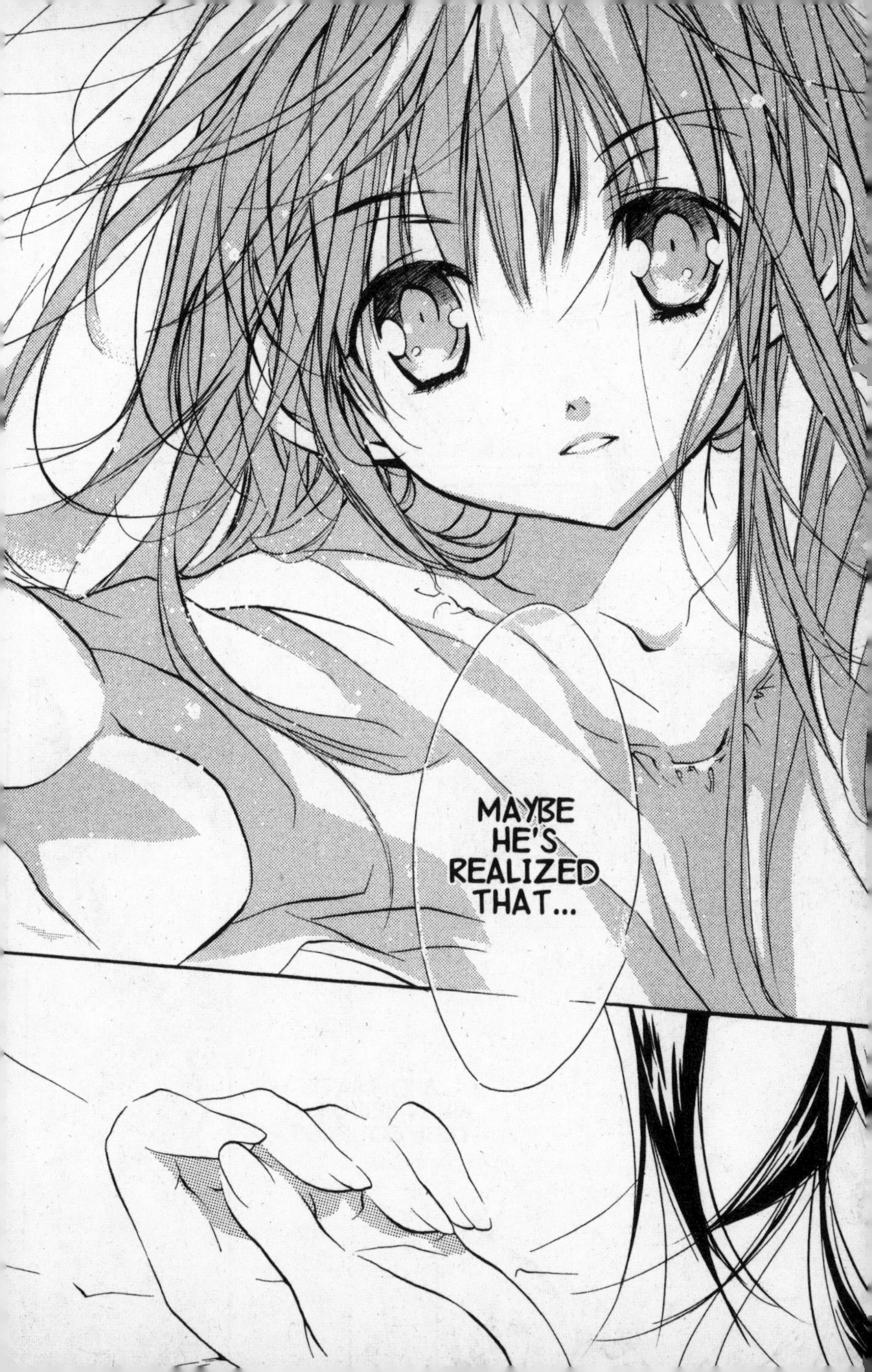
MAYBE HE'S REALIZED THAT...

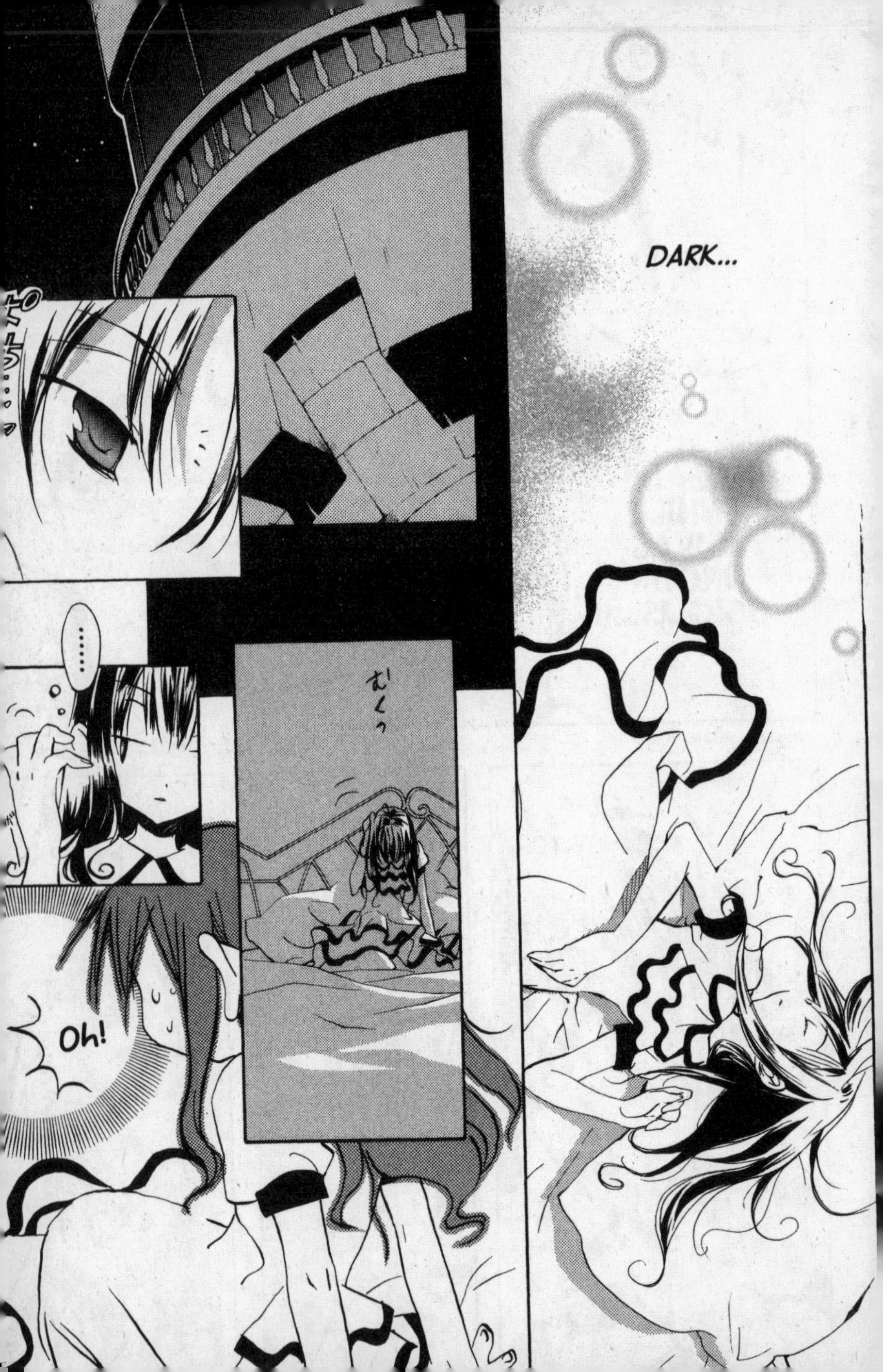
DARK...
むくっ
......
Oh!

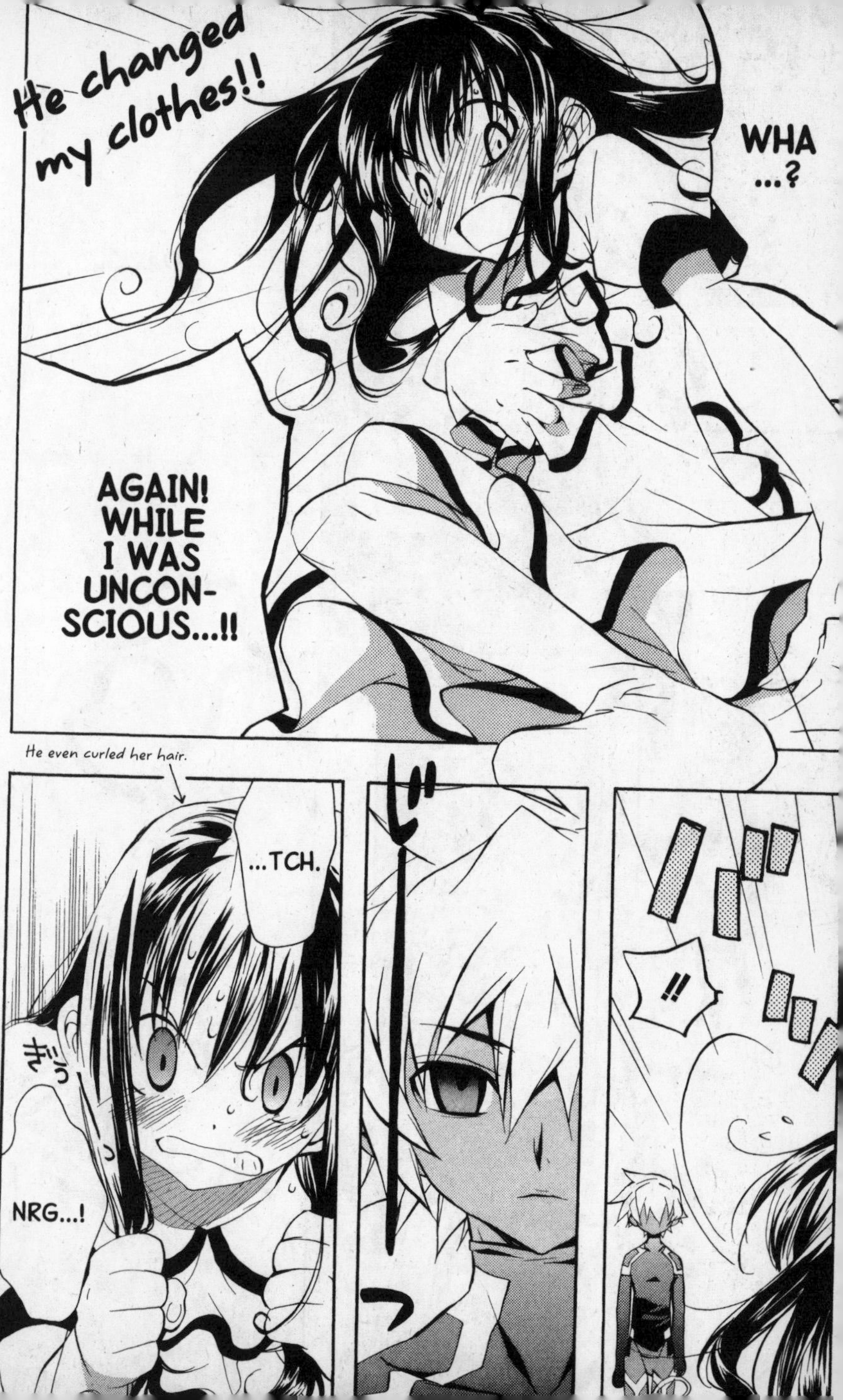
WHA ...?
He changed my clothes!!
AGAIN! WHILE I WAS UNCON-SCIOUS...!!
!!
...TCH.
He even curled her hair.
NRG...!

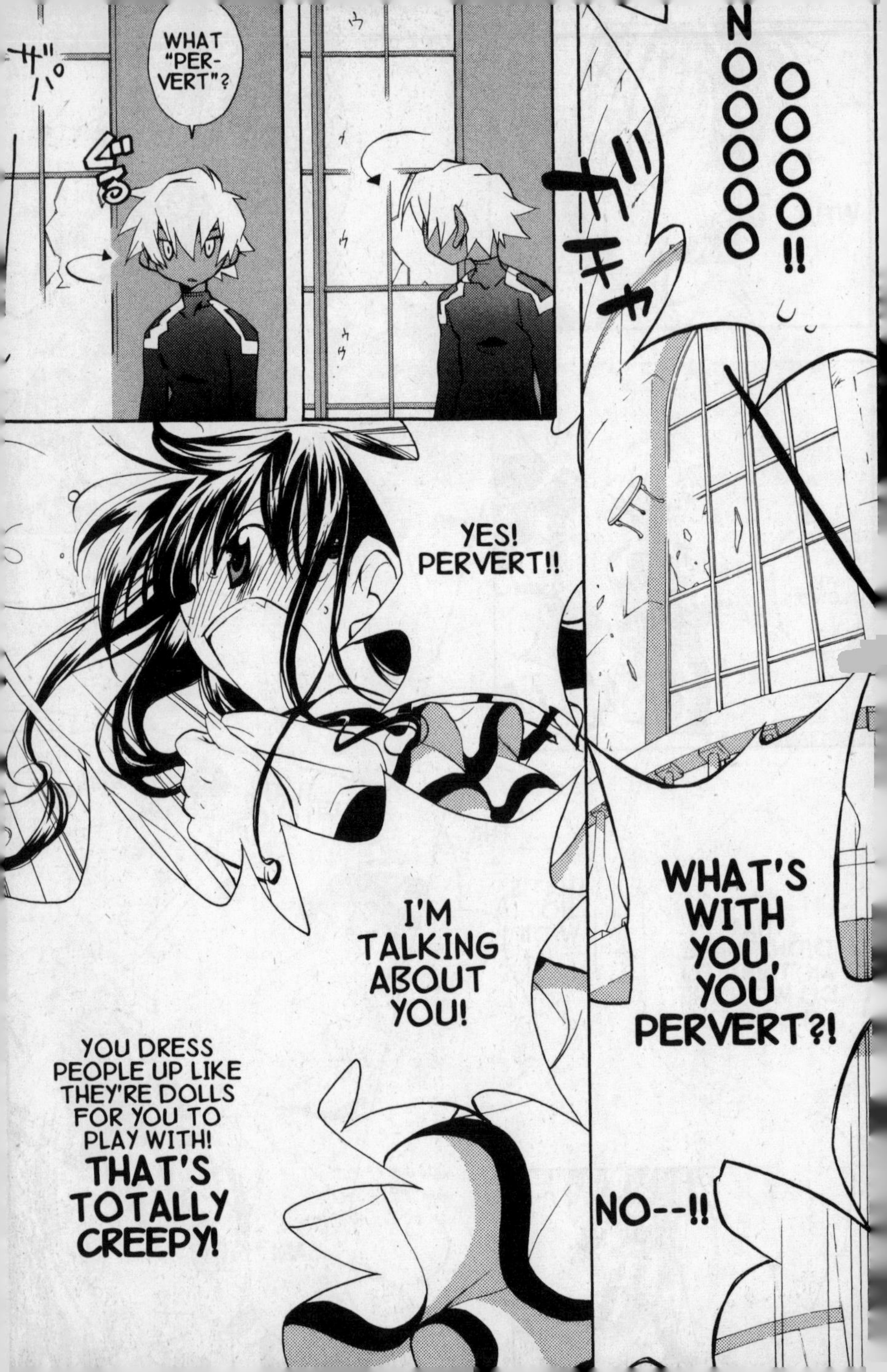
NOOOOOOOOOO!!
WHAT'S WITH YOU, YOU PERVERT?!
NO--!!
WHAT "PER-VERT"?
YES! PERVERT!!
I'M TALKING ABOUT YOU!
YOU DRESS PEOPLE UP LIKE THEY'RE DOLLS FOR YOU TO PLAY WITH! THAT'S TOTALLY CREEPY!

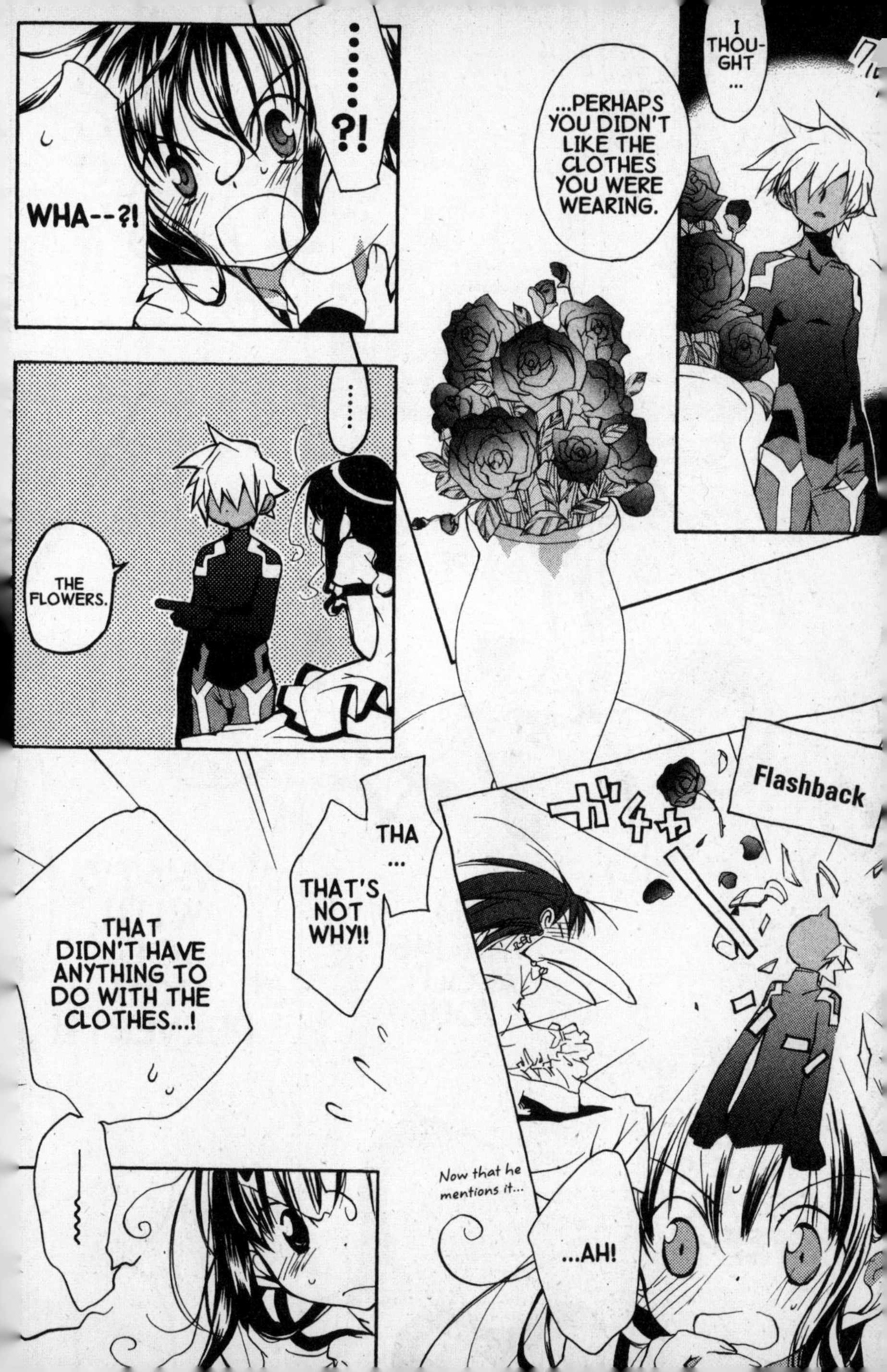

I THOUGHT...
...PERHAPS YOU DIDN'T LIKE THE CLOTHES YOU WERE WEARING.
......?!
WHA--?!
......
THE FLOWERS.
Flashback
THA... THAT'S NOT WHY!!
THAT DIDN'T HAVE ANYTHING TO DO WITH THE CLOTHES...!
Now that he mentions it...
...AH!
......

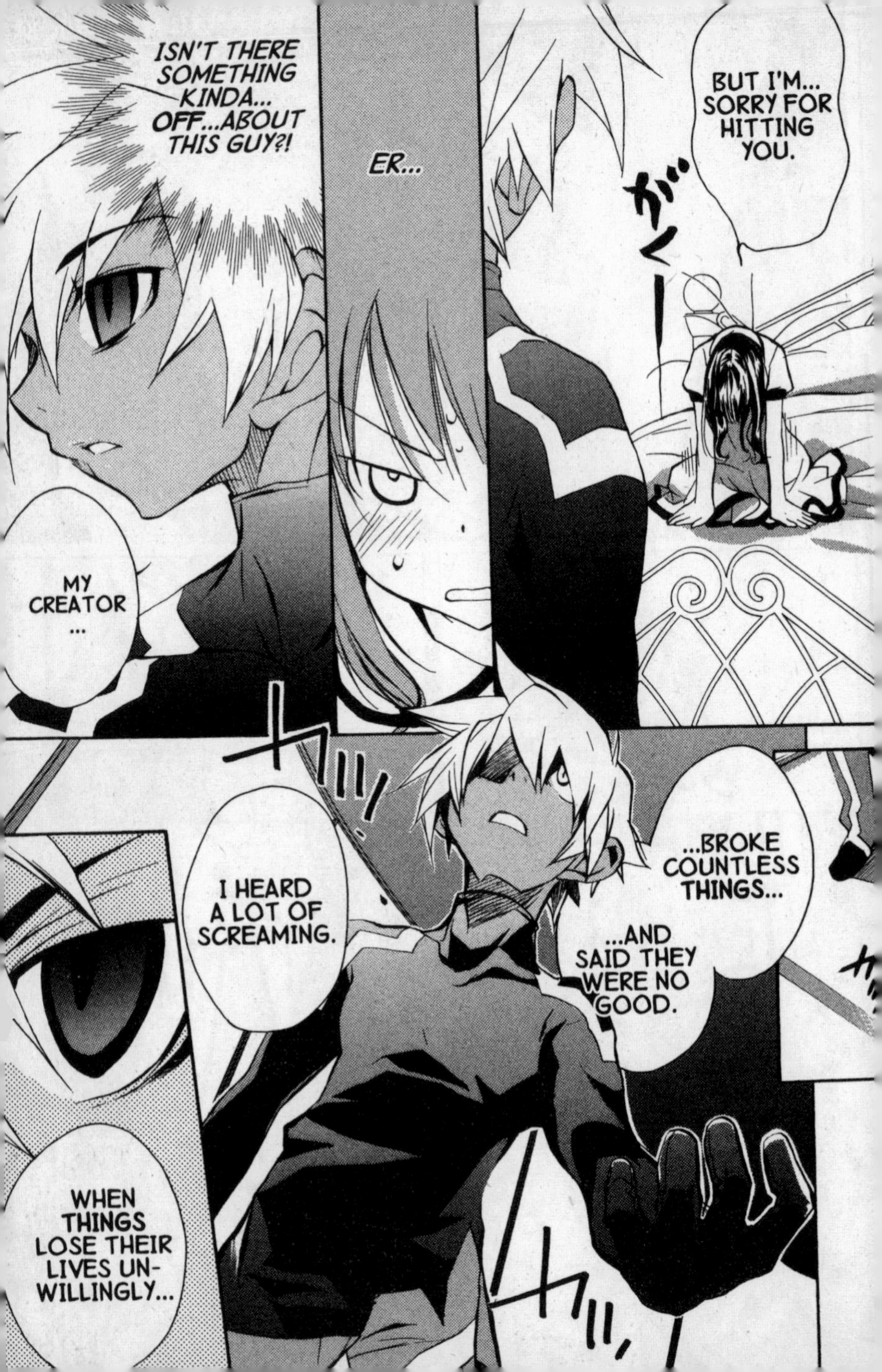
BUT I'M... SORRY FOR HITTING YOU.
がくー
ER...
ISN'T THERE SOMETHING KINDA... OFF...ABOUT THIS GUY?!
MY CREATOR ...
...BROKE COUNTLESS THINGS...
...AND SAID THEY WERE NO GOOD.
I HEARD A LOT OF SCREAMING.
WHEN THINGS LOSE THEIR LIVES UN-WILLINGLY...

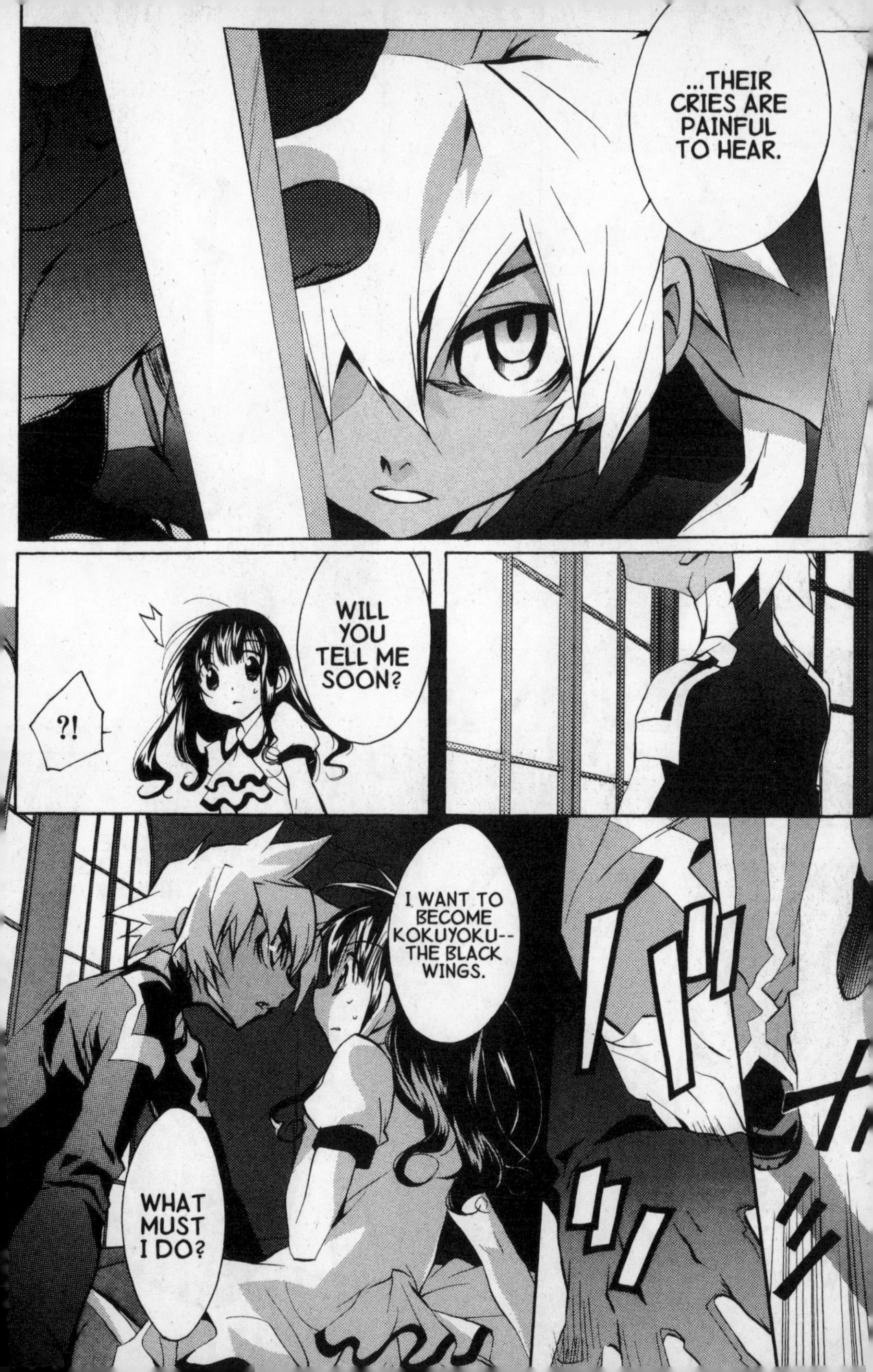
...THEIR CRIES ARE PAINFUL TO HEAR.
WILL YOU TELL ME SOON?
?!
I WANT TO BECOME KOKUYOKU-- THE BLACK WINGS.
WHAT MUST I DO?

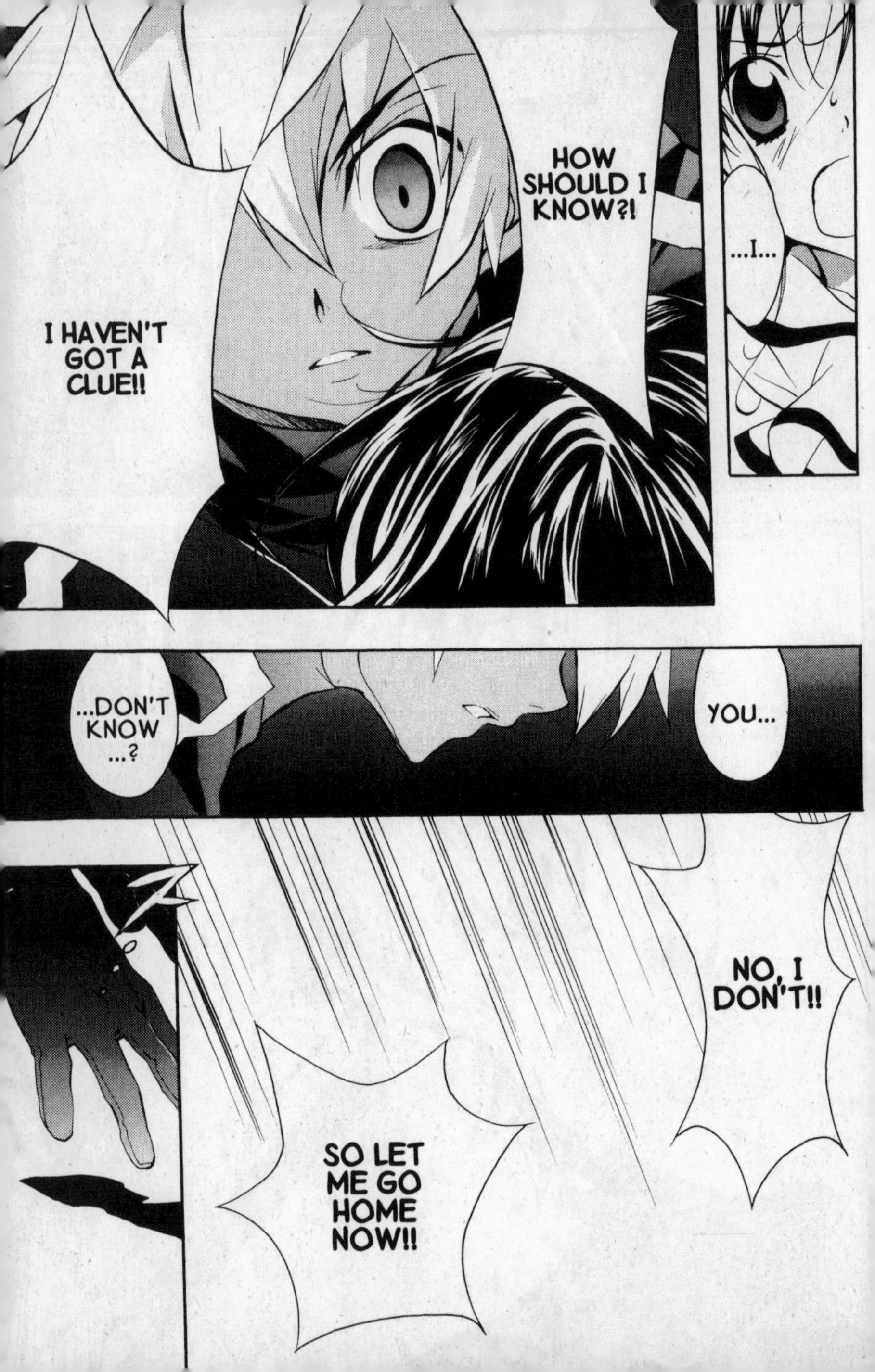
...I...
HOW SHOULD I KNOW?!
I HAVEN'T GOT A CLUE!!
YOU...
...DON'T KNOW ...?
NO, I DON'T!!
SO LET ME GO HOME NOW!!

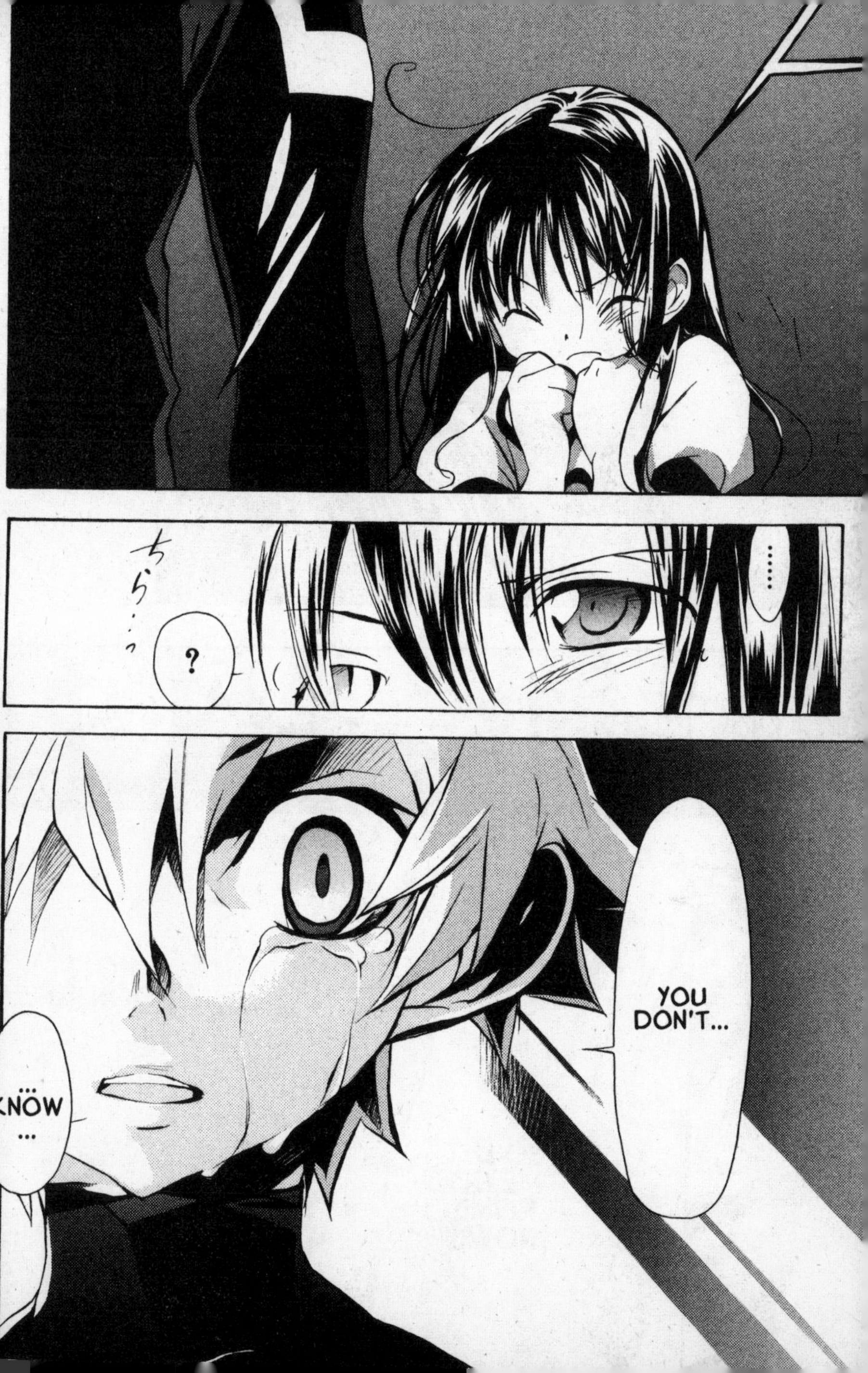
……
ちら…っ
?
YOU DON'T...
...KNOW...

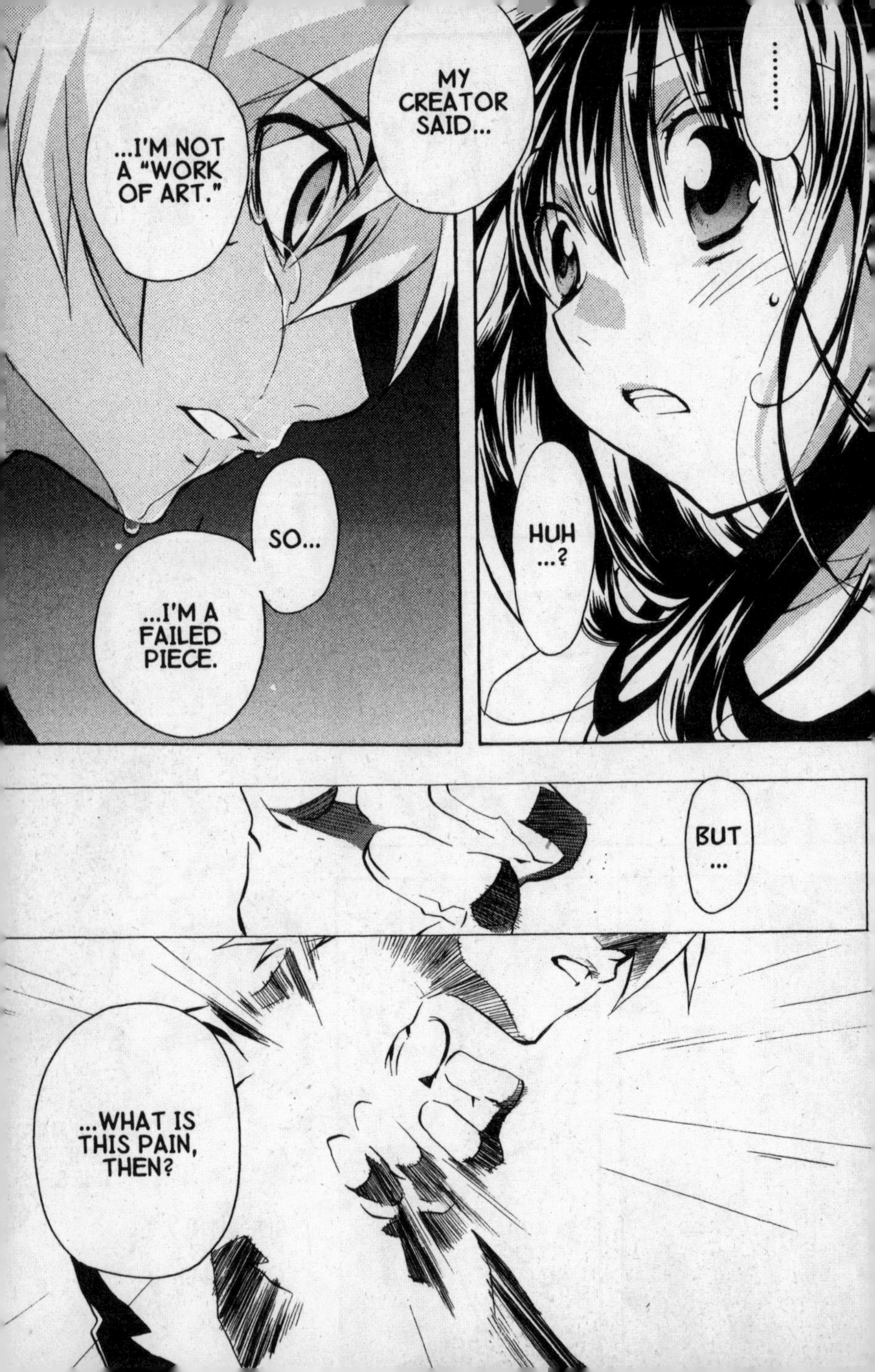
......
MY CREATOR SAID...
...I'M NOT A "WORK OF ART."
HUH ...?
SO...
...I'M A FAILED PIECE.
BUT ...
...WHAT IS THIS PAIN, THEN?

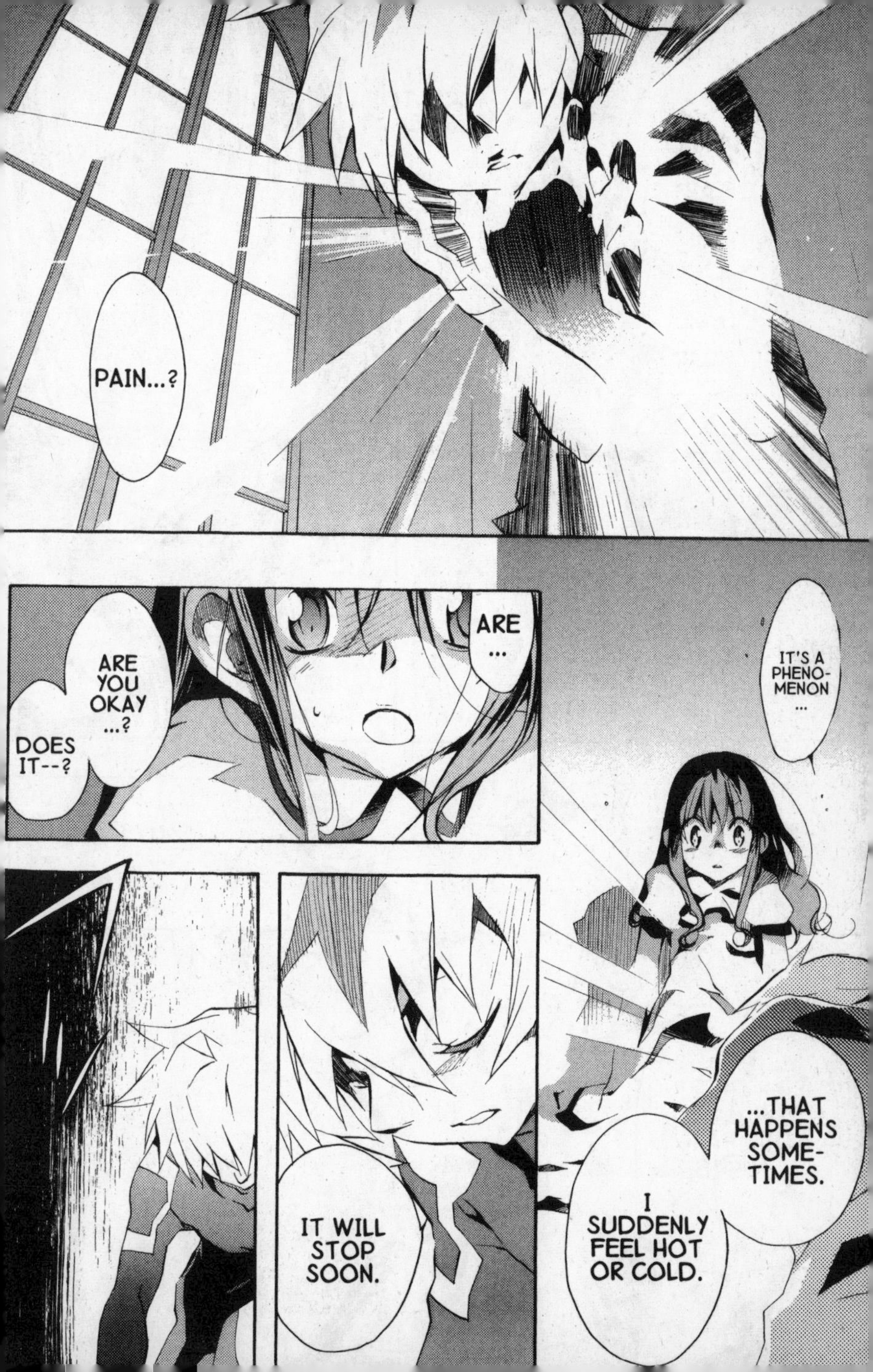
PAIN...?
ARE ...
ARE YOU OKAY ...?
DOES IT--?
IT'S A PHENOMENON ...
...THAT HAPPENS SOMETIMES.
I SUDDENLY FEEL HOT OR COLD.
IT WILL STOP SOON.

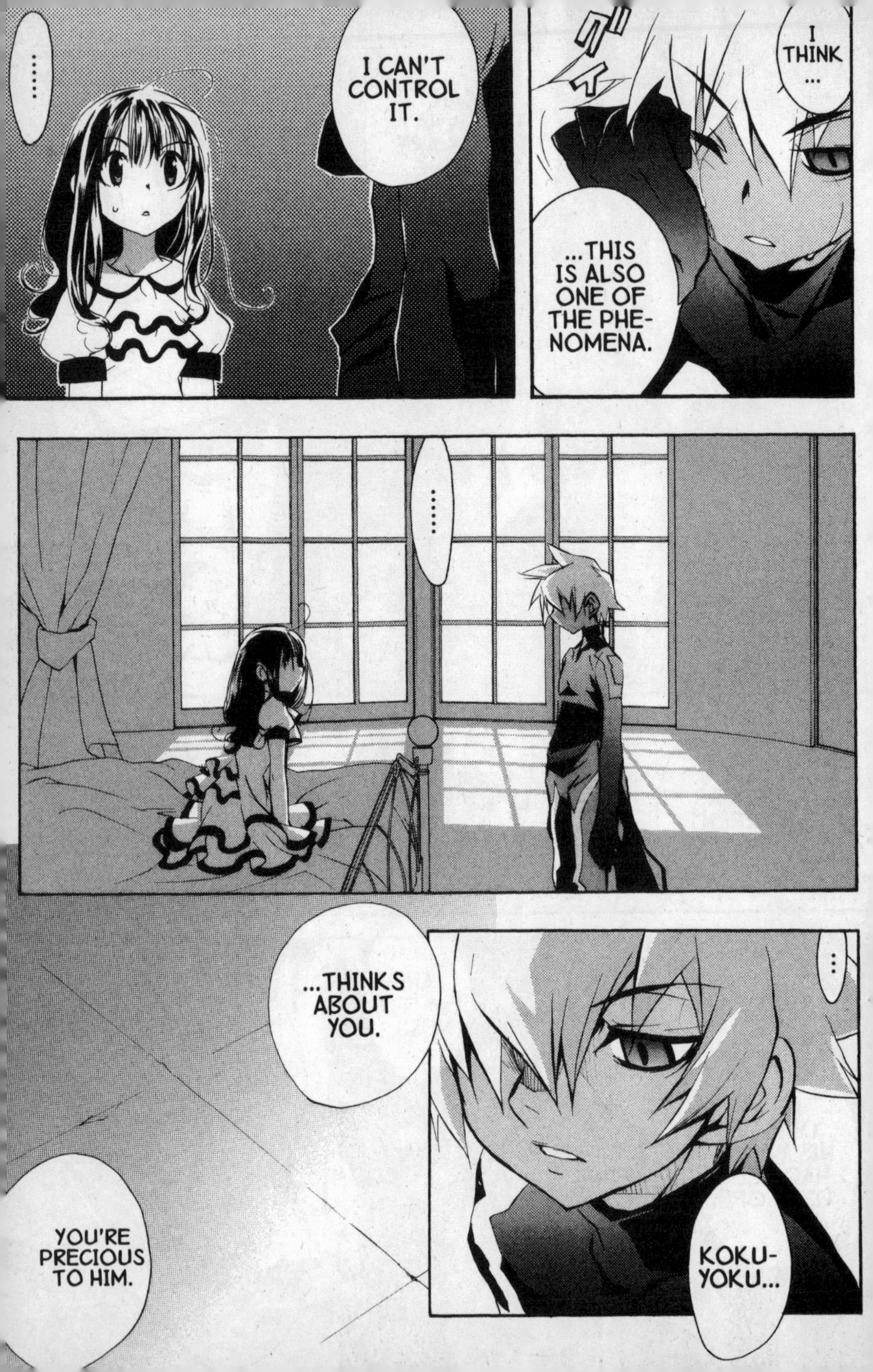
I THINK ...
...THIS IS ALSO ONE OF THE PHE-NOMENA.
I CAN'T CONTROL IT.
......
......
...
KOKU-YOKU...
...THINKS ABOUT YOU.
YOU'RE PRECIOUS TO HIM.

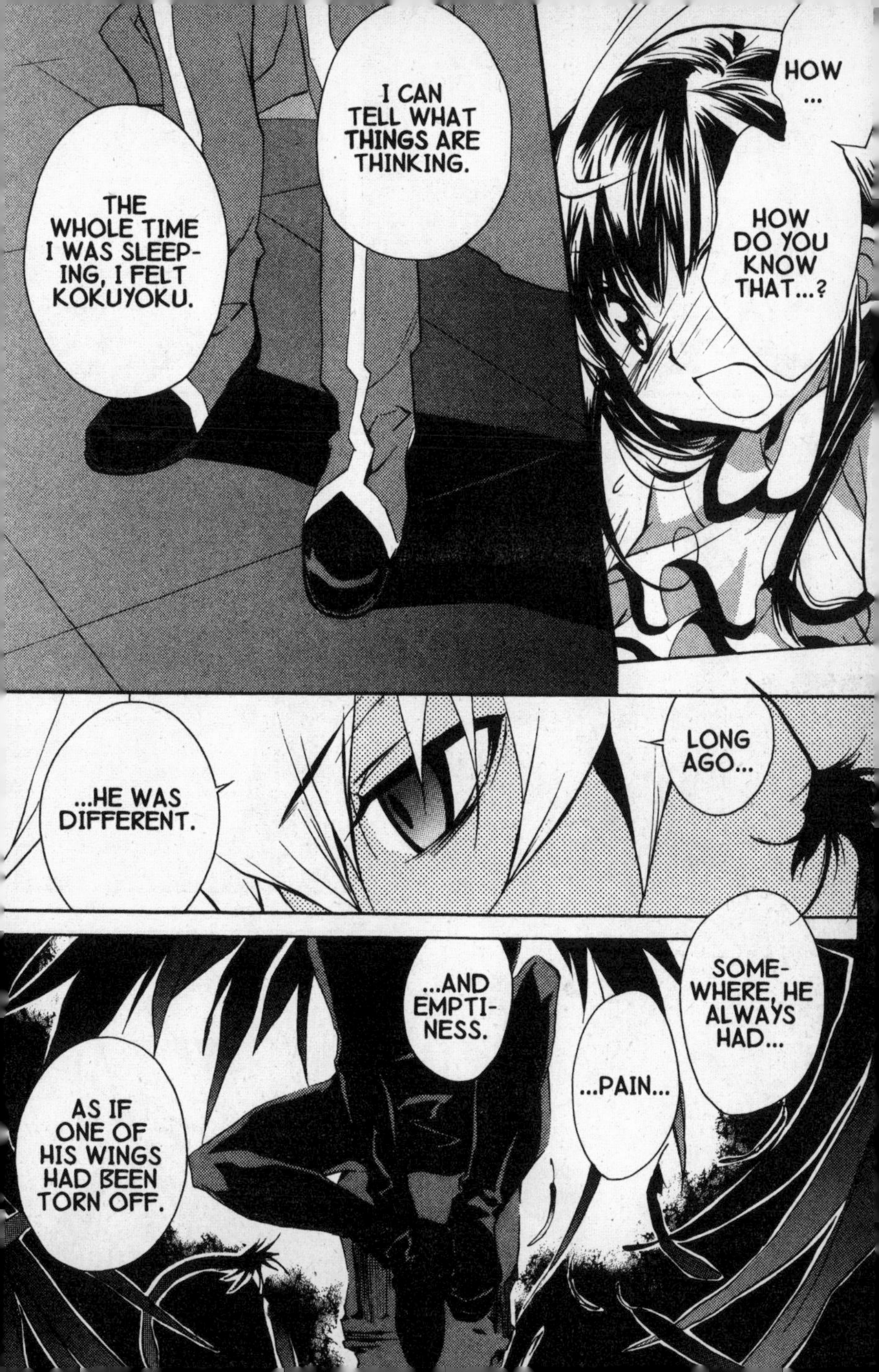
HOW ...
HOW DO YOU KNOW THAT...?
I CAN TELL WHAT THINGS ARE THINKING.
THE WHOLE TIME I WAS SLEEPING, I FELT KOKUYOKU.
LONG AGO...
...HE WAS DIFFERENT.
SOMEWHERE, HE ALWAYS HAD...
...PAIN...
...AND EMPTINESS.
AS IF ONE OF HIS WINGS HAD BEEN TORN OFF.

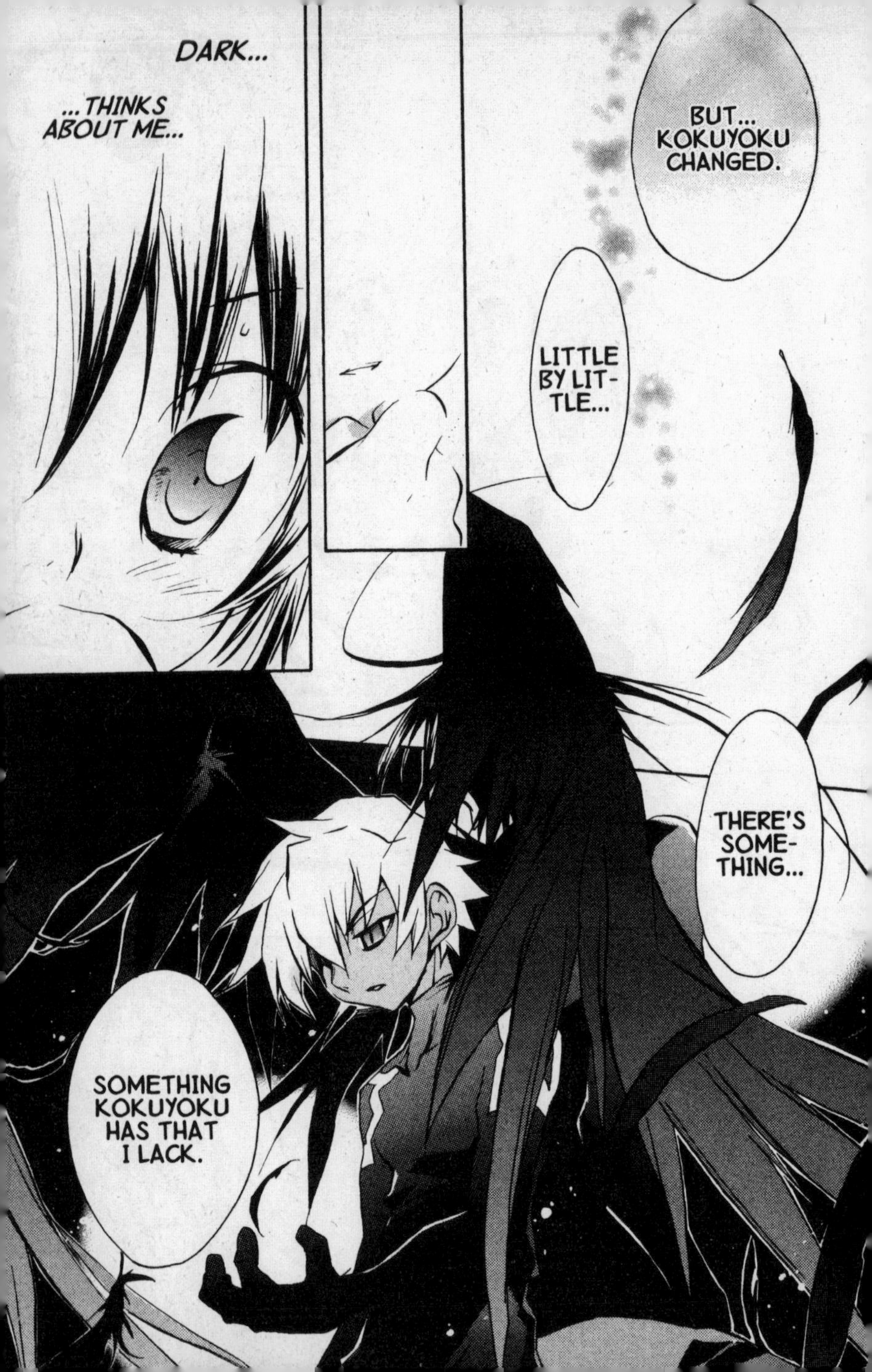
BUT... KOKUYOKU CHANGED.
LITTLE BY LIT-TLE...
DARK...
...THINKS ABOUT ME...
THERE'S SOME-THING...
SOMETHING KOKUYOKU HAS THAT I LACK.

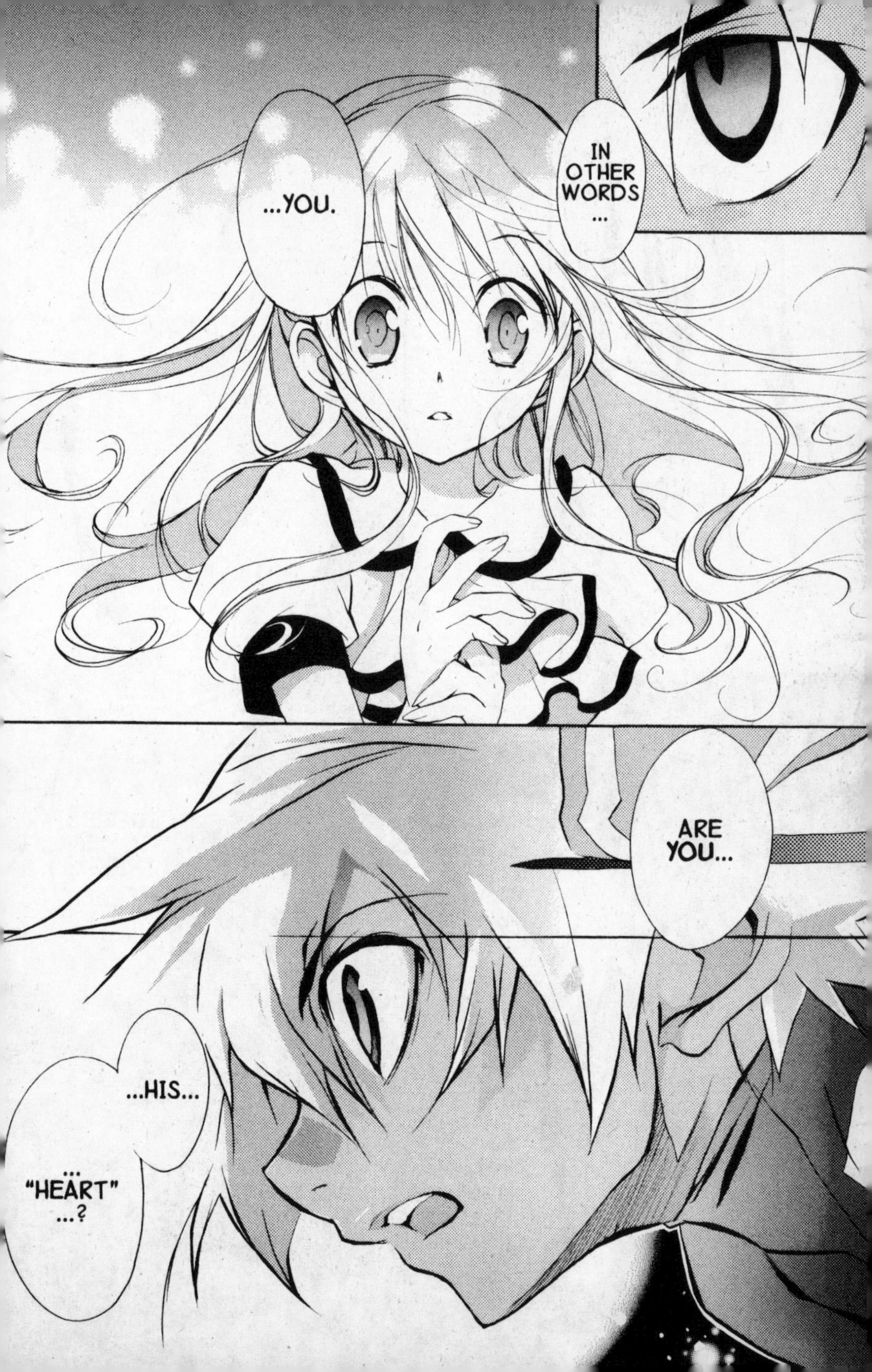
IN OTHER WORDS ...
...YOU.
ARE YOU...
...HIS...
... "HEART" ...?

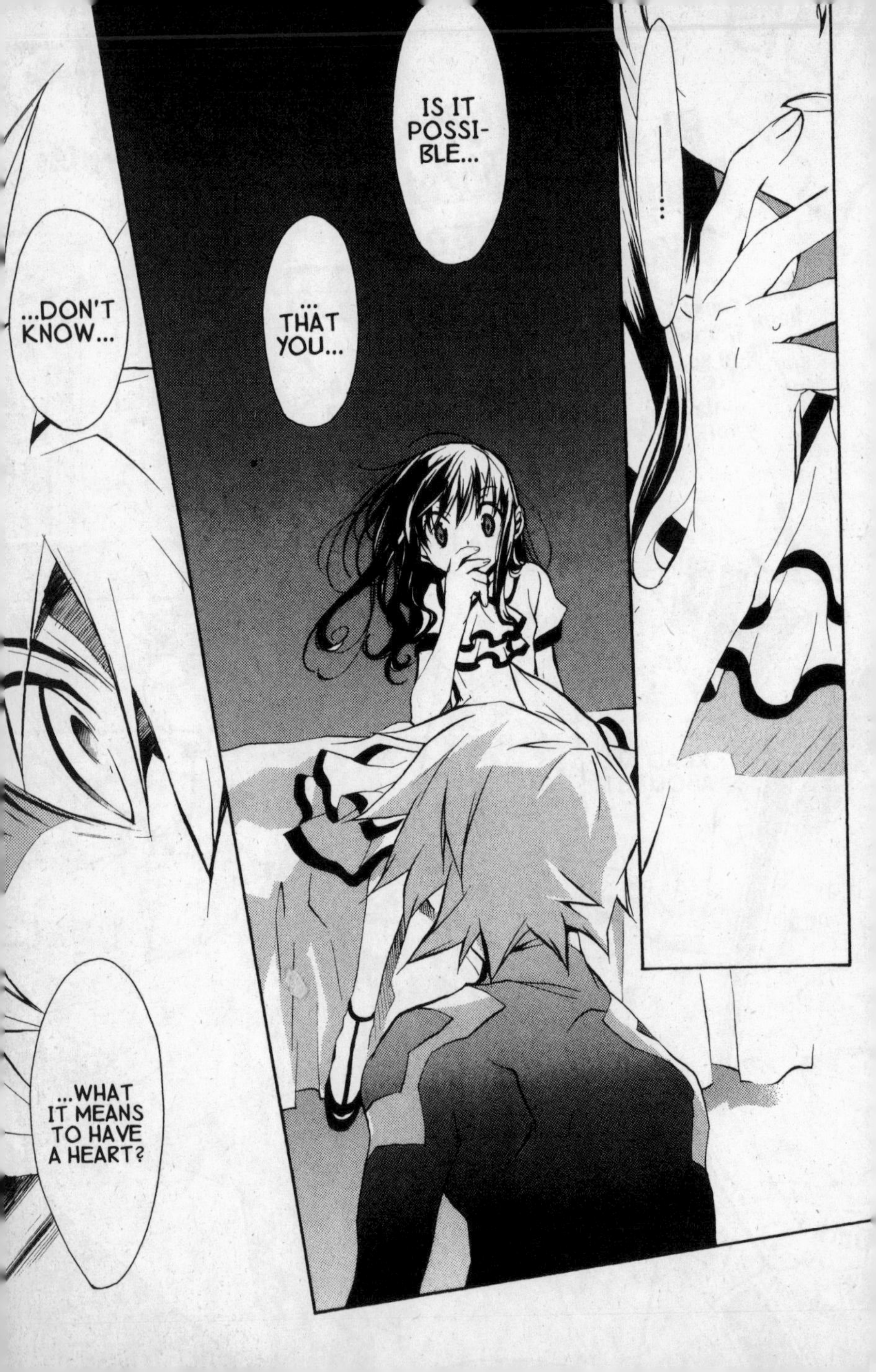
......
IS IT POSSIBLE...
...THAT YOU...
...DON'T KNOW...
...WHAT IT MEANS TO HAVE A HEART?

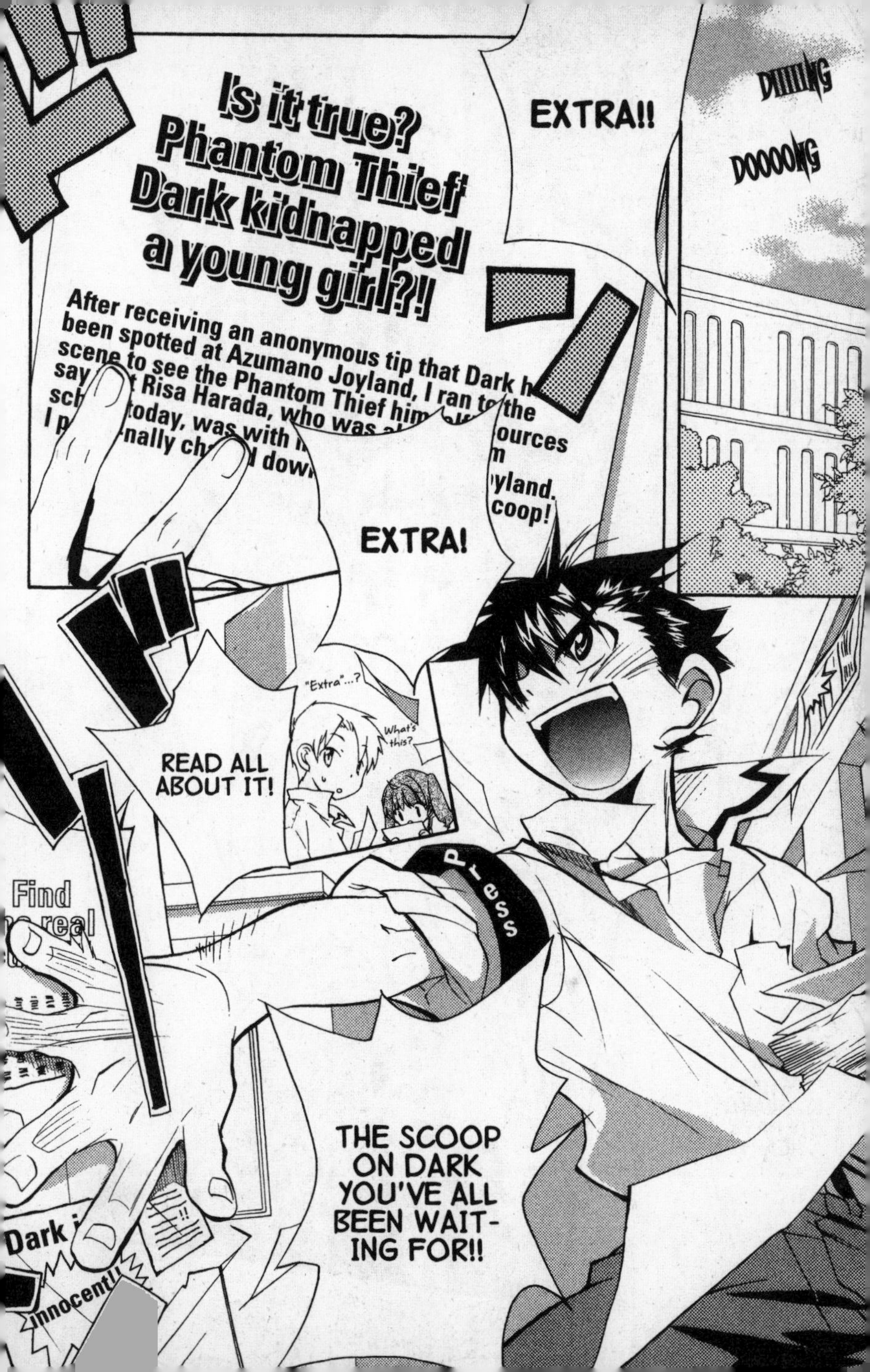
DIIIIING
DOOOONG
EXTRA!!
Is it true? Phantom Thief Dark kidnapped a young girl?!
After receiving an anonymous tip that Dark h
been spotted at Azumano Joyland, I ran to the
scene to see the Phantom Thief him
say Risa Harada, who was al ources
sch today, was with h m
I p nally ch d dow yland.
coop!
EXTRA!
"Extra"...?
What's this?
READ ALL ABOUT IT!
Press
THE SCOOP ON DARK YOU'VE ALL BEEN WAIT-ING FOR!!
Find
real
Dark i
innocent!!

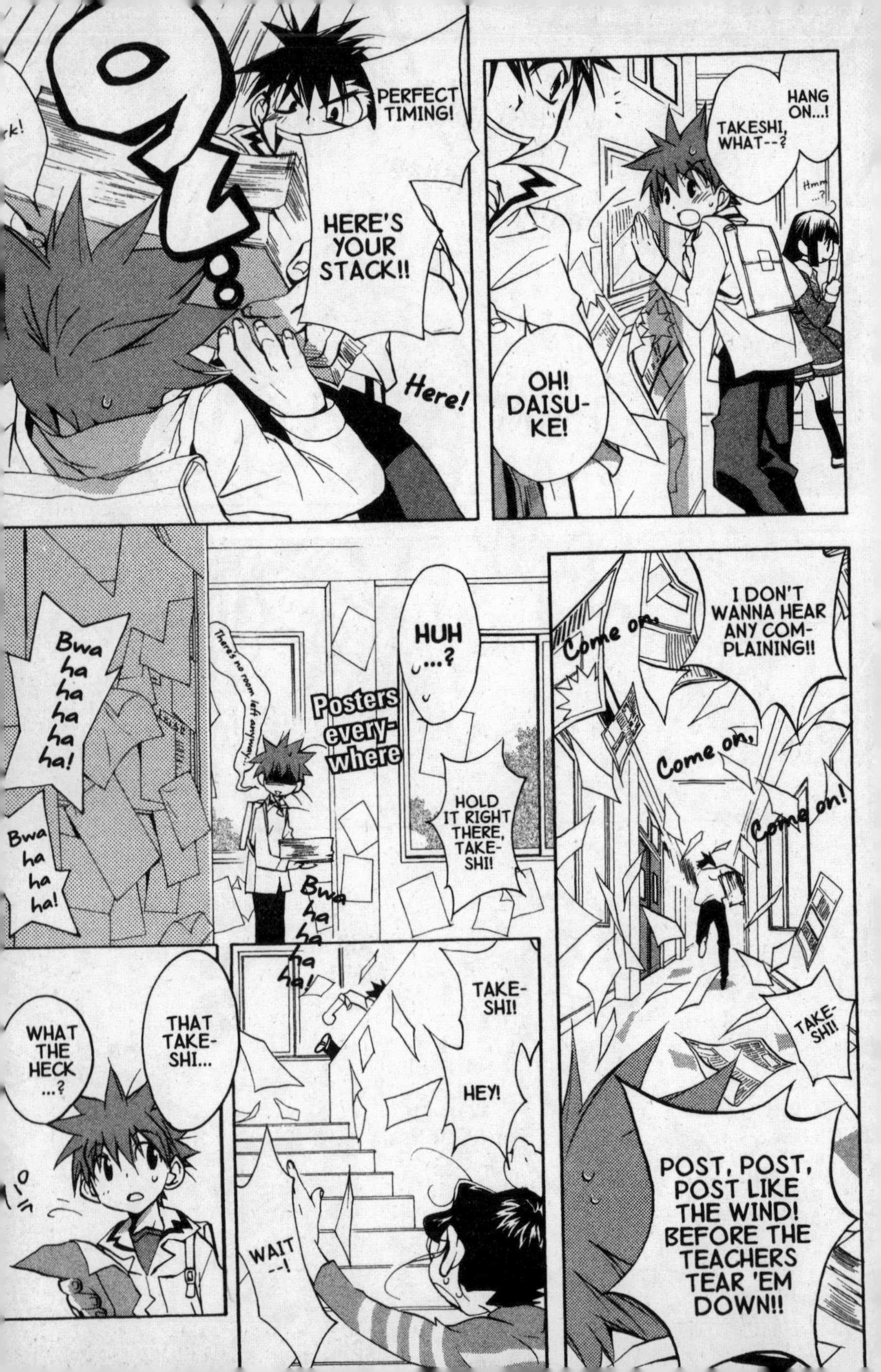
HANG ON...! TAKESHI, WHAT--?
Hmm ...?
OH! DAISUKE!
PERFECT TIMING!
HERE'S YOUR STACK!!
Here!
I DON'T WANNA HEAR ANY COMPLAINING!!
Come on,
Come on,
Come on!
TAKESHI!
POST, POST, POST LIKE THE WIND! BEFORE THE TEACHERS TEAR 'EM DOWN!!
HUH ...?
HOLD IT RIGHT THERE, TAKESHI!
Posters everywhere
There's no room left anyway...
Bwa ha ha ha ha ha ha!
Bwa ha ha ha ha!
Bwa ha ha ha ha!
TAKESHI!
HEY!
WAIT--!
THAT TAKESHI...
WHAT THE HECK...?

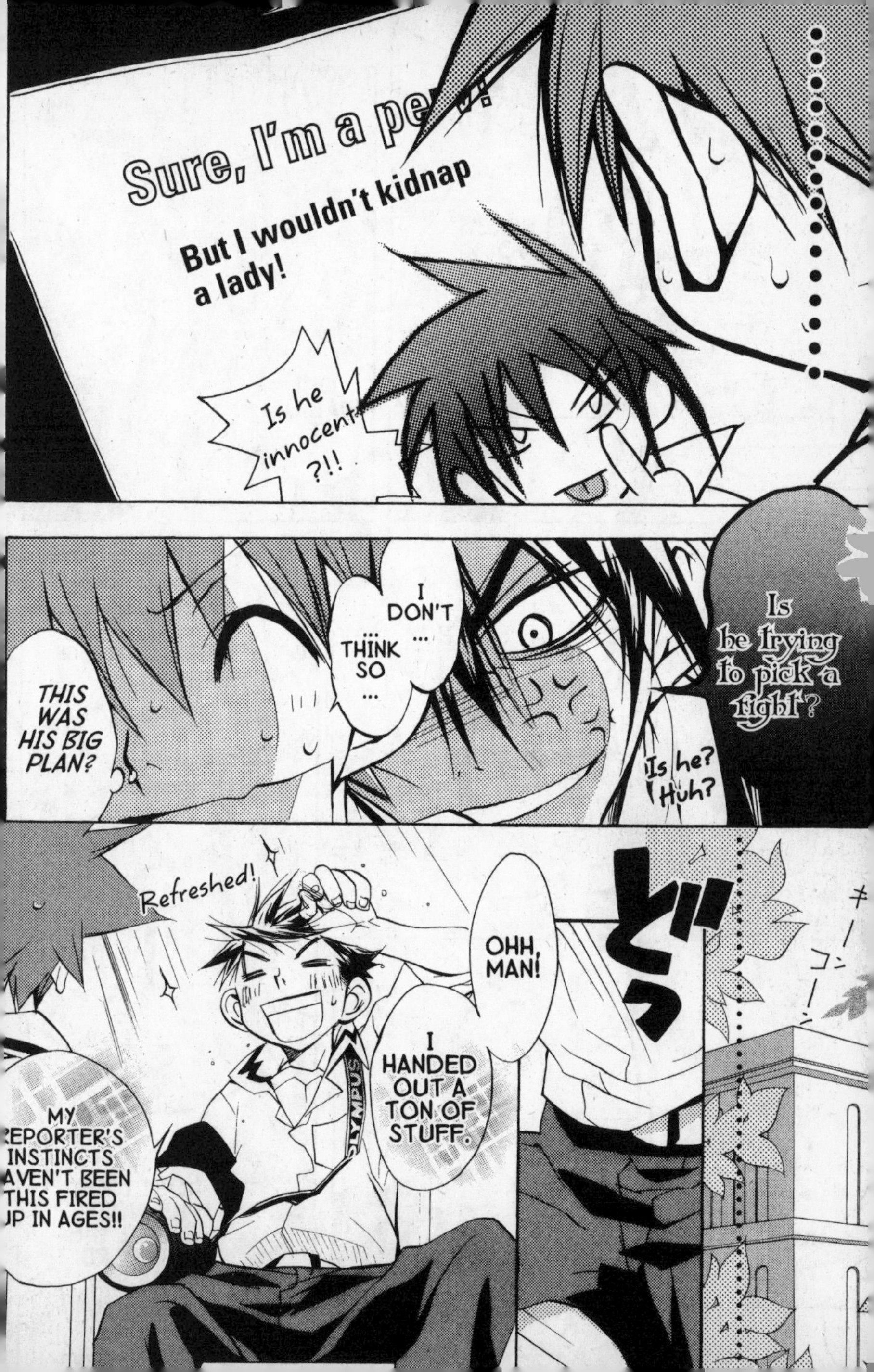
.....
Sure, I'm a pe
But I wouldn't kidnap a lady!
Is he innocent?!!
Is he trying to pick a fight?
Is he? Huh?
I DON'T ... THINK SO ...
THIS WAS HIS BIG PLAN?
どっ
OHH, MAN!
I HANDED OUT A TON OF STUFF.
Refreshed!
MY REPORTER'S INSTINCTS AVEN'T BEEN THIS FIRED JP IN AGES!!

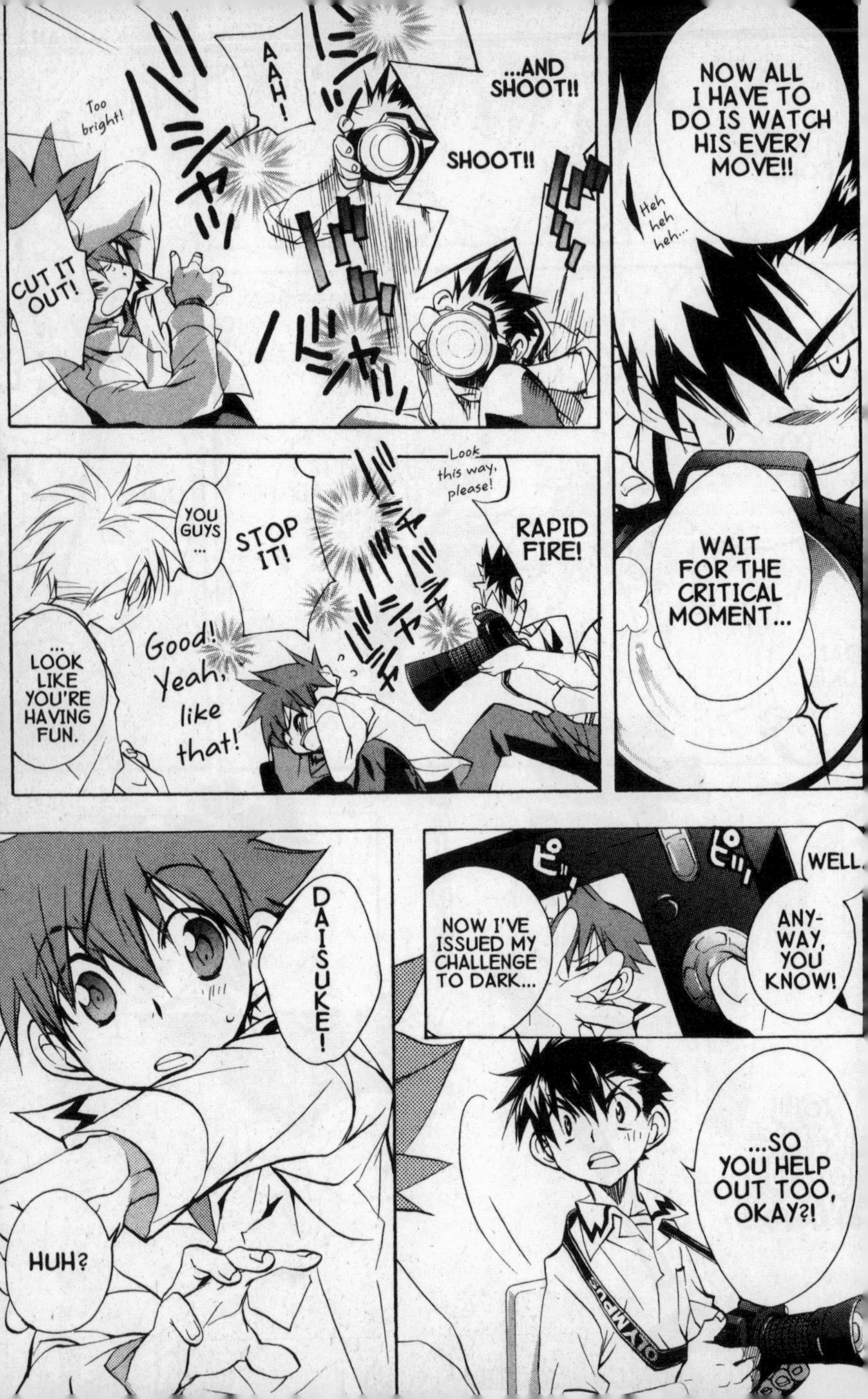
NOW ALL I HAVE TO DO IS WATCH HIS EVERY MOVE!!
Heh heh heh...
WAIT FOR THE CRITICAL MOMENT...
...AND SHOOT!!
SHOOT!!
AAH!
Too bright!
CUT IT OUT!
RAPID FIRE!
Look this way, please!
STOP IT!
YOU GUYS ...
Good! Yeah, like that!
... LOOK LIKE YOU'RE HAVING FUN.
WELL.
ANY-WAY, YOU KNOW!
NOW I'VE ISSUED MY CHALLENGE TO DARK...
...SO YOU HELP OUT TOO, OKAY?!
DAISUKE!
HUH?

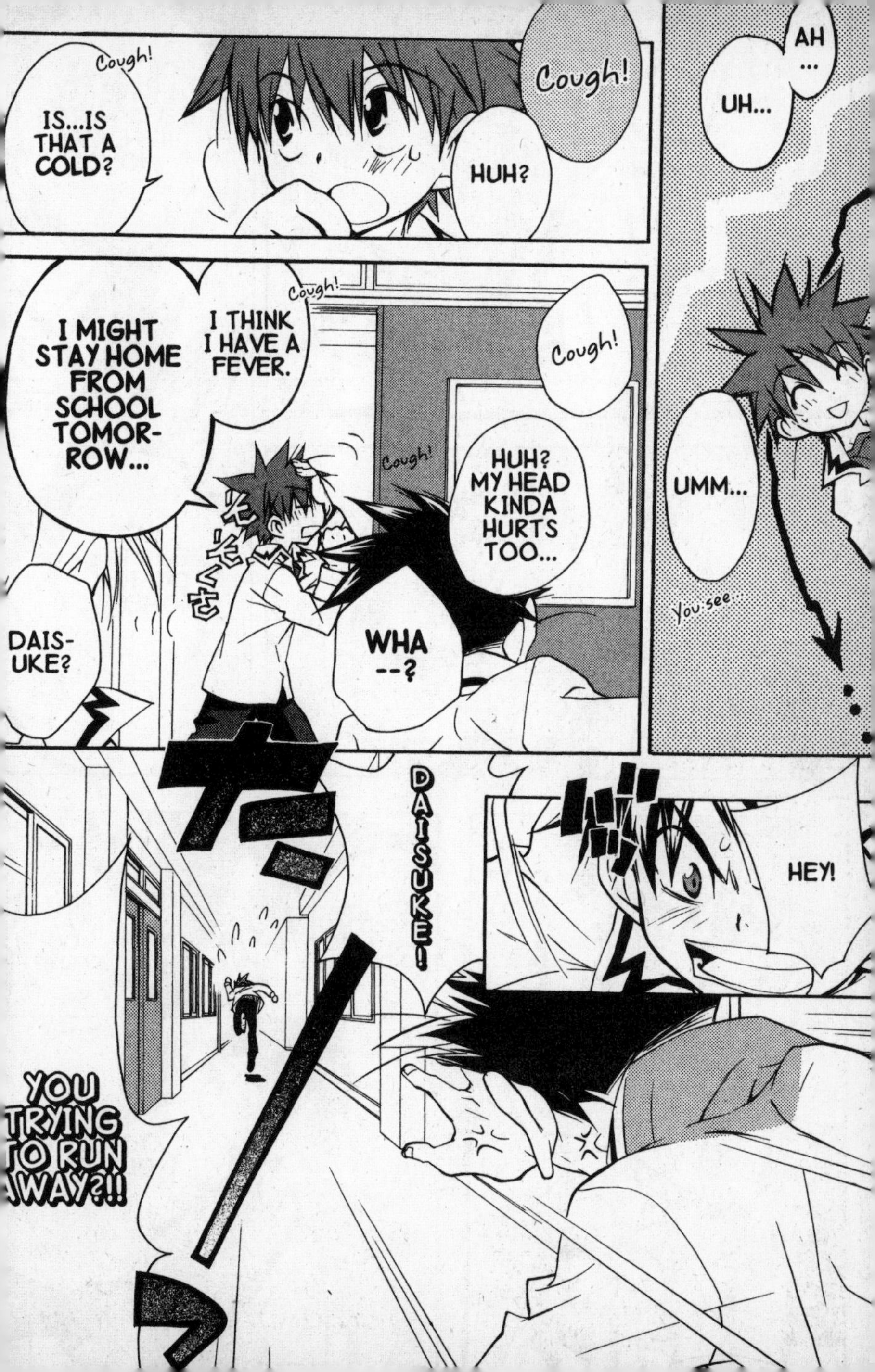
AH...
UH...
UMM...
You see...
Cough!
HUH?
Cough!
IS...IS THAT A COLD?
Cough!
HUH? MY HEAD KINDA HURTS TOO...
Cough!
Cough!
I THINK I HAVE A FEVER.
I MIGHT STAY HOME FROM SCHOOL TOMOR-ROW...
そそくさ
WHA --?
DAIS-UKE?
HEY!
DAISUKE!
YOU TRYING TO RUN AWAY?!!

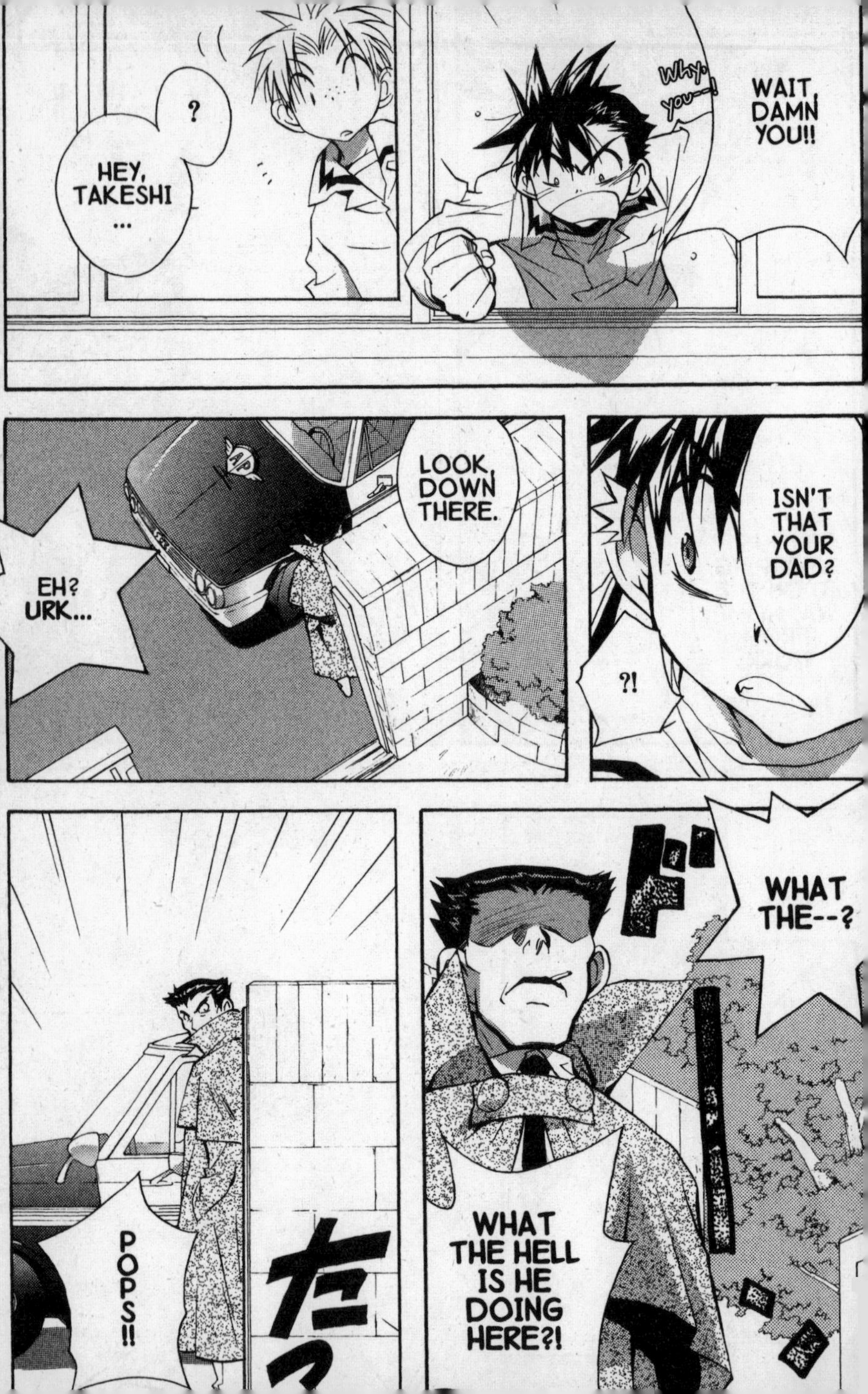
WAIT, DAMN YOU!!
Why, you--!
?
HEY, TAKESHI ...
ISN'T THAT YOUR DAD?
?!
LOOK, DOWN THERE.
EH? URK...
WHAT THE--?
ド
WHAT THE HELL IS HE DOING HERE?!
たっ
POPS!!

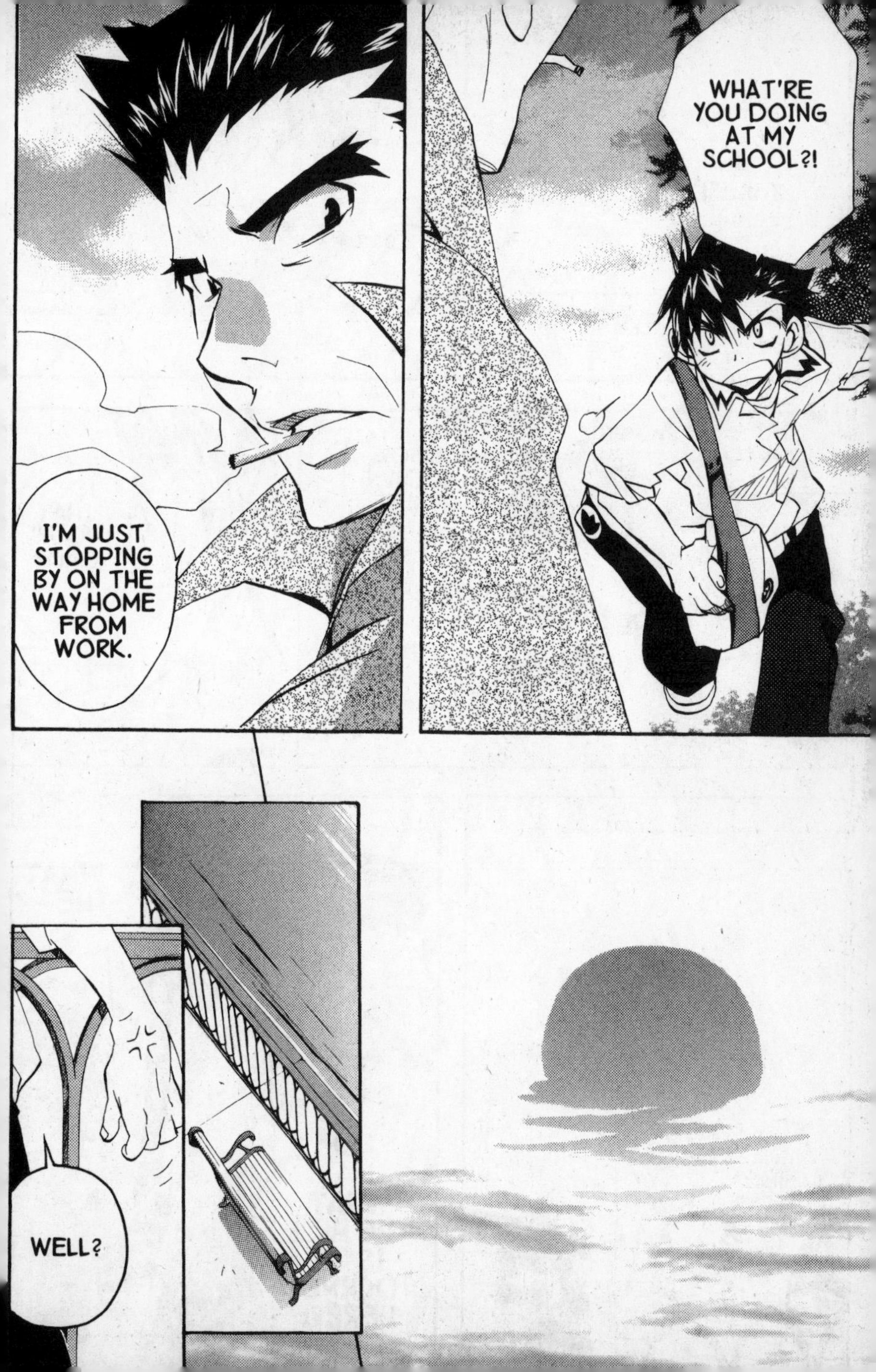
WHAT'RE YOU DOING AT MY SCHOOL?!
I'M JUST STOPPING BY ON THE WAY HOME FROM WORK.
WELL?

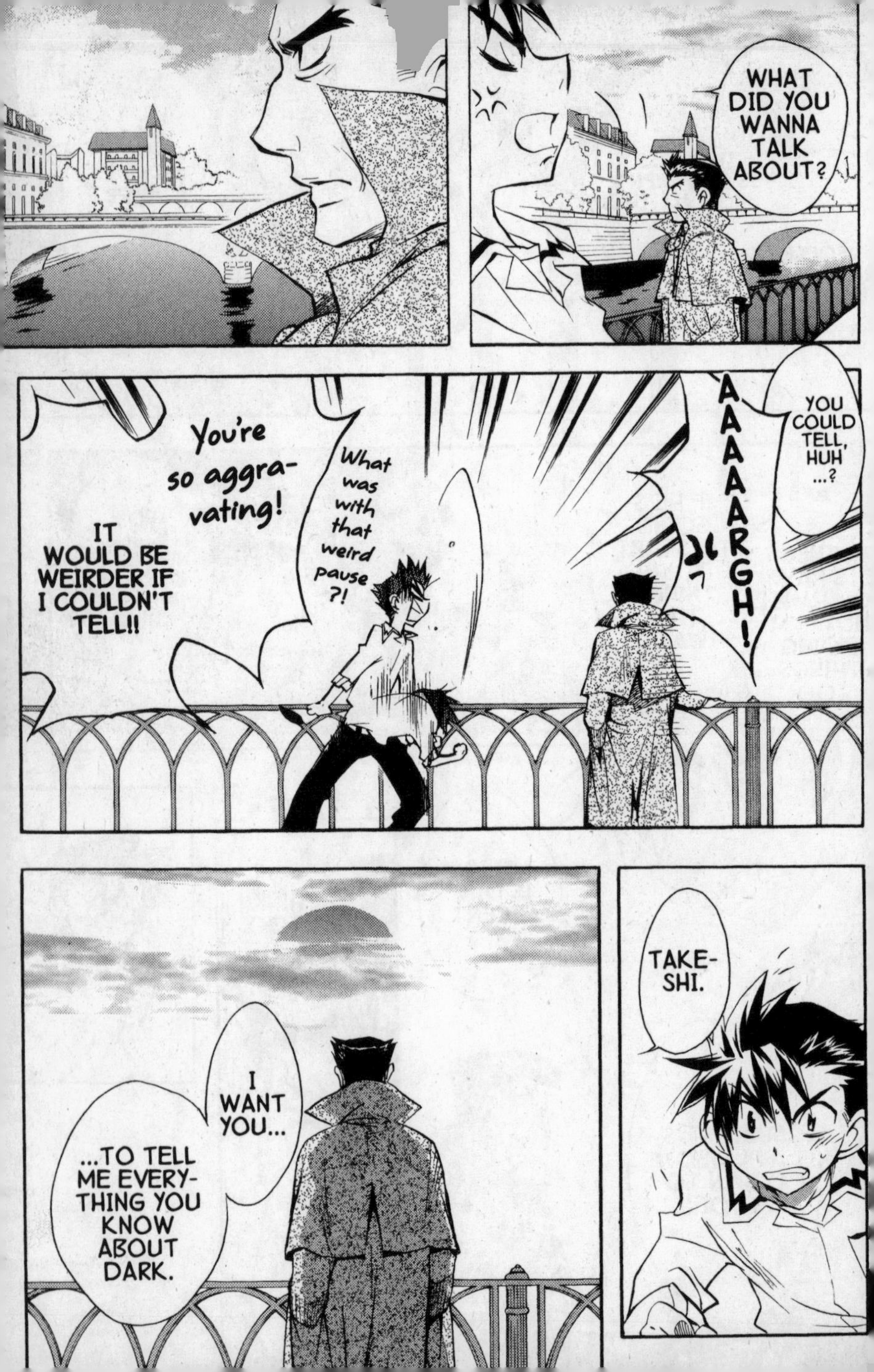

WHAT DID YOU WANNA TALK ABOUT?
YOU COULD TELL, HUH ...?
AAAAARGH!
What was with that weird pause?!
You're so aggra-vating!
IT WOULD BE WEIRDER IF I COULDN'T TELL!!
TAKE-SHI.
I WANT YOU...
...TO TELL ME EVERY-THING YOU KNOW ABOUT DARK.

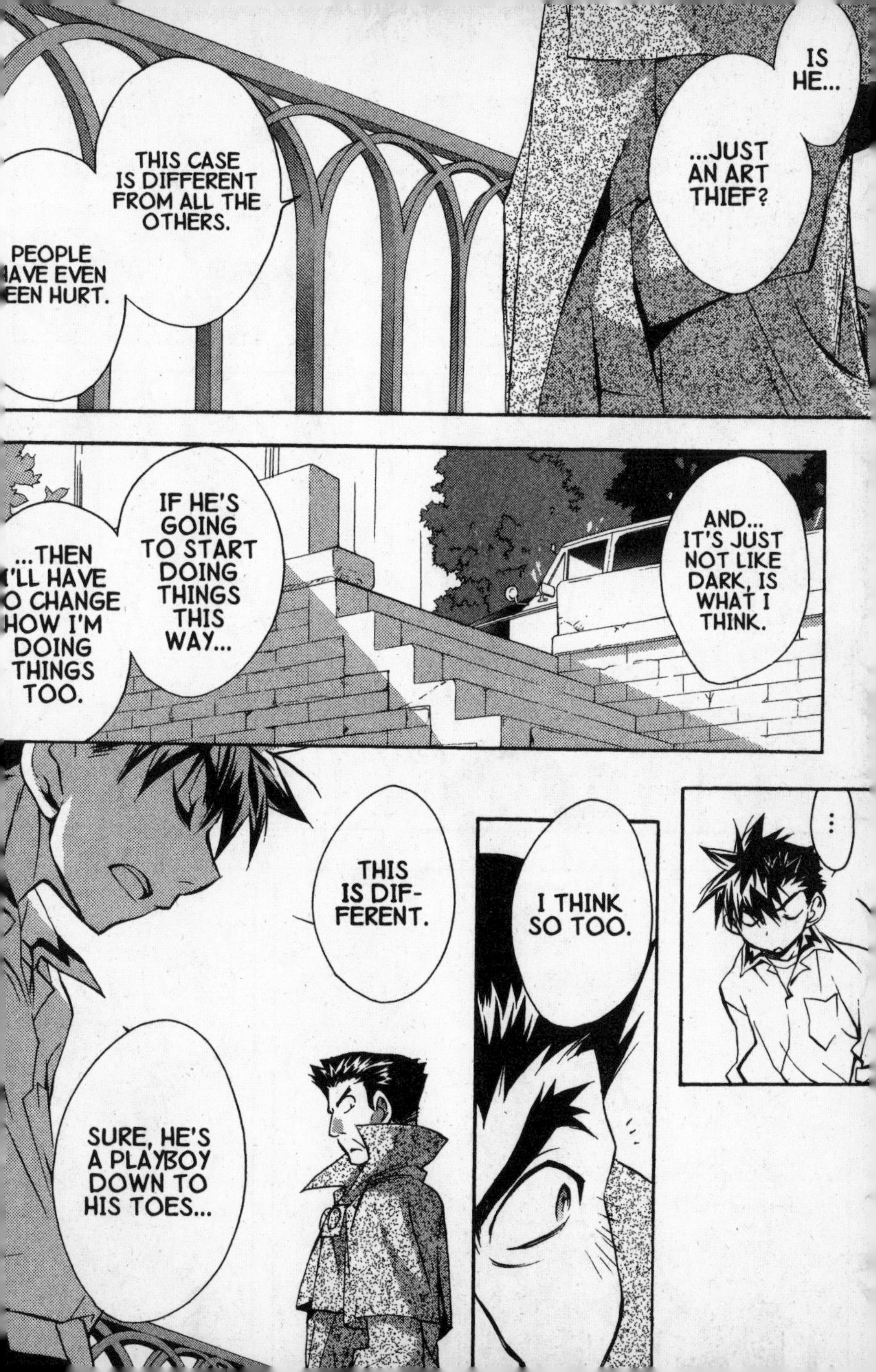
IS HE...
...JUST AN ART THIEF?
THIS CASE IS DIFFERENT FROM ALL THE OTHERS.
PEOPLE AVE EVEN EEN HURT.
AND... IT'S JUST NOT LIKE DARK, IS WHAT I THINK.
IF HE'S GOING TO START DOING THINGS THIS WAY...
...THEN 'LL HAVE O CHANGE HOW I'M DOING THINGS TOO.
...
I THINK SO TOO.
THIS IS DIF-FERENT.
SURE, HE'S A PLAYBOY DOWN TO HIS TOES...

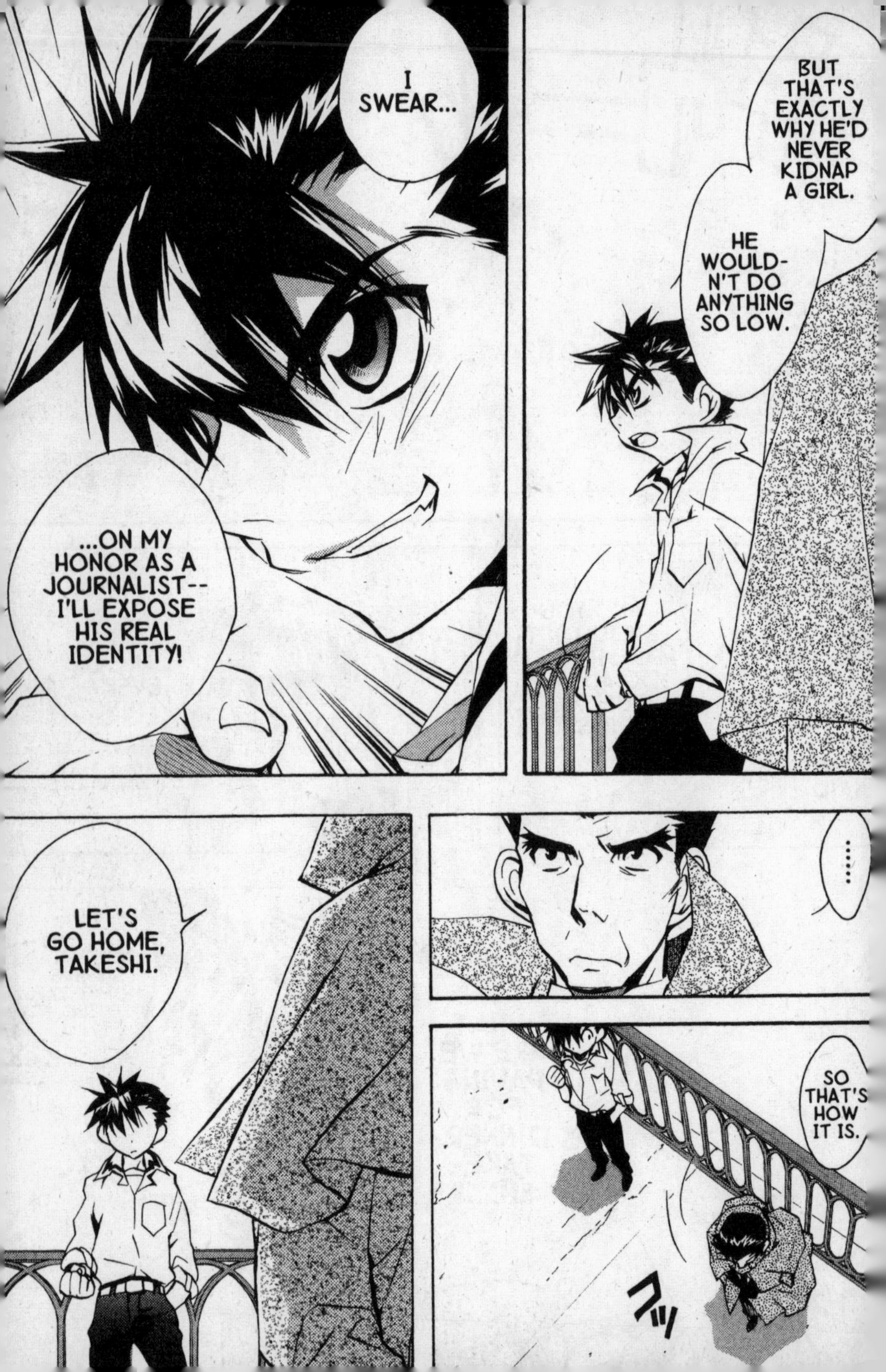
BUT THAT'S EXACTLY WHY HE'D NEVER KIDNAP A GIRL.
HE WOULD-N'T DO ANYTHING SO LOW.
I SWEAR...
...ON MY HONOR AS A JOURNALIST-- I'LL EXPOSE HIS REAL IDENTITY!
......
SO THAT'S HOW IT IS.
LET'S GO HOME, TAKESHI.

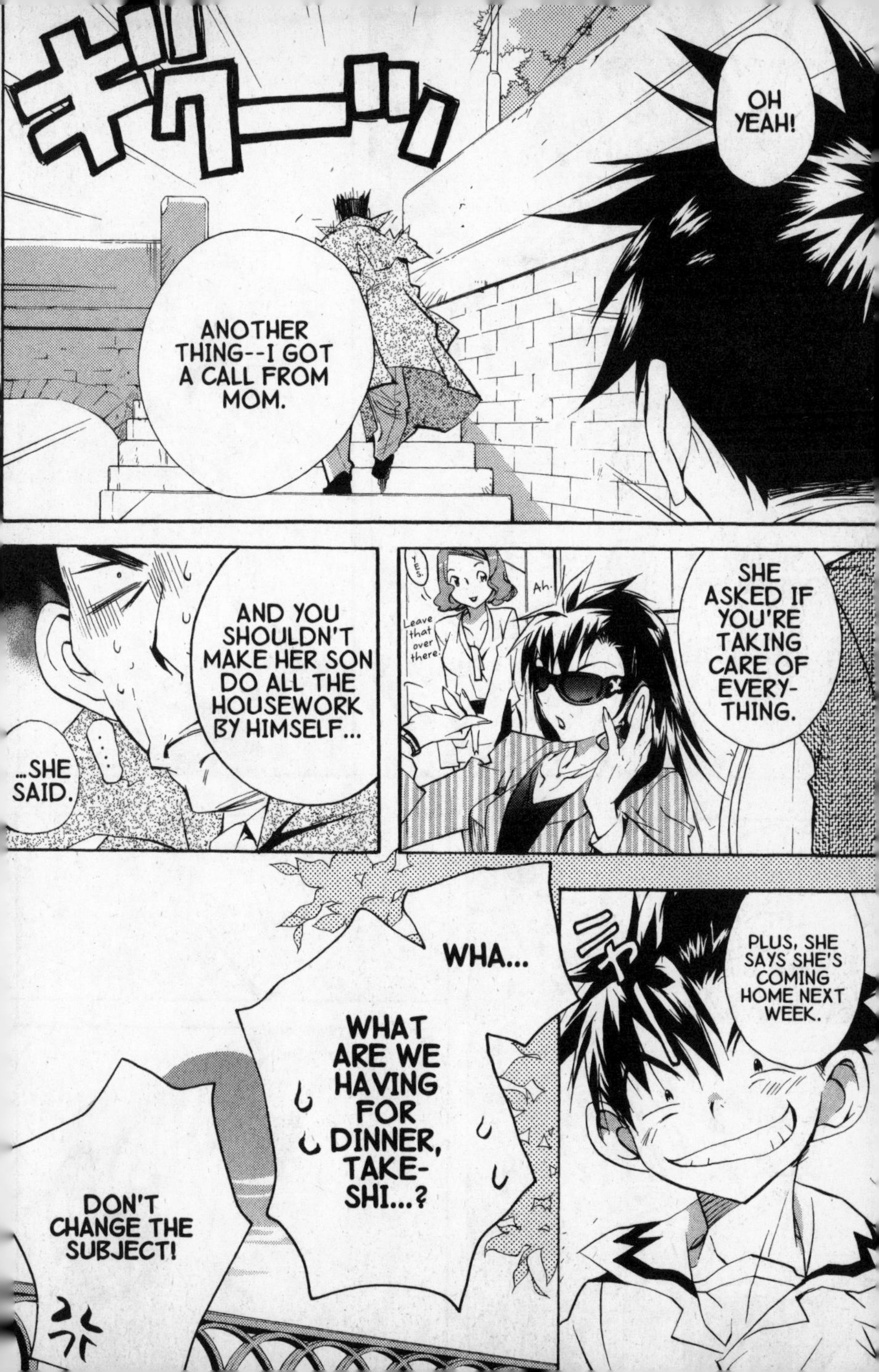

OH YEAH!
ANOTHER THING--I GOT A CALL FROM MOM.
SHE ASKED IF YOU'RE TAKING CARE OF EVERY-THING.
Ah.
YES.
Leave that over there.
AND YOU SHOULDN'T MAKE HER SON DO ALL THE HOUSEWORK BY HIMSELF...
...SHE SAID.
PLUS, SHE SAYS SHE'S COMING HOME NEXT WEEK.
WHA...
WHAT ARE WE HAVING FOR DINNER, TAKE-SHI...?
DON'T CHANGE THE SUBJECT!

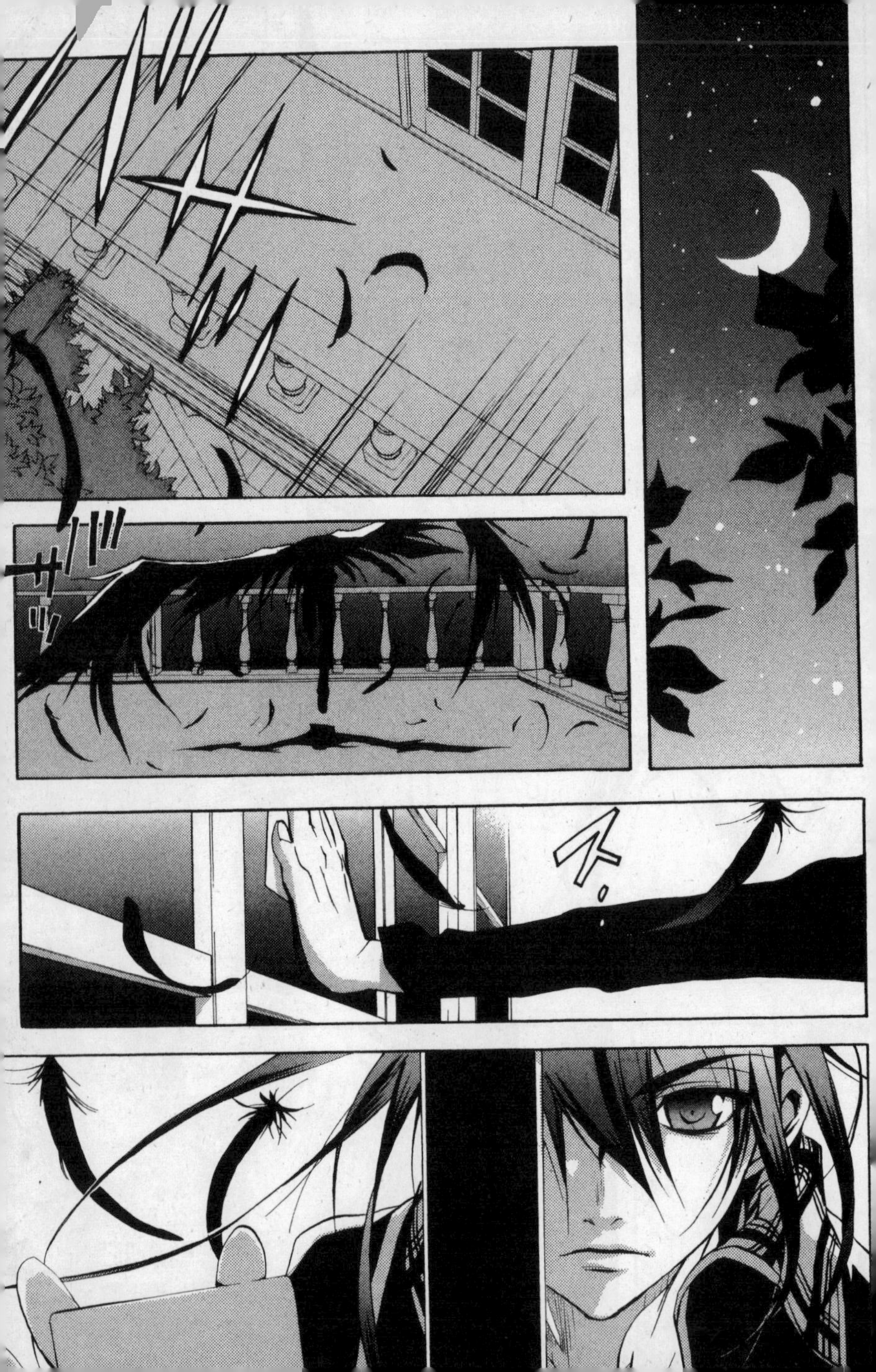
ザッ

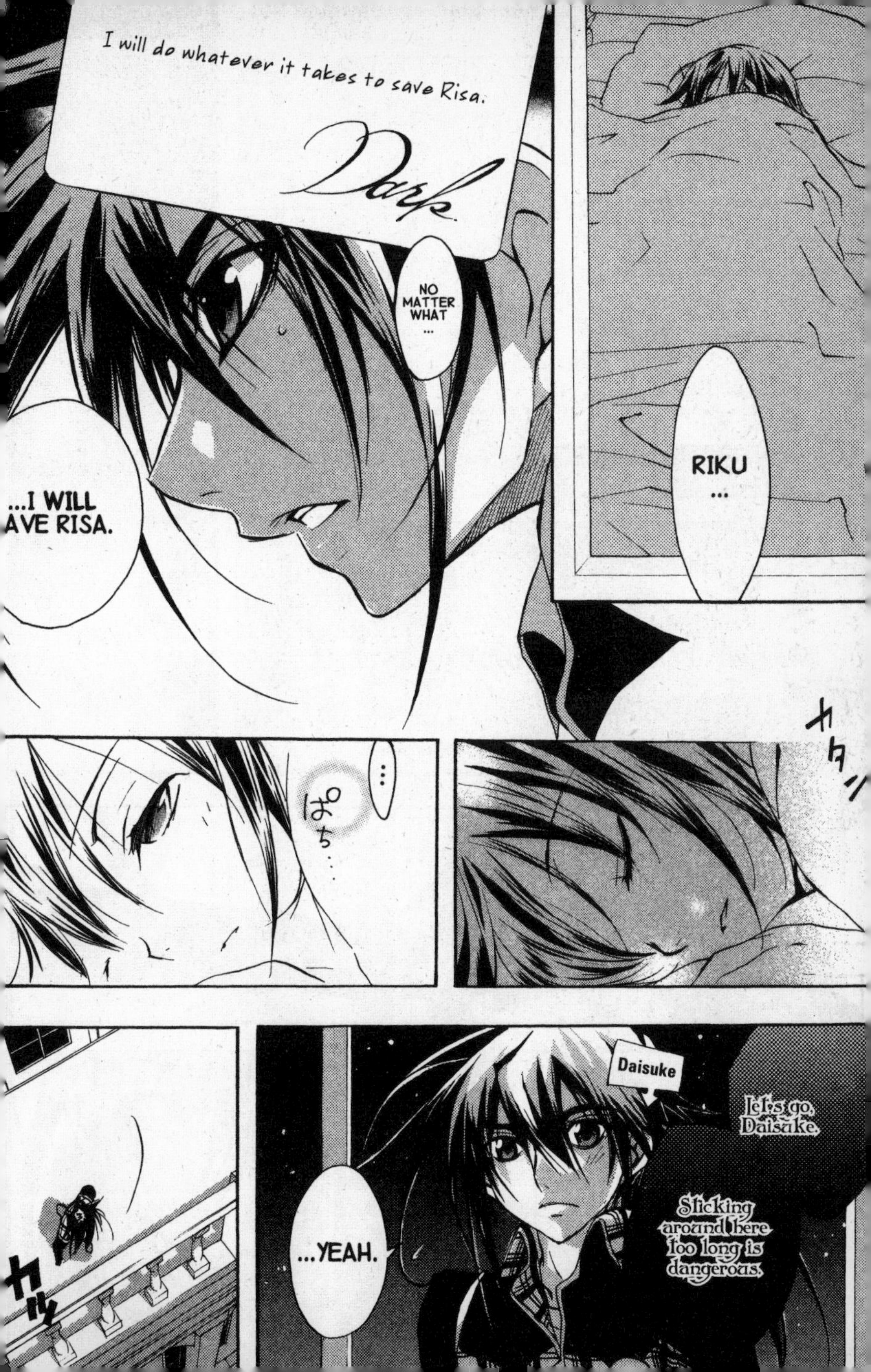
RIKU ...
I will do whatever it takes to save Risa.
Dark
NO MATTER WHAT ...
...I WILL AVE RISA.
カタン
...
ぱち…
Daisuke
Let's go, Daisuke.
Sticking around here too long is dangerous.
...YEAH.

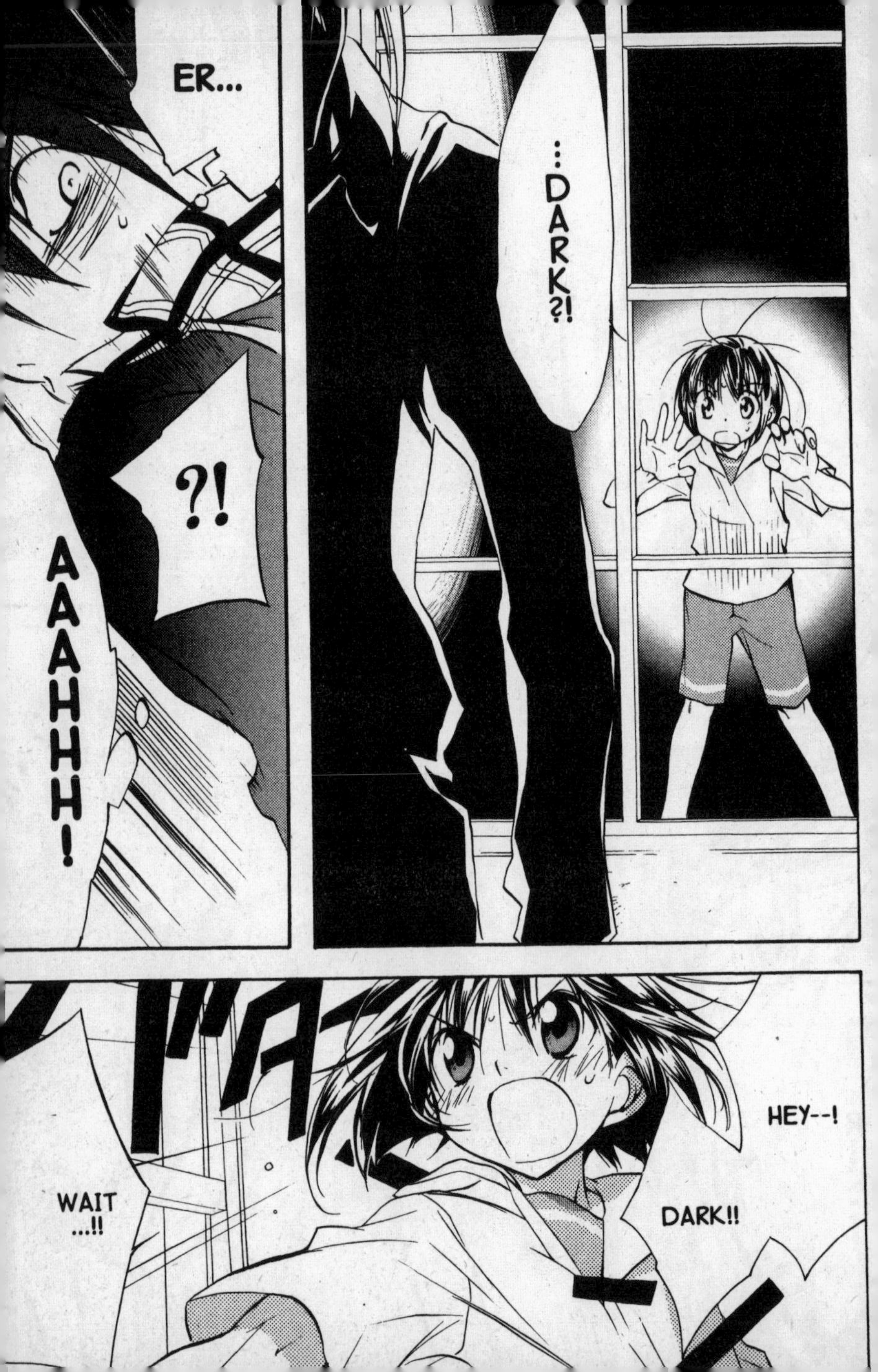

...DARK?!
ER...
?!
AAAAHHH!
HEY--!
DARK!!
WAIT ...!!

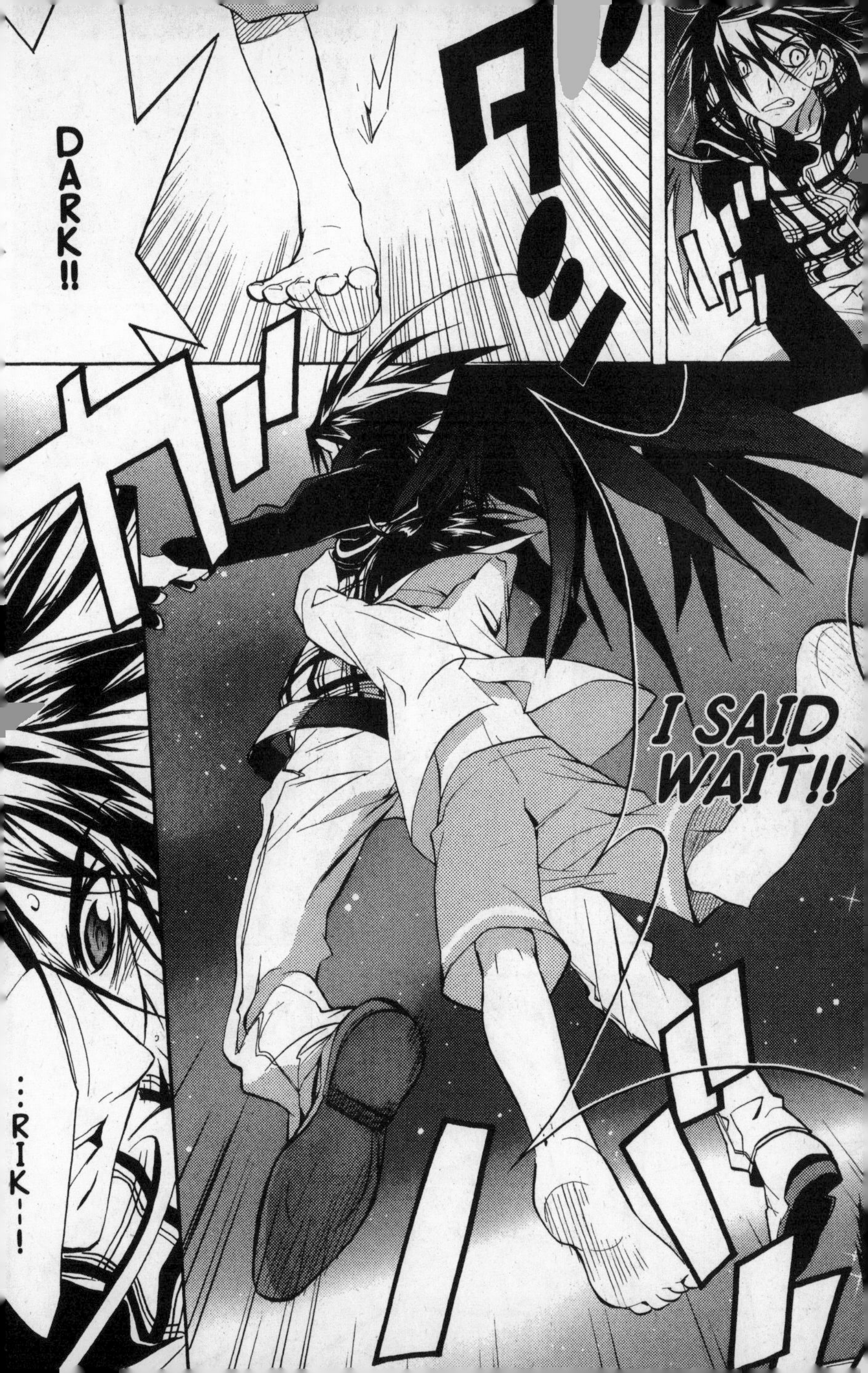
DARK!!
I SAID WAIT!!
...RIK--!

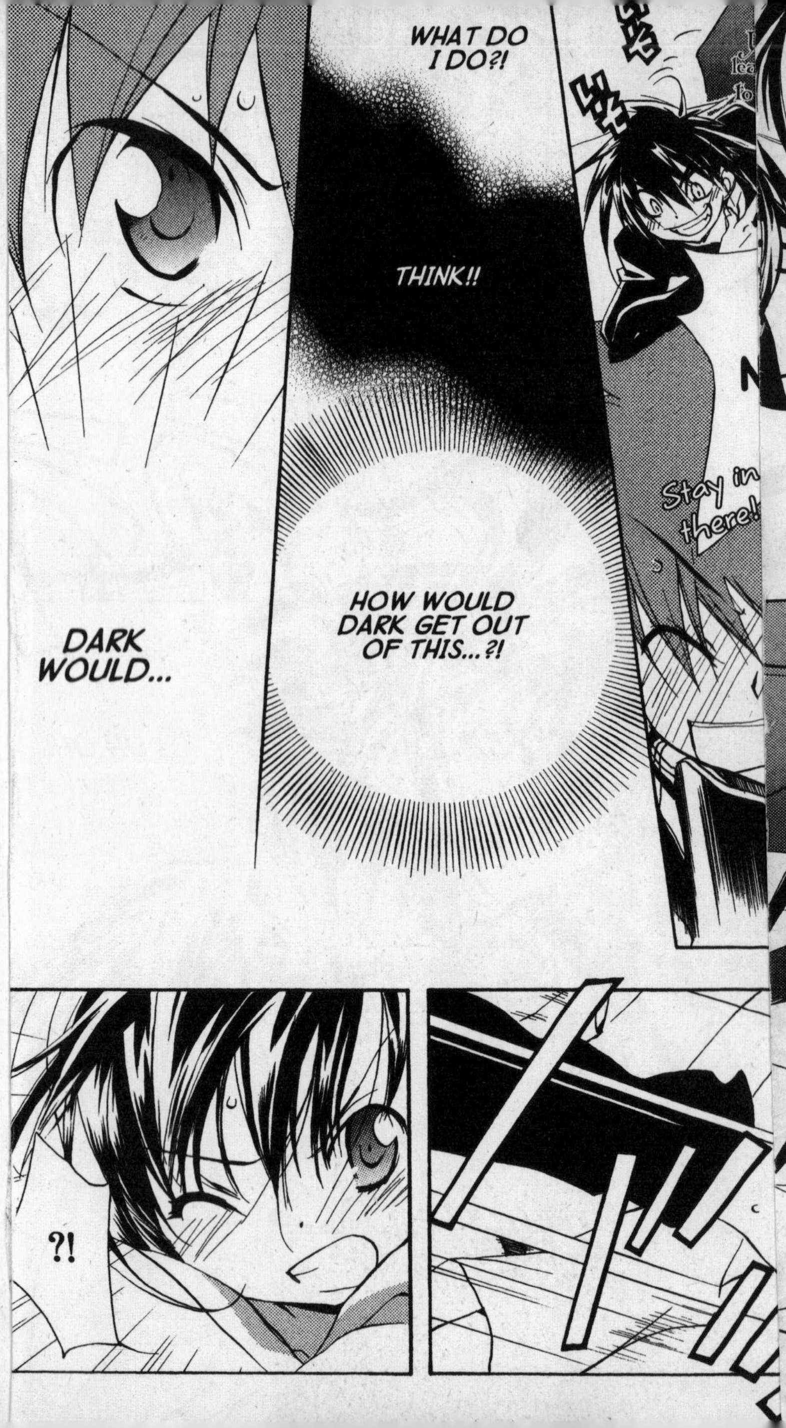
Stay in there!!
WHAT DO I DO?!
THINK!!
HOW WOULD DARK GET OUT OF THIS...?!
DARK WOULD...
?!
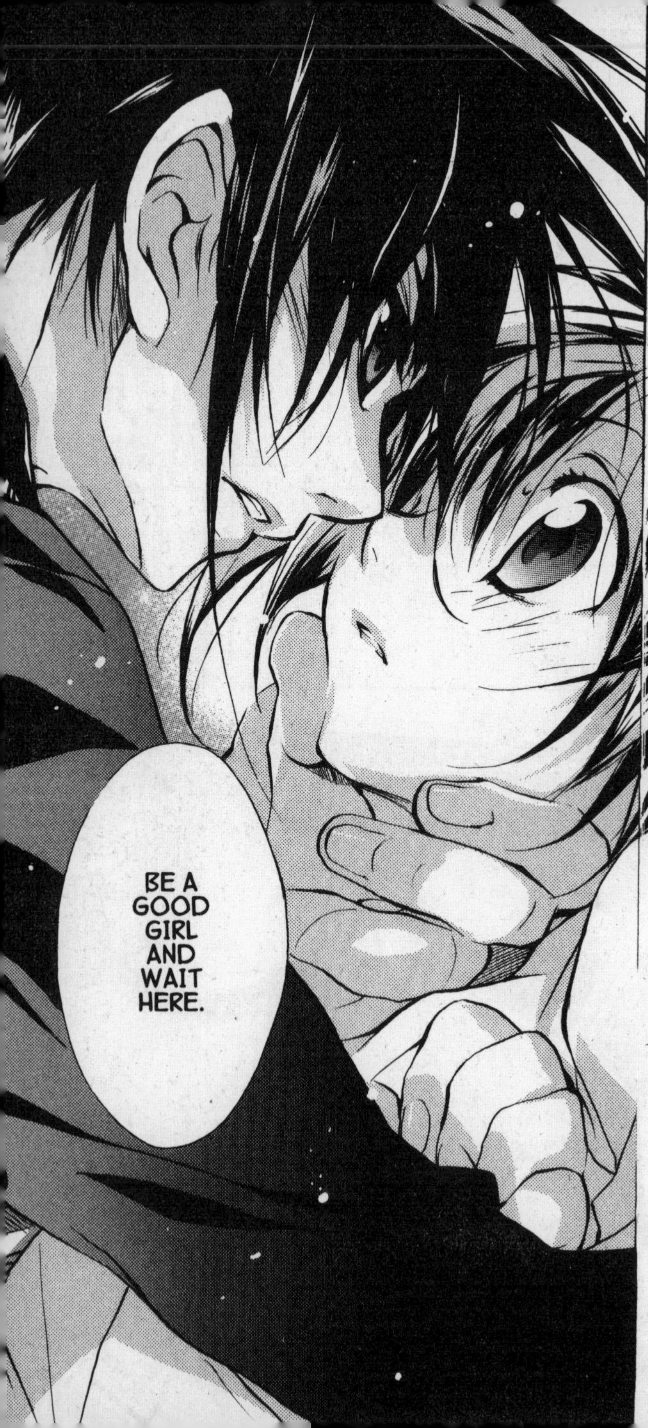
EVERY-THING WILL BE FINE.
BE A GOOD GIRL AND WAIT HERE.

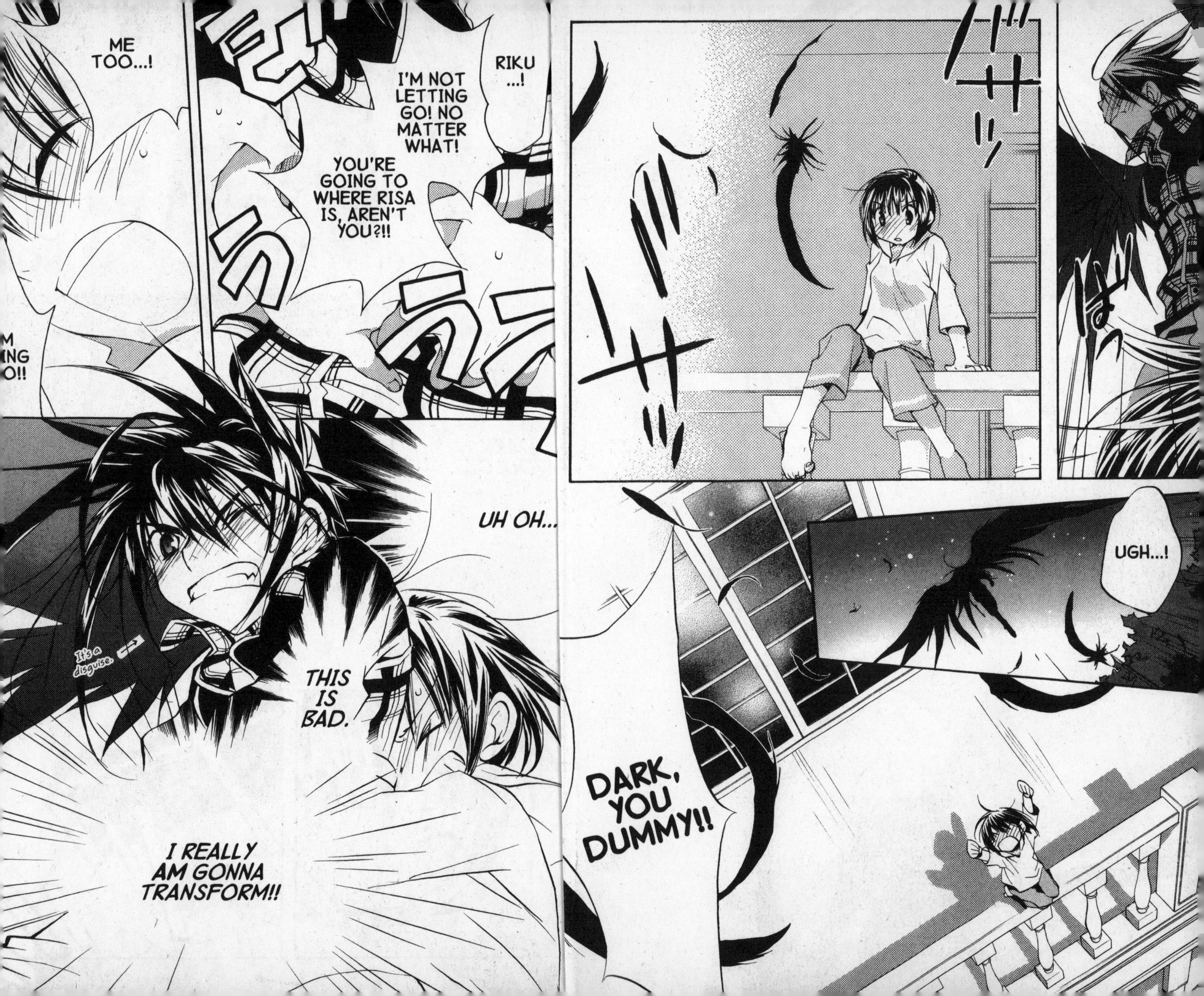
UGH...!
DARK, YOU DUMMY!!
RIKU ...!
I'M NOT LETTING GO! NO MATTER WHAT!
YOU'RE GOING TO WHERE RISA IS, AREN'T YOU?!!
ME TOO...!
UH OH...
THIS IS BAD.
It's a disguise.
I REALLY AM GONNA TRANSFORM!!

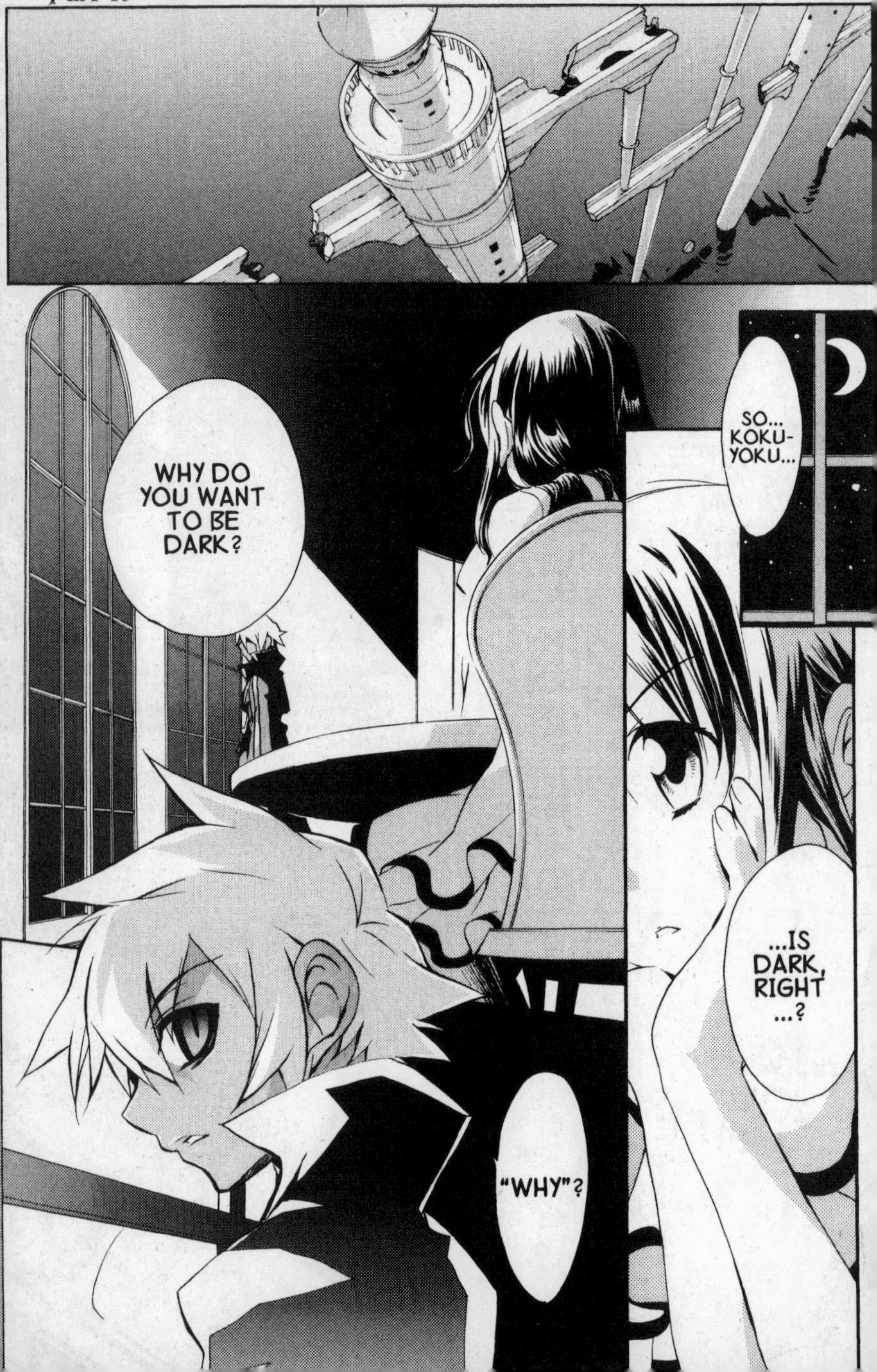
SO... KOKU-YOKU...
...IS DARK, RIGHT ...?
WHY DO YOU WANT TO BE DARK?
"WHY"?

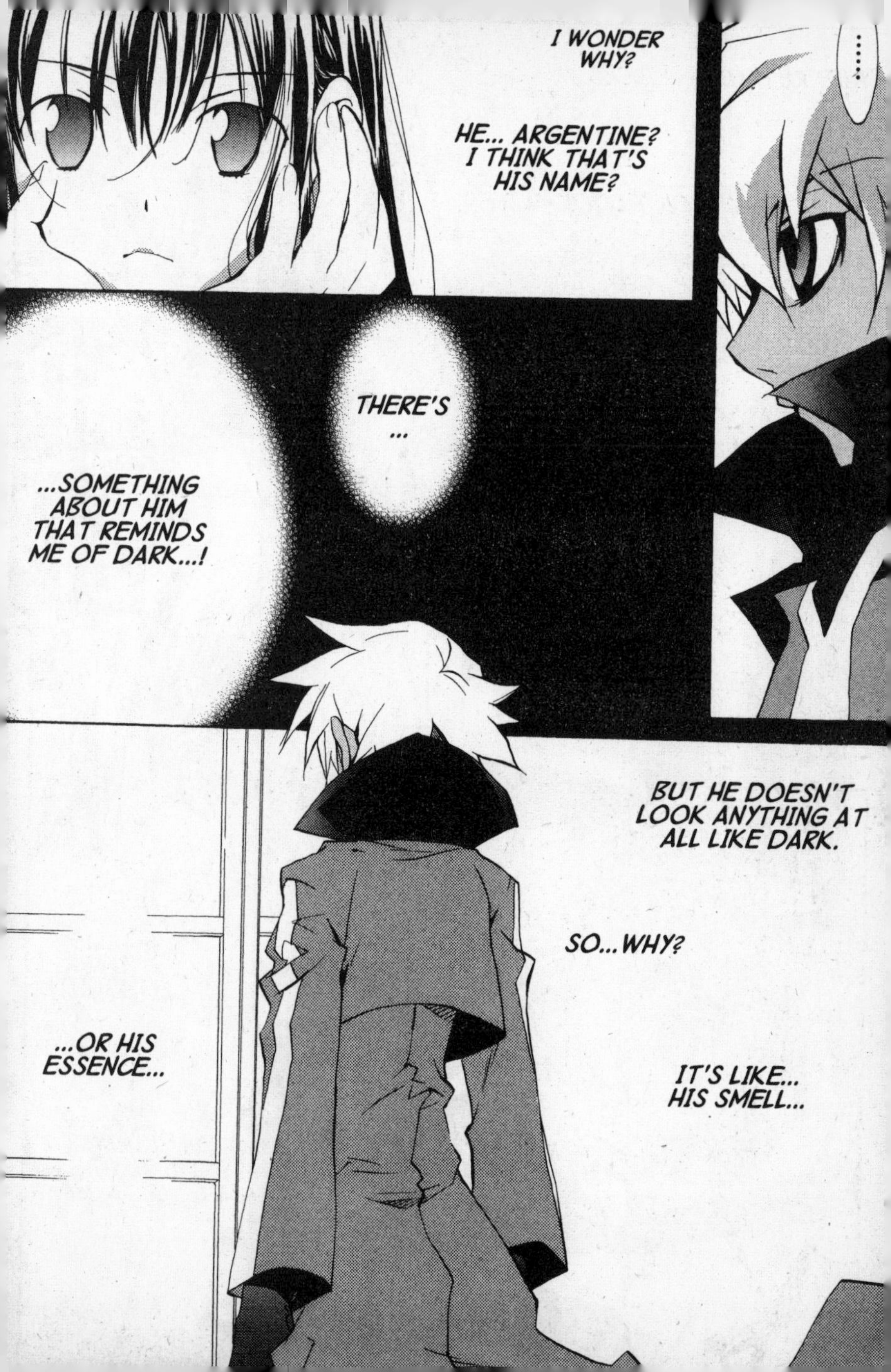
......
I WONDER WHY?
HE... ARGENTINE? I THINK THAT'S HIS NAME?
THERE'S ...
...SOMETHING ABOUT HIM THAT REMINDS ME OF DARK...!
BUT HE DOESN'T LOOK ANYTHING AT ALL LIKE DARK.
SO...WHY?
IT'S LIKE... HIS SMELL...
...OR HIS ESSENCE...

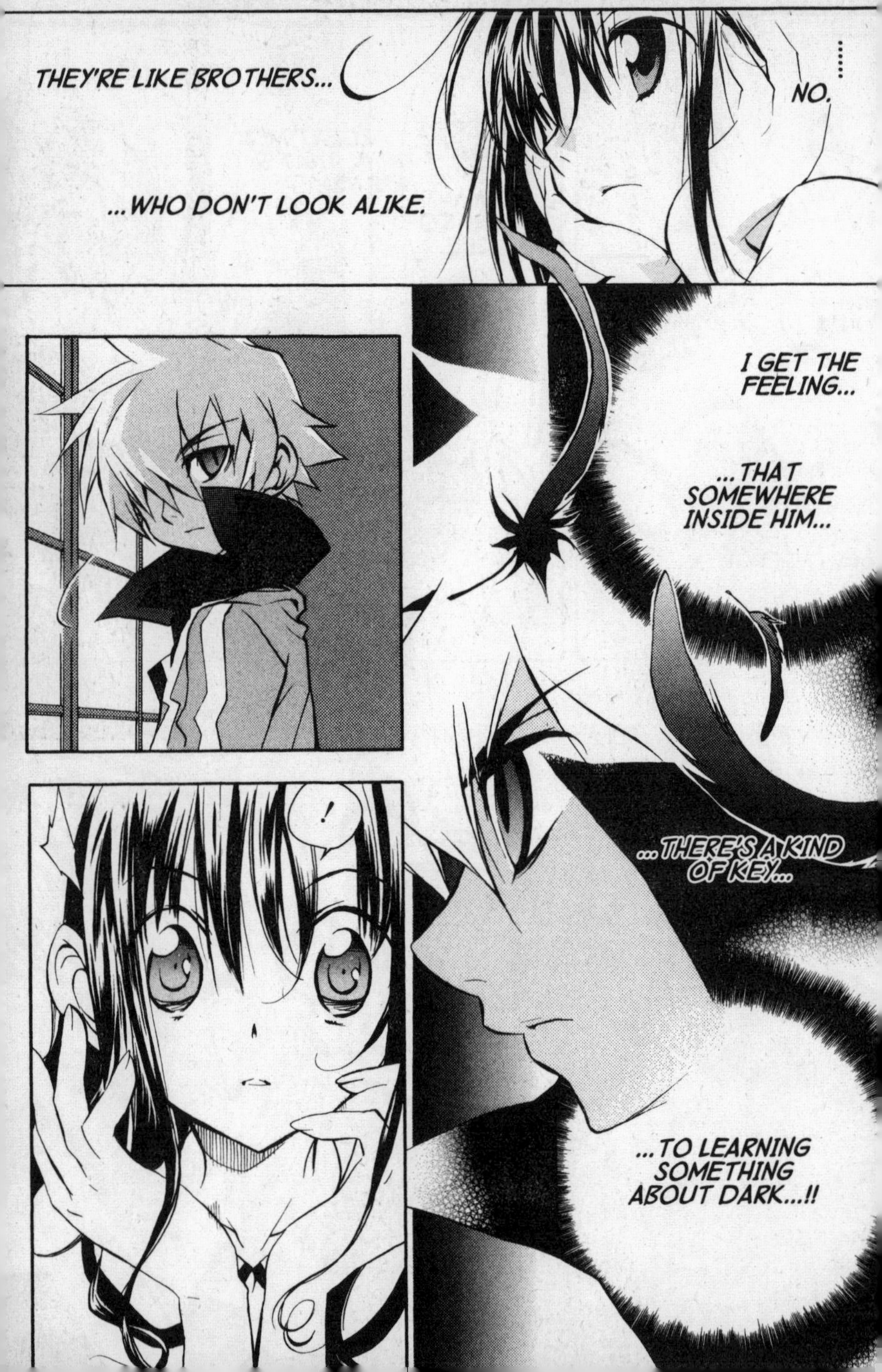
......
NO.
THEY'RE LIKE BROTHERS...
...WHO DON'T LOOK ALIKE.
I GET THE FEELING...
...THAT SOMEWHERE INSIDE HIM...
...THERE'S A KIND OF KEY...
...TO LEARNING SOMETHING ABOUT DARK...!!
!

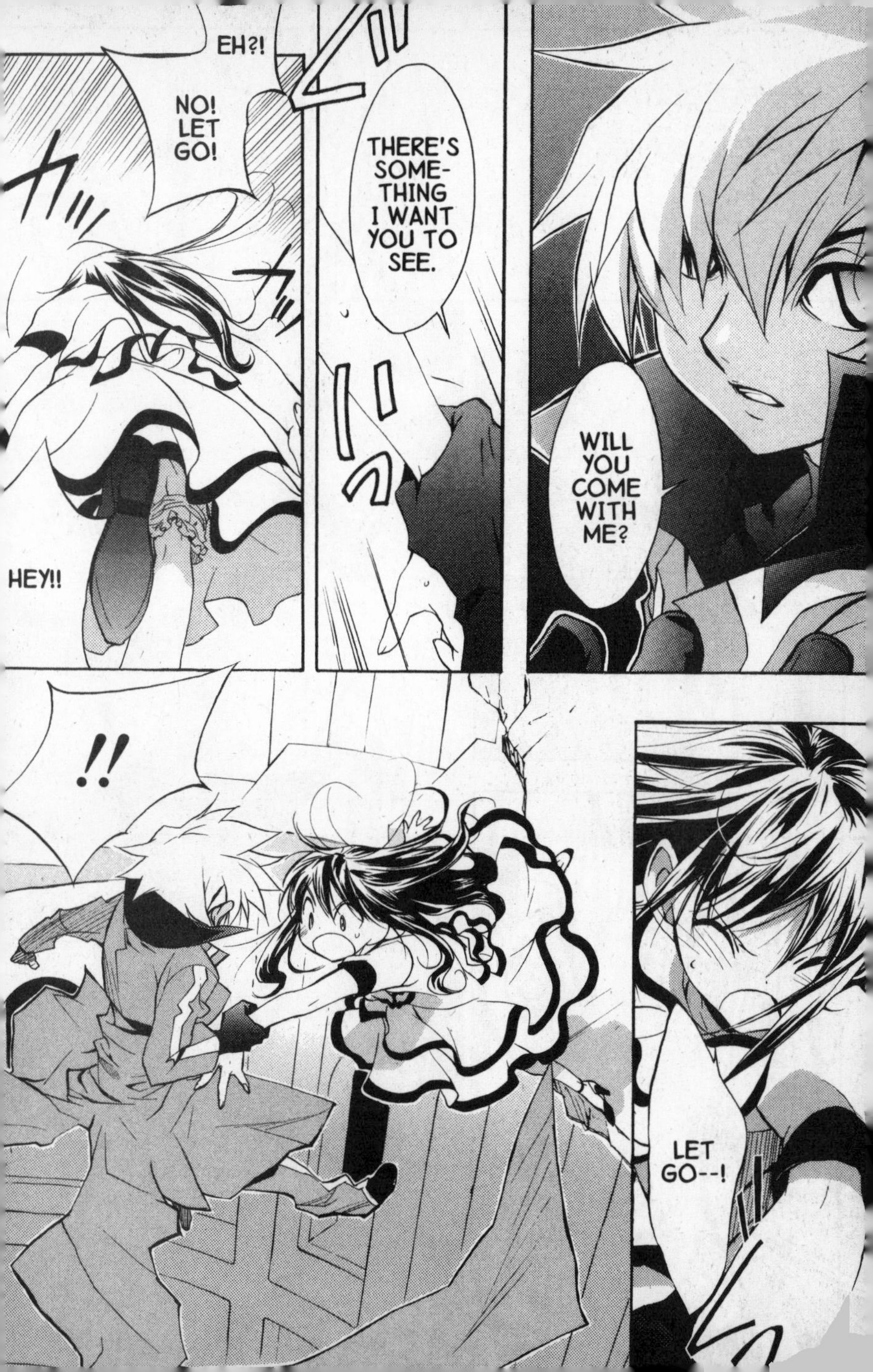
WILL YOU COME WITH ME?
THERE'S SOME-THING I WANT YOU TO SEE.
EH?!
NO! LET GO!
HEY!!
LET GO--!
!!

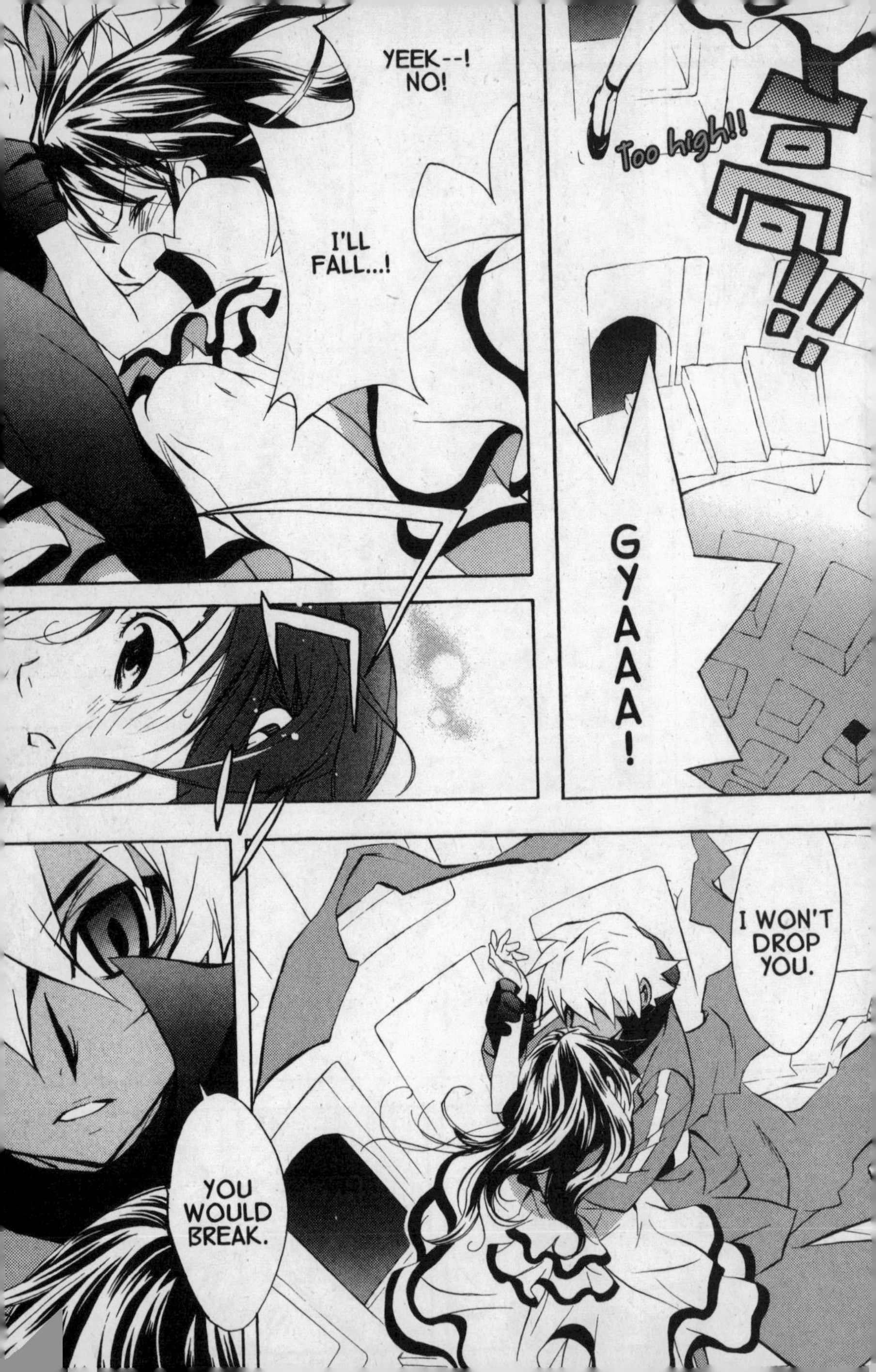
Too high!!
GYAAAA!
YEEK--! NO!
I'LL FALL...!
I WON'T DROP YOU.
YOU WOULD BREAK.

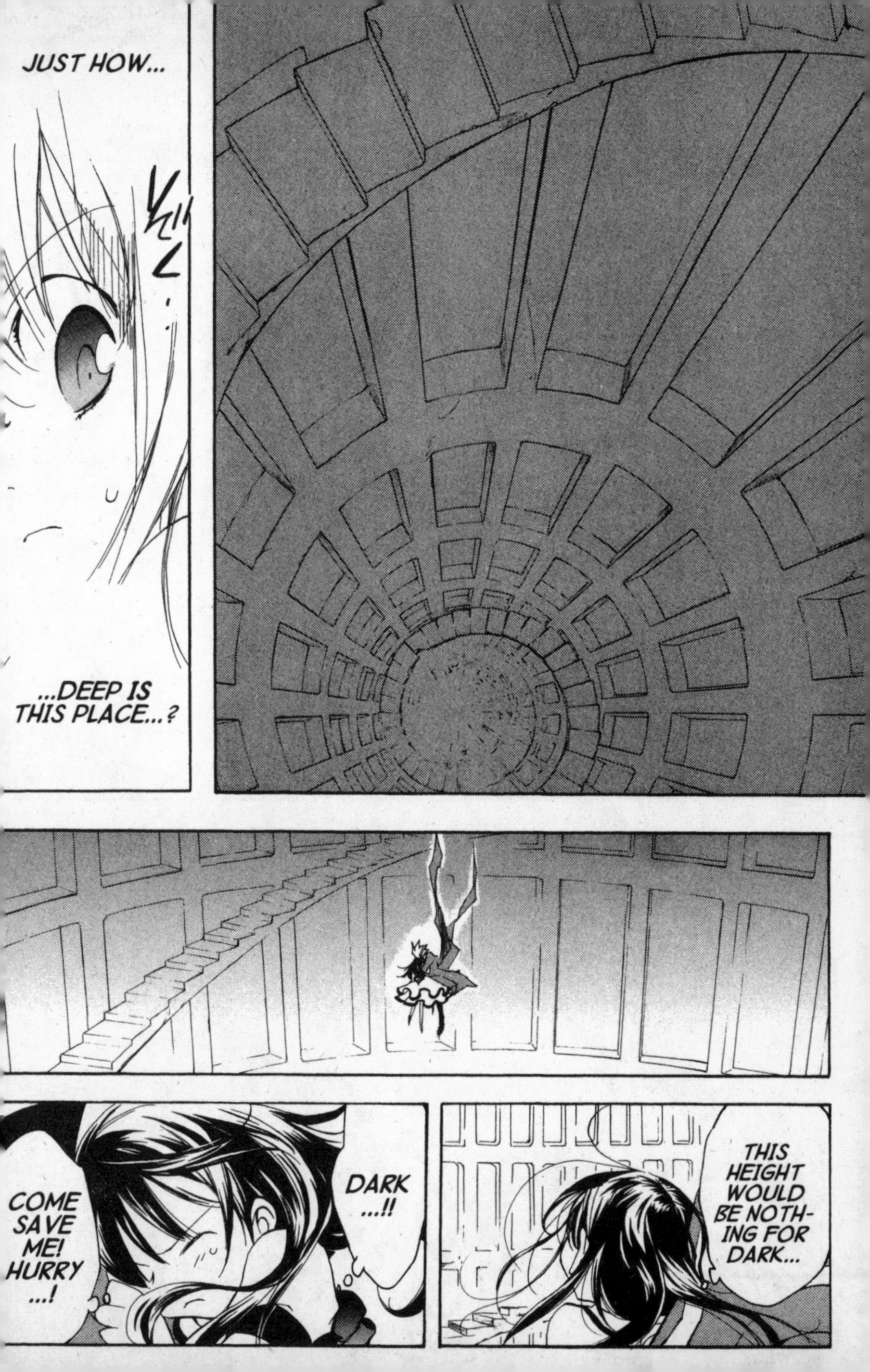
JUST HOW...
...DEEP IS THIS PLACE...?
THIS HEIGHT WOULD BE NOTHING FOR DARK...
DARK ...!!
COME SAVE ME! HURRY ...!

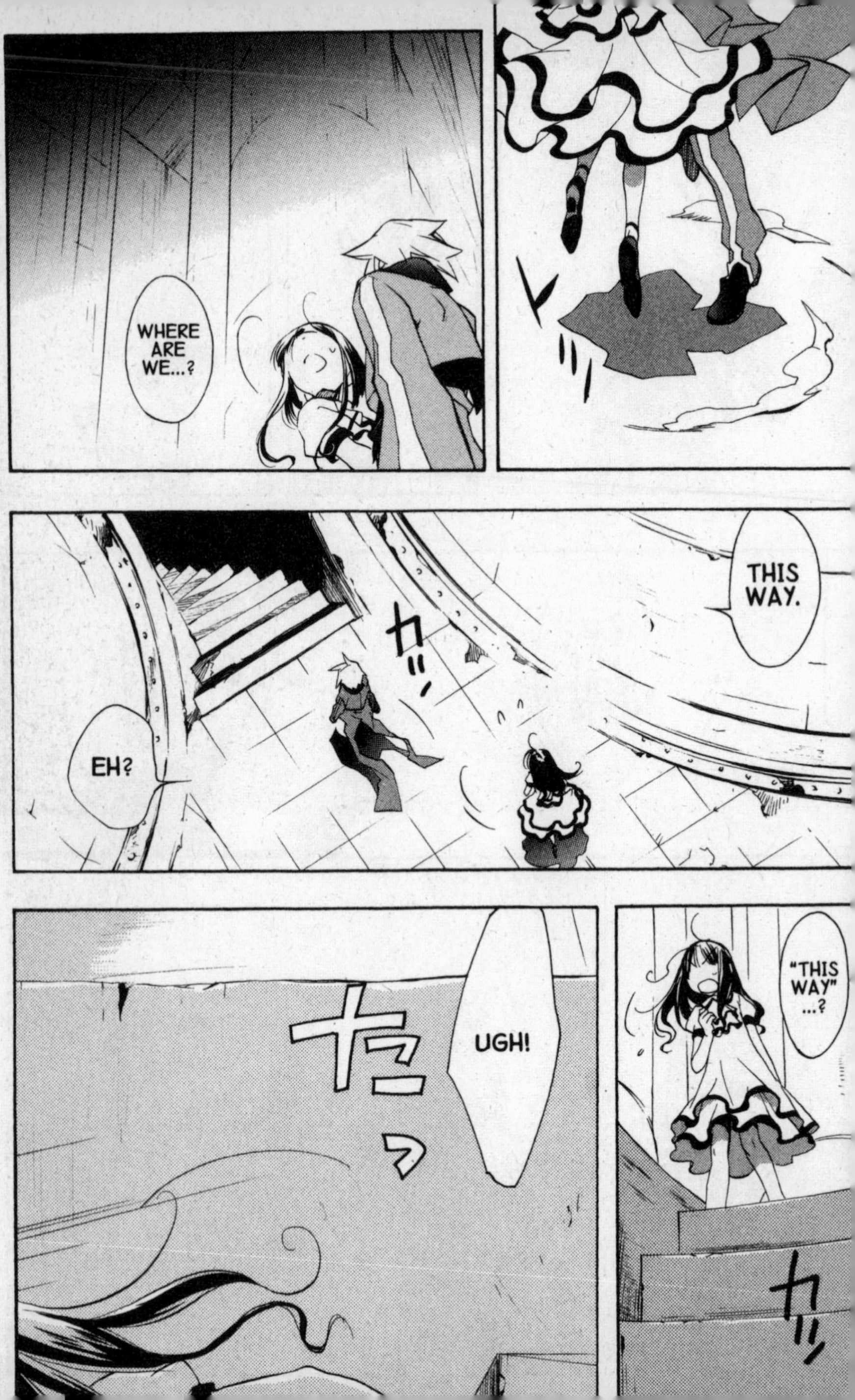
WHERE ARE WE...?
THIS WAY.
カッ
EH?
"THIS WAY" ...?
カッ
UGH!
タッ

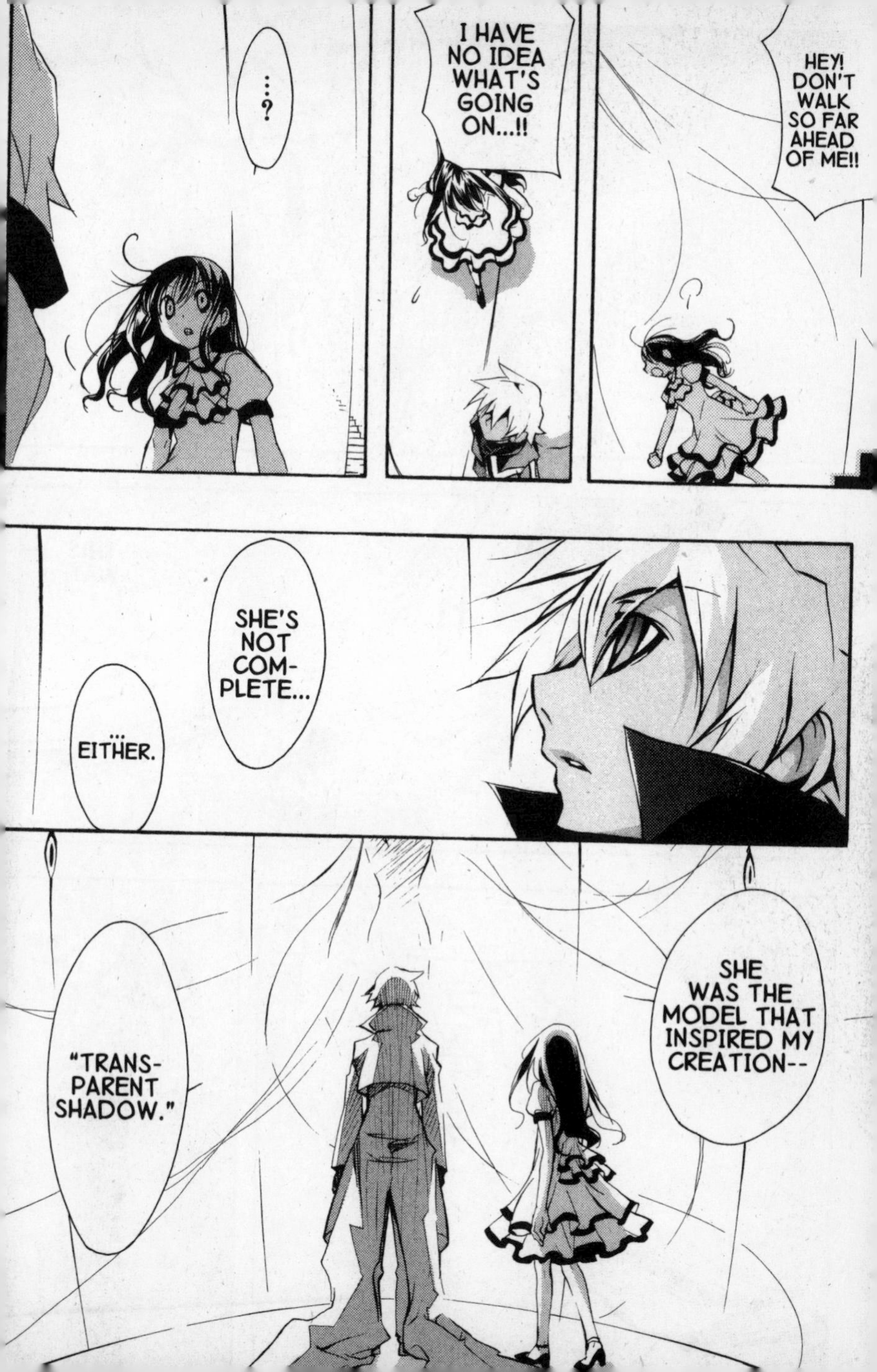
HEY! DON'T WALK SO FAR AHEAD OF ME!!
I HAVE NO IDEA WHAT'S GOING ON...!!
...?
SHE'S NOT COM-PLETE...
...EITHER.
SHE WAS THE MODEL THAT INSPIRED MY CREATION--
"TRANS-PARENT SHADOW."

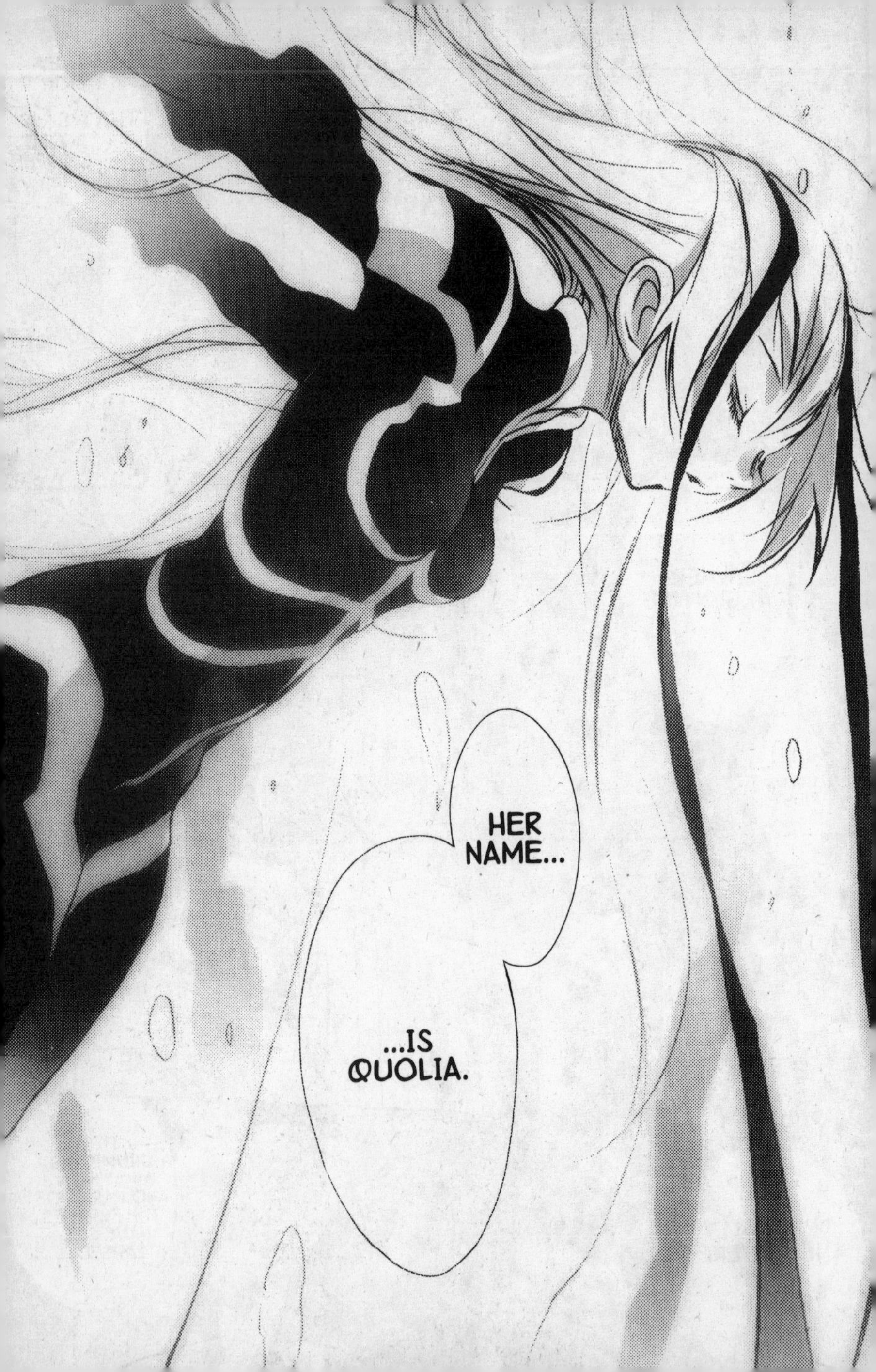
HER NAME...
...IS QUOLIA.

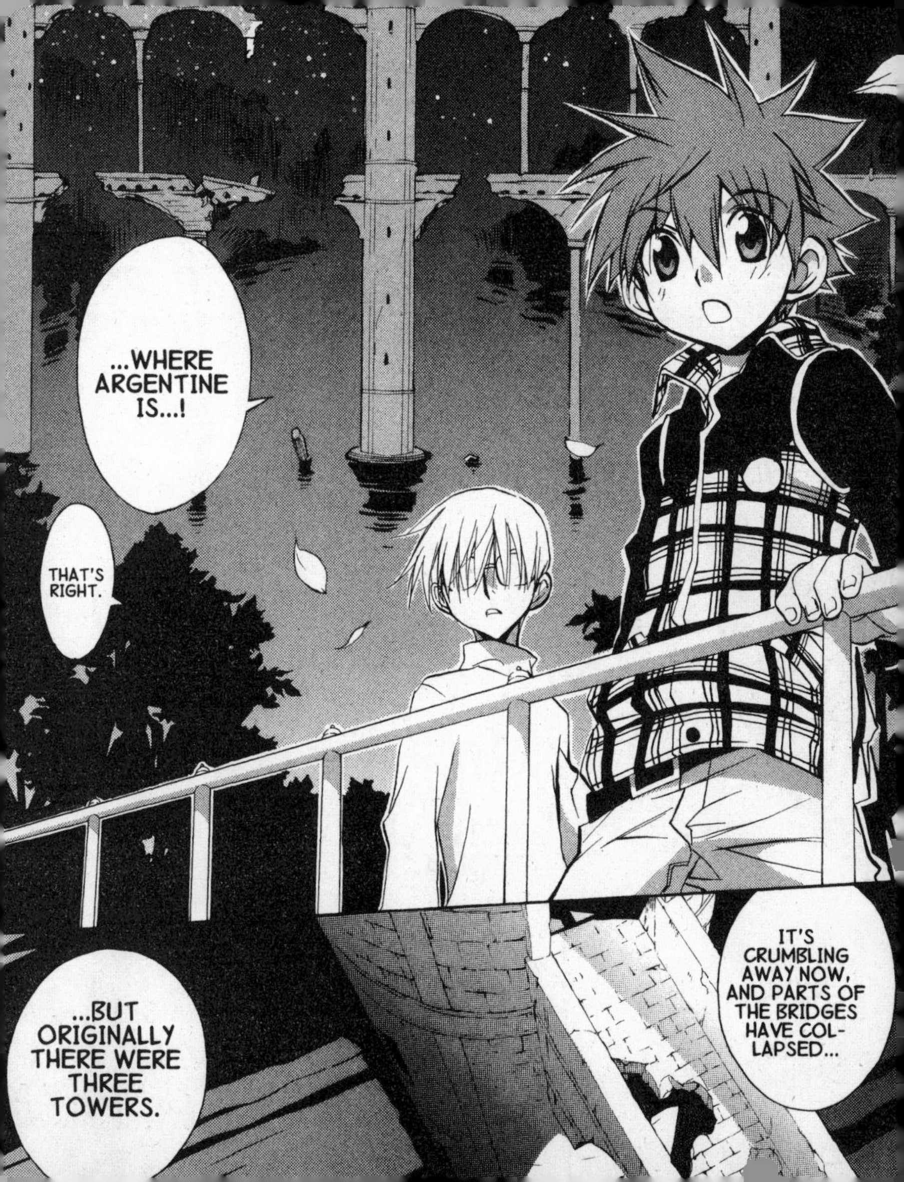
...WHERE ARGENTINE IS...!
THAT'S RIGHT.
IT'S CRUMBLING AWAY NOW, AND PARTS OF THE BRIDGES HAVE COL-LAPSED...
...BUT ORIGINALLY THERE WERE THREE TOWERS.

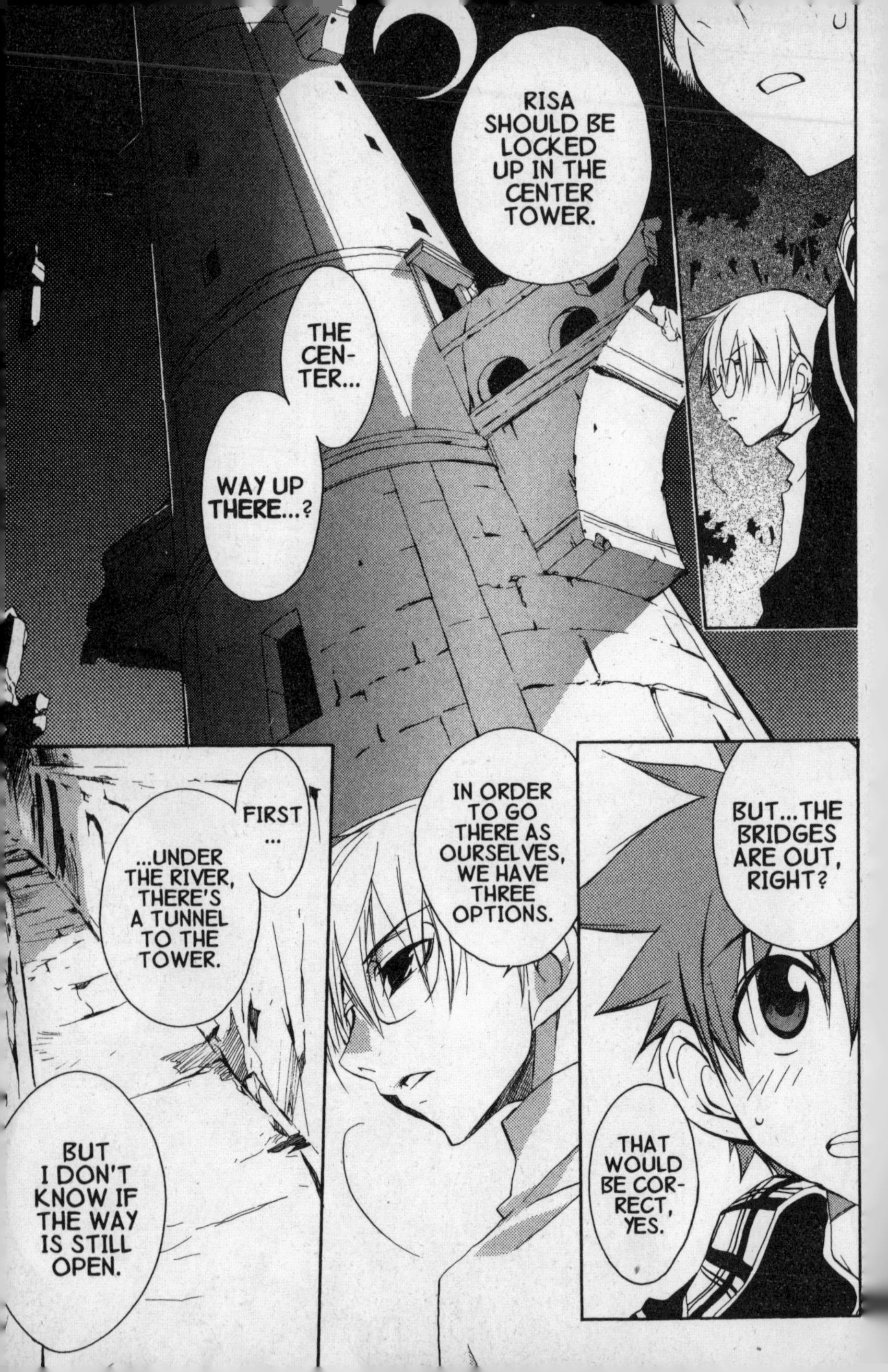
RISA SHOULD BE LOCKED UP IN THE CENTER TOWER.
THE CEN-TER...
WAY UP THERE...?
BUT...THE BRIDGES ARE OUT, RIGHT?
THAT WOULD BE COR-RECT, YES.
IN ORDER TO GO THERE AS OURSELVES, WE HAVE THREE OPTIONS.
FIRST...
...UNDER THE RIVER, THERE'S A TUNNEL TO THE TOWER.
BUT I DON'T KNOW IF THE WAY IS STILL OPEN.

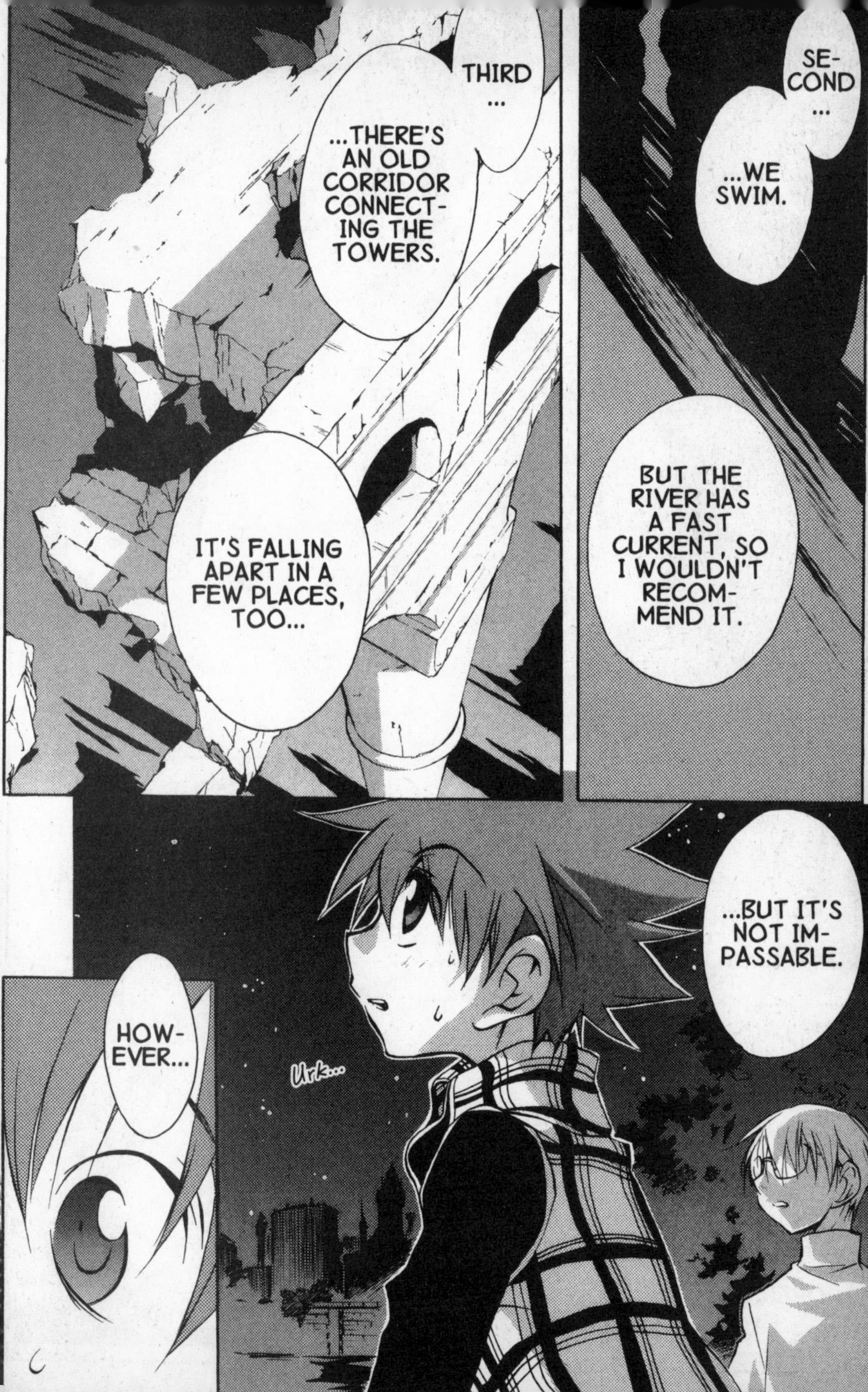
SE-COND...
...WE SWIM.
BUT THE RIVER HAS A FAST CURRENT, SO I WOULDN'T RECOM-MEND IT.
THIRD...
...THERE'S AN OLD CORRIDOR CONNECT-ING THE TOWERS.
IT'S FALLING APART IN A FEW PLACES, TOO...
...BUT IT'S NOT IM-PASSABLE.
Urk...
HOW-EVER...

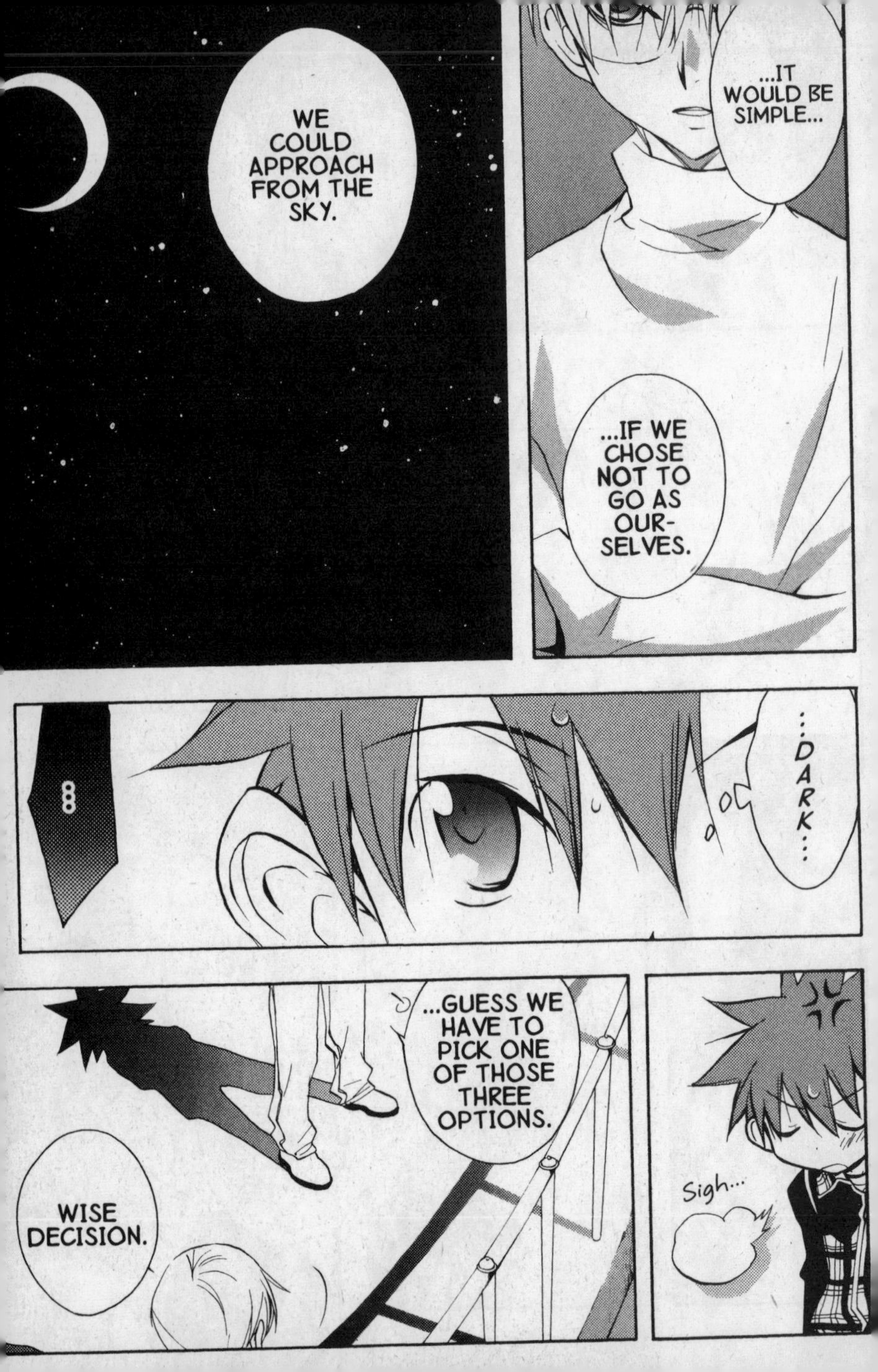
...IT WOULD BE SIMPLE...
...IF WE CHOSE NOT TO GO AS OUR-SELVES.
WE COULD APPROACH FROM THE SKY.
...DARK...
...
Sigh...
...GUESS WE HAVE TO PICK ONE OF THOSE THREE OPTIONS.
WISE DECISION.

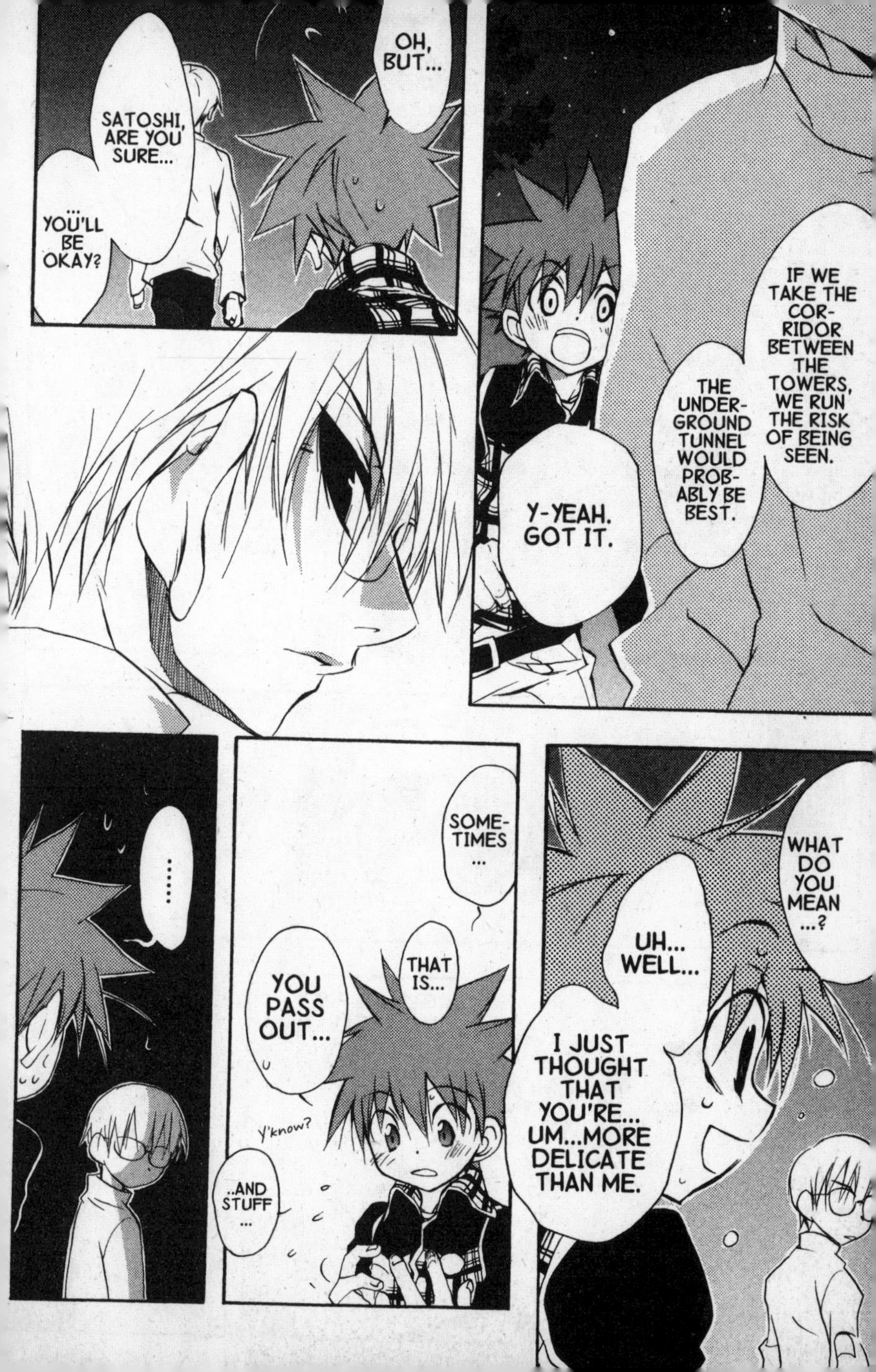
IF WE TAKE THE COR-RIDOR BETWEEN THE TOWERS, WE RUN THE RISK OF BEING SEEN.
THE UNDER-GROUND TUNNEL WOULD PROB-ABLY BE BEST.
Y-YEAH. GOT IT.
OH, BUT...
SATOSHI, ARE YOU SURE...
...YOU'LL BE OKAY?
WHAT DO YOU MEAN ...?
UH... WELL...
I JUST THOUGHT THAT YOU'RE... UM...MORE DELICATE THAN ME.
SOME-TIMES ...
THAT IS...
YOU PASS OUT...
Y'know?
..AND STUFF ...
......

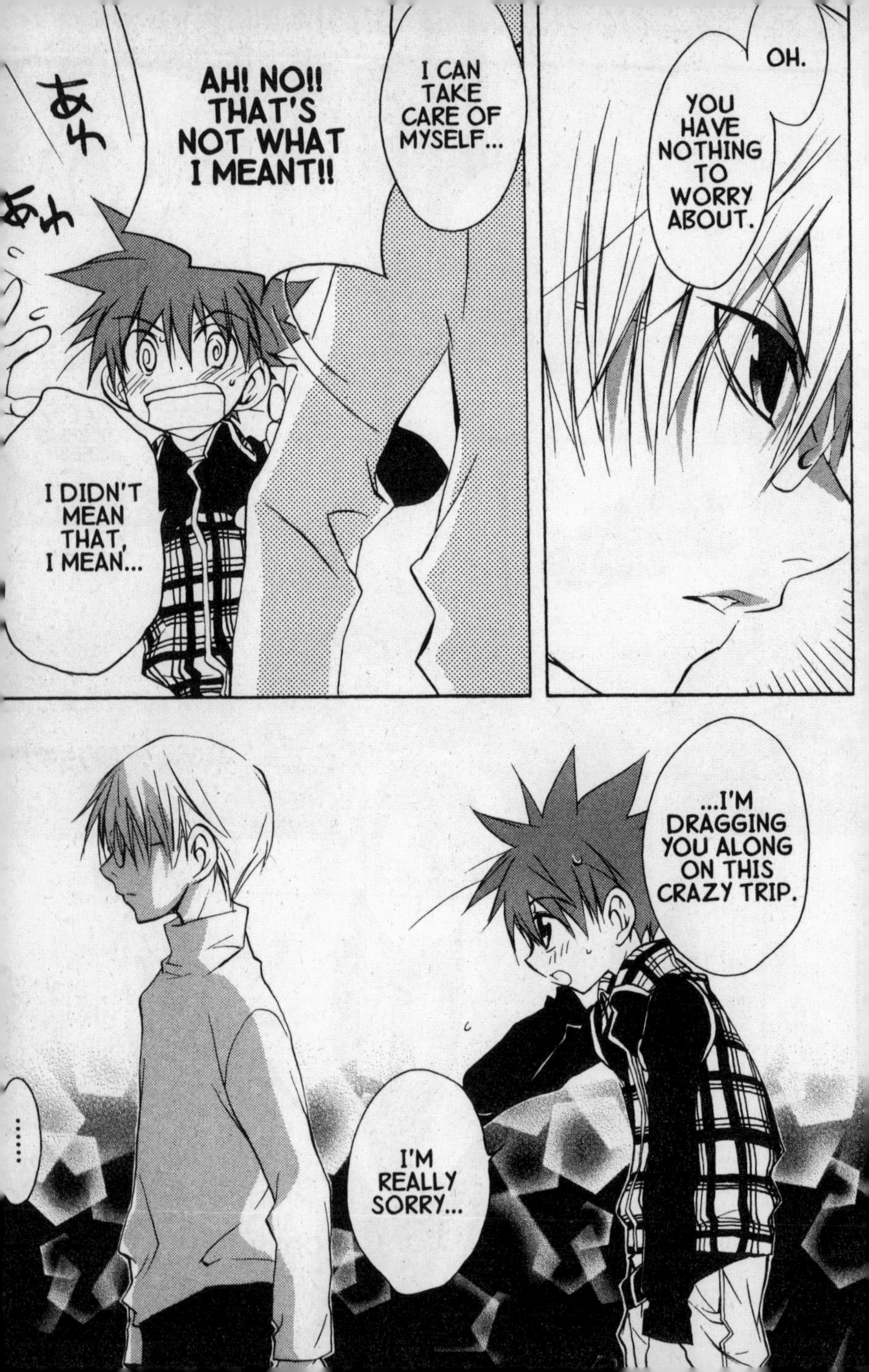
OH.
YOU HAVE NOTHING TO WORRY ABOUT.
I CAN TAKE CARE OF MYSELF...
AH! NO!! THAT'S NOT WHAT I MEANT!!
あわ
あわ
I DIDN'T MEAN THAT, I MEAN...
...I'M DRAGGING YOU ALONG ON THIS CRAZY TRIP.
I'M REALLY SORRY...
......

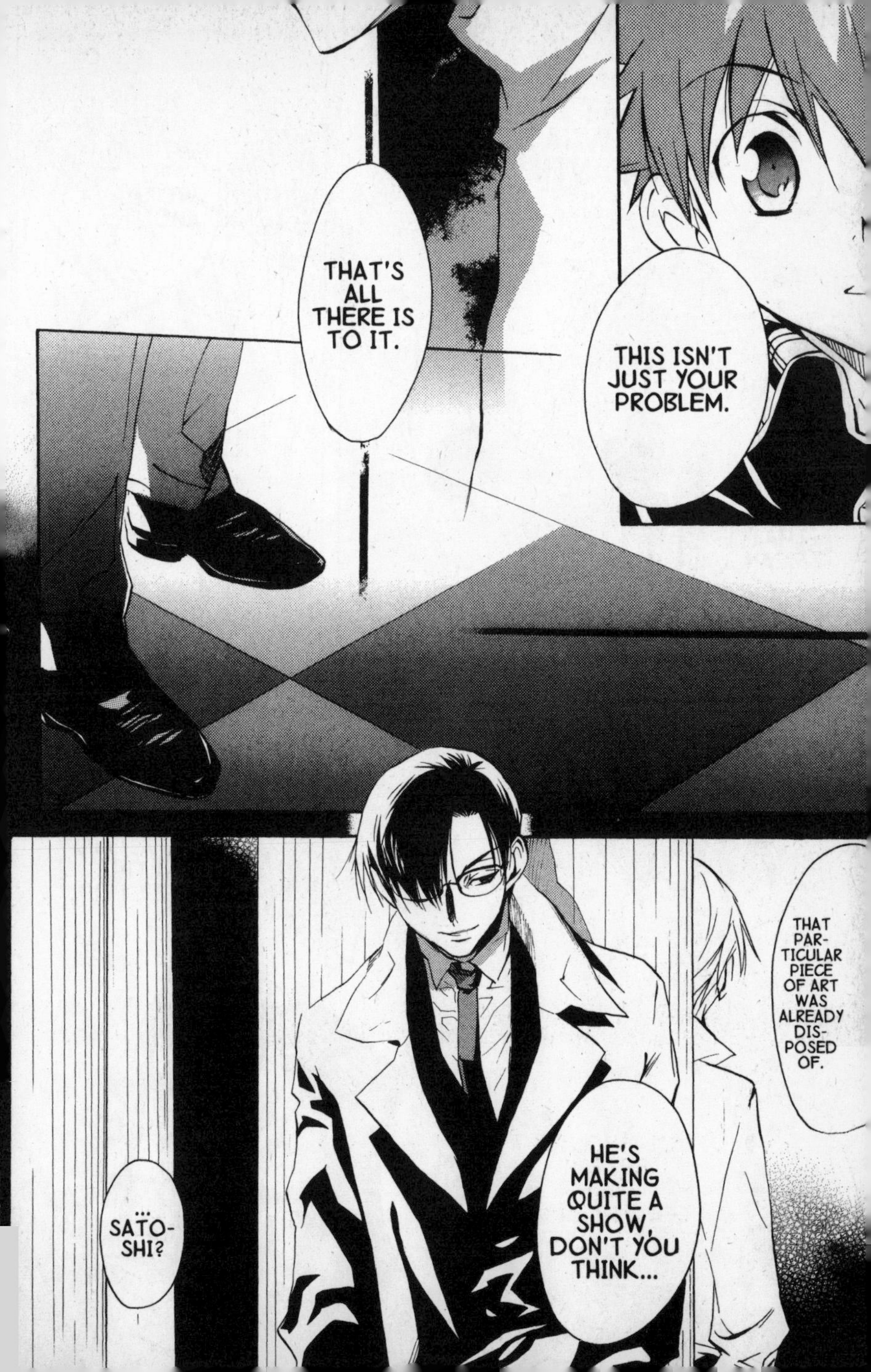
THIS ISN'T JUST YOUR PROBLEM.
THAT'S ALL THERE IS TO IT.
THAT PAR-TICULAR PIECE OF ART WAS ALREADY DIS-POSED OF.
HE'S MAKING QUITE A SHOW, DON'T YOU THINK...
...SATO-SHI?

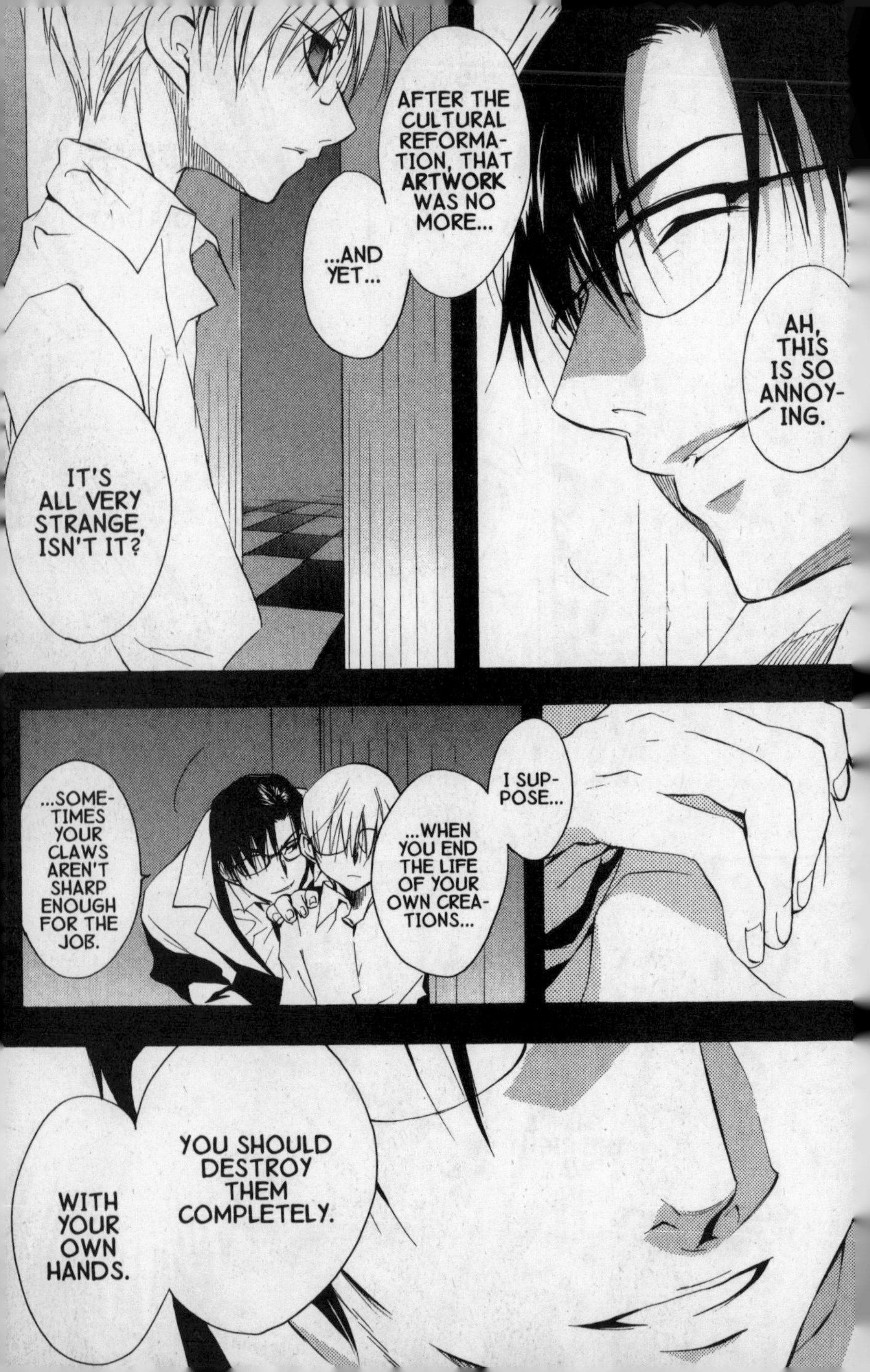
AH, THIS IS SO ANNOYING.
AFTER THE CULTURAL REFORMATION, THAT ARTWORK WAS NO MORE...
...AND YET...
IT'S ALL VERY STRANGE, ISN'T IT?
I SUPPOSE...
...WHEN YOU END THE LIFE OF YOUR OWN CREATIONS...
...SOMETIMES YOUR CLAWS AREN'T SHARP ENOUGH FOR THE JOB.
YOU SHOULD DESTROY THEM COMPLETELY.
WITH YOUR OWN HANDS.

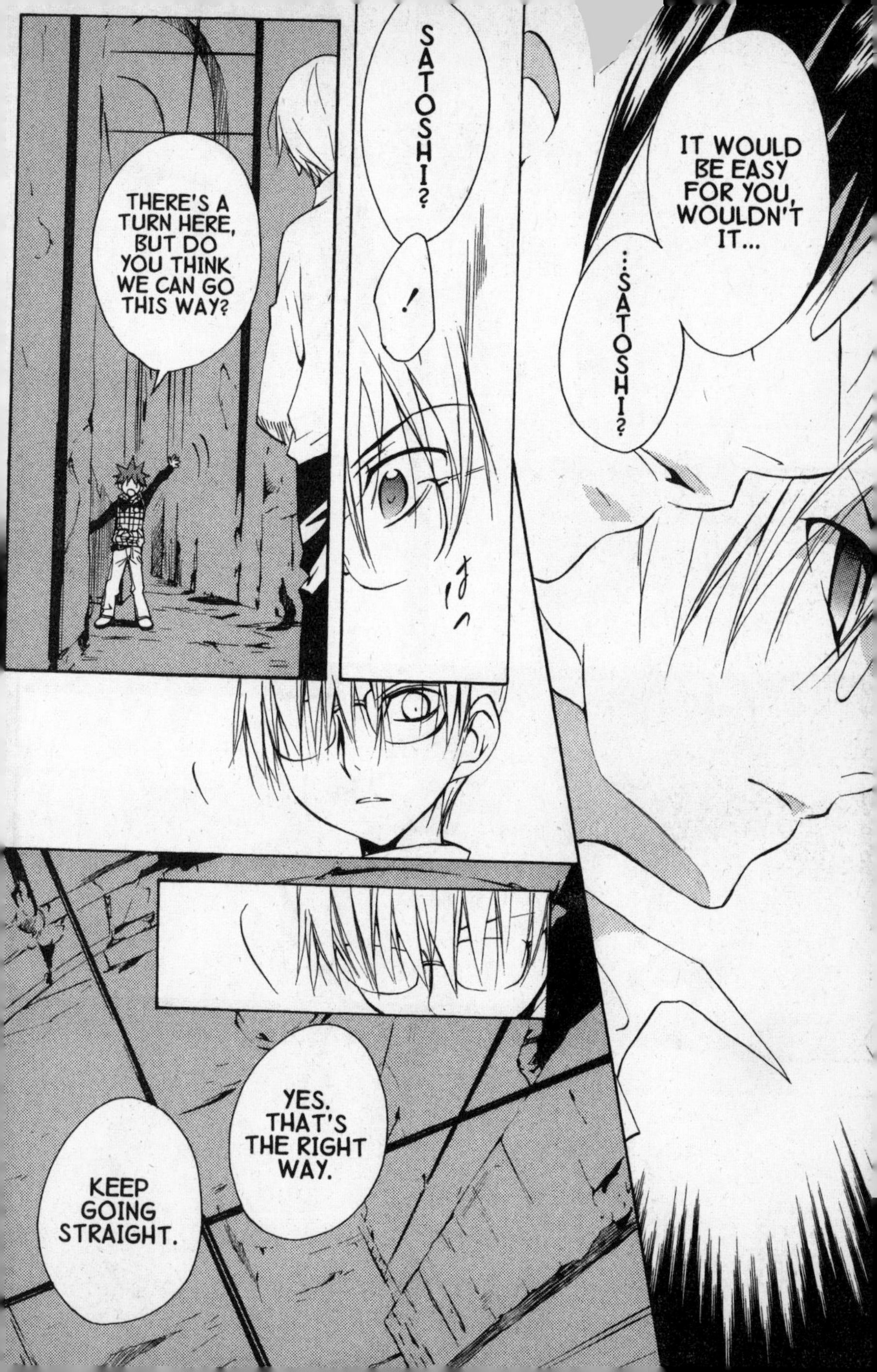

IT WOULD BE EASY FOR YOU, WOULDN'T IT...
...SATOSHI?
SATOSHI?
!
はっ
THERE'S A TURN HERE, BUT DO YOU THINK WE CAN GO THIS WAY?
YES. THAT'S THE RIGHT WAY.
KEEP GOING STRAIGHT.

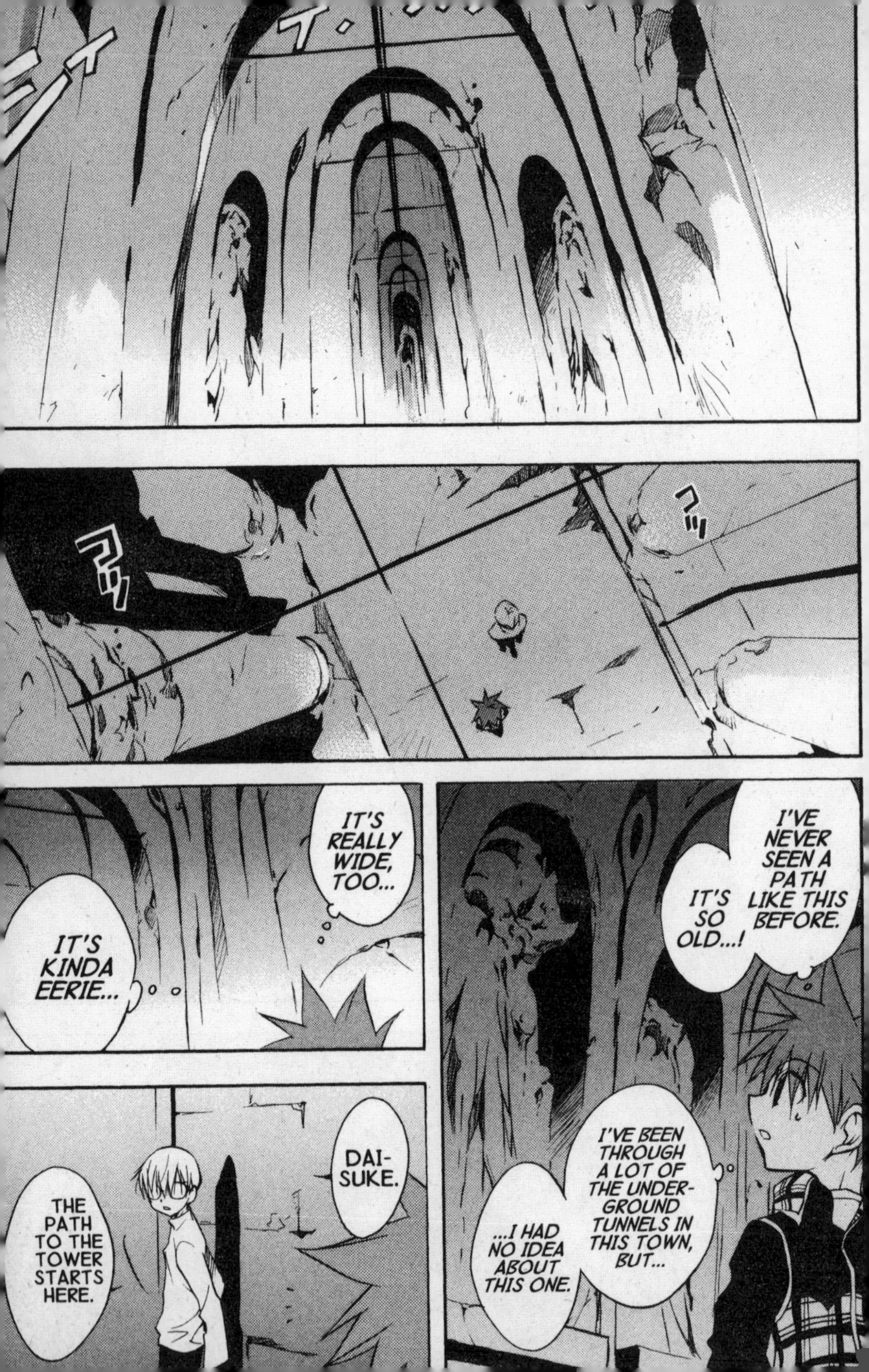
I'VE NEVER SEEN A PATH LIKE THIS BEFORE.
IT'S SO OLD...!
I'VE BEEN THROUGH A LOT OF THE UNDER-GROUND TUNNELS IN THIS TOWN, BUT...
...I HAD NO IDEA ABOUT THIS ONE.
IT'S REALLY WIDE, TOO...
IT'S KINDA EERIE...
DAI-SUKE.
THE PATH TO THE TOWER STARTS HERE.

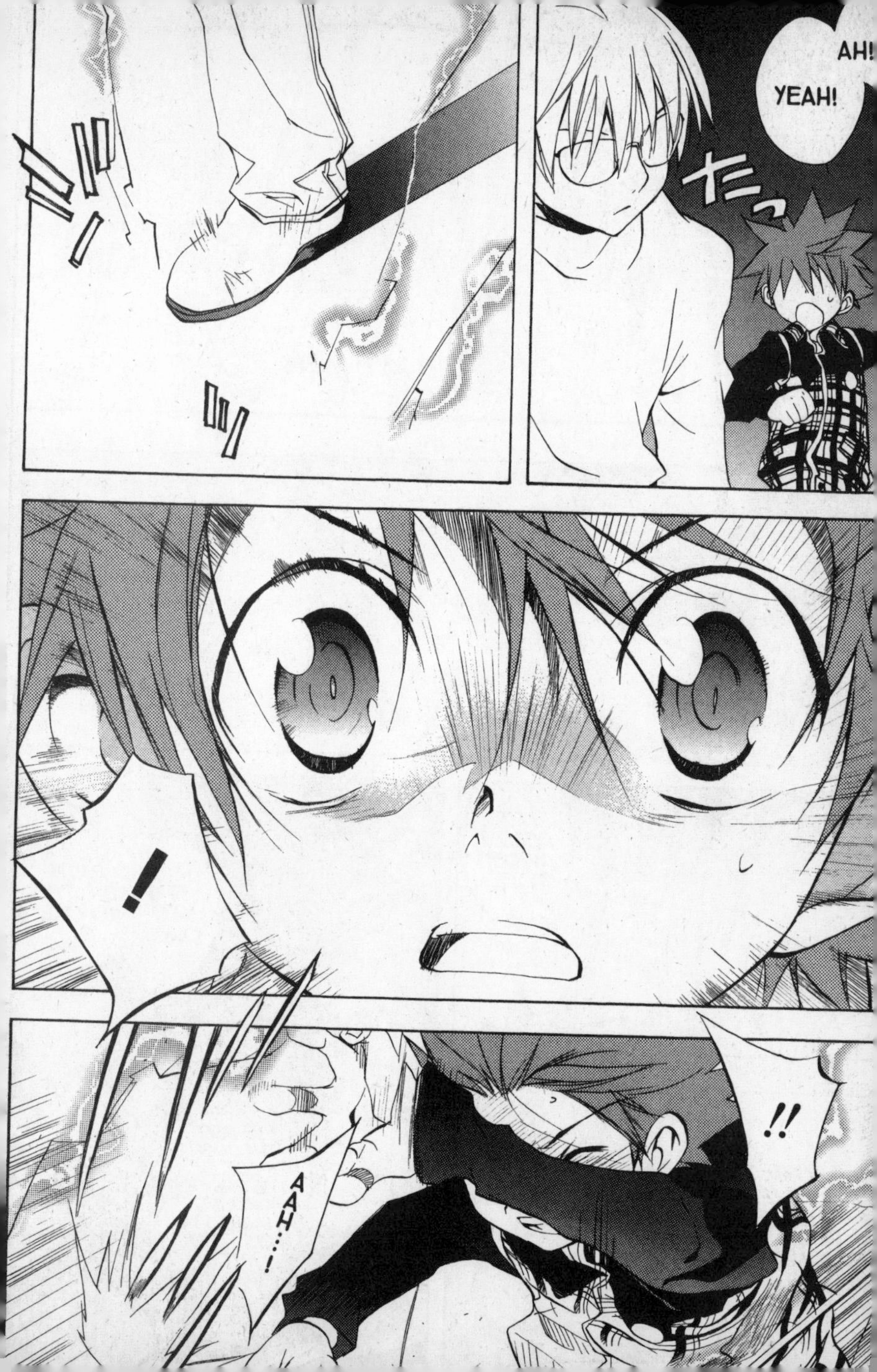
AH! YEAH!
!
!!
AAH...!

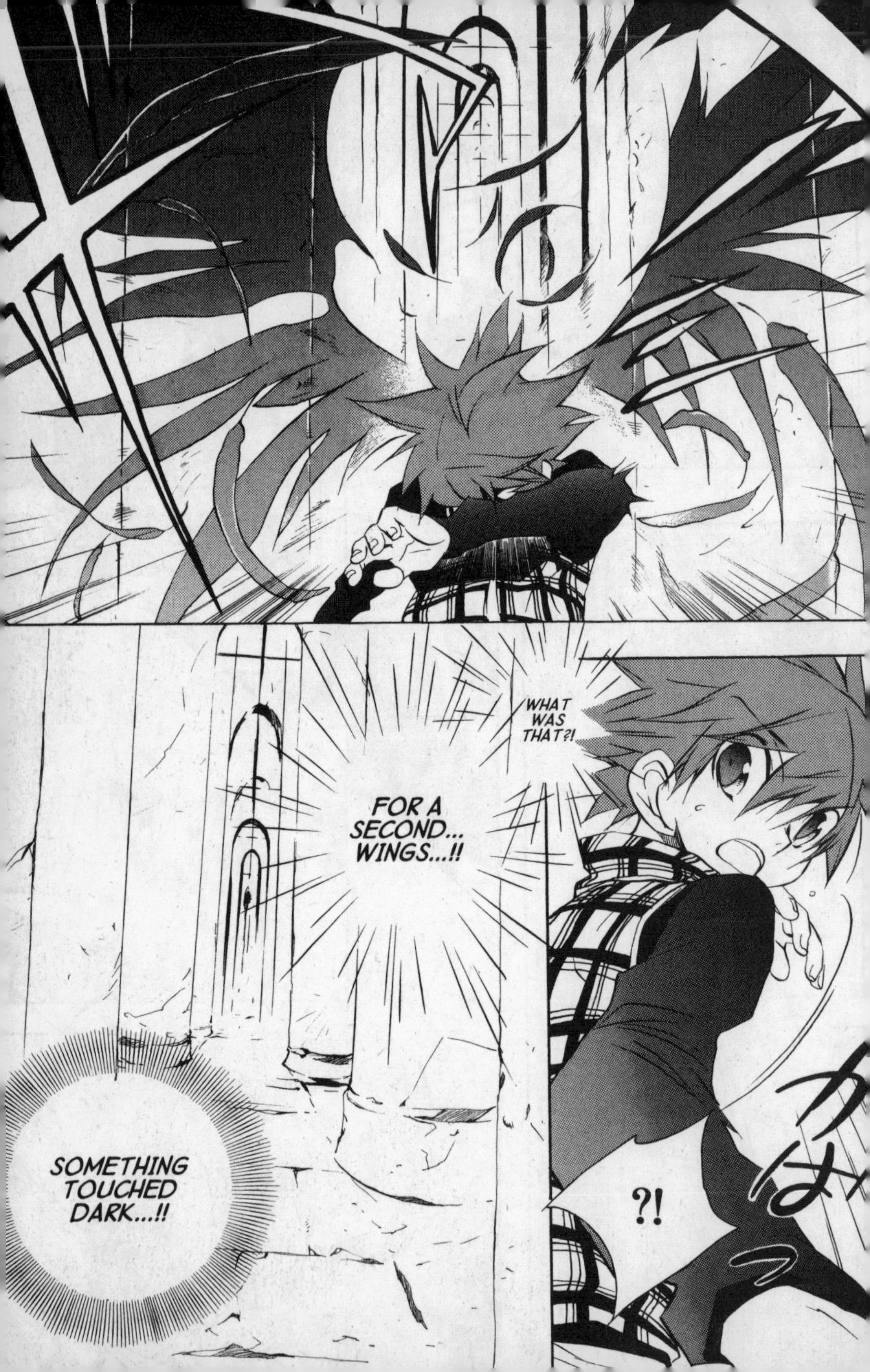
WHAT WAS THAT?!
FOR A SECOND... WINGS...!!
?!
SOMETHING TOUCHED DARK...!!

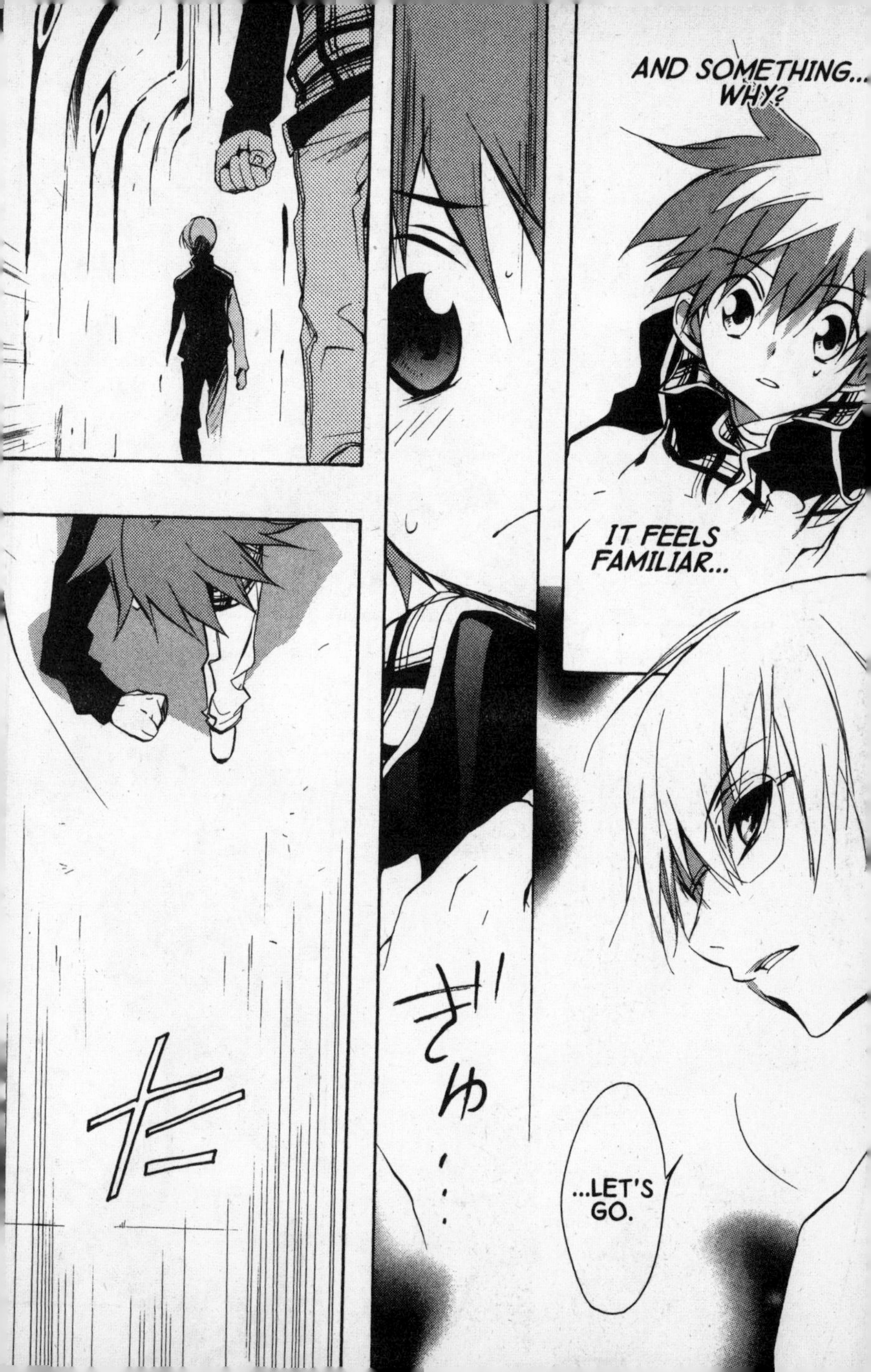
AND SOMETHING... WHY?
IT FEELS FAMILIAR...
...LET'S GO.
ぎゅ…
た

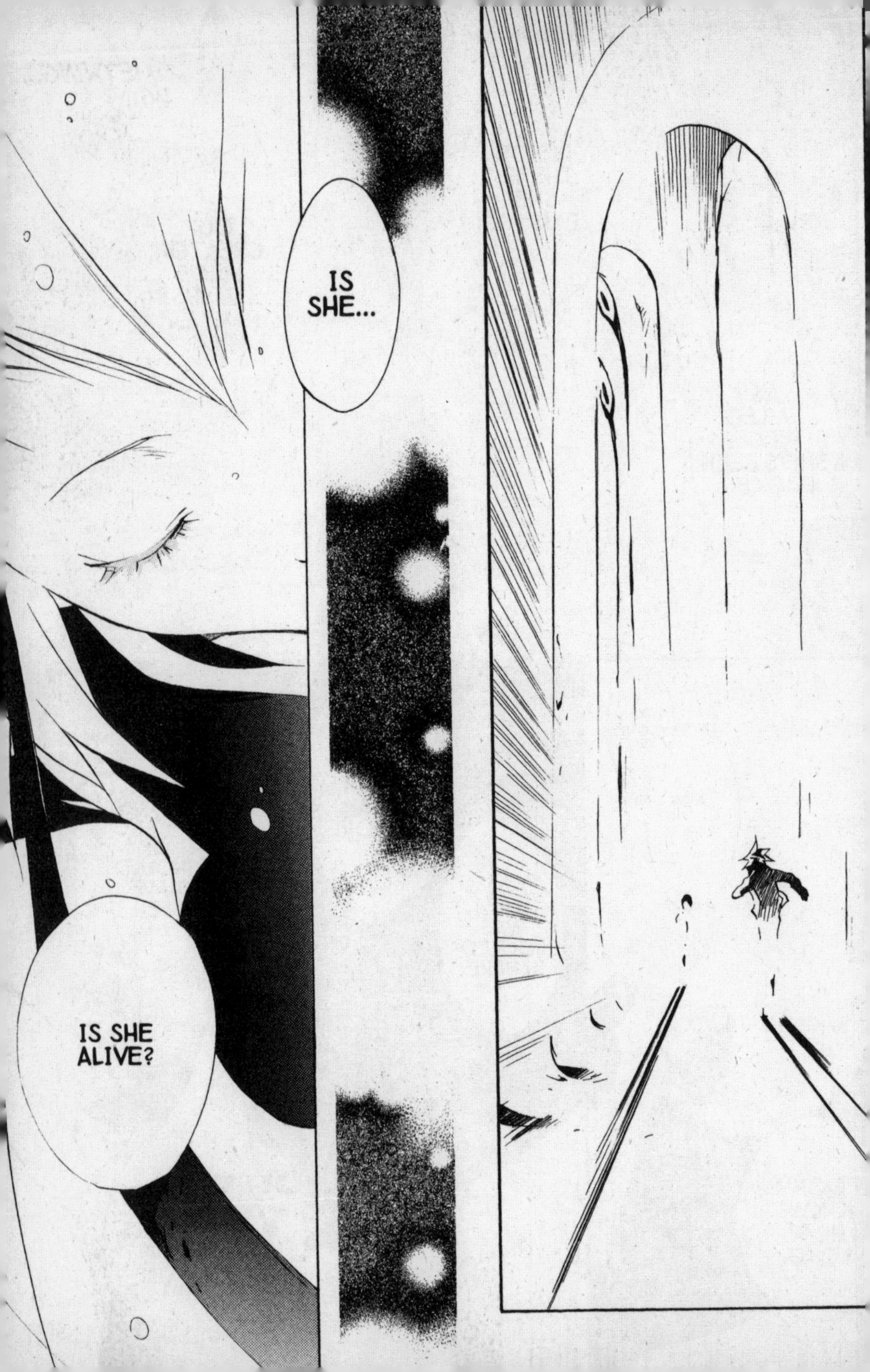
IS SHE...
IS SHE ALIVE?

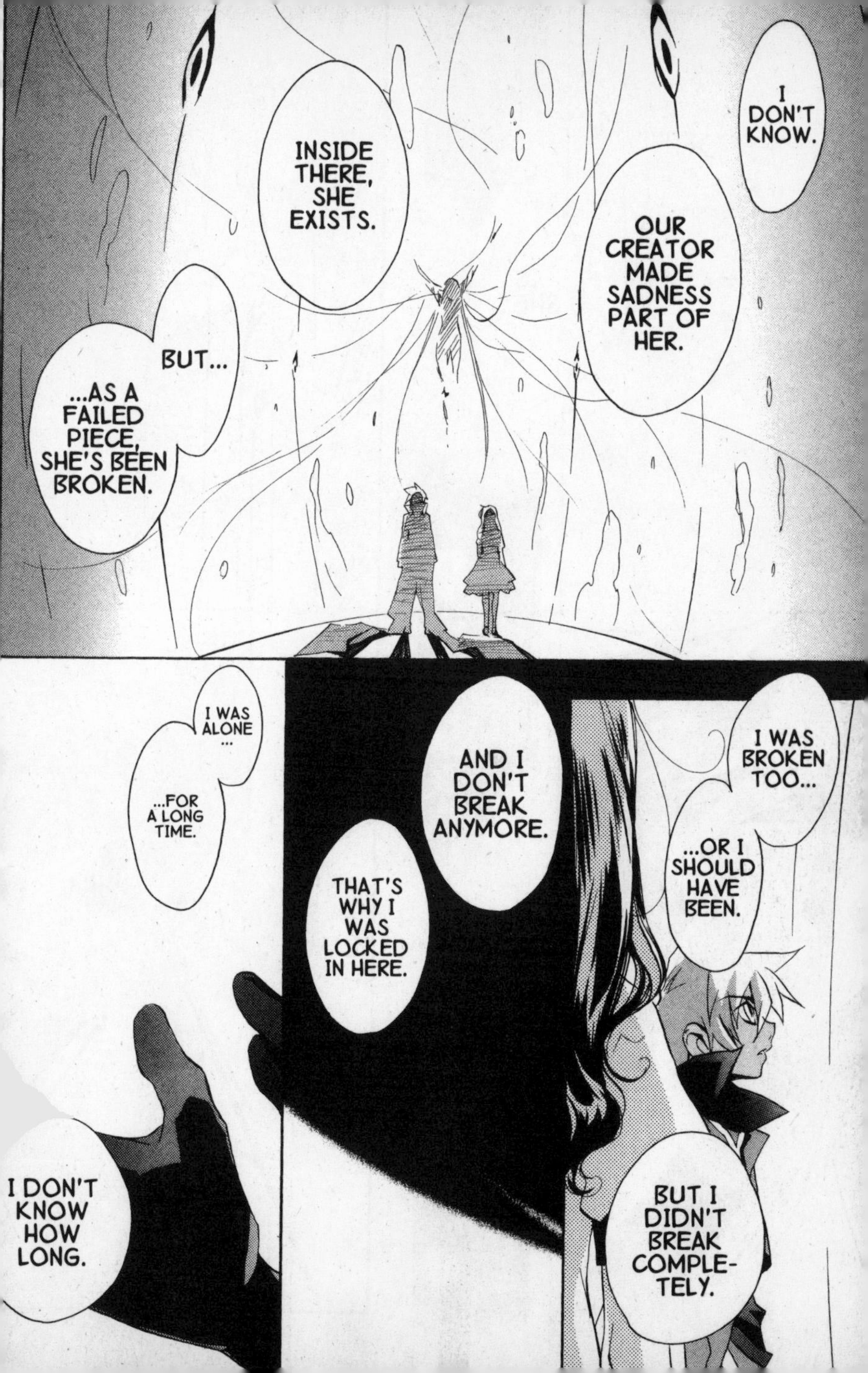
I DON'T KNOW.
OUR CREATOR MADE SADNESS PART OF HER.
INSIDE THERE, SHE EXISTS.
BUT...
...AS A FAILED PIECE, SHE'S BEEN BROKEN.
I WAS BROKEN TOO...
...OR I SHOULD HAVE BEEN.
BUT I DIDN'T BREAK COMPLE-TELY.
AND I DON'T BREAK ANYMORE.
THAT'S WHY I WAS LOCKED IN HERE.
I WAS ALONE ...
...FOR A LONG TIME.
I DON'T KNOW HOW LONG.

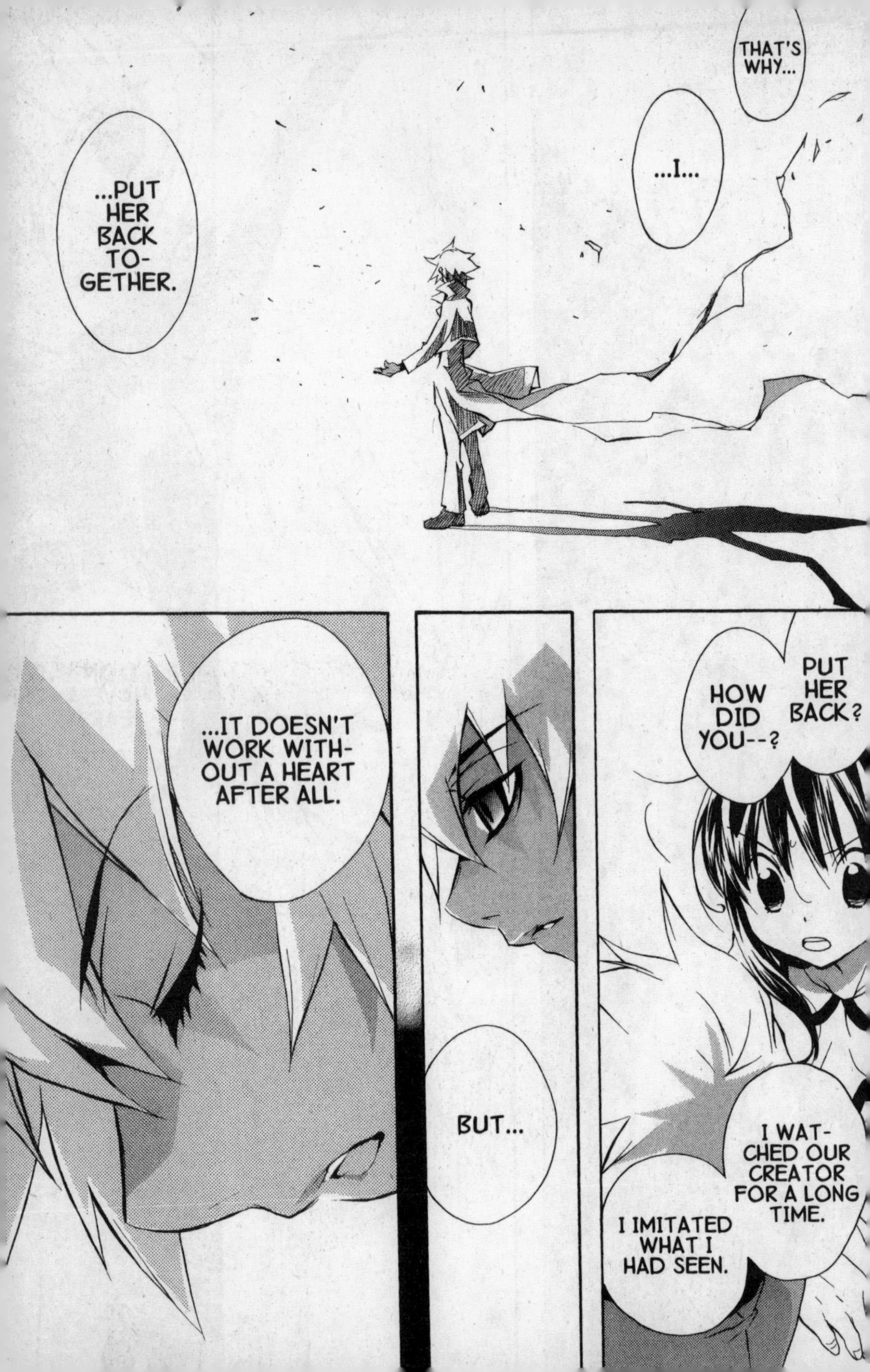
THAT'S WHY...
...I...
...PUT HER BACK TO-GETHER.
PUT HER BACK?
HOW DID YOU--?
I WAT-CHED OUR CREATOR FOR A LONG TIME.
I IMITATED WHAT I HAD SEEN.
BUT...
...IT DOESN'T WORK WITH-OUT A HEART AFTER ALL.

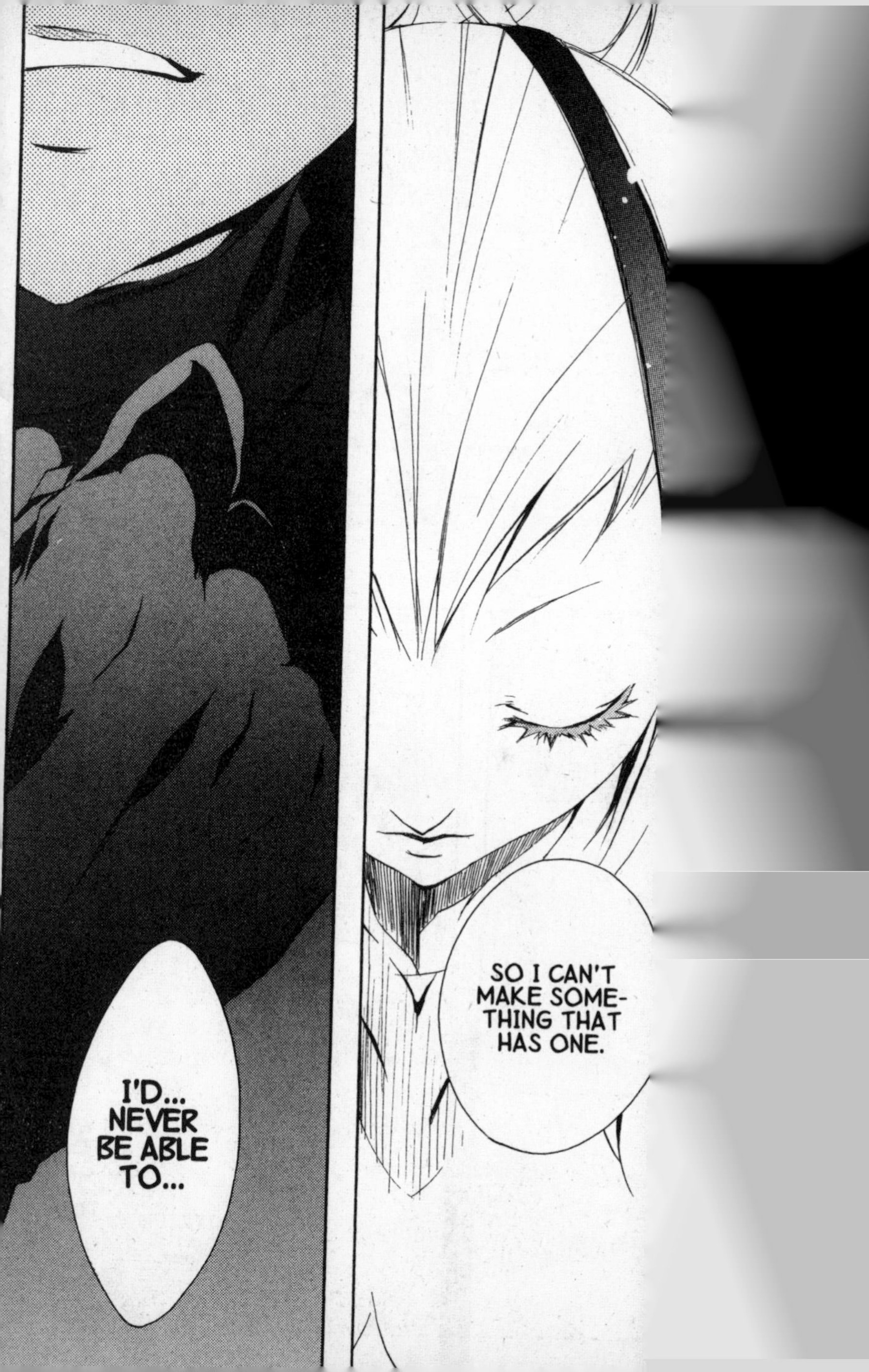
SO I CAN'T MAKE SOME-THING THAT HAS ONE.
I'D... NEVER BE ABLE TO...

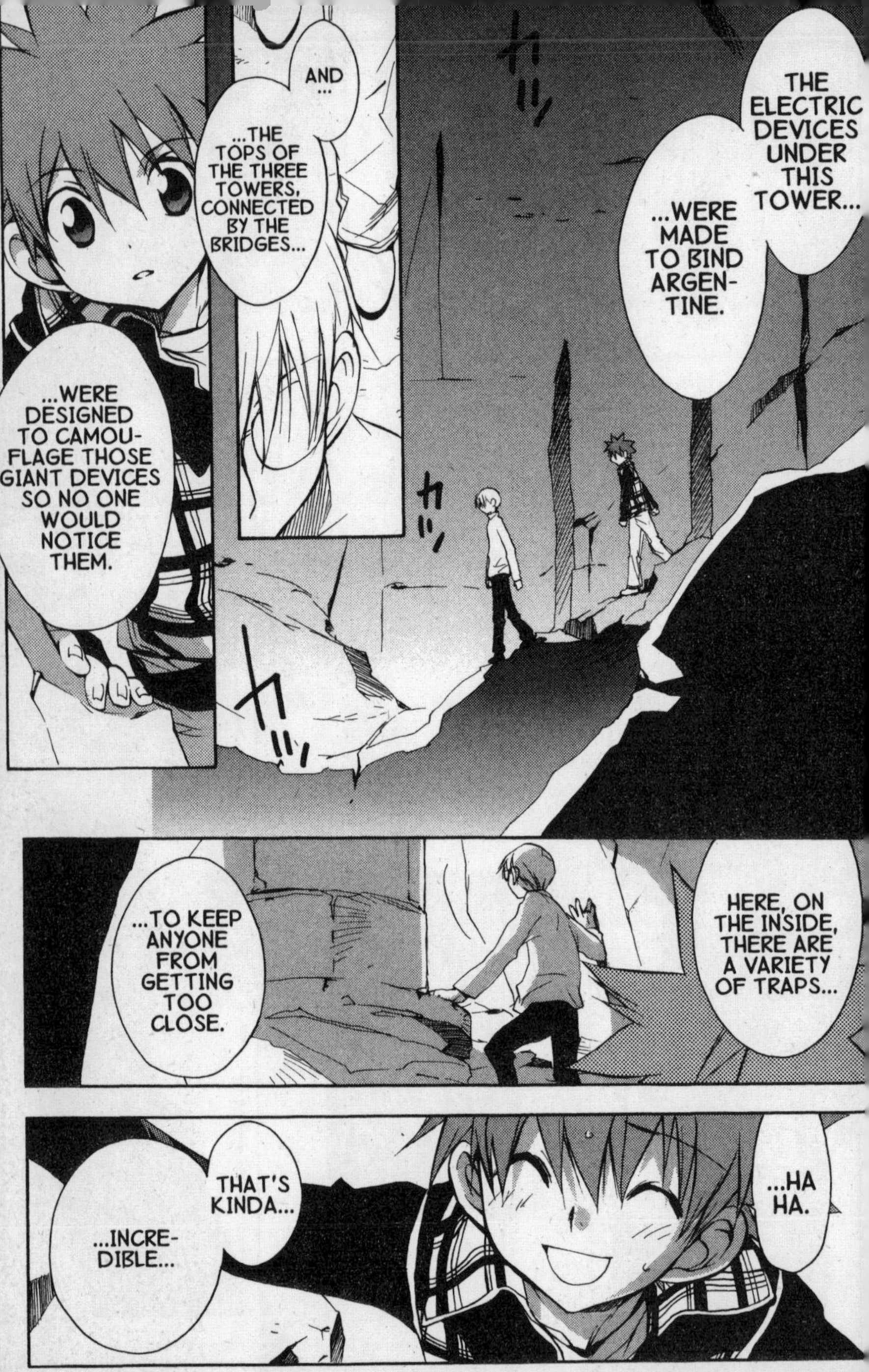
THE ELECTRIC DEVICES UNDER THIS TOWER...
...WERE MADE TO BIND ARGEN-TINE.
AND ...
...THE TOPS OF THE THREE TOWERS, CONNECTED BY THE BRIDGES...
...WERE DESIGNED TO CAMOU-FLAGE THOSE GIANT DEVICES SO NO ONE WOULD NOTICE THEM.
HERE, ON THE INSIDE, THERE ARE A VARIETY OF TRAPS...
...TO KEEP ANYONE FROM GETTING TOO CLOSE.
...HA HA.
THAT'S KINDA...
...INCRE-DIBLE...

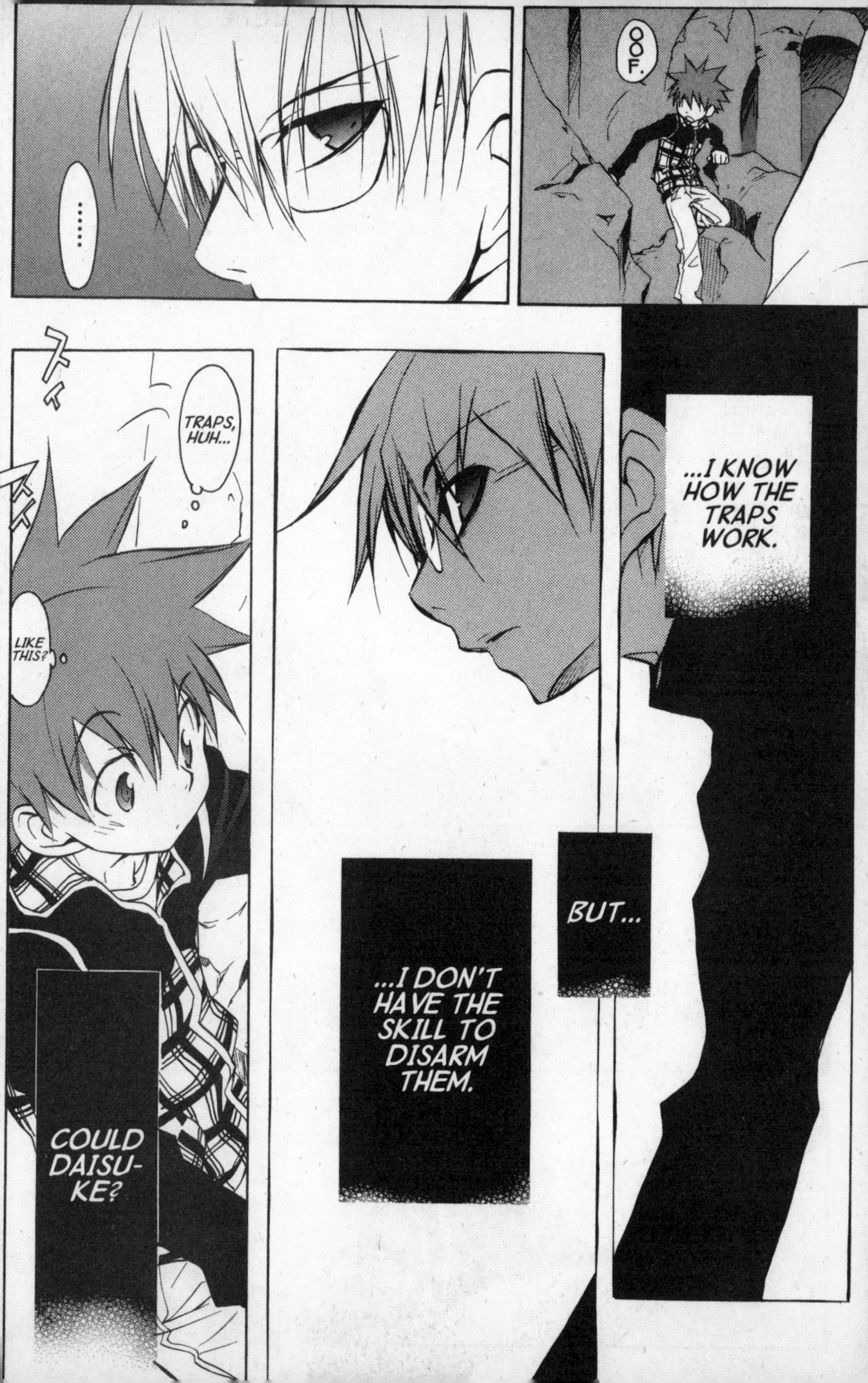
OOF.
......
...I KNOW HOW THE TRAPS WORK.
BUT...
...I DON'T HAVE THE SKILL TO DISARM THEM.
TRAPS, HUH...
LIKE THIS?
COULD DAISUKE?

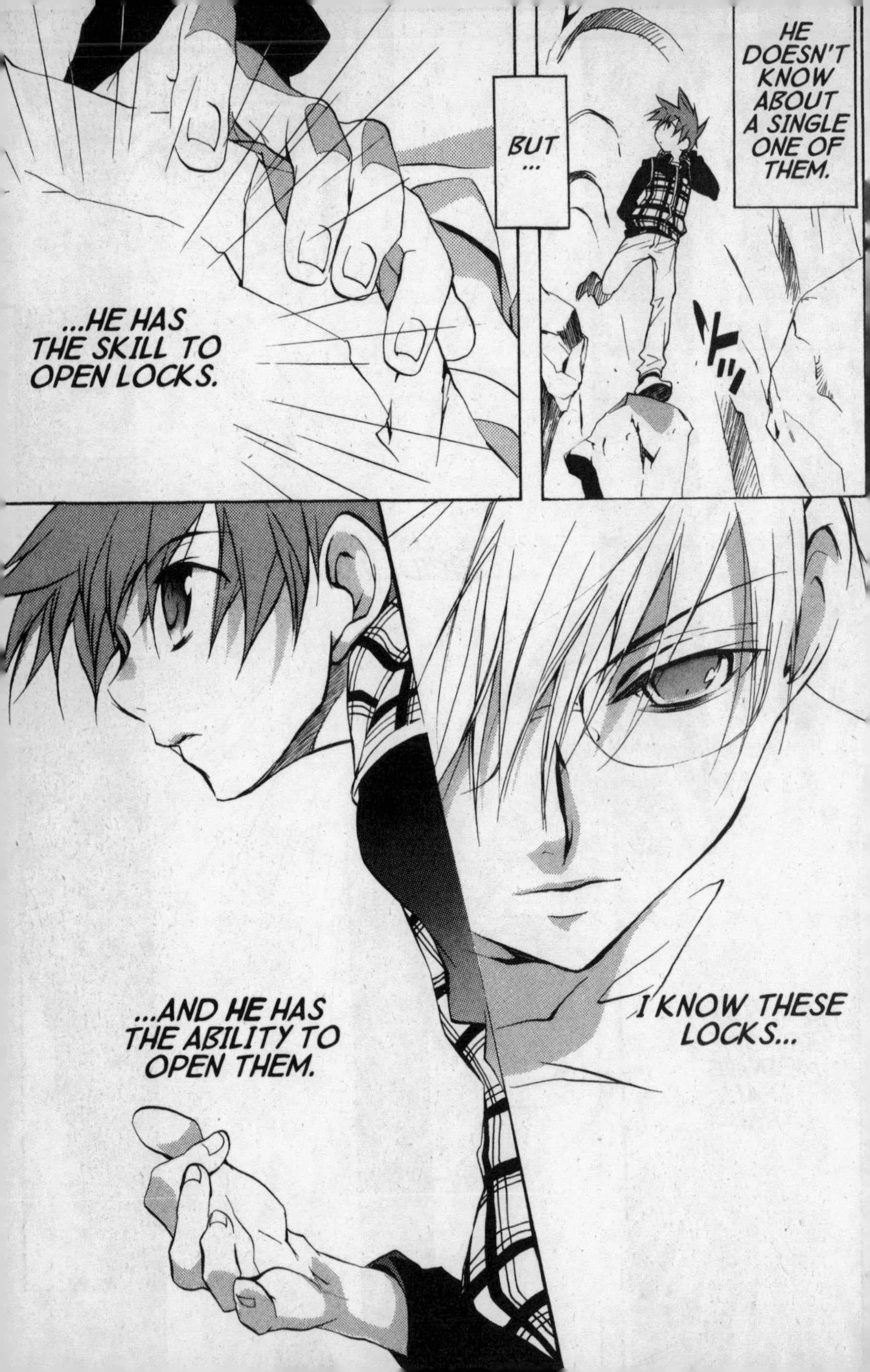
HE DOESN'T KNOW ABOUT A SINGLE ONE OF THEM.
BUT ...
...HE HAS THE SKILL TO OPEN LOCKS.
I KNOW THESE LOCKS...
...AND HE HAS THE ABILITY TO OPEN THEM.

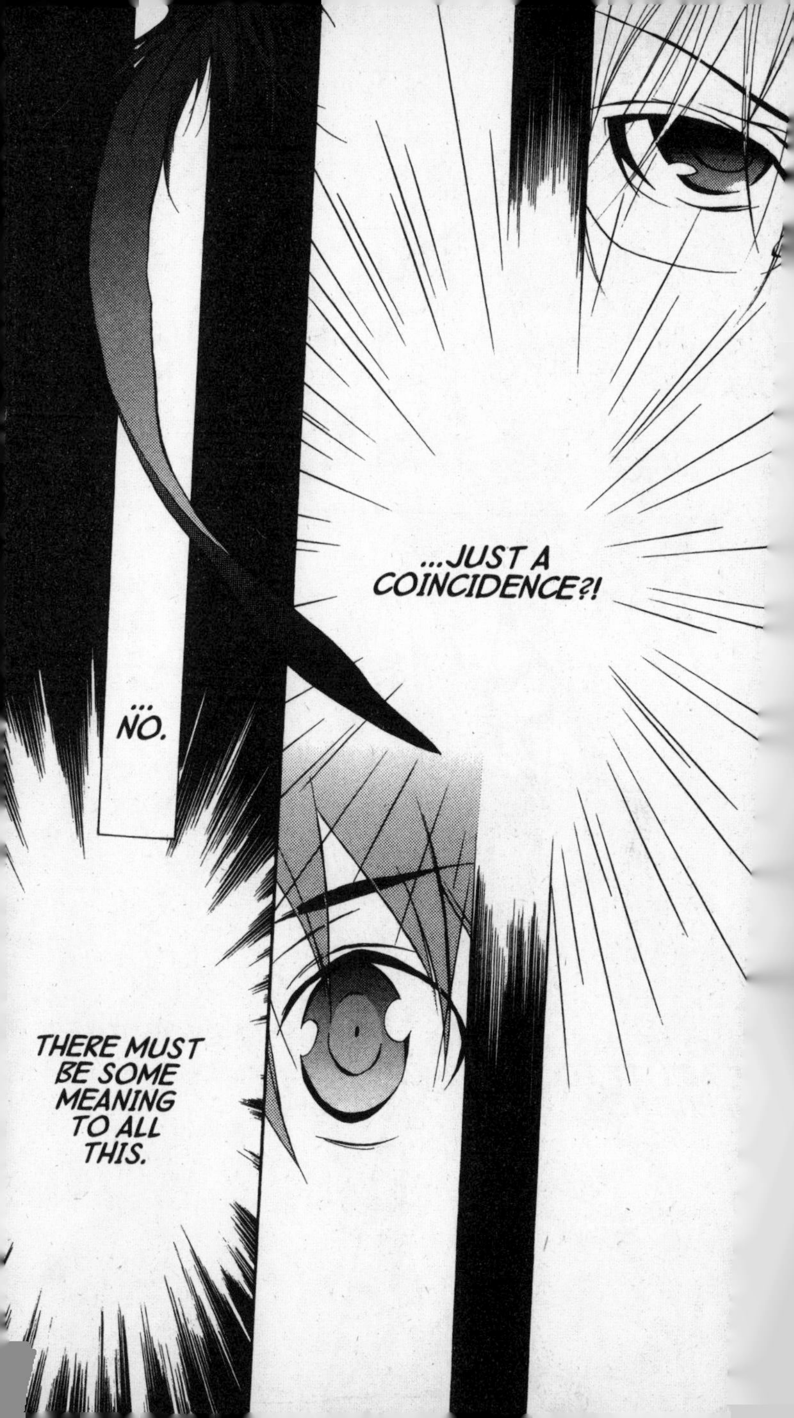
...JUST A COINCIDENCE?!
...NO.
THERE MUST BE SOME MEANING TO ALL THIS.

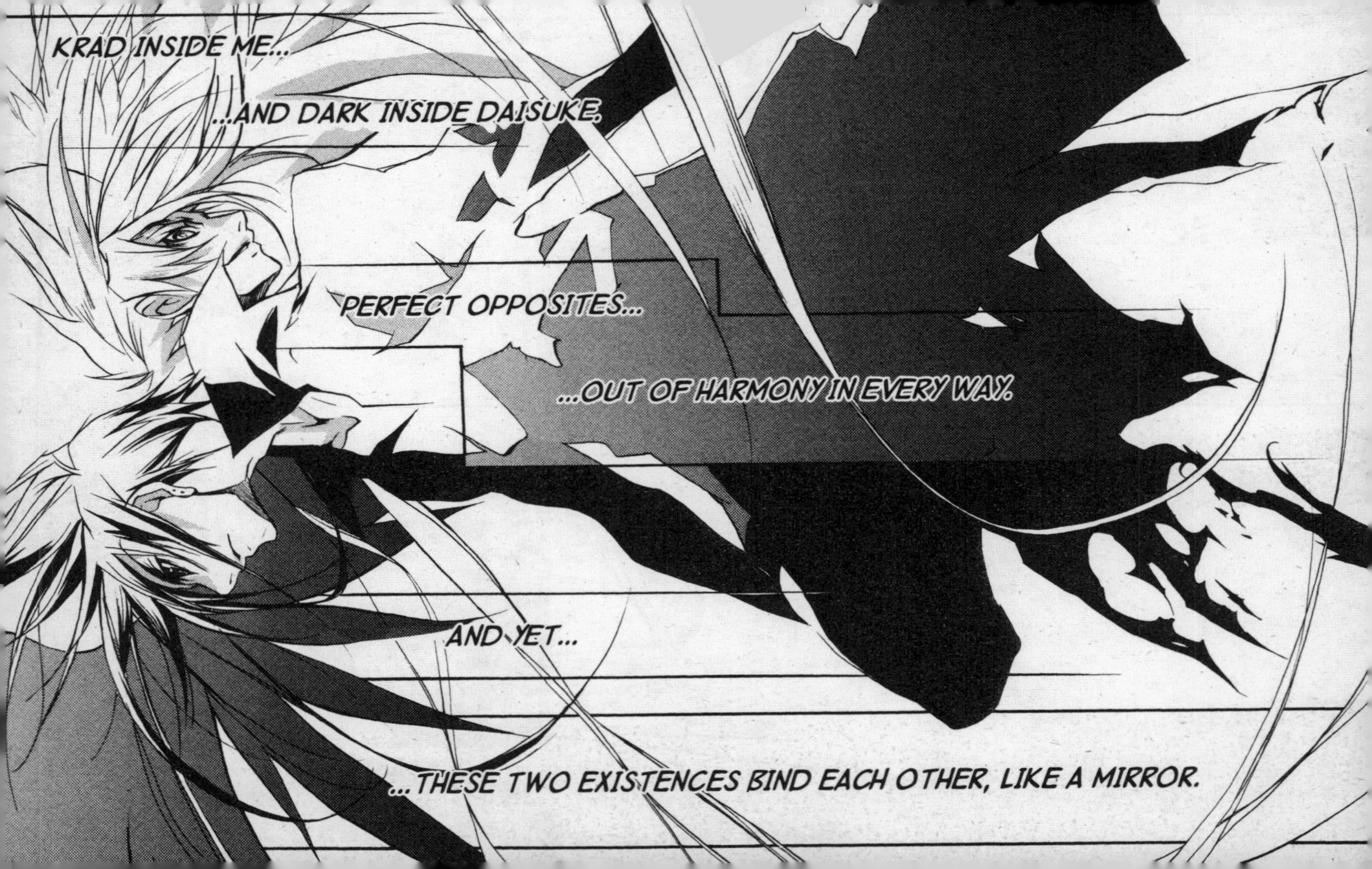
KRAD INSIDE ME...
...AND DARK INSIDE DAISUKE.
PERFECT OPPOSITES...
...OUT OF HARMONY IN EVERY WAY.
AND YET...
...THESE TWO EXISTENCES BIND EACH OTHER, LIKE A MIRROR.

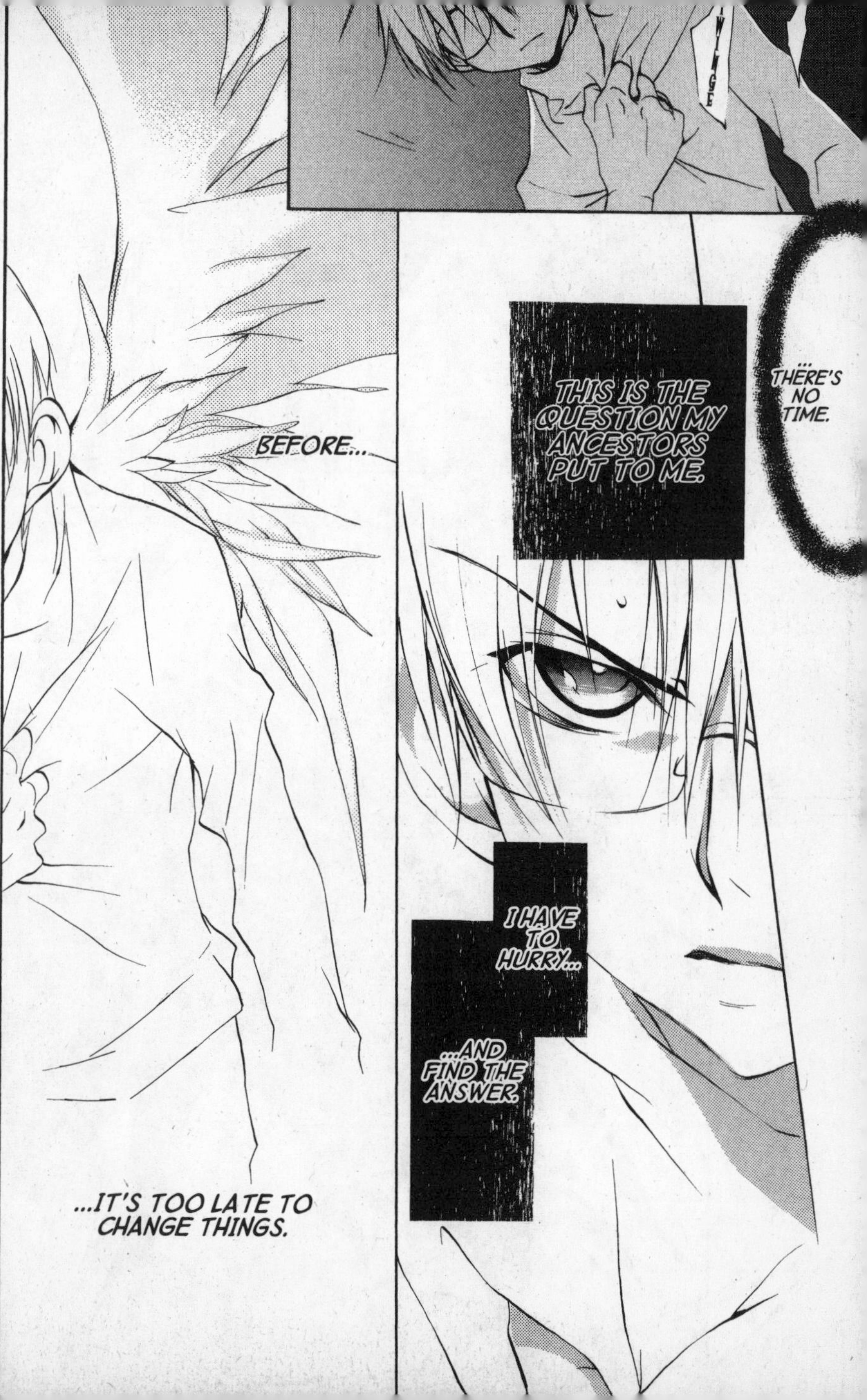
TWINGE
...THERE'S NO TIME.
THIS IS THE QUESTION MY ANCESTORS PUT TO ME.
I HAVE TO HURRY...
...AND FIND THE ANSWER.
BEFORE...
...IT'S TOO LATE TO CHANGE THINGS.

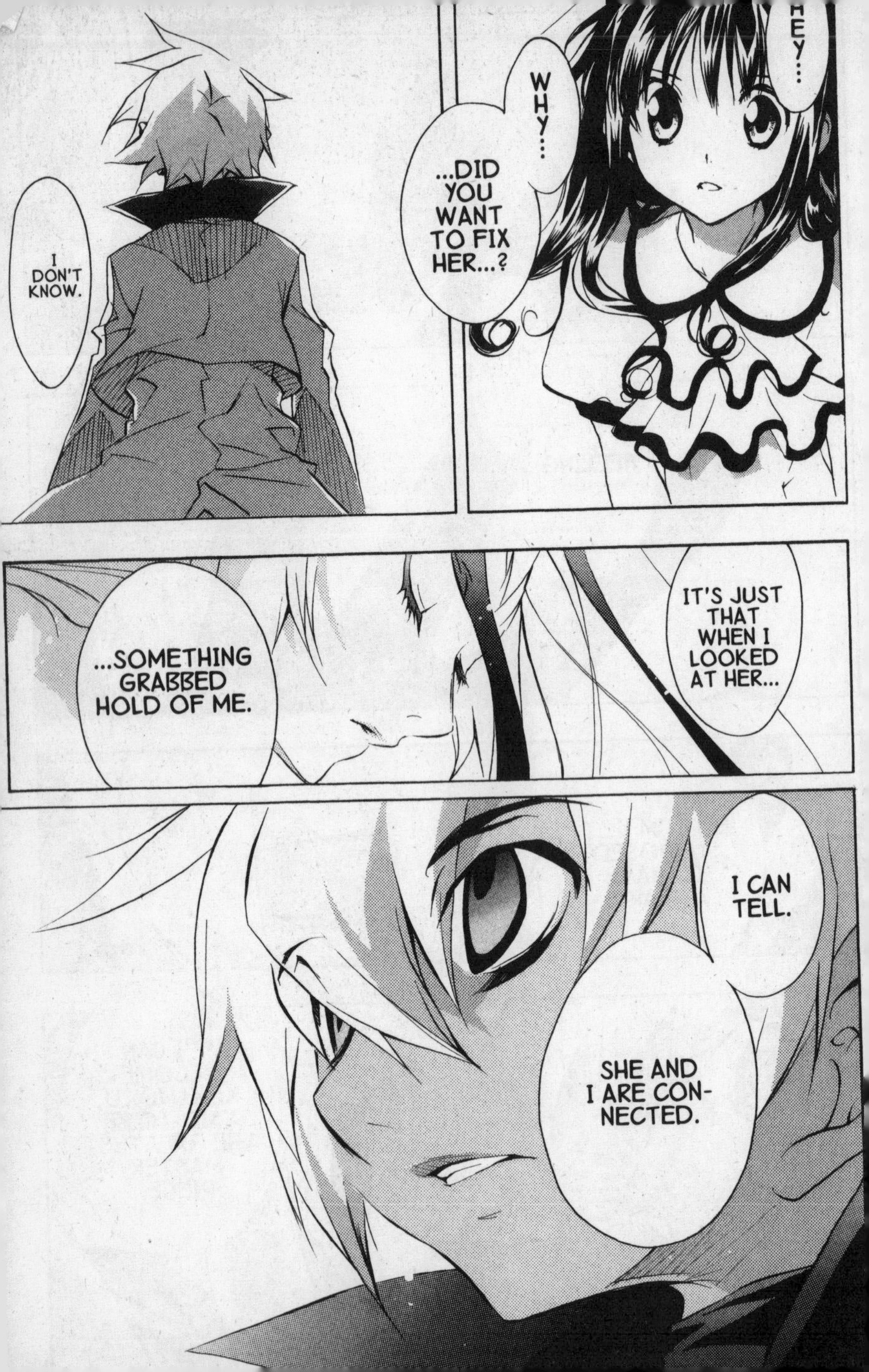
HEY...
WHY...
...DID YOU WANT TO FIX HER...?
I DON'T KNOW.
IT'S JUST THAT WHEN I LOOKED AT HER...
...SOMETHING GRABBED HOLD OF ME.
I CAN TELL.
SHE AND I ARE CONNECTED.

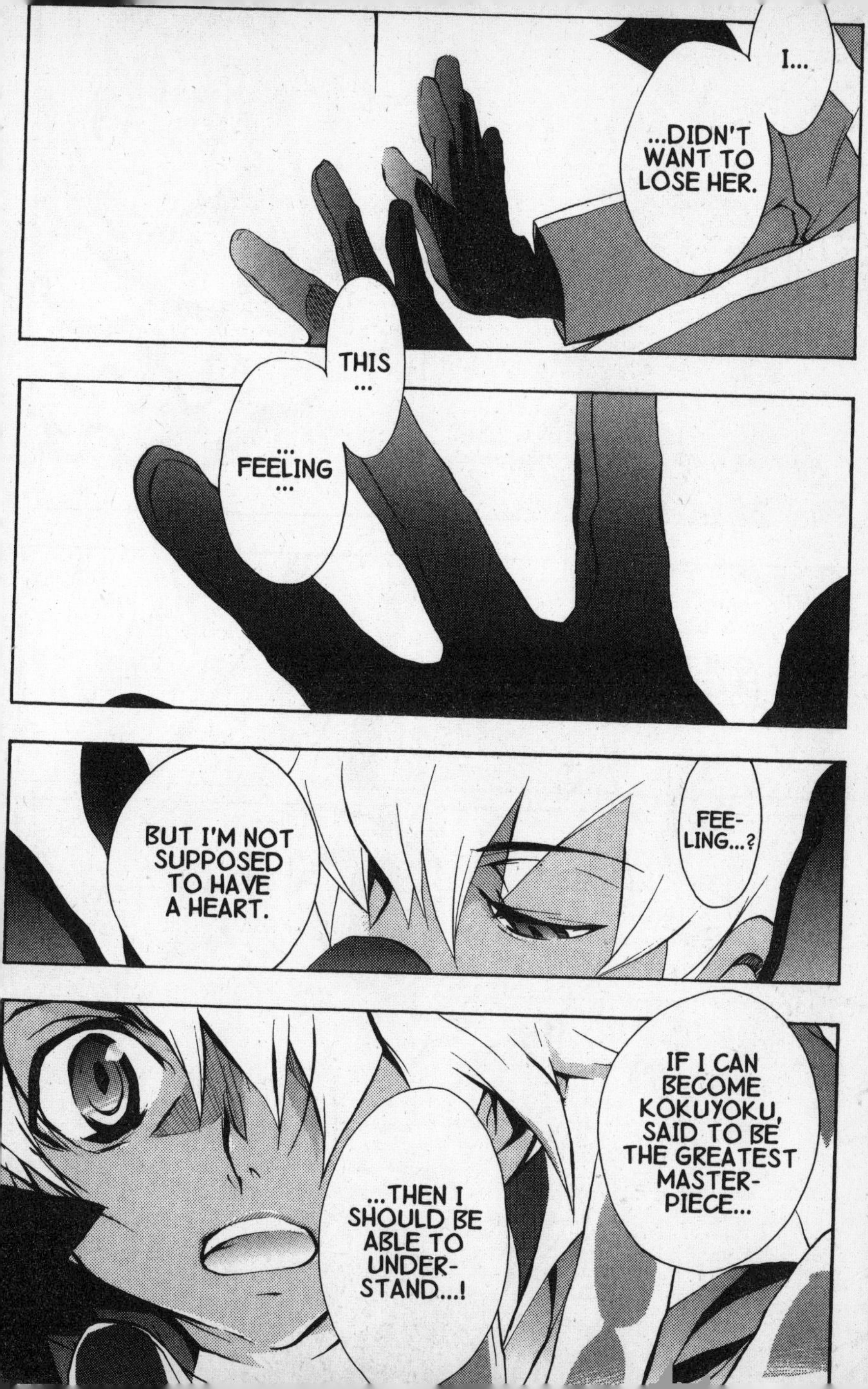
I...
...DIDN'T WANT TO LOSE HER.
THIS ...
... FEELING ...
FEE-LING...?
BUT I'M NOT SUPPOSED TO HAVE A HEART.
IF I CAN BECOME KOKUYOKU, SAID TO BE THE GREATEST MASTER-PIECE...
...THEN I SHOULD BE ABLE TO UNDER-STAND...!

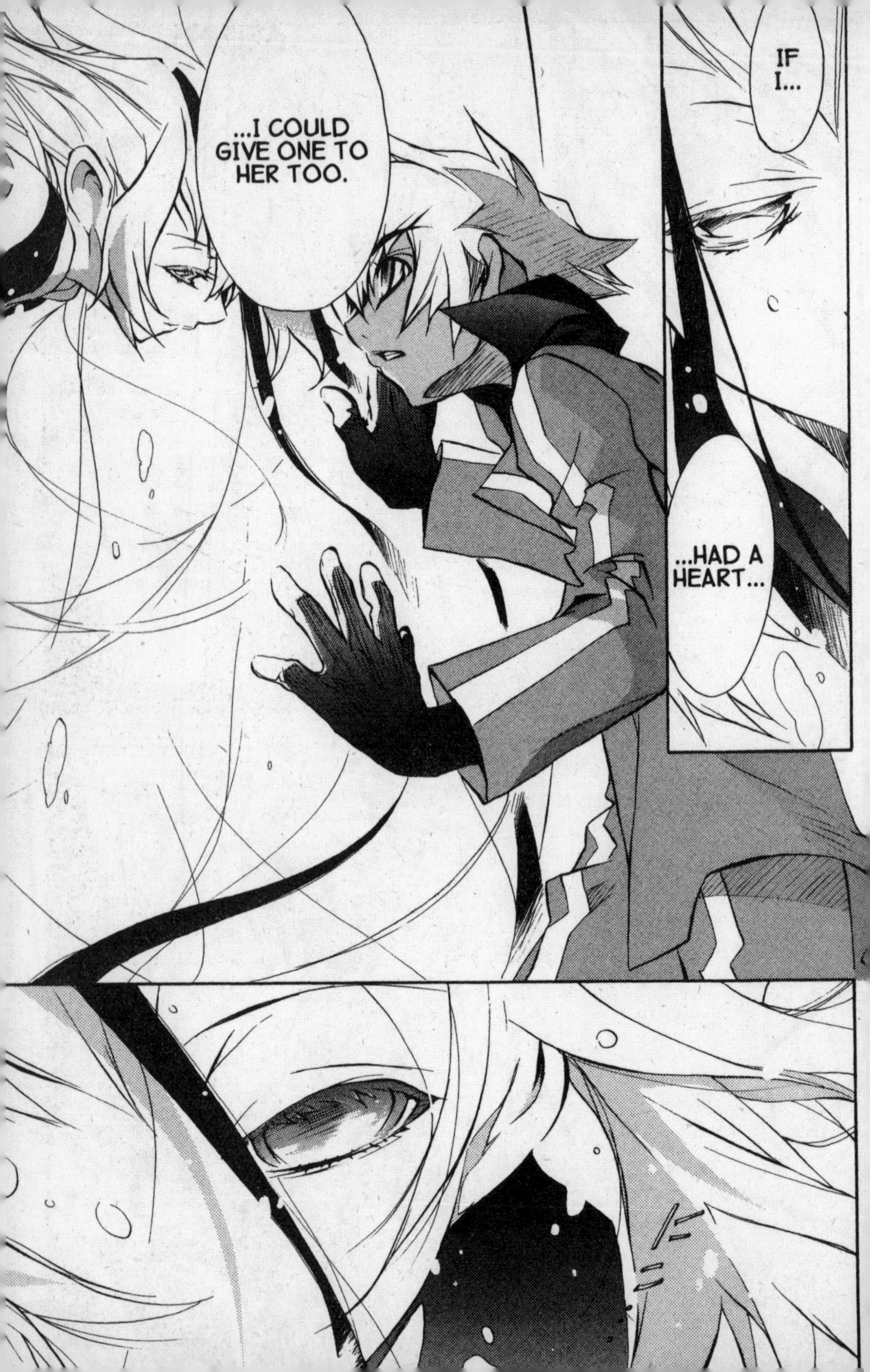
IF I...
...HAD A HEART...
...I COULD GIVE ONE TO HER TOO.

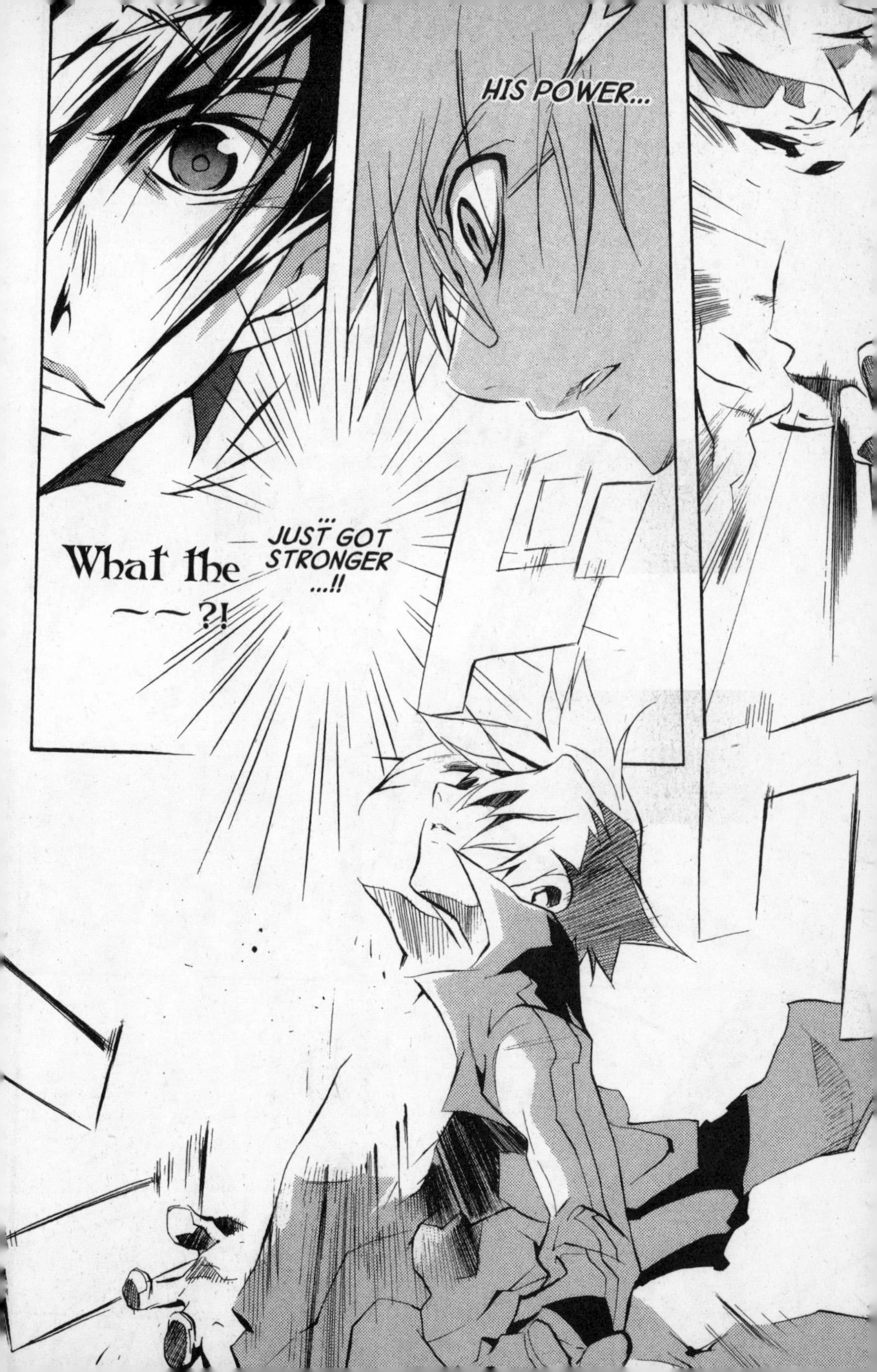
HIS POWER...
...JUST GOT STRONGER...!!
What the ~~?!

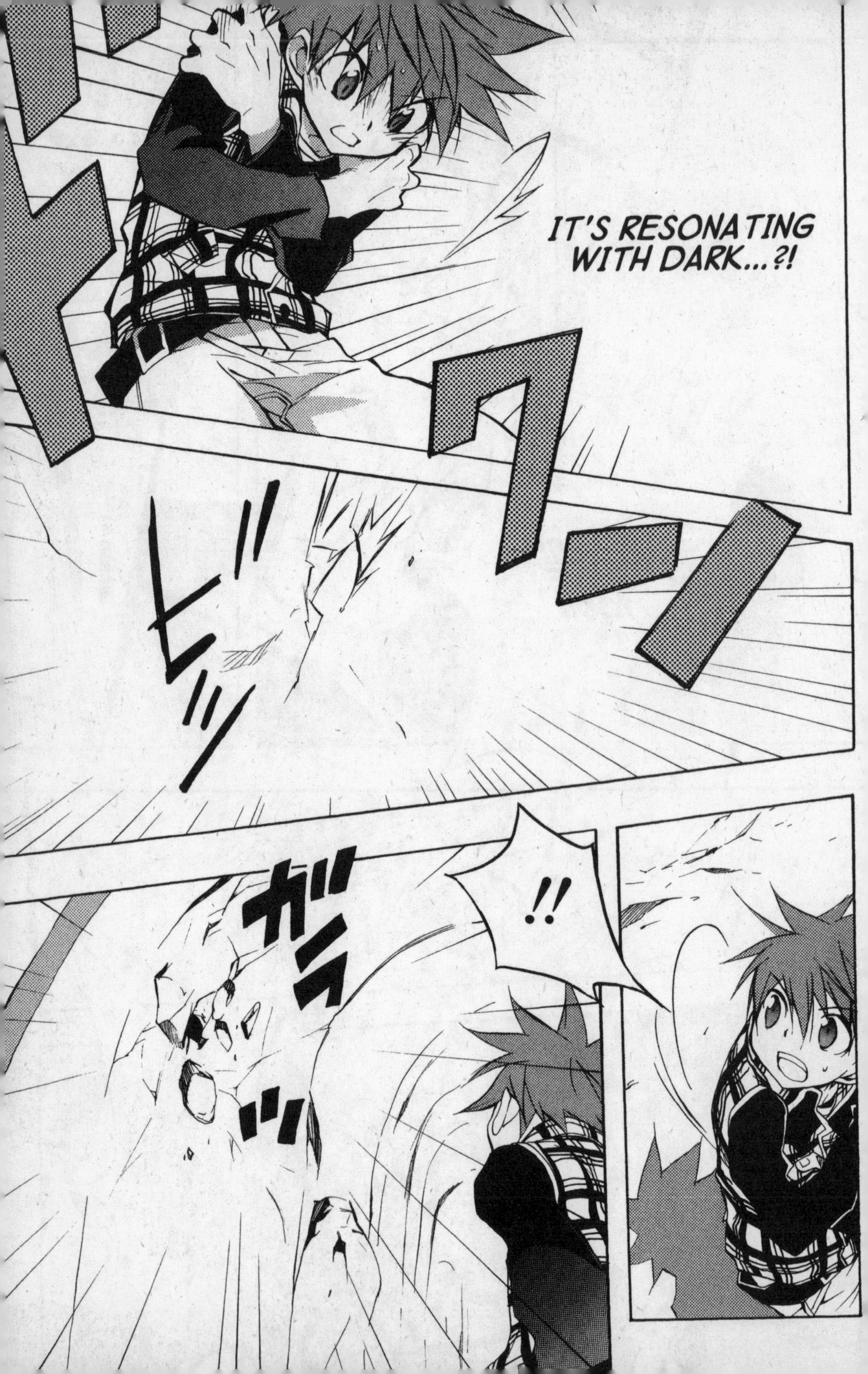
IT'S RESONATING WITH DARK...?!
!!

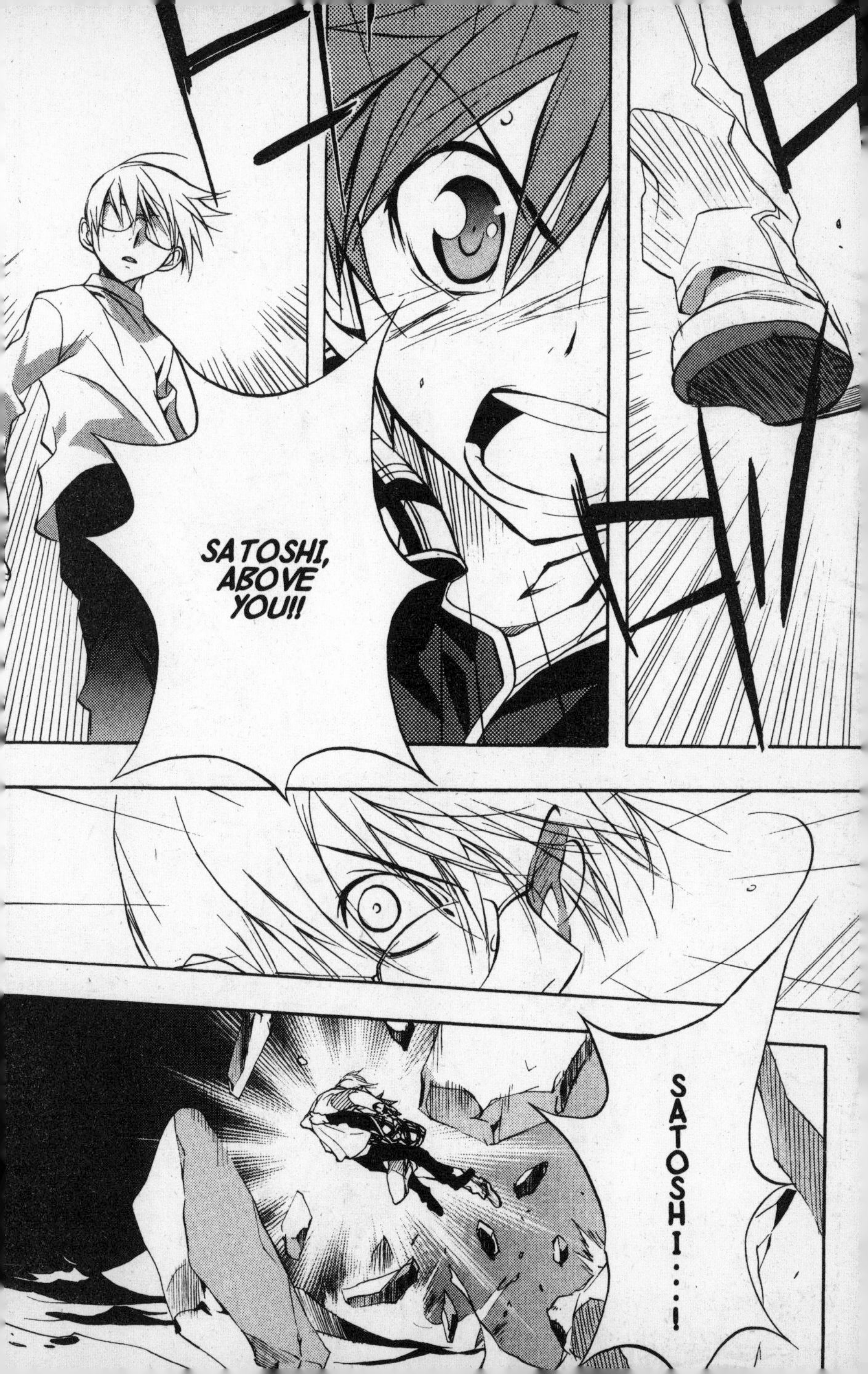
SATOSHI, ABOVE YOU!!
SATOSHI...!

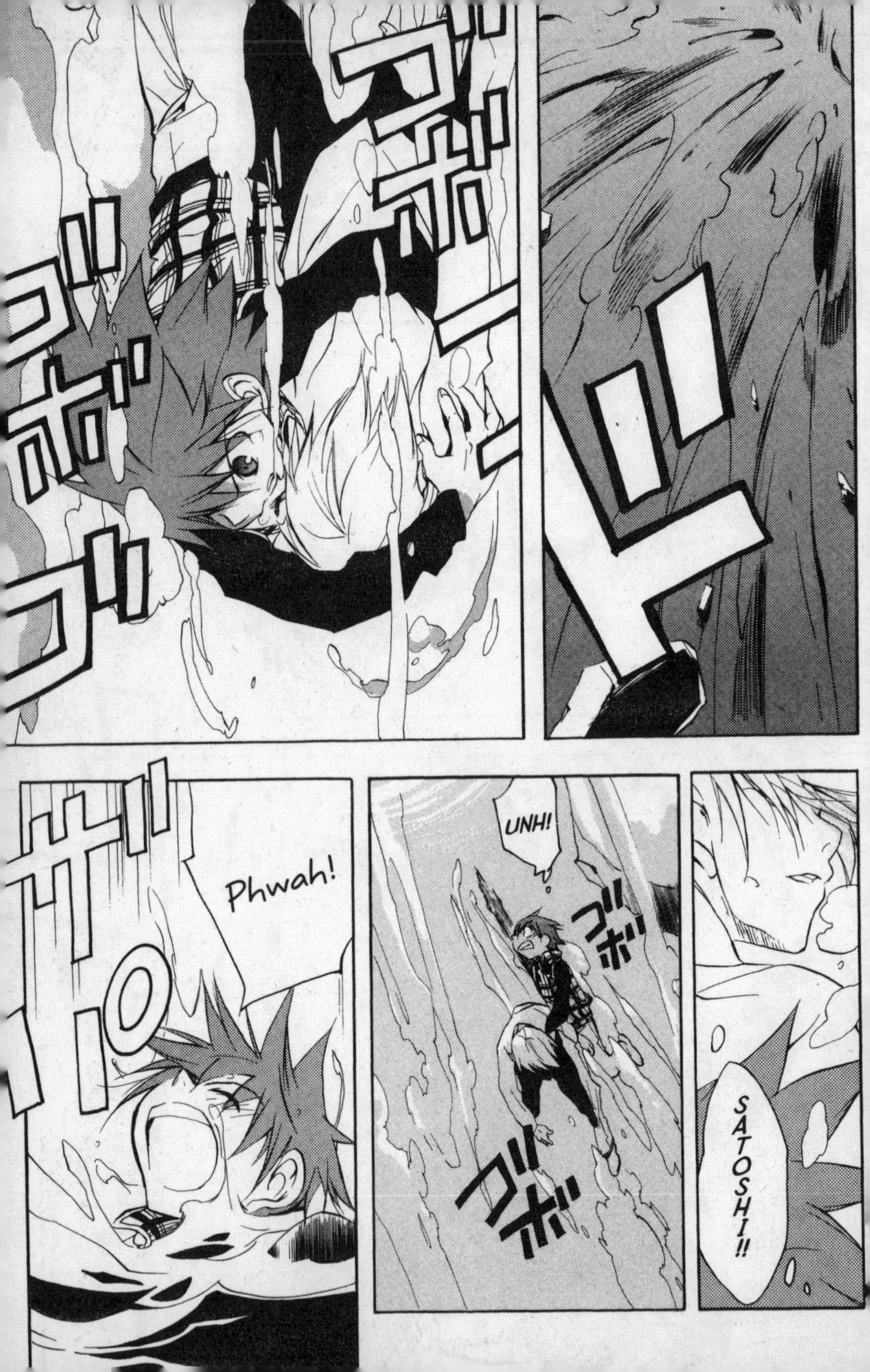
SATOSHI!!
UNH!
ゴボ
ゴボ
Phwah!

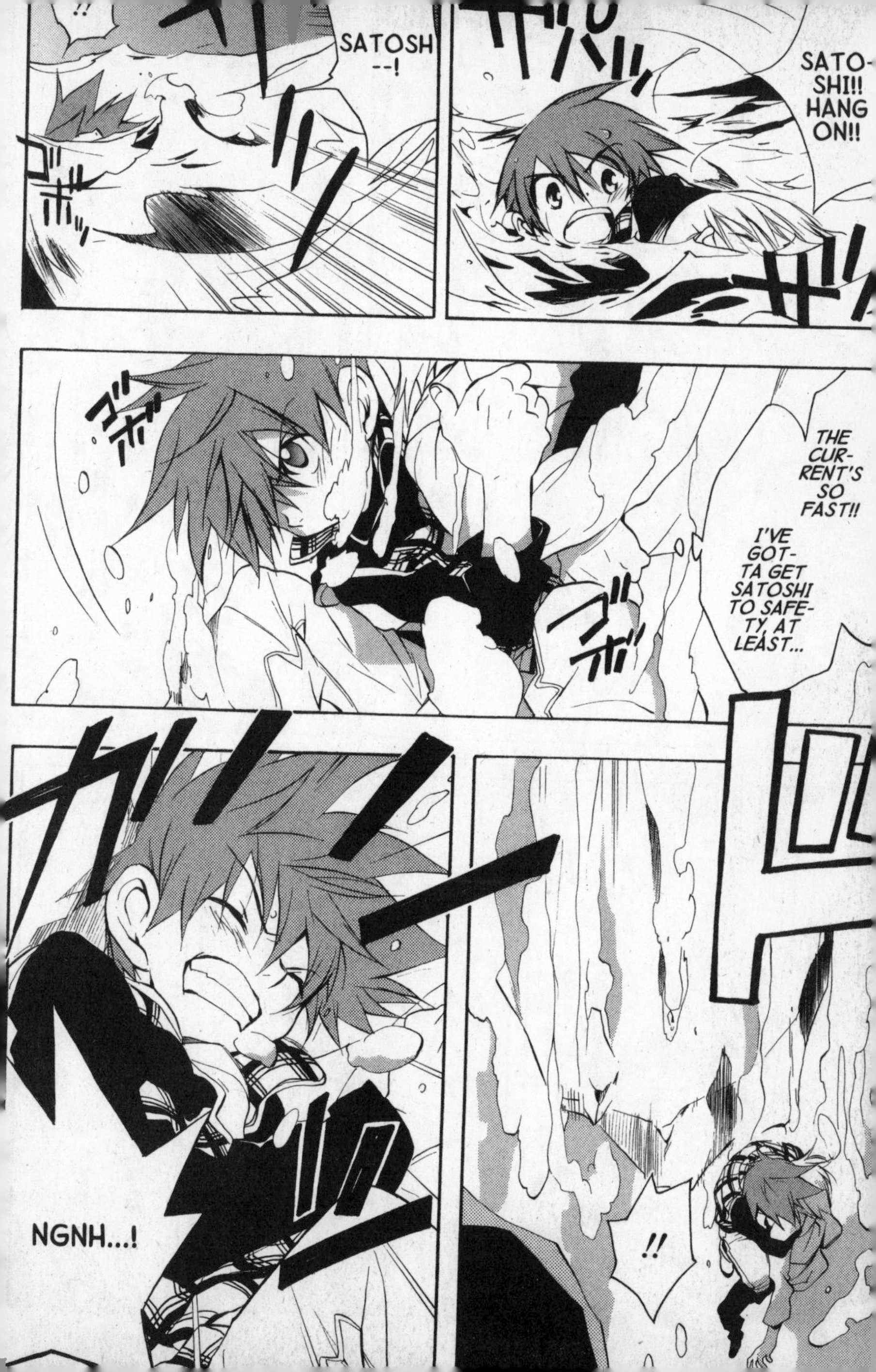
SATO-SHI!! HANG ON!!
SATOSH --!
!!
THE CUR-RENT'S SO FAST!!
I'VE GOT-TA GET SATOSHI TO SAFE-TY, AT LEAST...
!!
NGNH...!

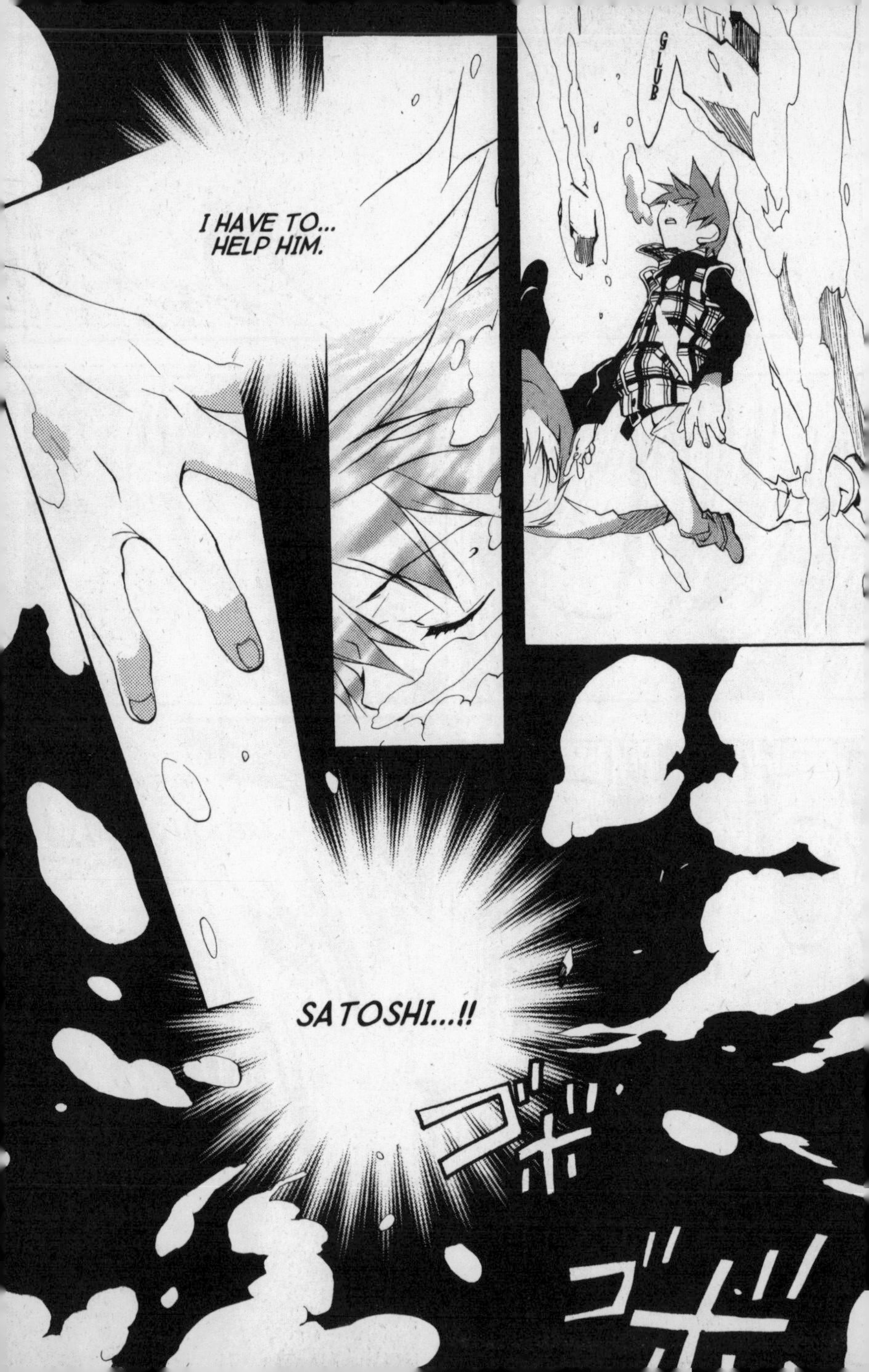
GLUB
I HAVE TO... HELP HIM.
SATOSHI...!!
ゴボ
ゴボ

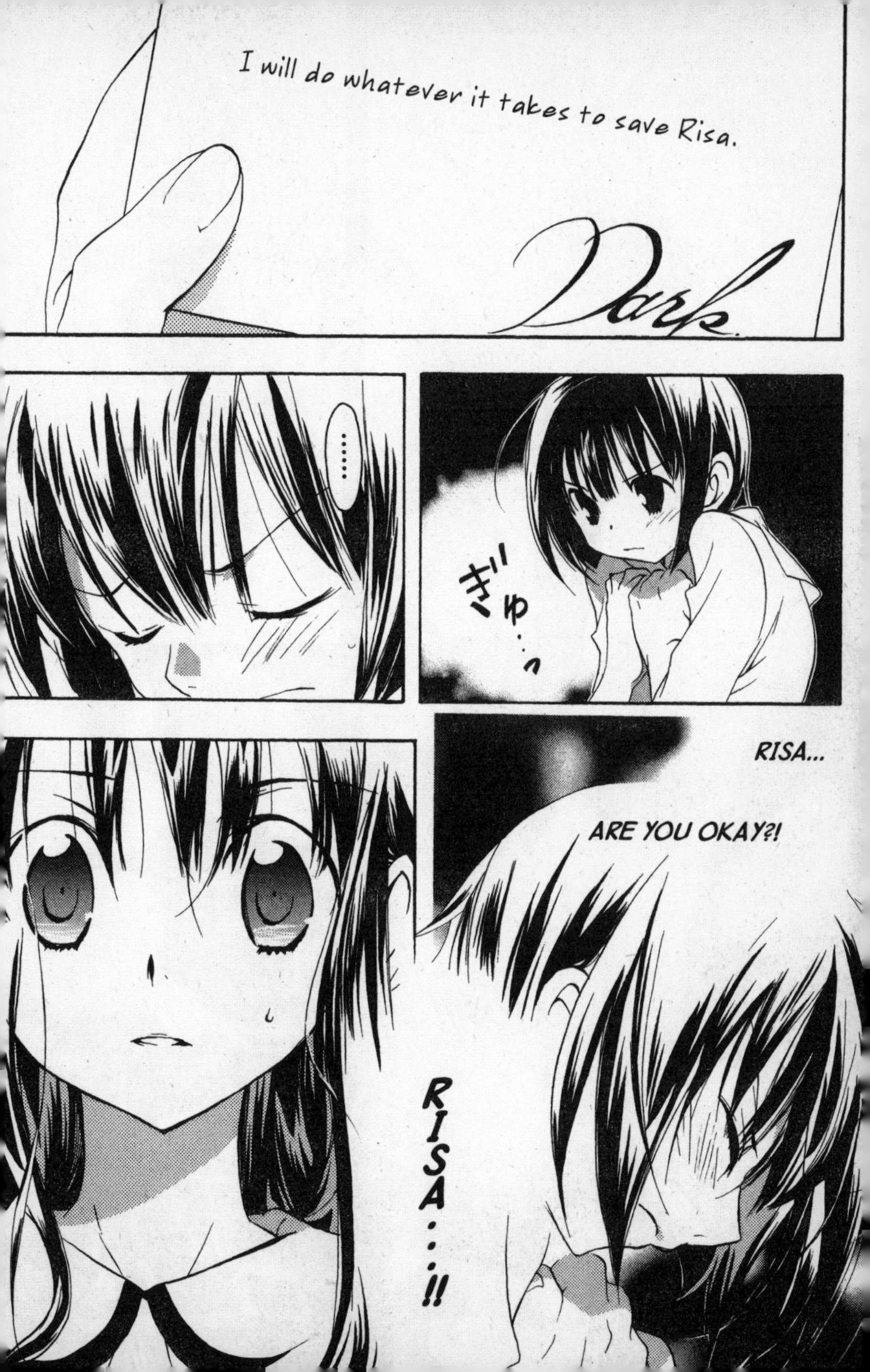
I will do whatever it takes to save Risa.
Dark.
ぎゅ…っ
……
RISA...
ARE YOU OKAY?!
RISA...!!

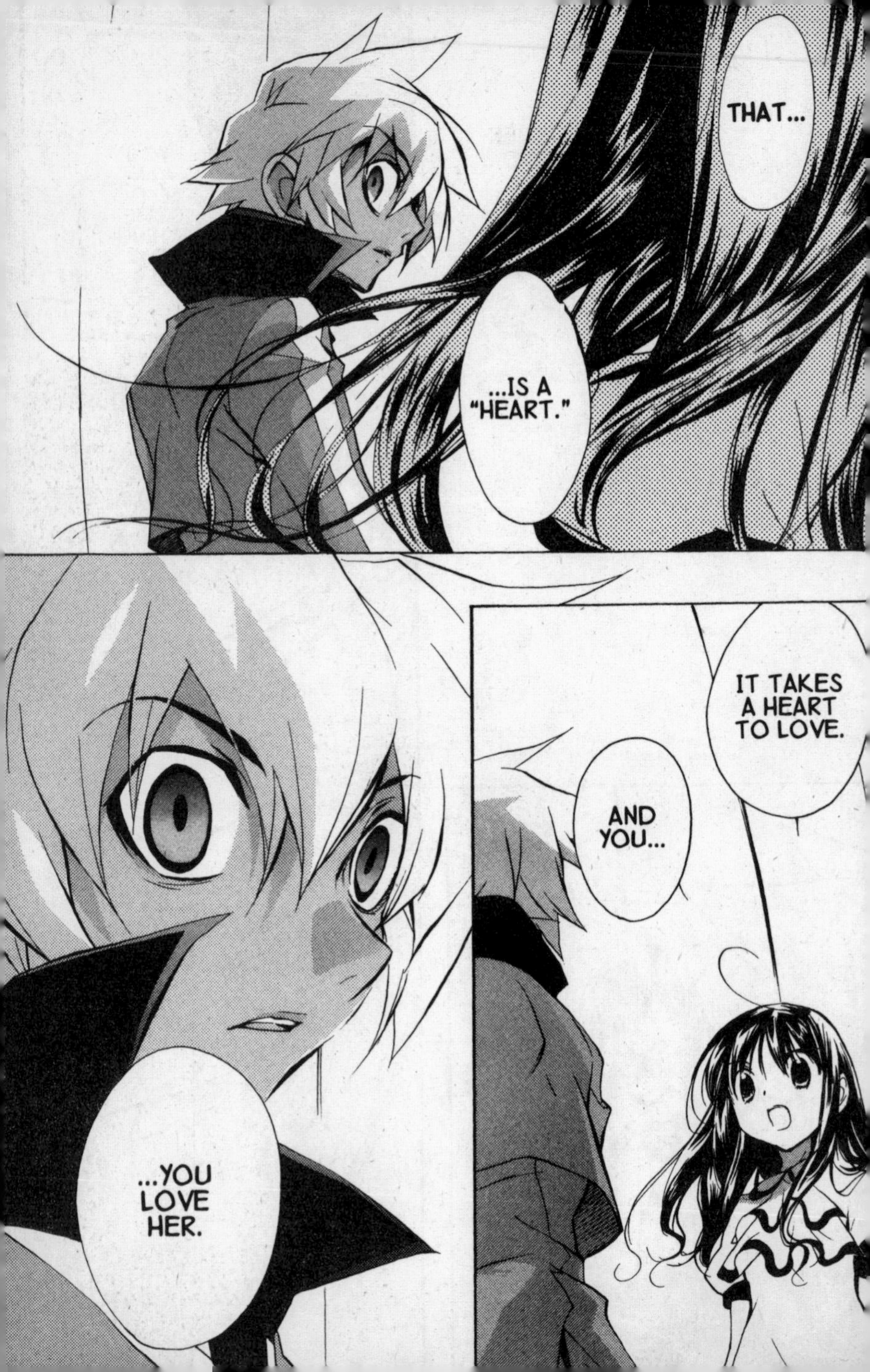
THAT...
...IS A "HEART."
IT TAKES A HEART TO LOVE.
AND YOU...
...YOU LOVE HER.

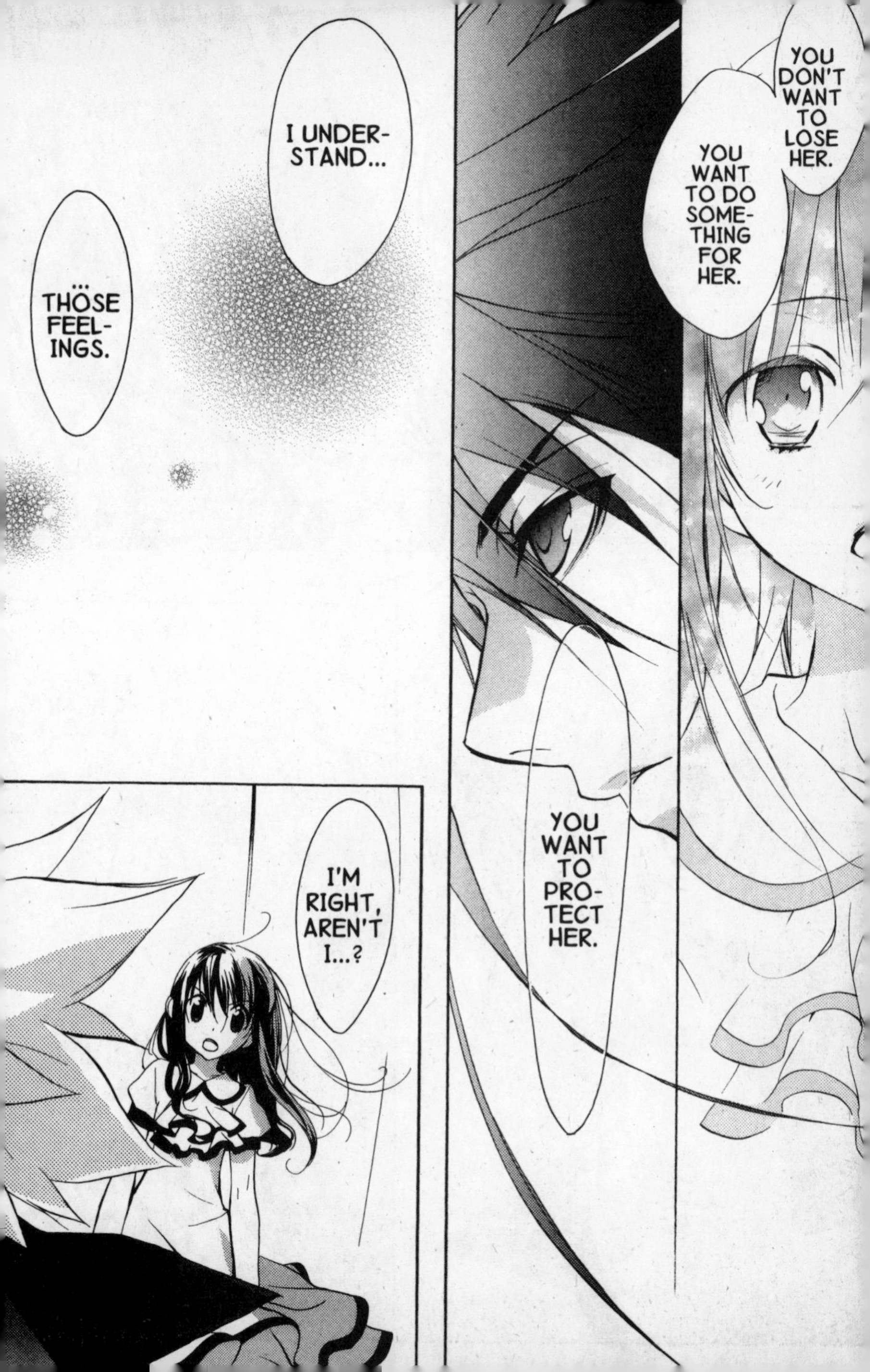
YOU DON'T WANT TO LOSE HER.
YOU WANT TO DO SOME-THING FOR HER.
YOU WANT TO PRO-TECT HER.
I UNDER-STAND...
...THOSE FEEL-INGS.
I'M RIGHT, AREN'T I...?

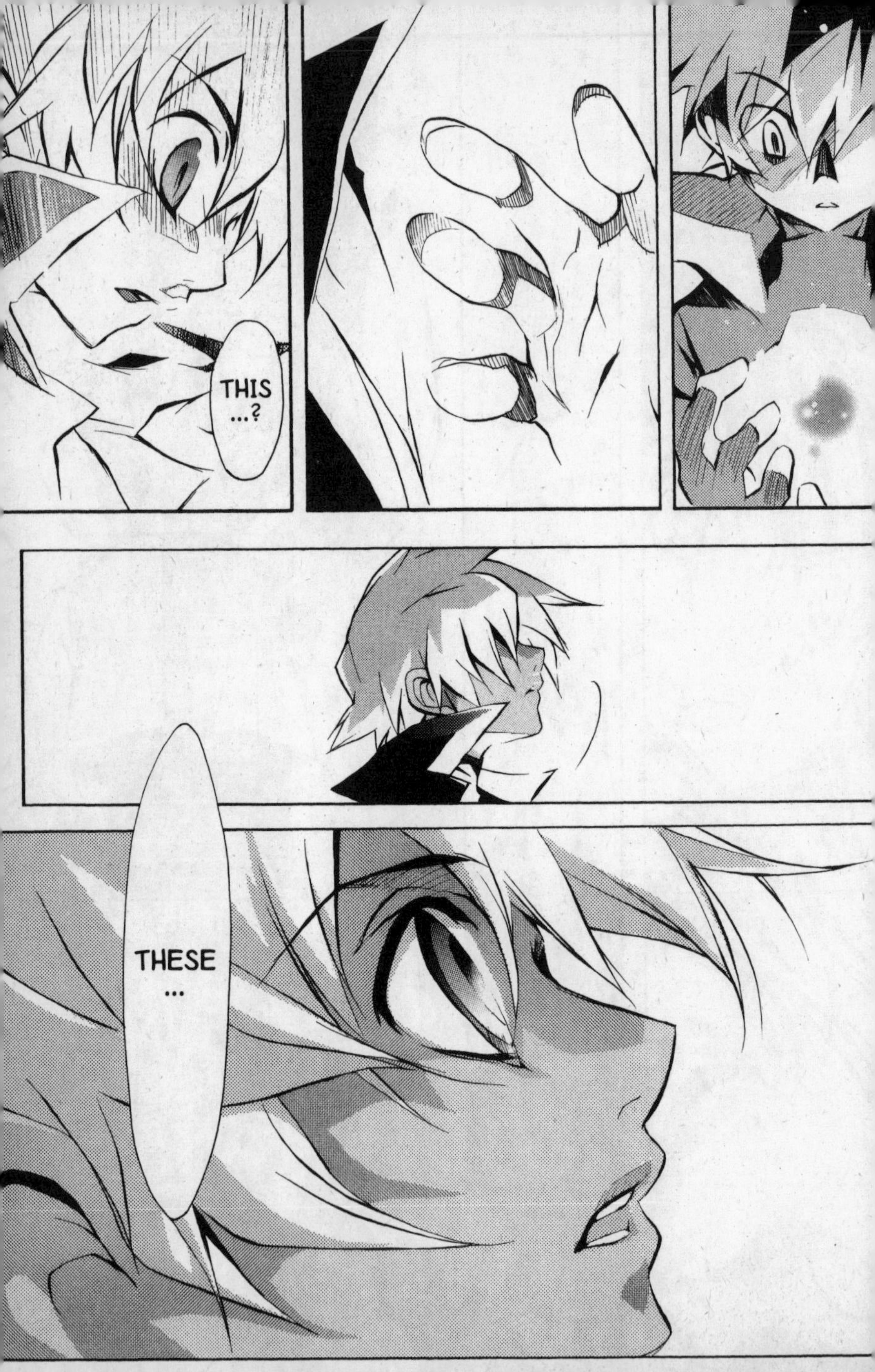
THIS ...?
THESE ...

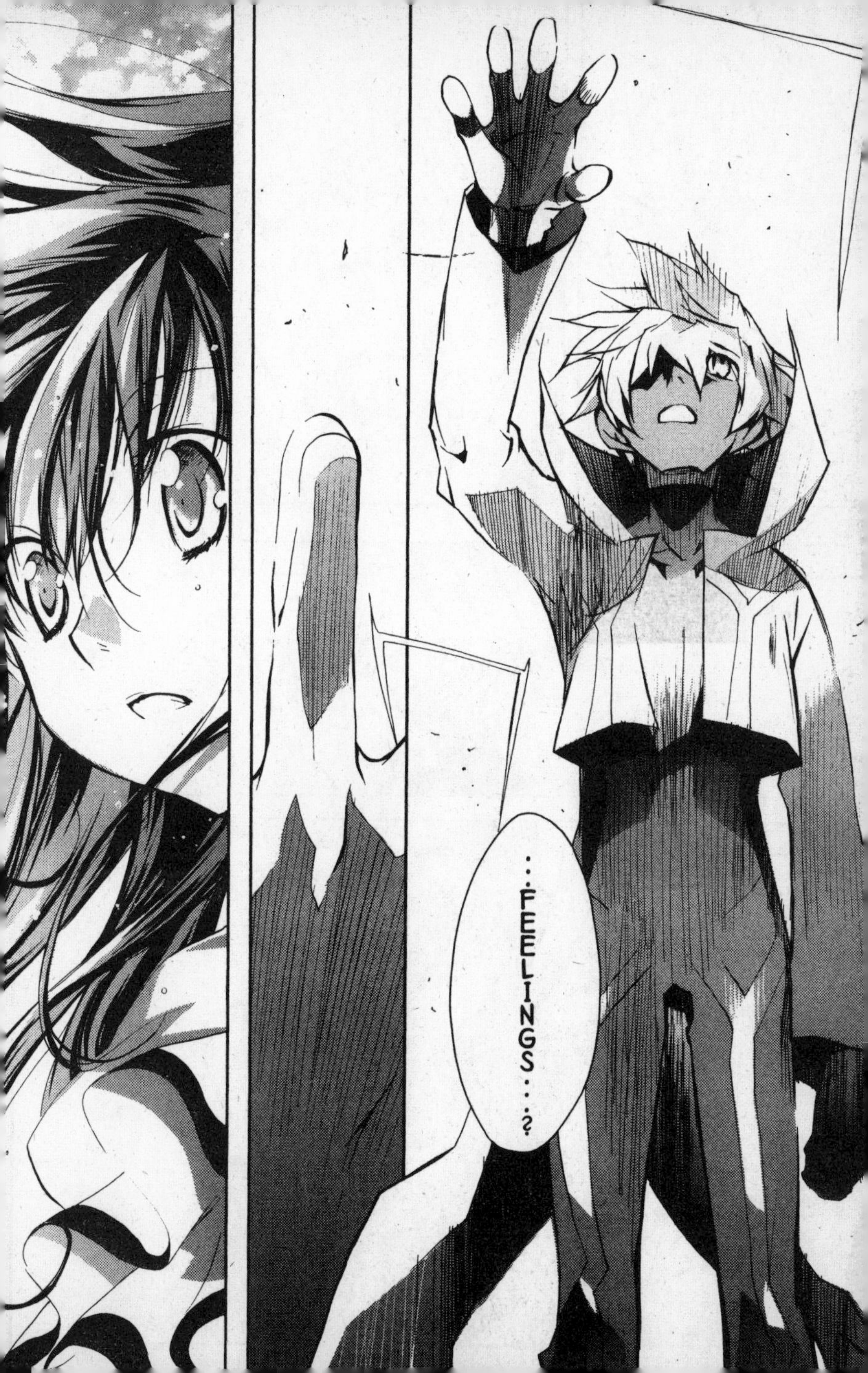
...FEELINGS...?

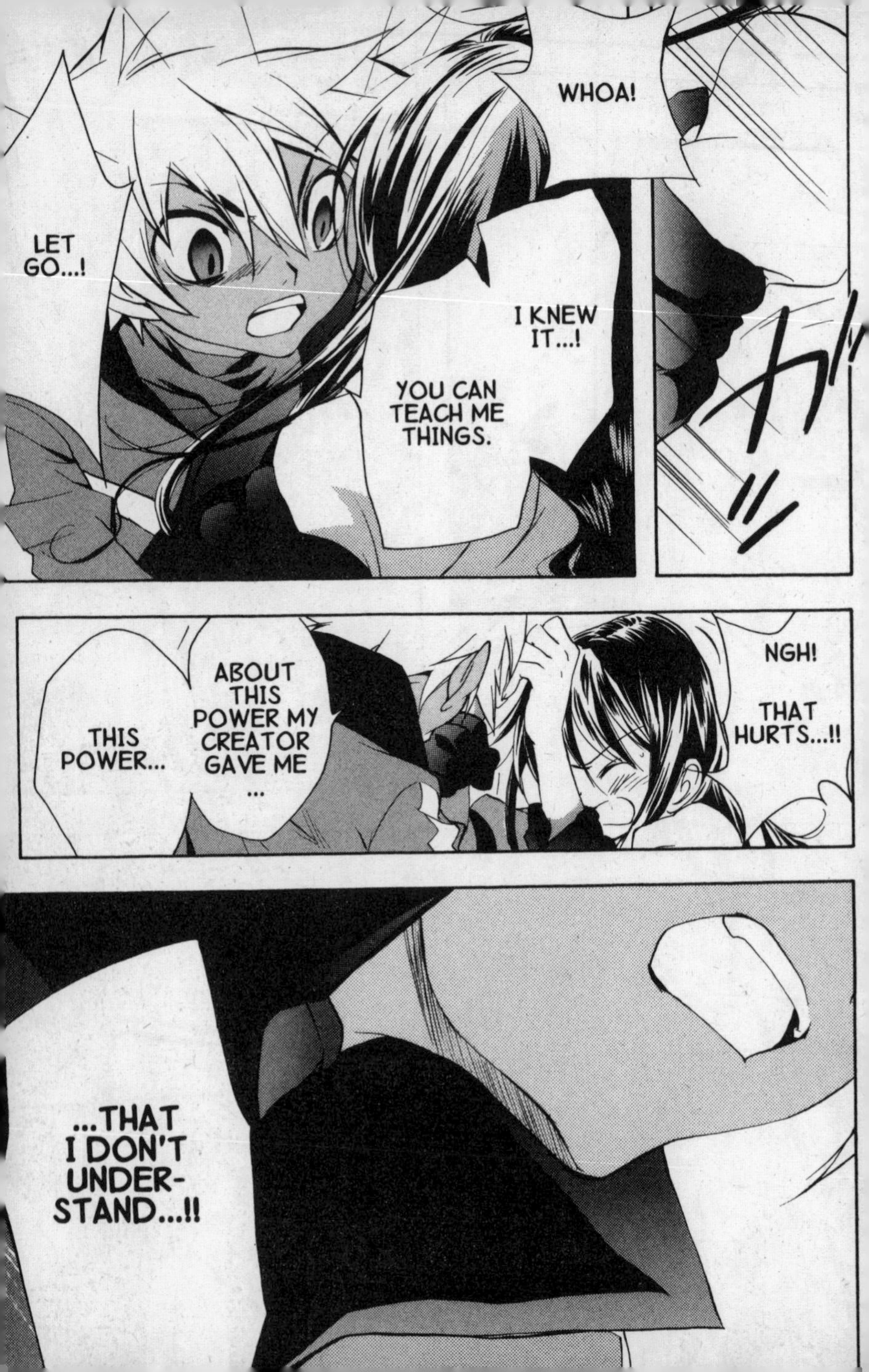
WHOA!
ガッ
I KNEW IT...!
YOU CAN TEACH ME THINGS.
LET GO...!
NGH!
THAT HURTS...!!
ABOUT THIS POWER MY CREATOR GAVE ME ...
THIS POWER...
...THAT I DON'T UNDER-STAND...!!

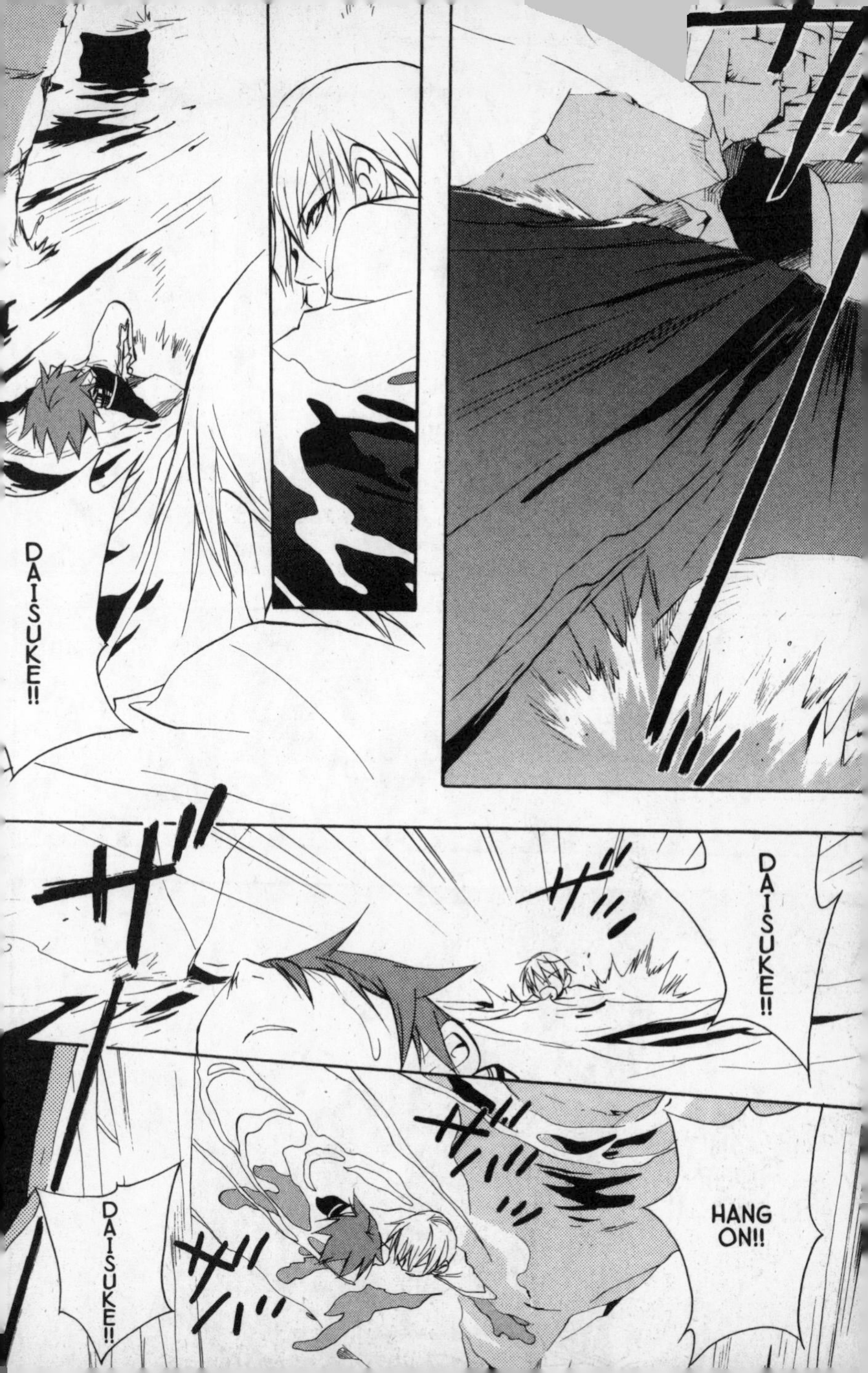
DAISUKE!!
DAISUKE!!
HANG ON!!
DAISUKE!!

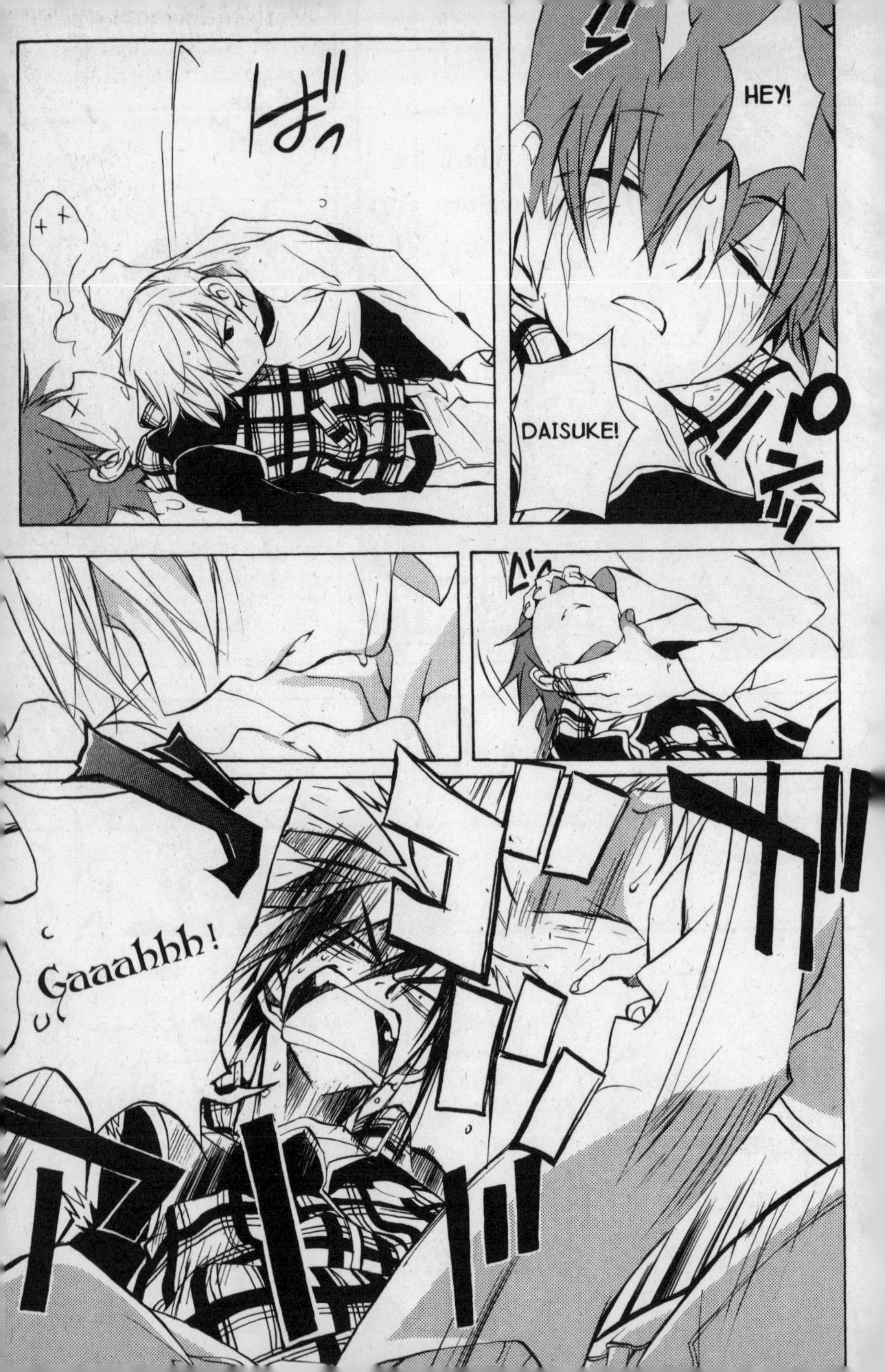
HEY!
DAISUKE!
ばっ
Gaaahhh!

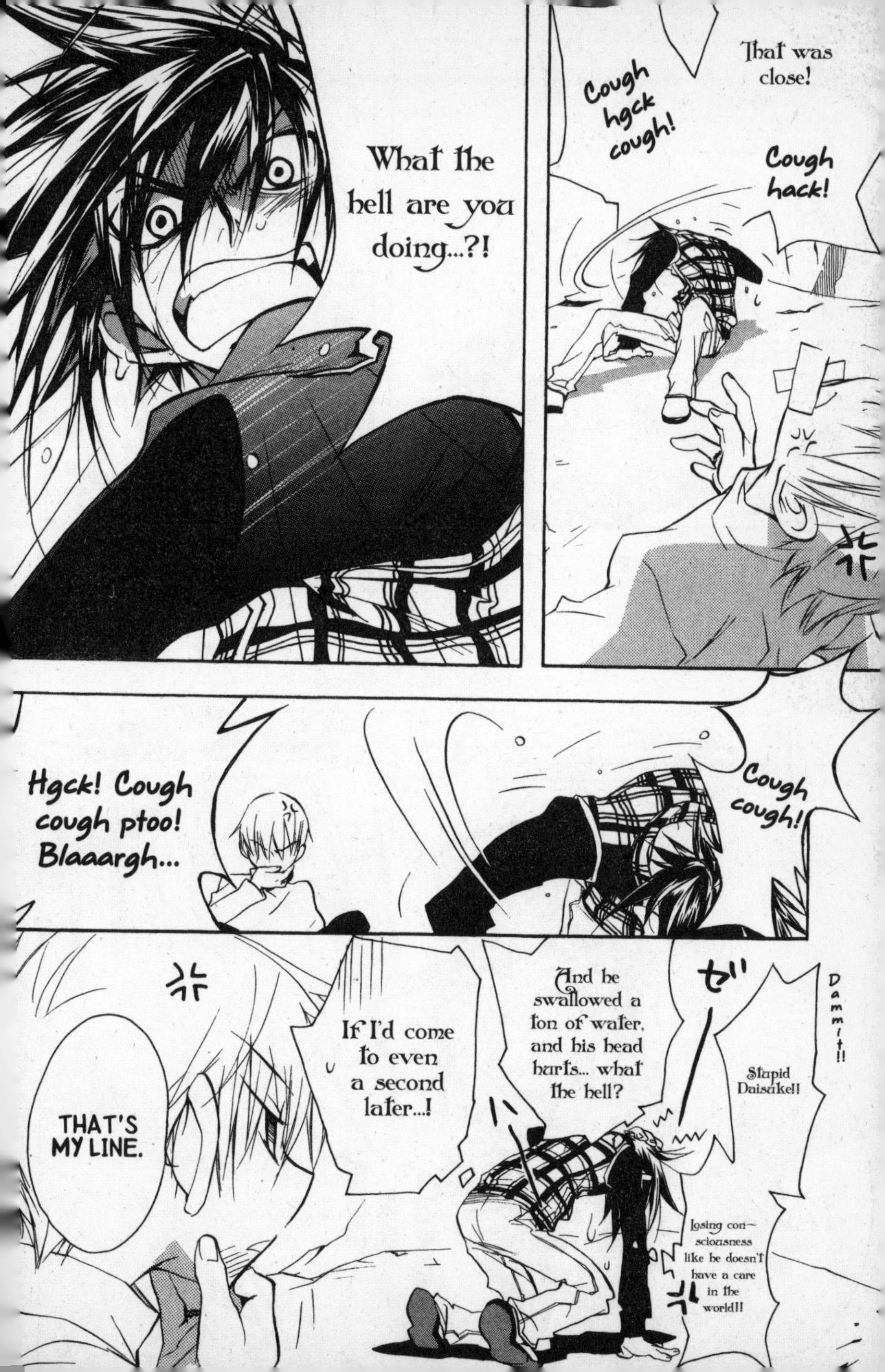
That was close!
Cough hgck cough!
Cough hack!
What the hell are you doing...?!
Cough cough!
Hgck! Cough cough ptoo! Blaaargh...
Dammit!!
Stupid Daisuke!!
And he swallowed a ton of water, and his head hurts... what the hell?
If I'd come to even a second later...!
Losing con-sciousness like he doesn't have a care in the world!!
THAT'S MY LINE.

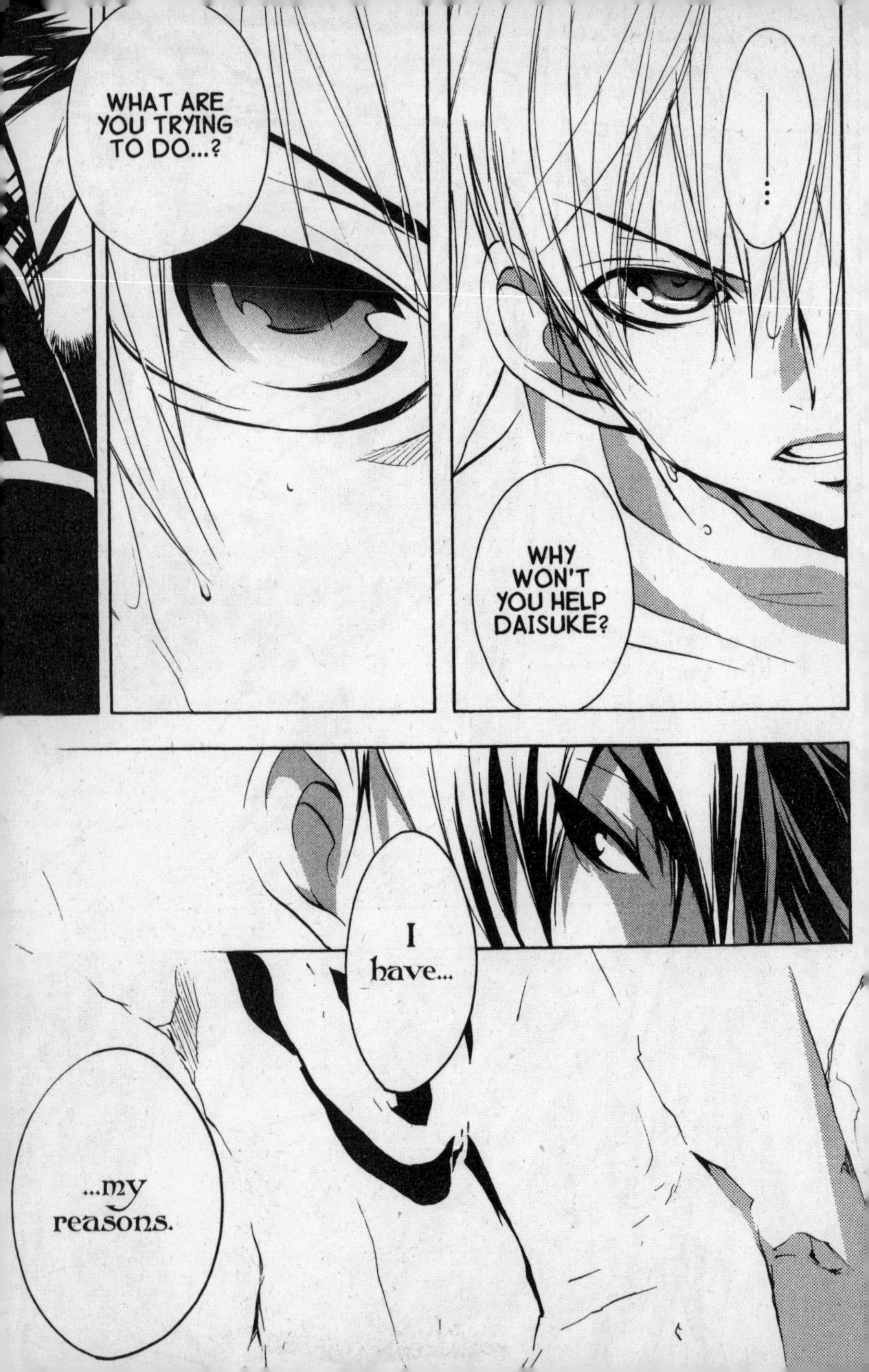

...
WHY WON'T YOU HELP DAISUKE?
WHAT ARE YOU TRYING TO DO...?
I have...
...my reasons.

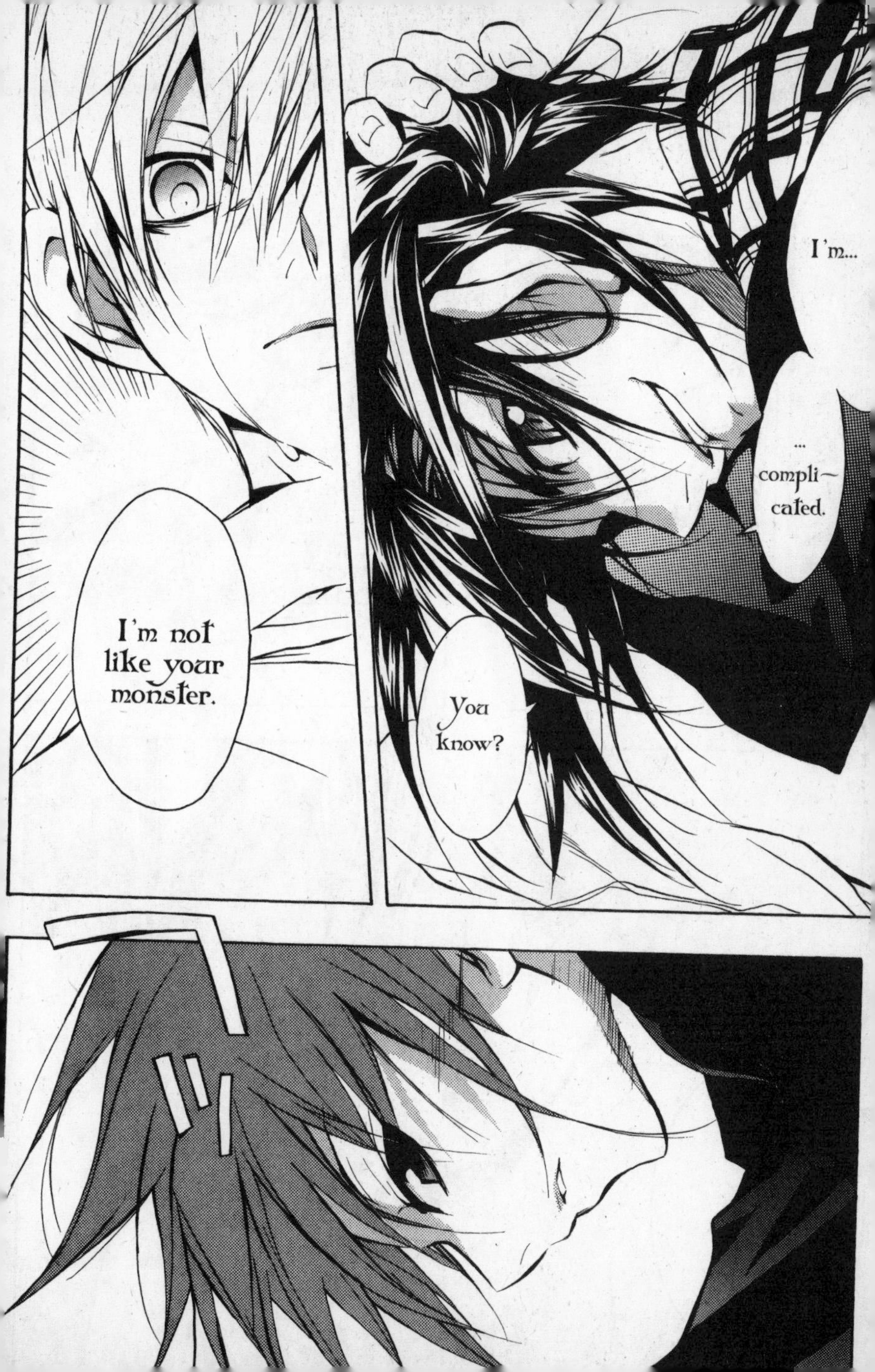
I'm...
... compli-cated.
You know?
I'm not like your monster.

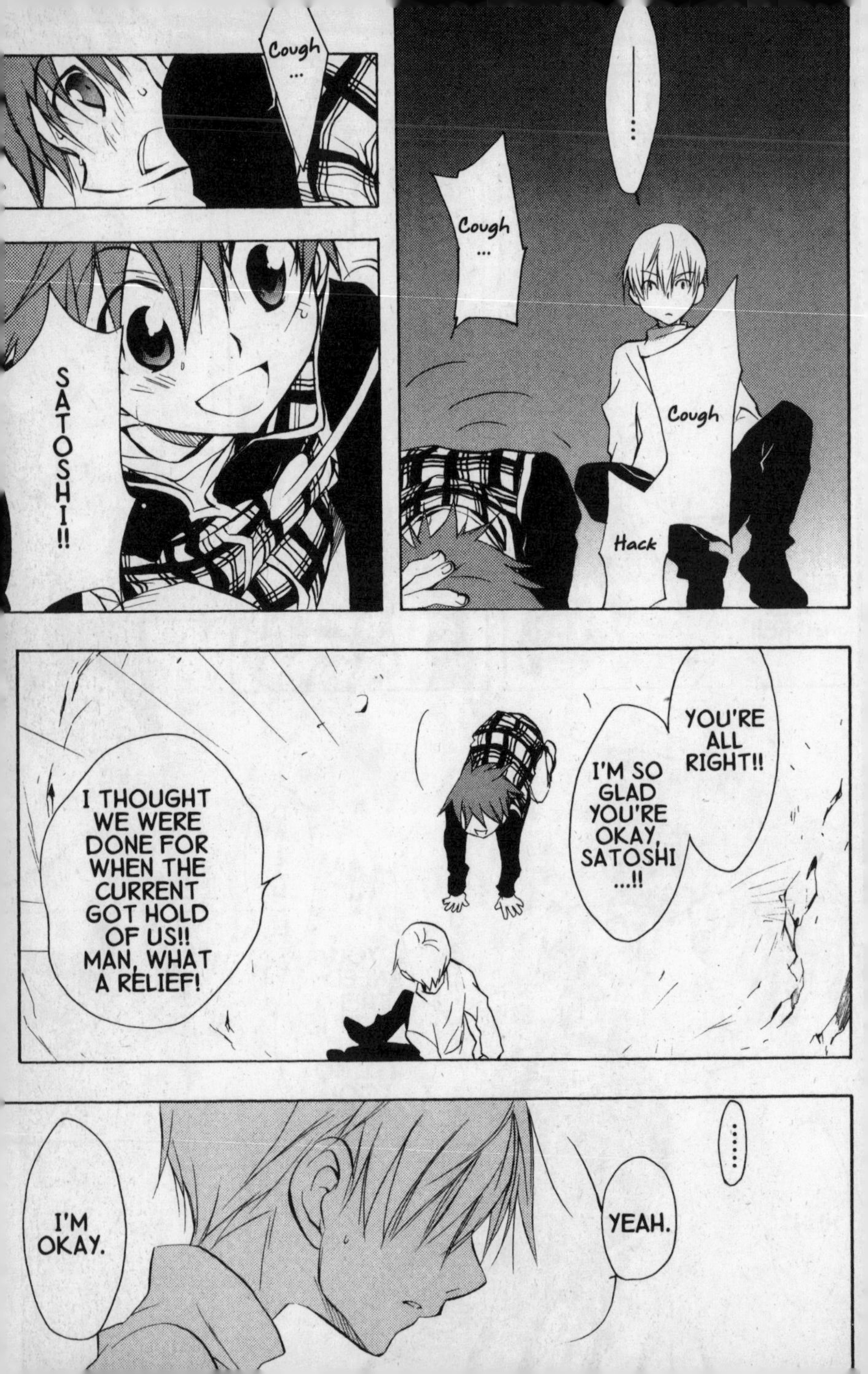
......
Cough ...
Cough
Hack
Cough ...
SATOSHI!!
YOU'RE ALL RIGHT!!
I'M SO GLAD YOU'RE OKAY, SATOSHI ...!!
I THOUGHT WE WERE DONE FOR WHEN THE CURRENT GOT HOLD OF US!! MAN, WHAT A RELIEF!
......
YEAH.
I'M OKAY.

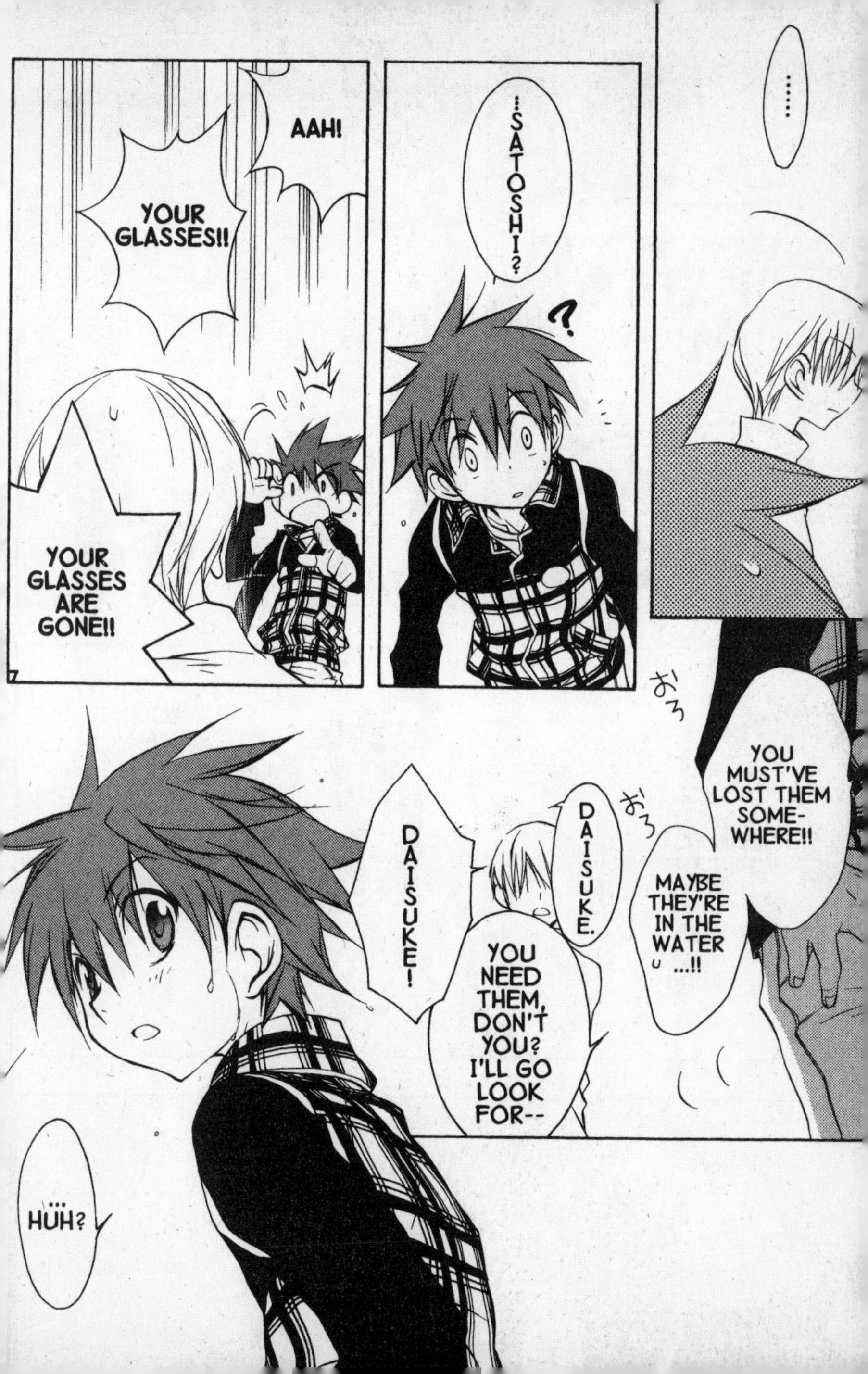
......
...SATOSHI?
?
AAH!
YOUR GLASSES!!
YOUR GLASSES ARE GONE!!
おろ
YOU MUST'VE LOST THEM SOME-WHERE!!
おろ
MAYBE THEY'RE IN THE WATER ...!!
DAISUKE.
YOU NEED THEM, DON'T YOU? I'LL GO LOOK FOR--
DAISUKE!
...HUH?

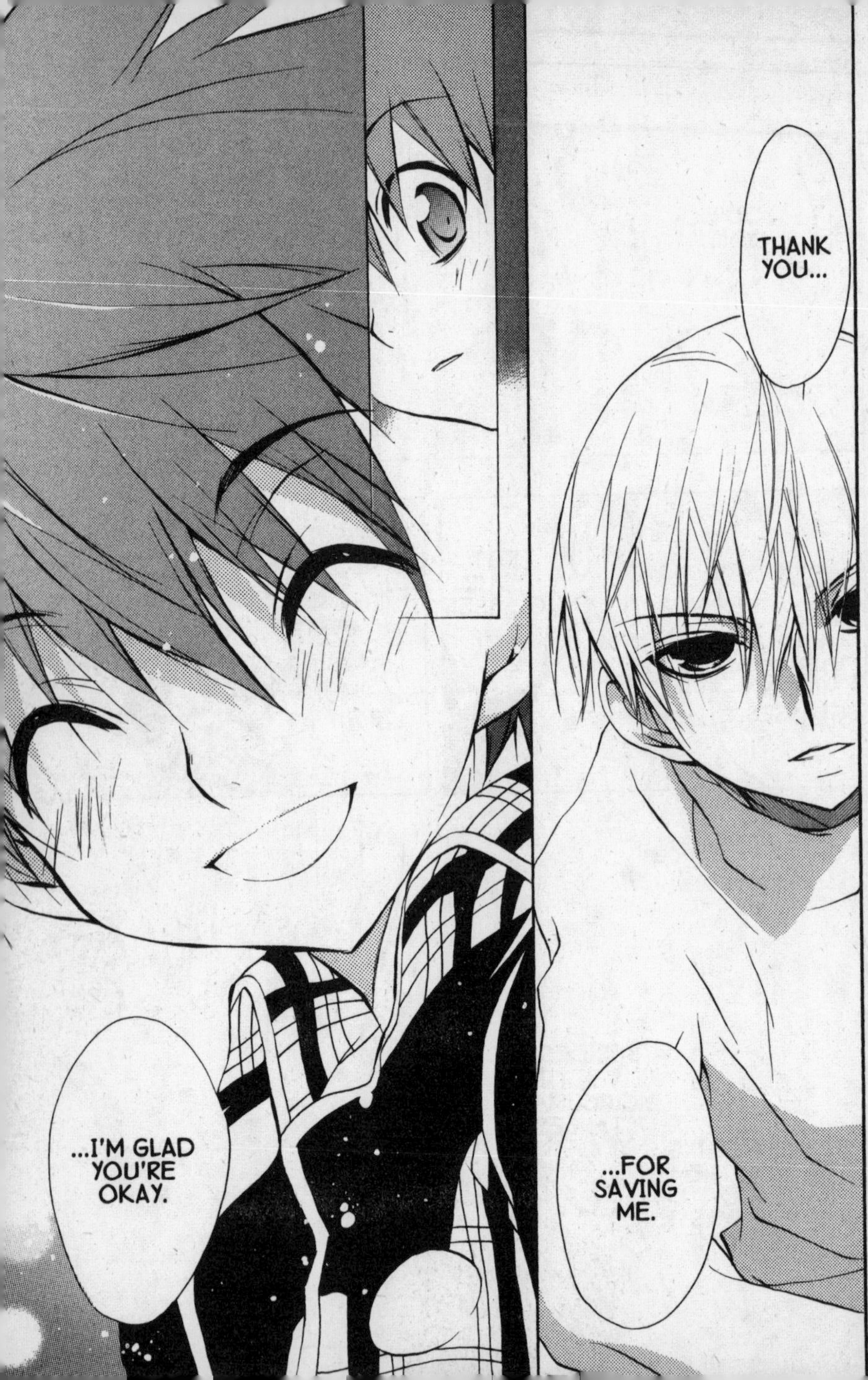
THANK YOU...
...FOR SAVING ME.
...I'M GLAD YOU'RE OKAY.

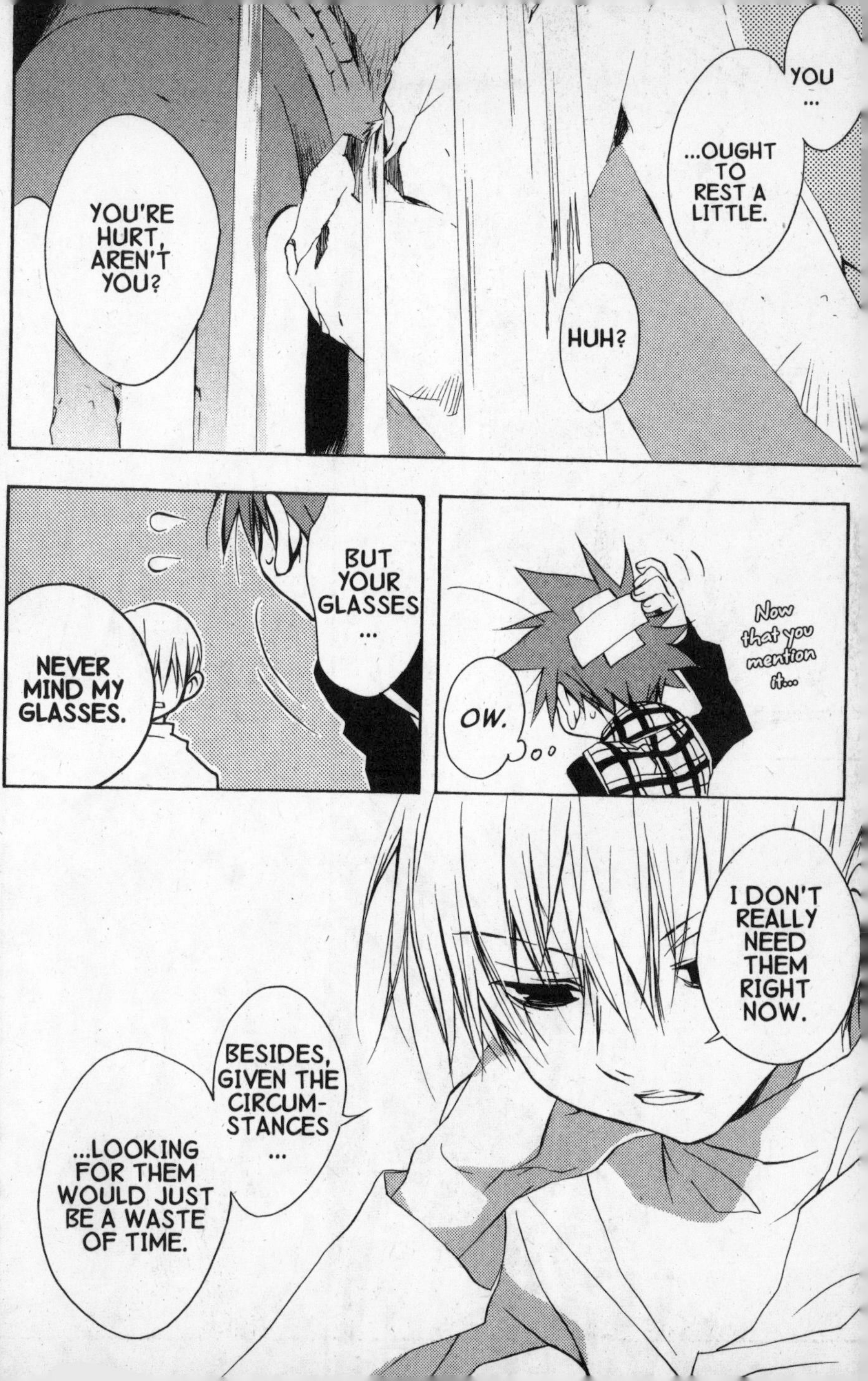
YOU ...
...OUGHT TO REST A LITTLE.
HUH?
YOU'RE HURT, AREN'T YOU?
Now that you mention it...
OW.
BUT YOUR GLASSES ...
NEVER MIND MY GLASSES.
I DON'T REALLY NEED THEM RIGHT NOW.
BESIDES, GIVEN THE CIRCUM- STANCES ...
...LOOKING FOR THEM WOULD JUST BE A WASTE OF TIME.

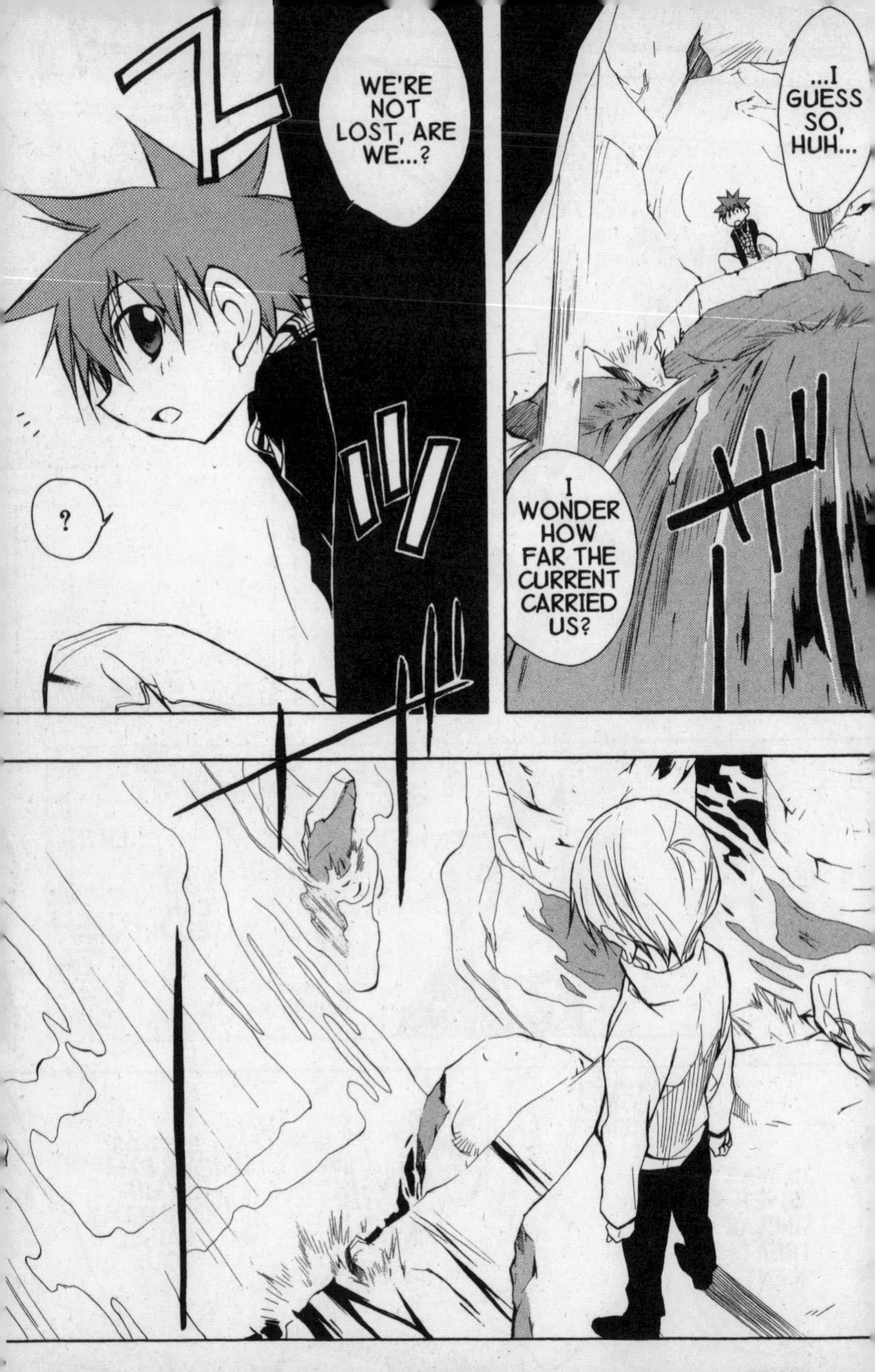
...I GUESS SO, HUH...
I WONDER HOW FAR THE CURRENT CARRIED US?
WE'RE NOT LOST, ARE WE...?
?

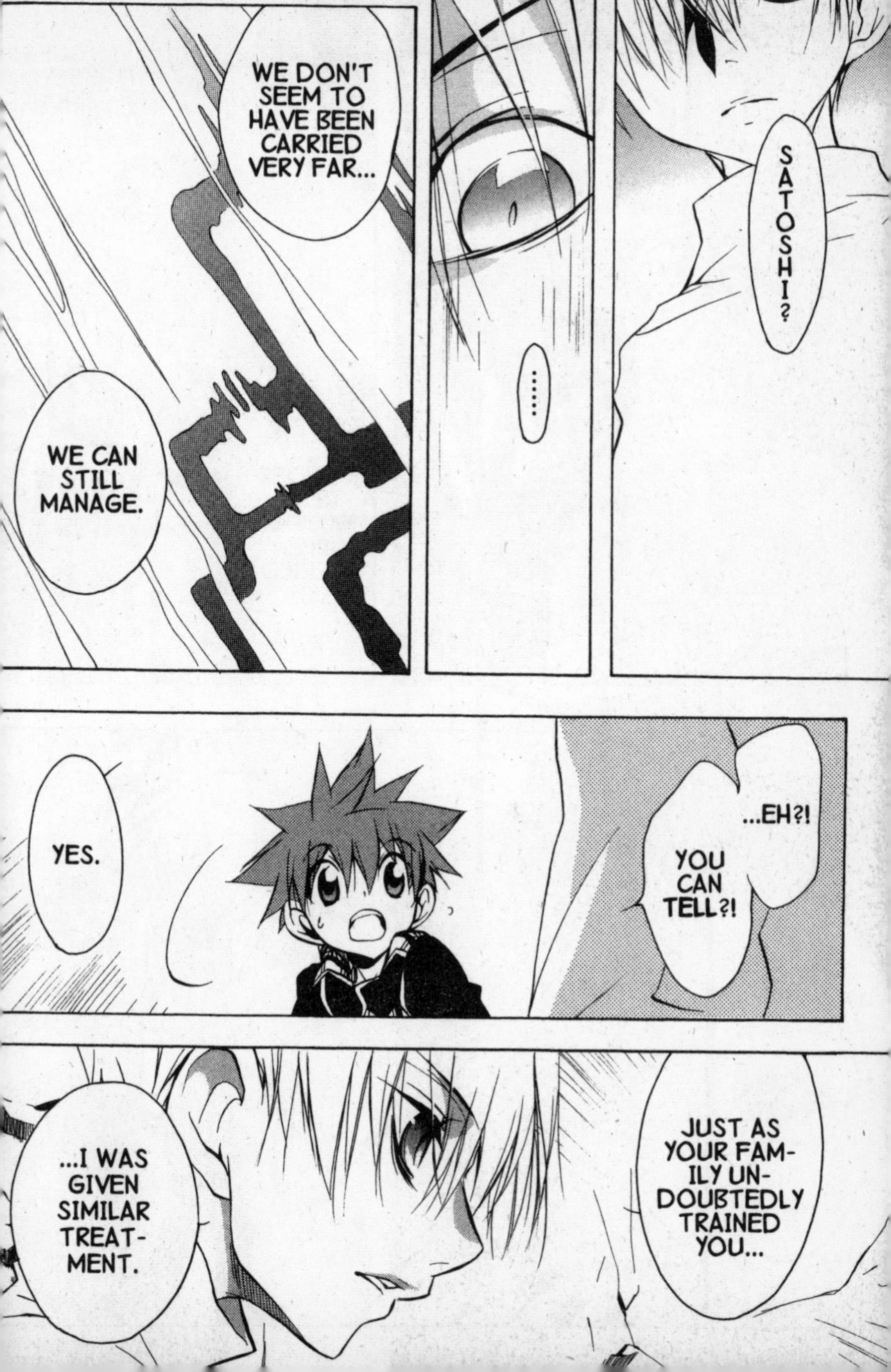
SATOSHI?
......
WE DON'T SEEM TO HAVE BEEN CARRIED VERY FAR...
WE CAN STILL MANAGE.
...EH?!
YOU CAN TELL?!
YES.
JUST AS YOUR FAMILY UNDOUBTEDLY TRAINED YOU...
...I WAS GIVEN SIMILAR TREATMENT.

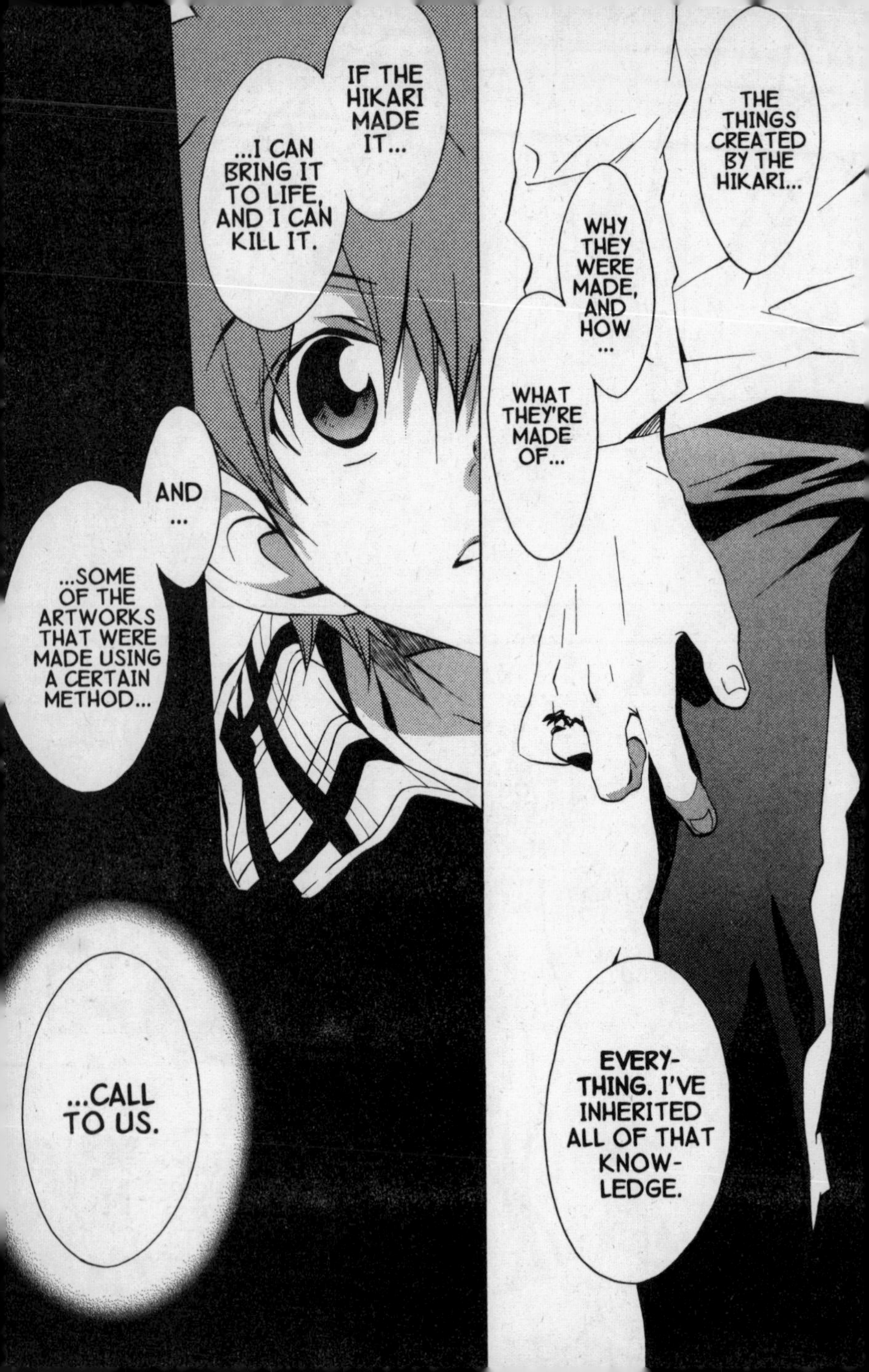
THE THINGS CREATED BY THE HIKARI...
WHY THEY WERE MADE, AND HOW...
WHAT THEY'RE MADE OF...
EVERYTHING. I'VE INHERITED ALL OF THAT KNOWLEDGE.
IF THE HIKARI MADE IT...
...I CAN BRING IT TO LIFE, AND I CAN KILL IT.
AND...
...SOME OF THE ARTWORKS THAT WERE MADE USING A CERTAIN METHOD...
...CALL TO US.

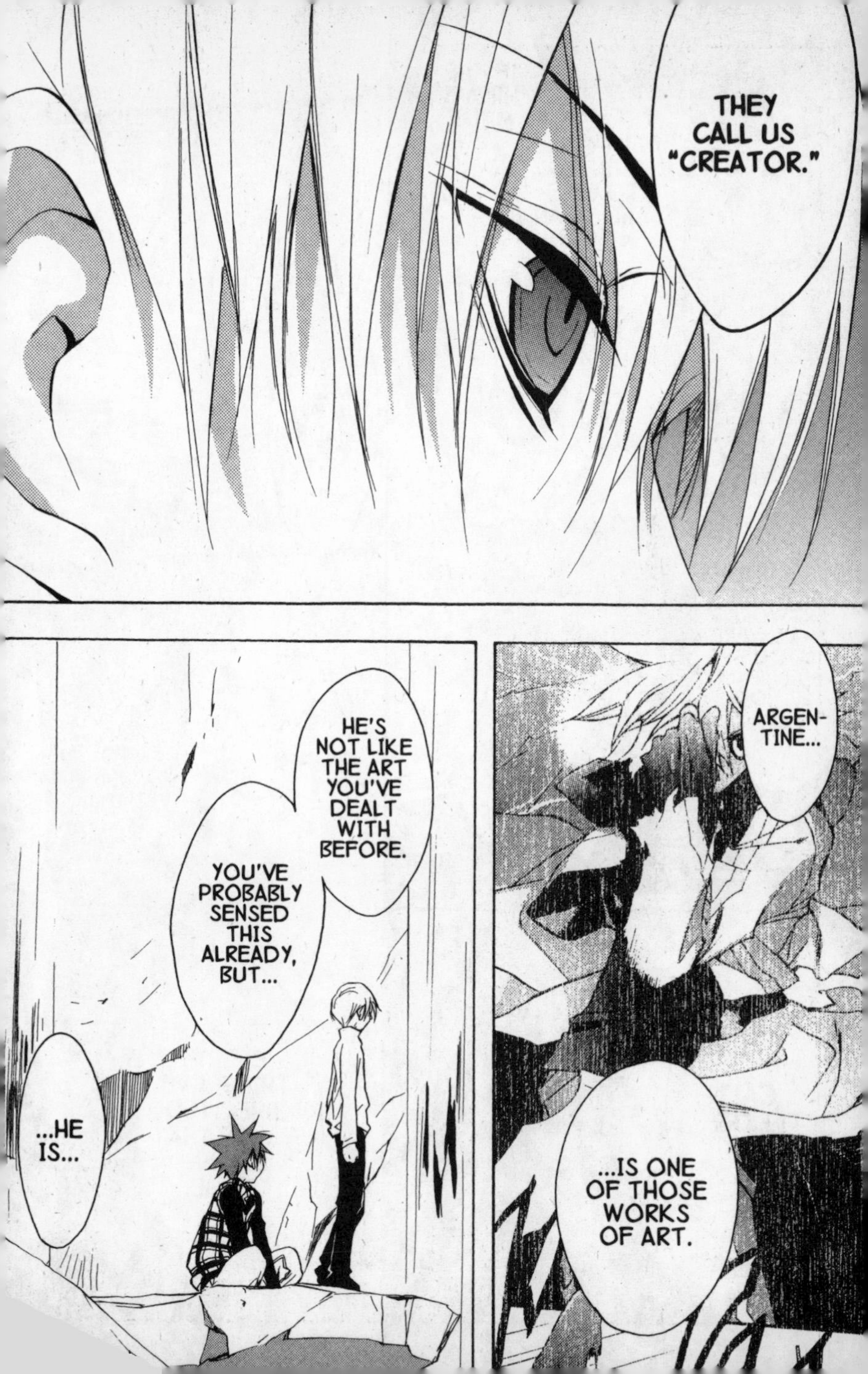
THEY CALL US "CREATOR."
ARGEN-TINE...
...IS ONE OF THOSE WORKS OF ART.
HE'S NOT LIKE THE ART YOU'VE DEALT WITH BEFORE.
YOU'VE PROBABLY SENSED THIS ALREADY, BUT...
...HE IS...

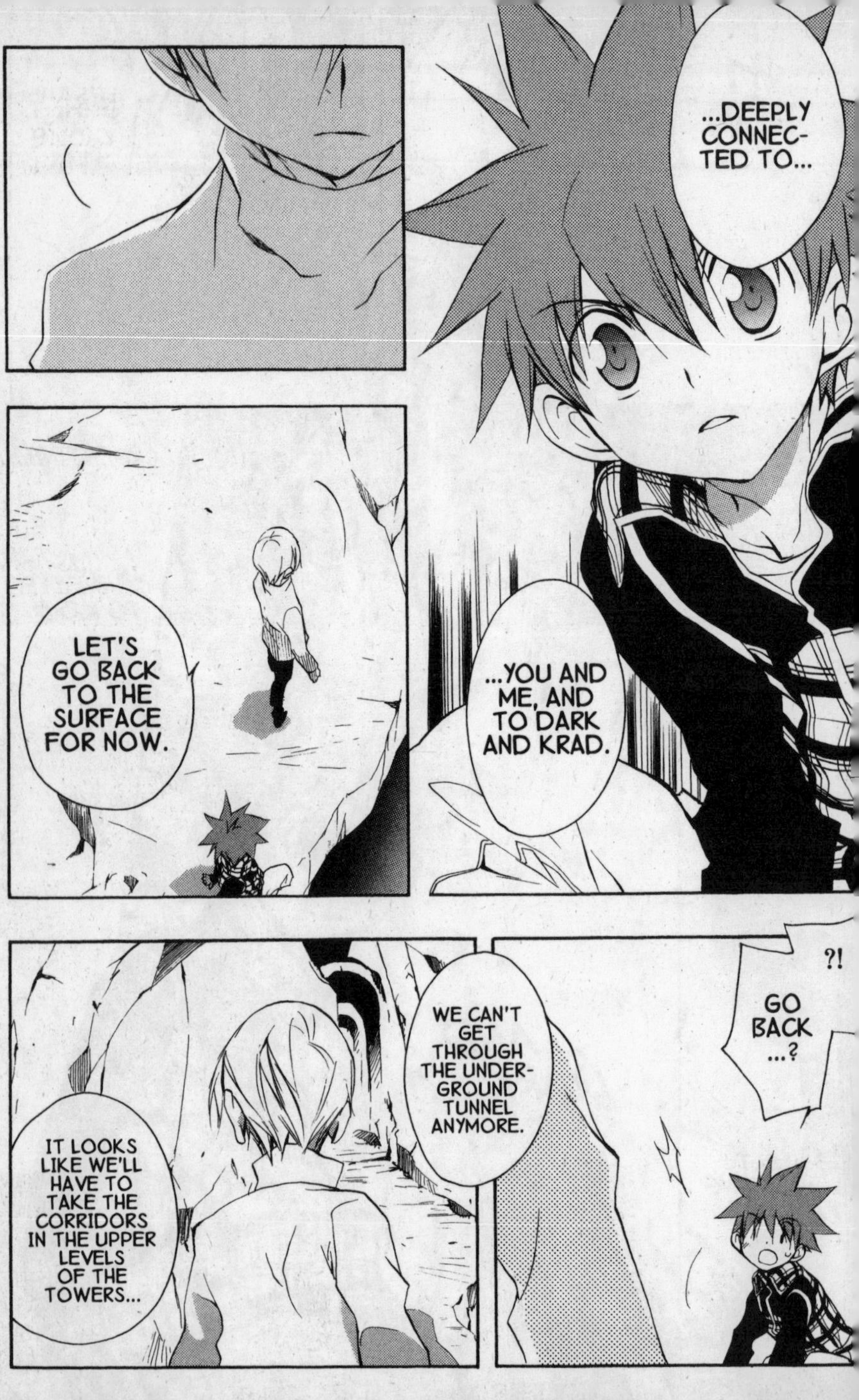
...DEEPLY CONNECTED TO...
...YOU AND ME, AND TO DARK AND KRAD.
LET'S GO BACK TO THE SURFACE FOR NOW.
?!
GO BACK ...?
WE CAN'T GET THROUGH THE UNDERGROUND TUNNEL ANYMORE.
IT LOOKS LIKE WE'LL HAVE TO TAKE THE CORRIDORS IN THE UPPER LEVELS OF THE TOWERS...

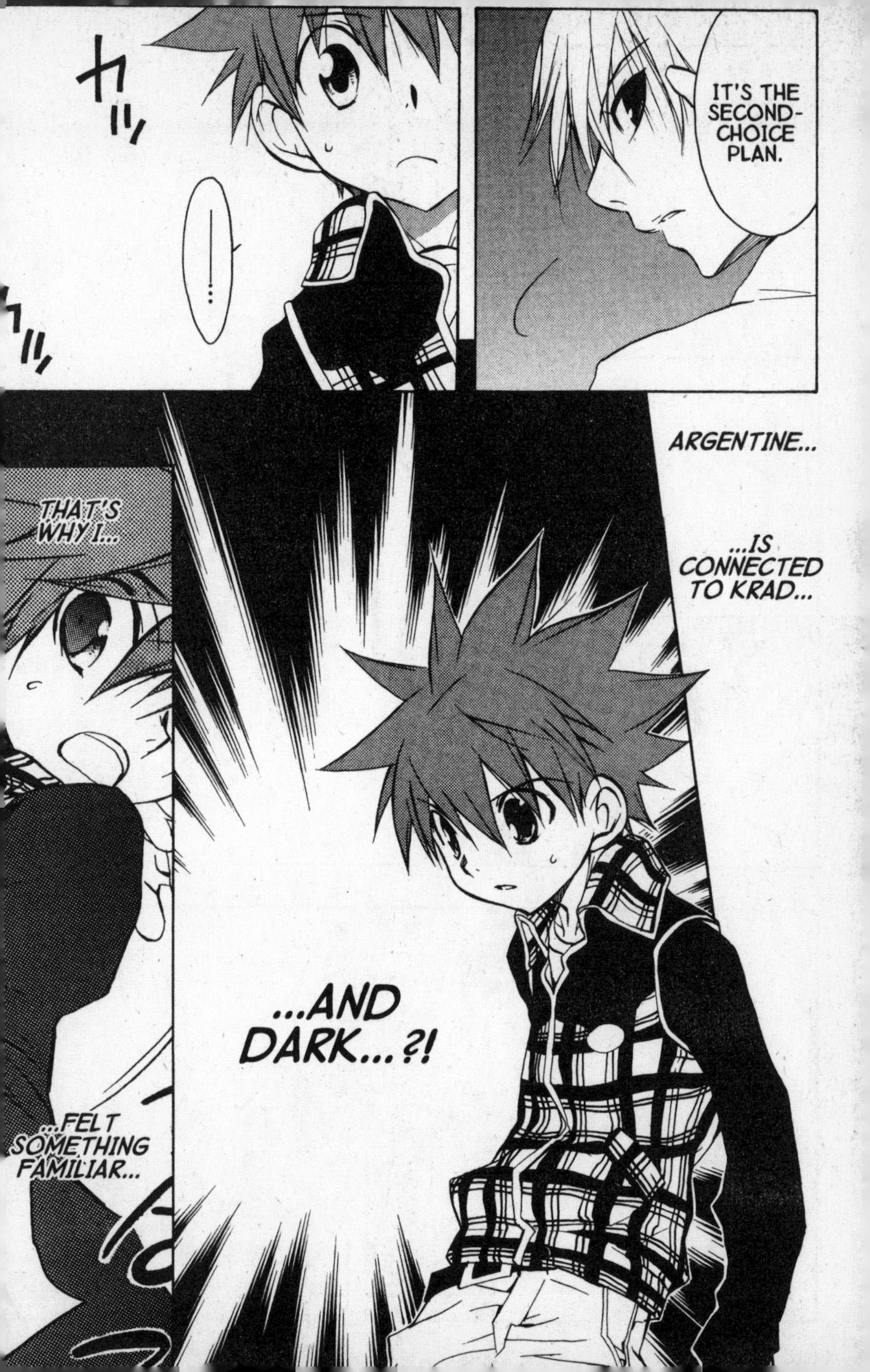
IT'S THE SECOND-CHOICE PLAN.
ARGENTINE...
...IS CONNECTED TO KRAD...
...AND DARK...?!
THAT'S WHY I...
...FELT SOMETHING FAMILIAR...

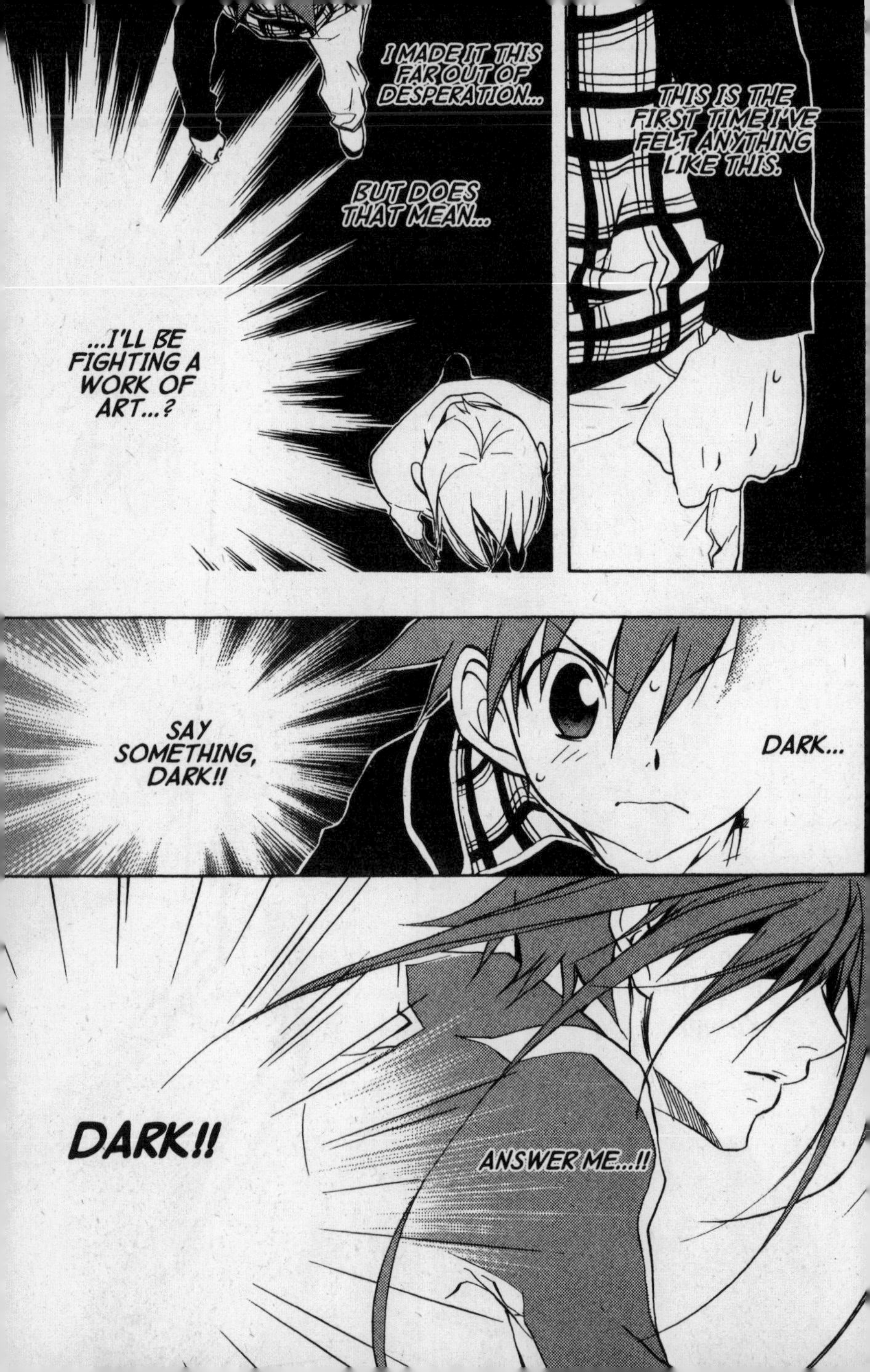
THIS IS THE FIRST TIME I'VE FELT ANYTHING LIKE THIS.
I MADE IT THIS FAR OUT OF DESPERATION...
BUT DOES THAT MEAN...
...I'LL BE FIGHTING A WORK OF ART...?
DARK...
SAY SOMETHING, DARK!!
ANSWER ME...!!
DARK!!

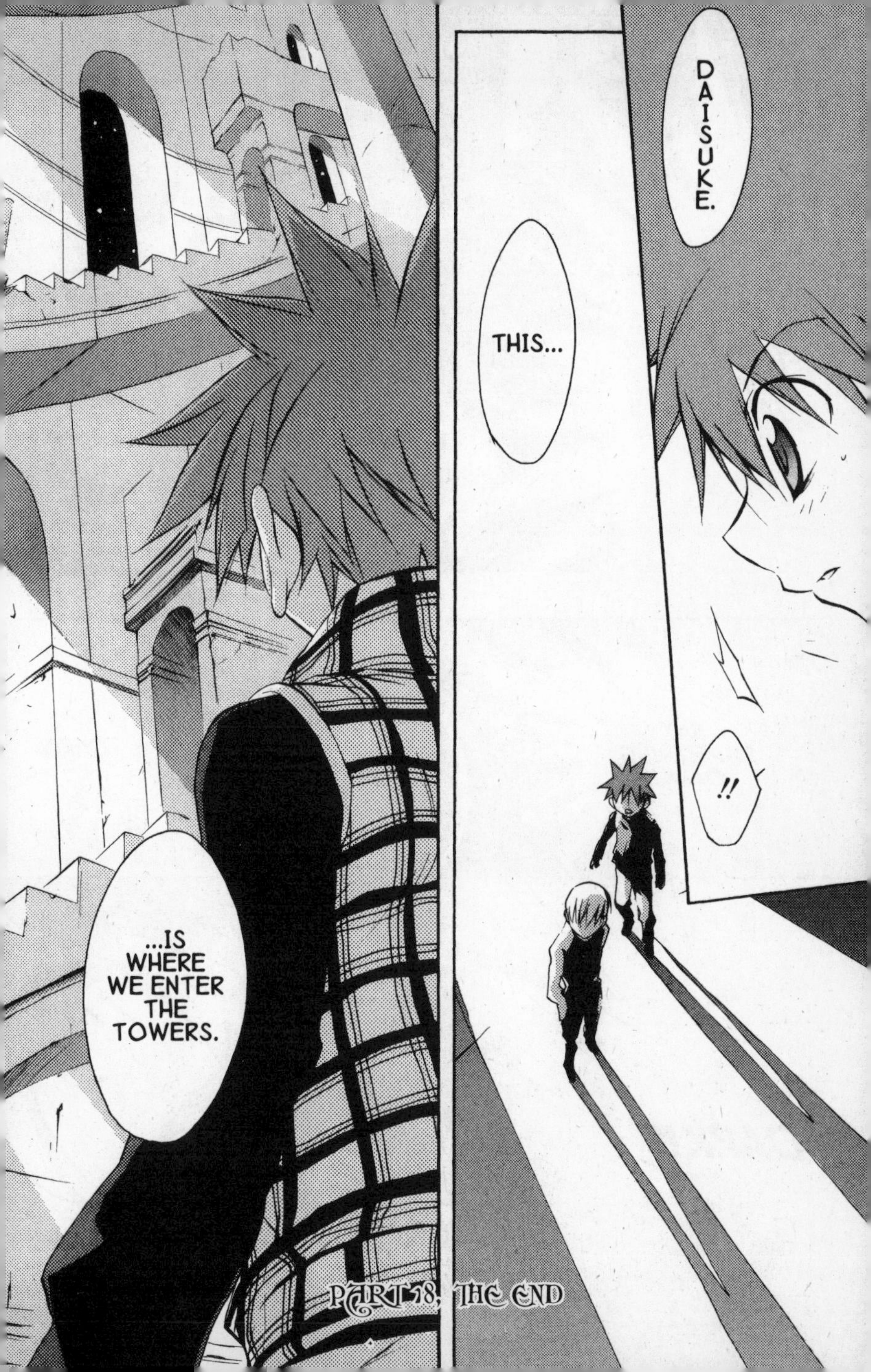
DAISUKE.
THIS...
!!
...IS WHERE WE ENTER THE TOWERS.
PART 18: THE END

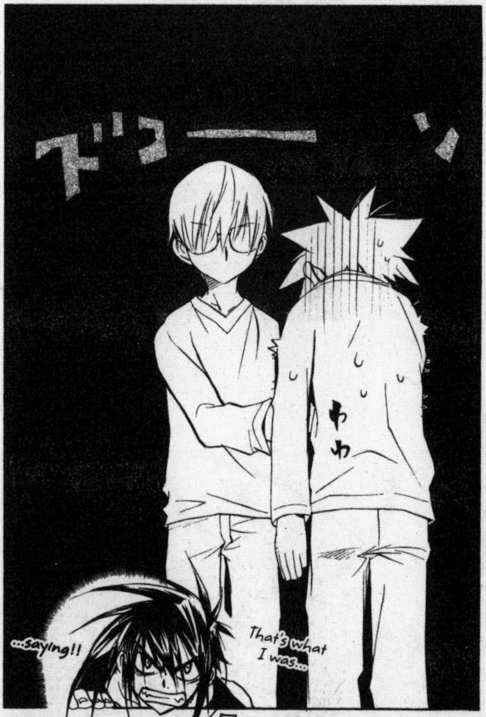
That's what I was...
...saying!!

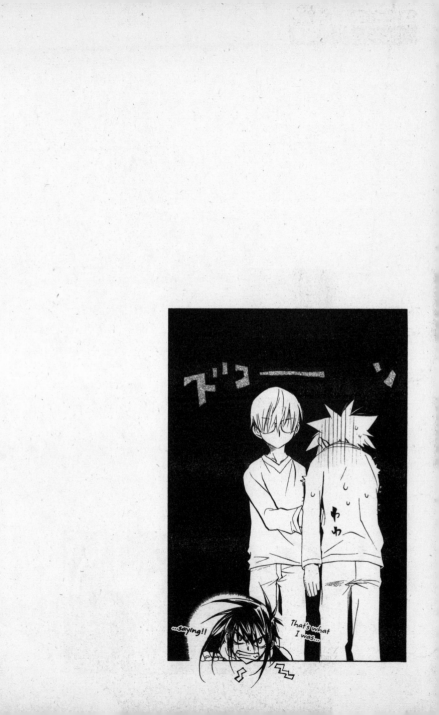

STAGE3 Vol. 19

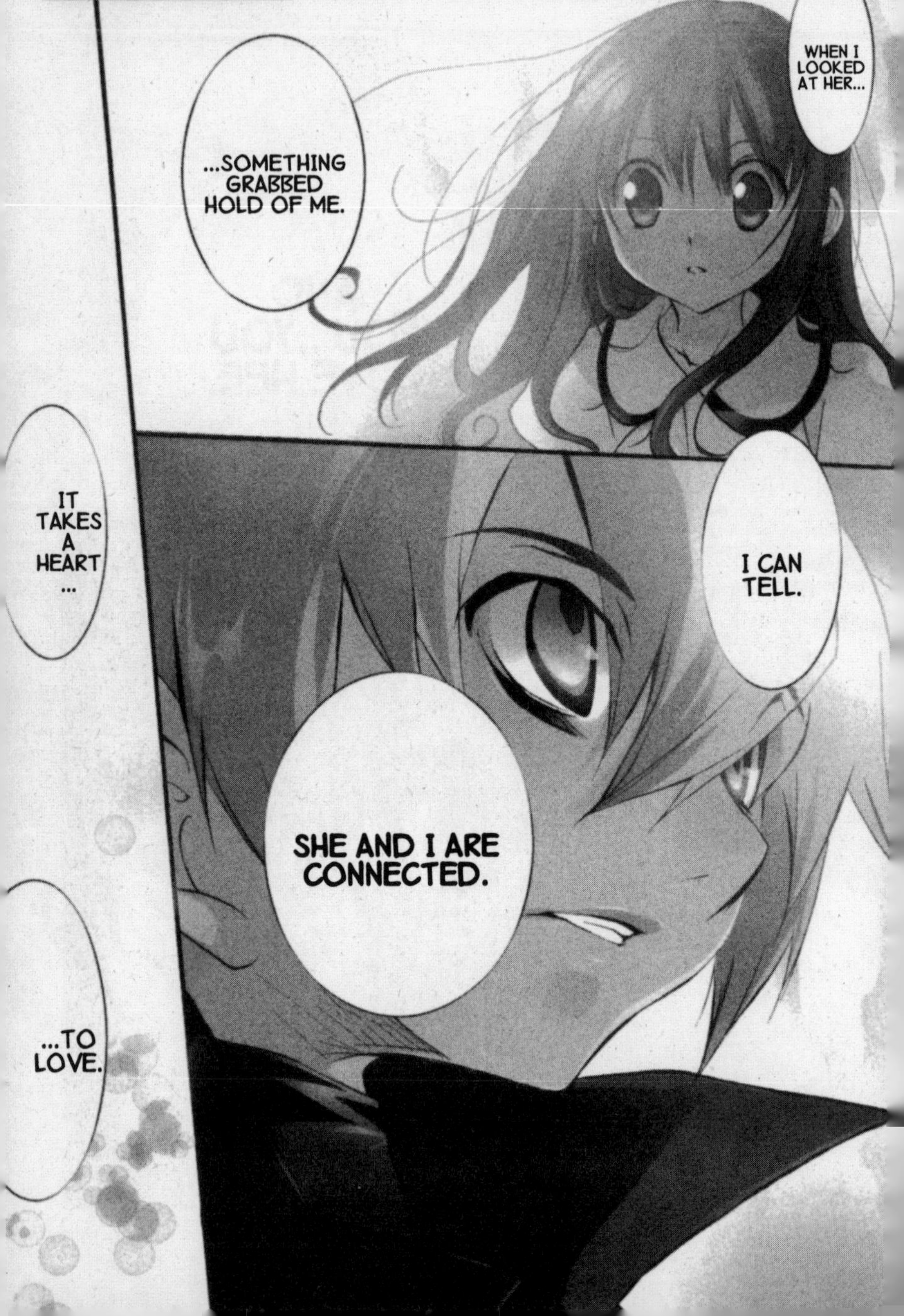
WHEN I LOOKED AT HER...
...SOMETHING GRABBED HOLD OF ME.
I CAN TELL.
SHE AND I ARE CONNECTED.
IT TAKES A HEART...
...TO LOVE.

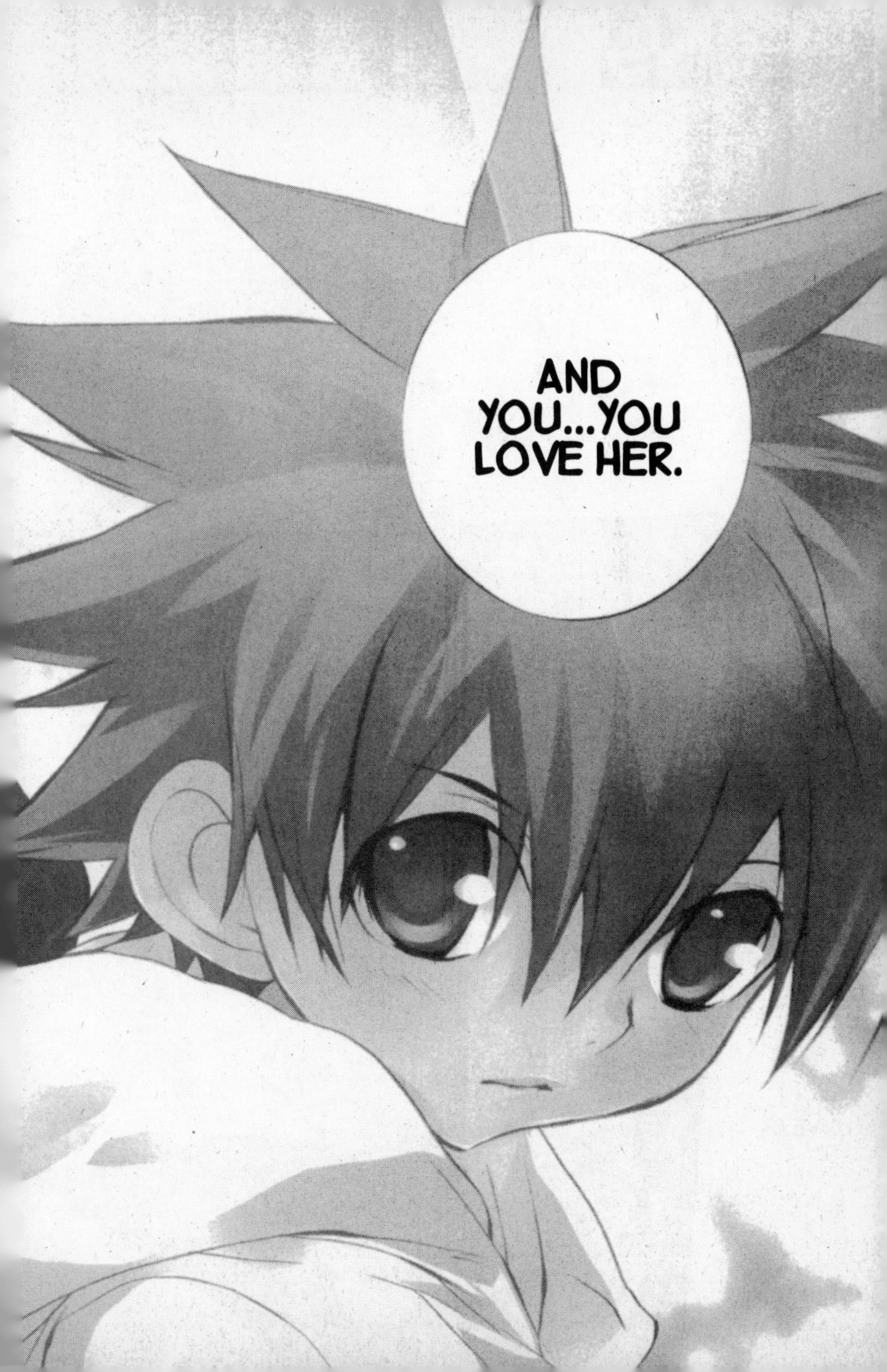
AND YOU...YOU LOVE HER.

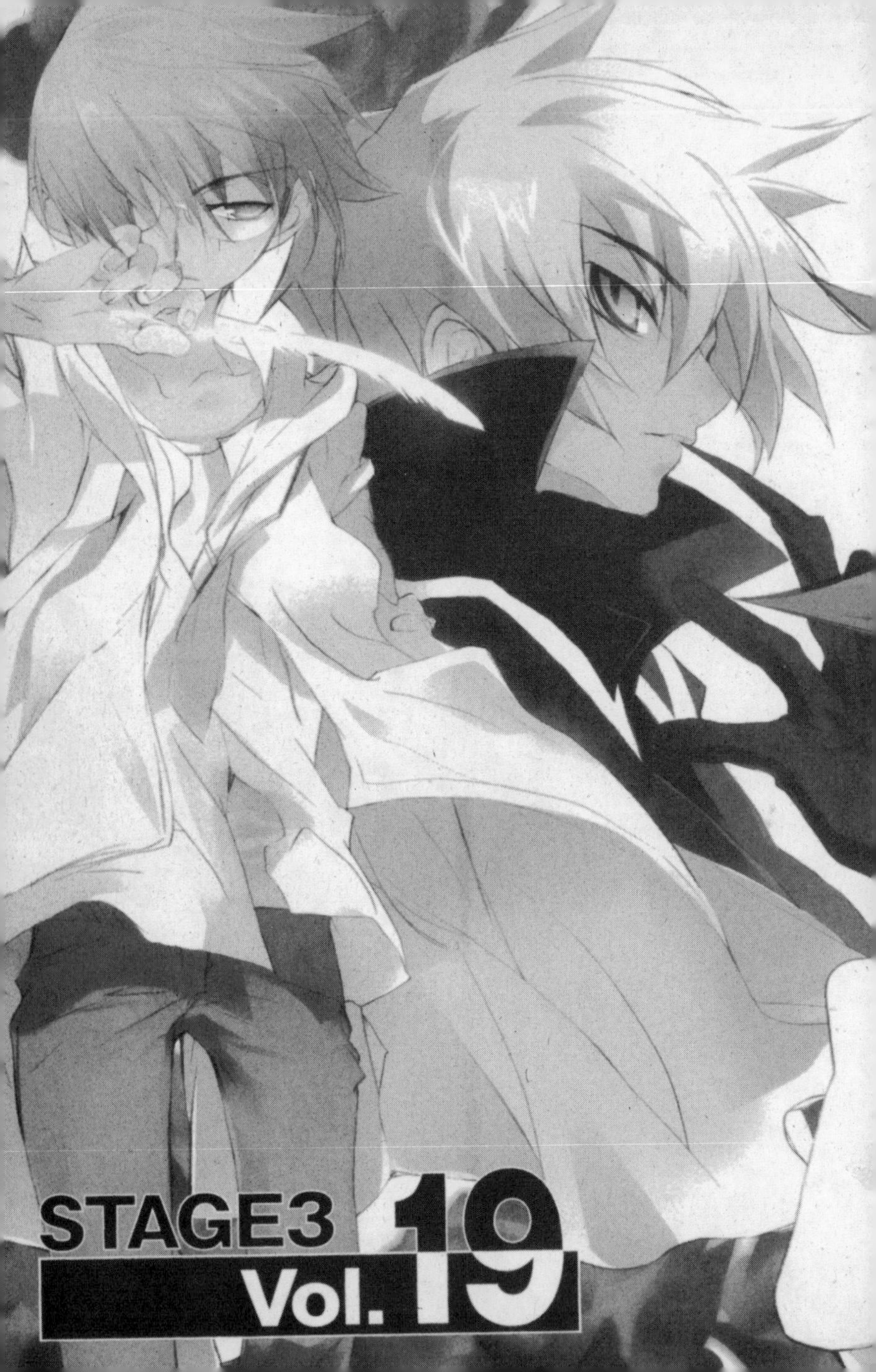
STAGE3
Vol. 19

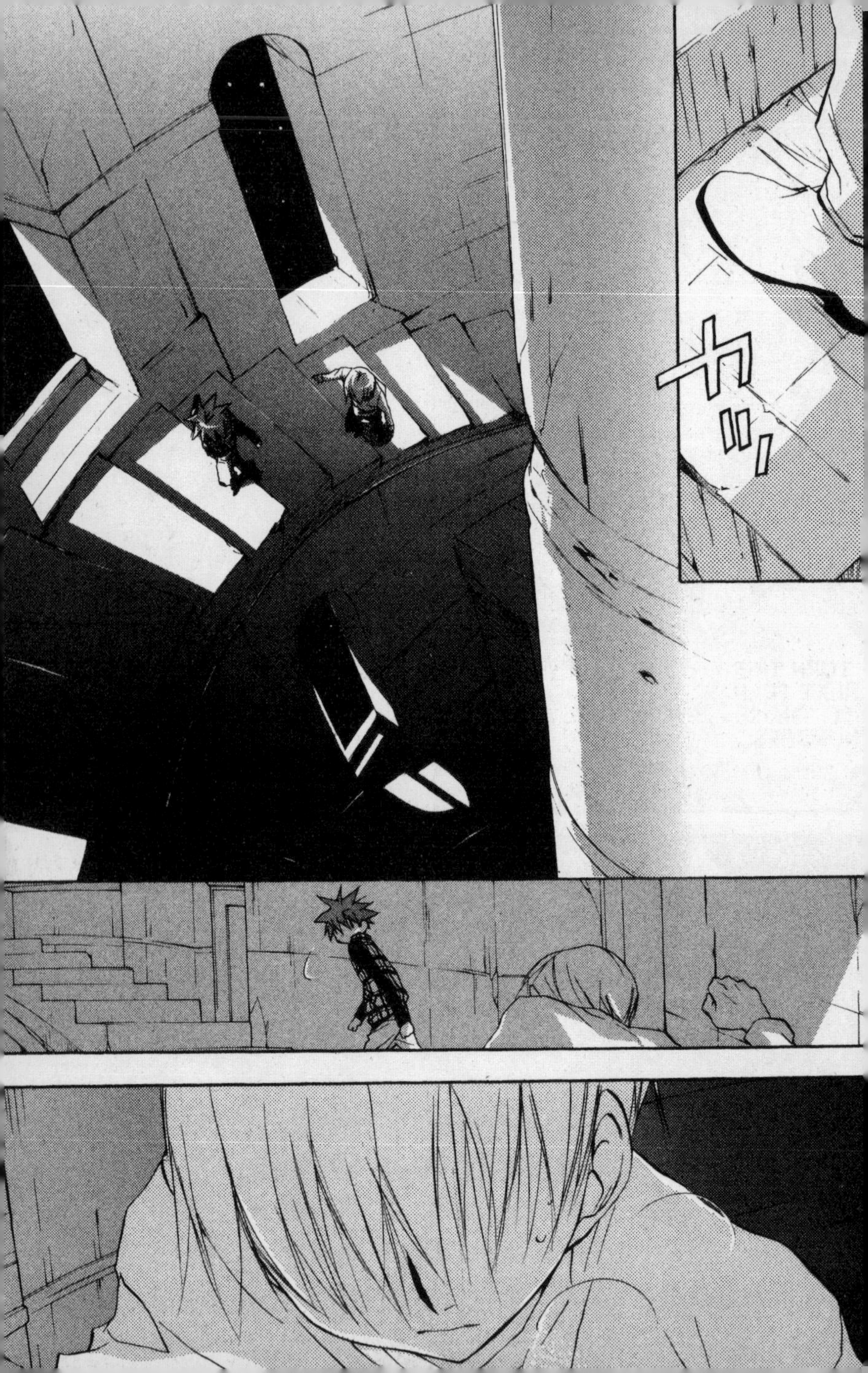
ガッ

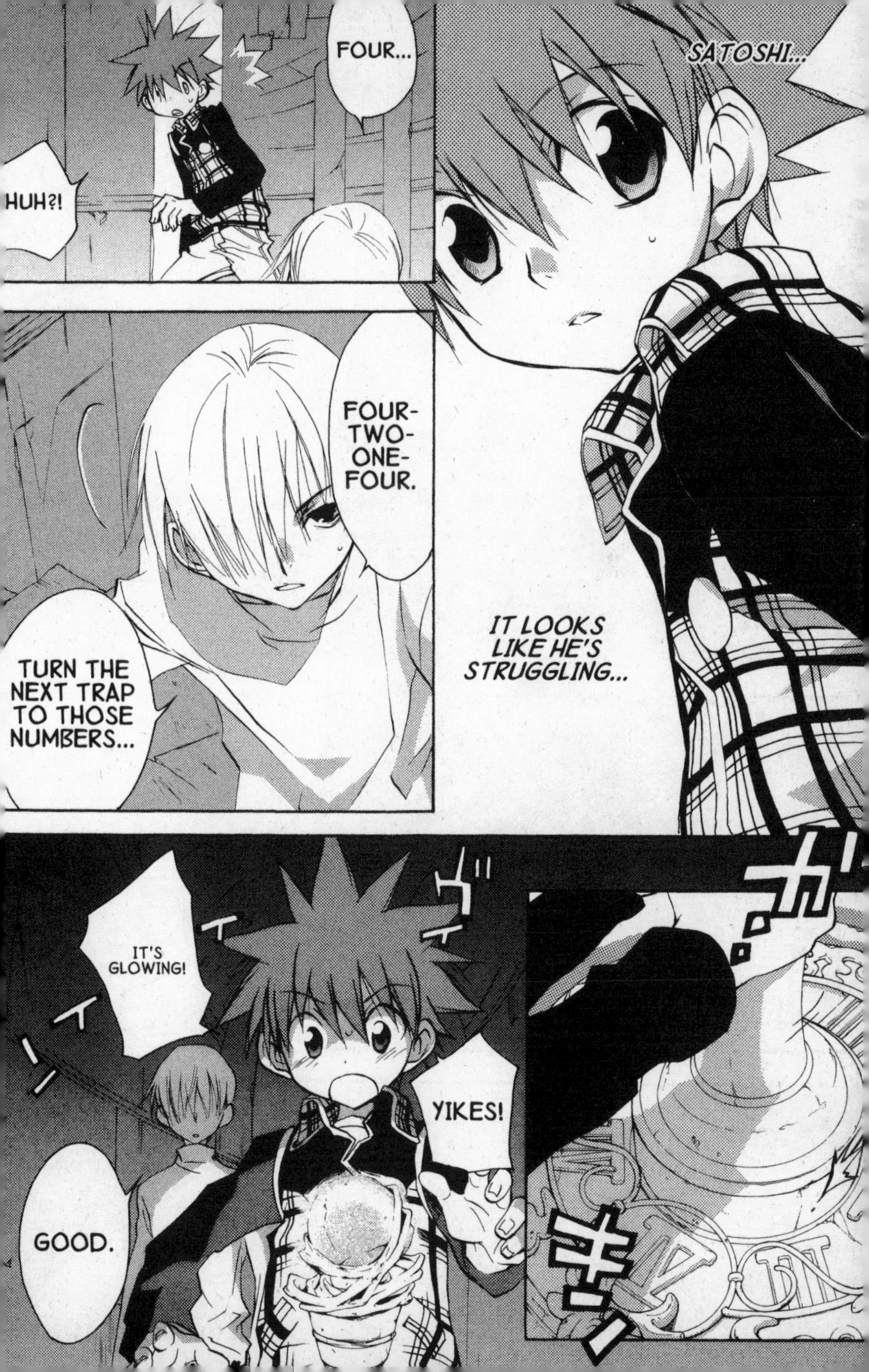
SATOSHI...
IT LOOKS LIKE HE'S STRUGGLING...
FOUR...
HUH?!
FOUR-TWO-ONE-FOUR.
TURN THE NEXT TRAP TO THOSE NUMBERS...
IT'S GLOWING!
YIKES!
GOOD.

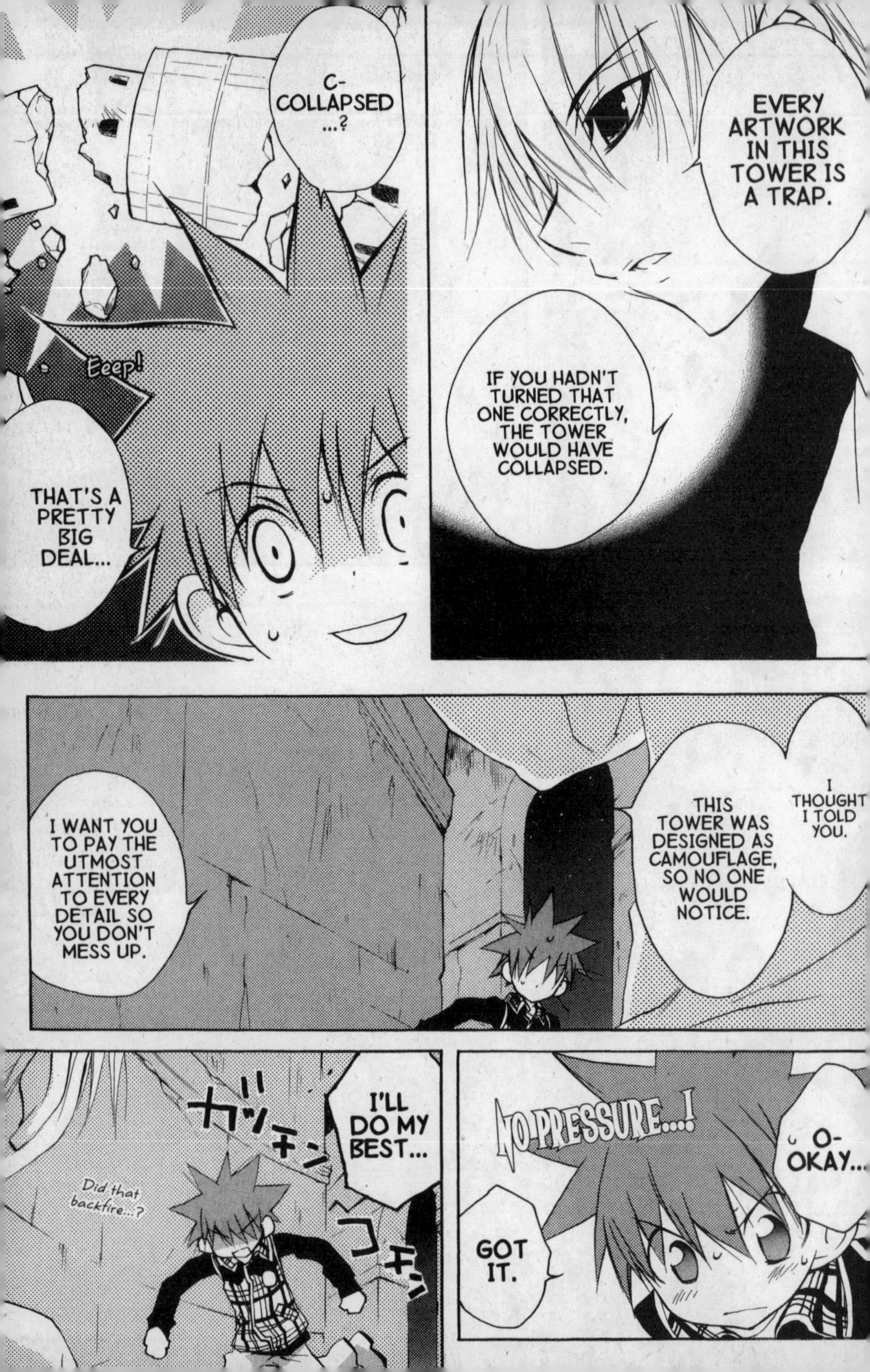
EVERY ARTWORK IN THIS TOWER IS A TRAP.
IF YOU HADN'T TURNED THAT ONE CORRECTLY, THE TOWER WOULD HAVE COLLAPSED.
C-COLLAPSED ...?
Eeep!
THAT'S A PRETTY BIG DEAL...
I THOUGHT I TOLD YOU.
THIS TOWER WAS DESIGNED AS CAMOUFLAGE, SO NO ONE WOULD NOTICE.
I WANT YOU TO PAY THE UTMOST ATTENTION TO EVERY DETAIL SO YOU DON'T MESS UP.
O-OKAY...
NO PRESSURE...!
GOT IT.
I'LL DO MY BEST...
Did that backfire...?

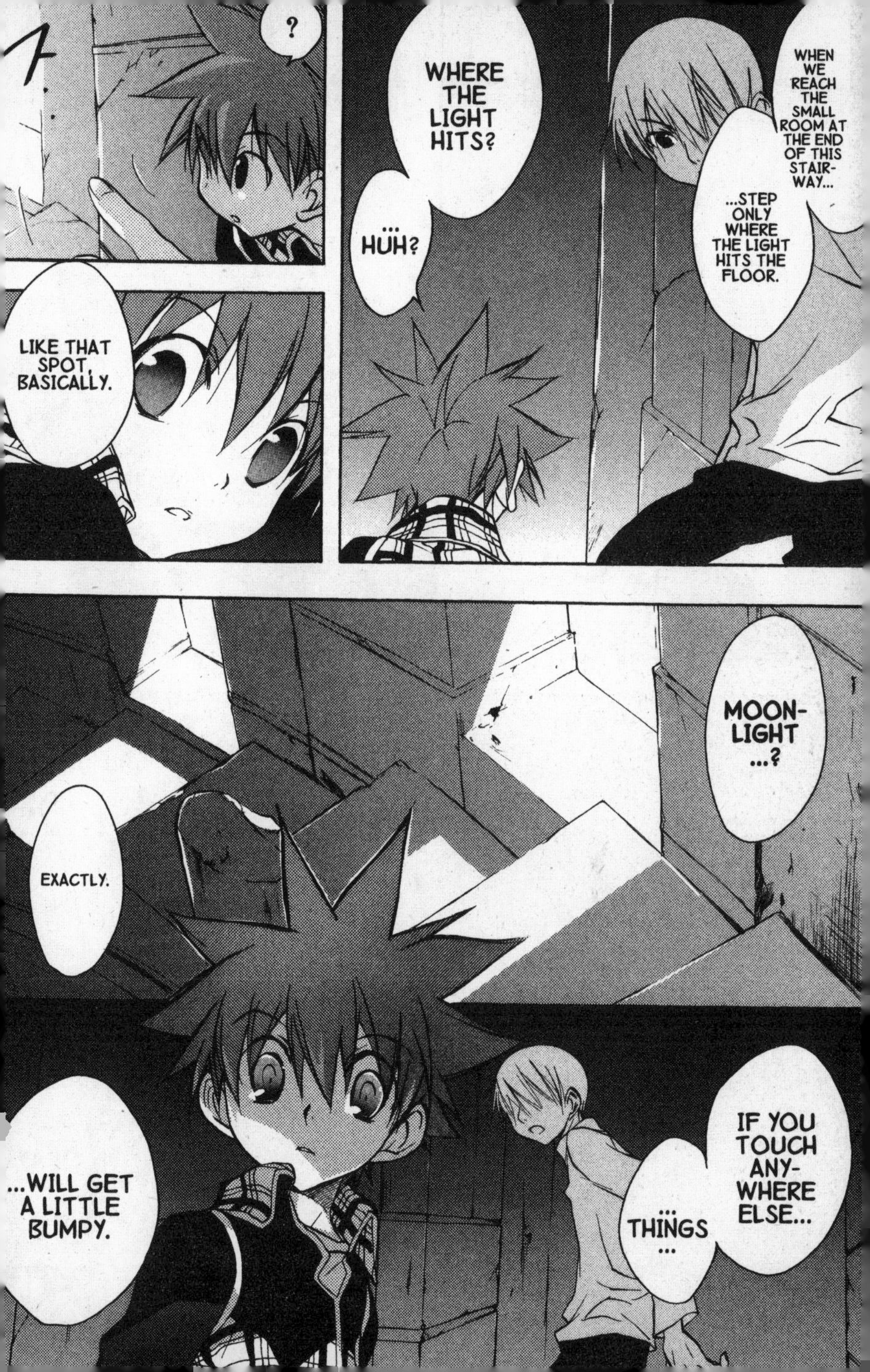
WHEN WE REACH THE SMALL ROOM AT THE END OF THIS STAIR-WAY...
...STEP ONLY WHERE THE LIGHT HITS THE FLOOR.
WHERE THE LIGHT HITS?
...HUH?
?
LIKE THAT SPOT, BASICALLY.
MOON-LIGHT ...?
EXACTLY.
IF YOU TOUCH ANY-WHERE ELSE...
...THINGS...
...WILL GET A LITTLE BUMPY.

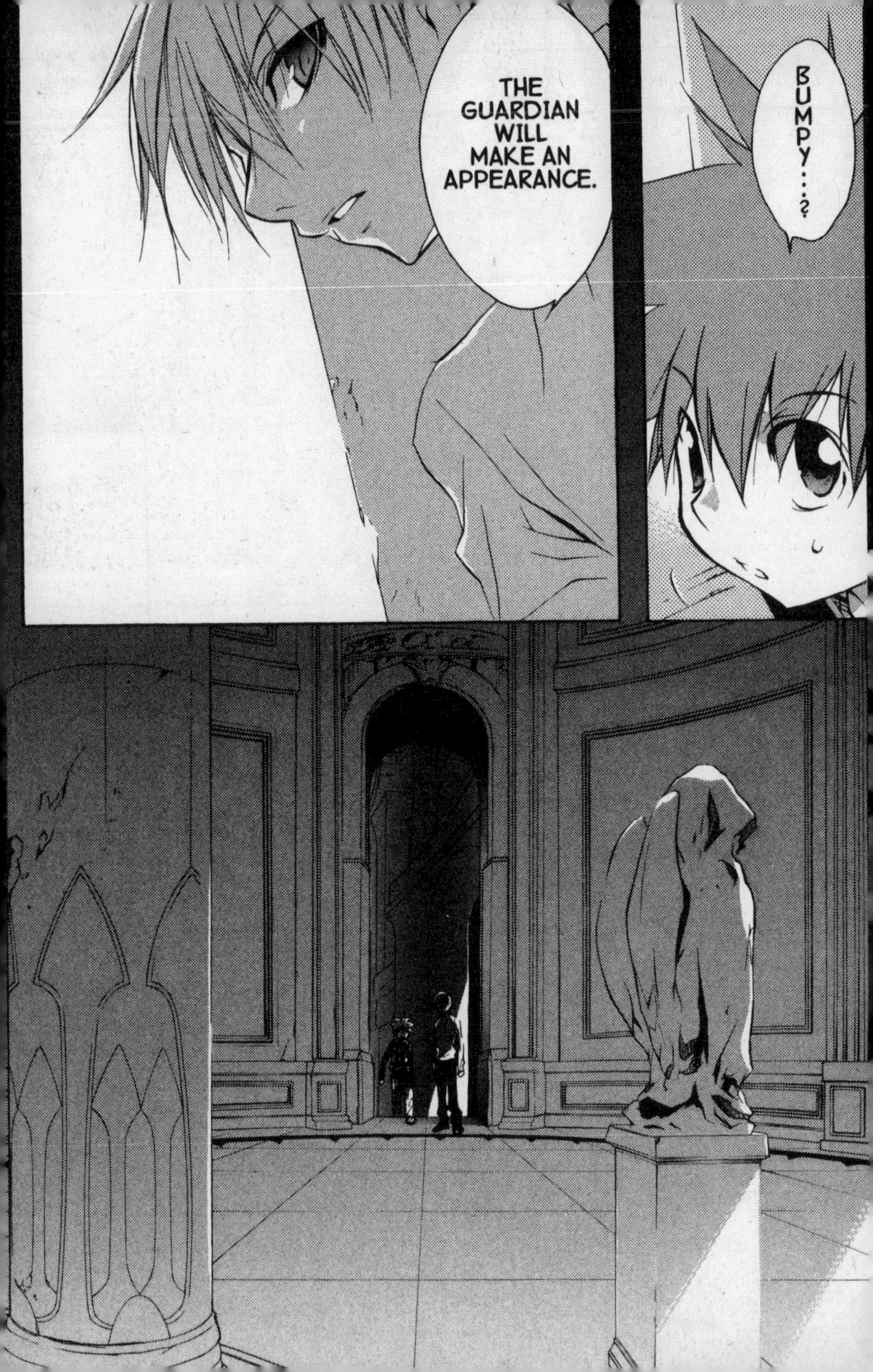
BUMPY...?
THE GUARDIAN WILL MAKE AN APPEARANCE.

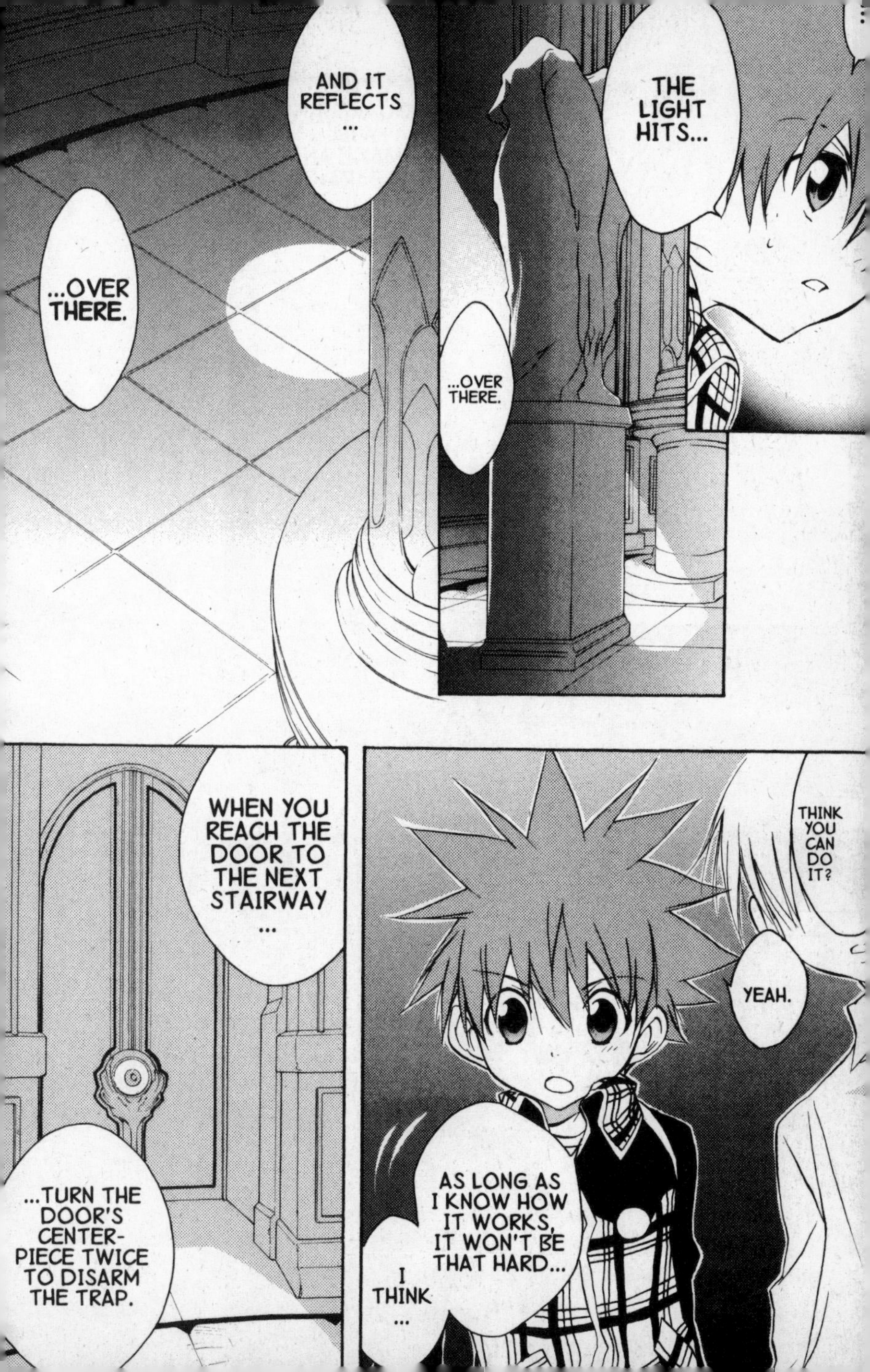
THE LIGHT HITS...
...OVER THERE.
AND IT REFLECTS ...
...OVER THERE.
THINK YOU CAN DO IT?
YEAH.
AS LONG AS I KNOW HOW IT WORKS, IT WON'T BE THAT HARD...
I THINK ...
WHEN YOU REACH THE DOOR TO THE NEXT STAIRWAY ...
...TURN THE DOOR'S CENTER-PIECE TWICE TO DISARM THE TRAP.

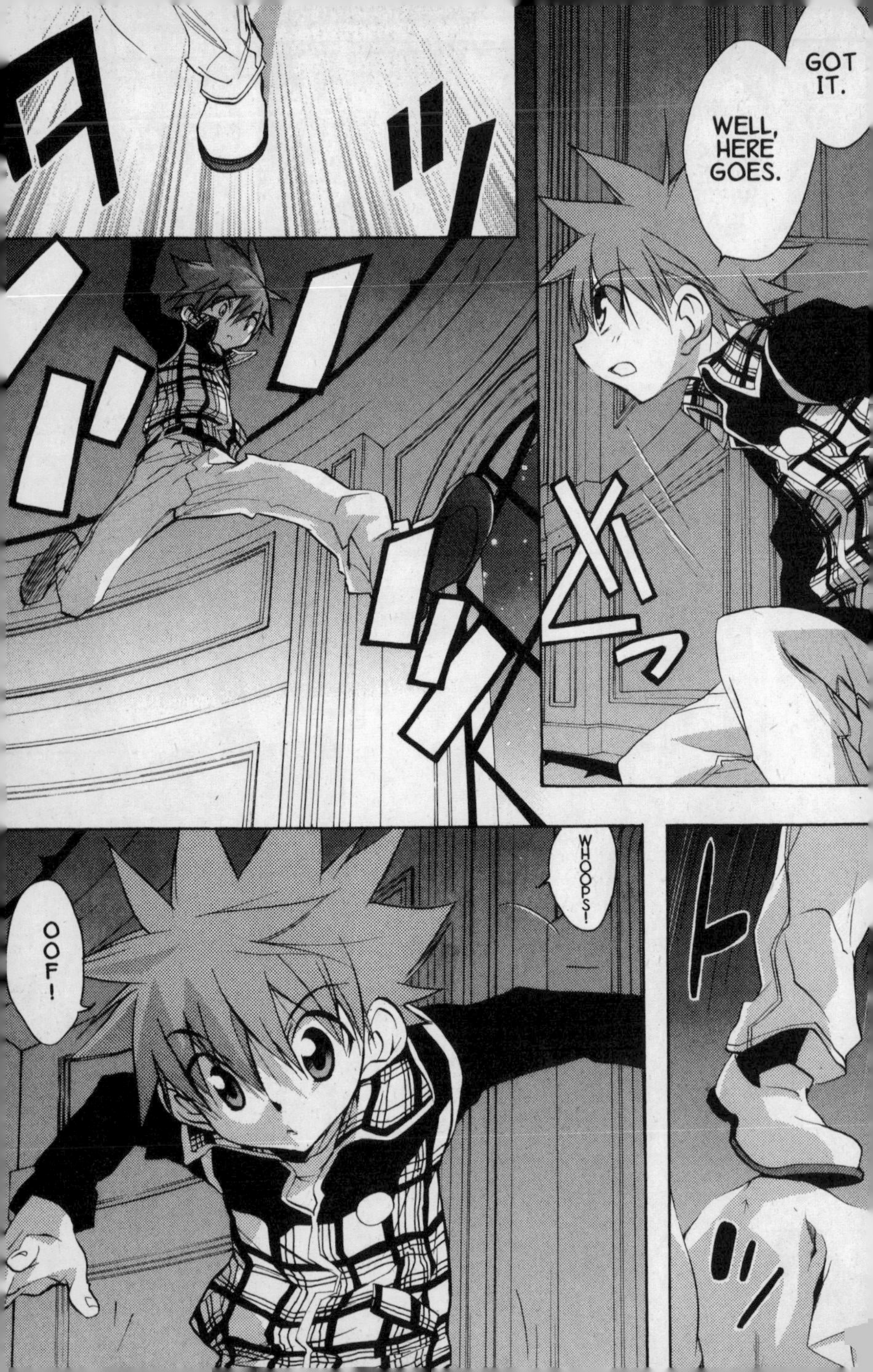
GOT IT.
WELL, HERE GOES.
WHOOPS!
OOF!

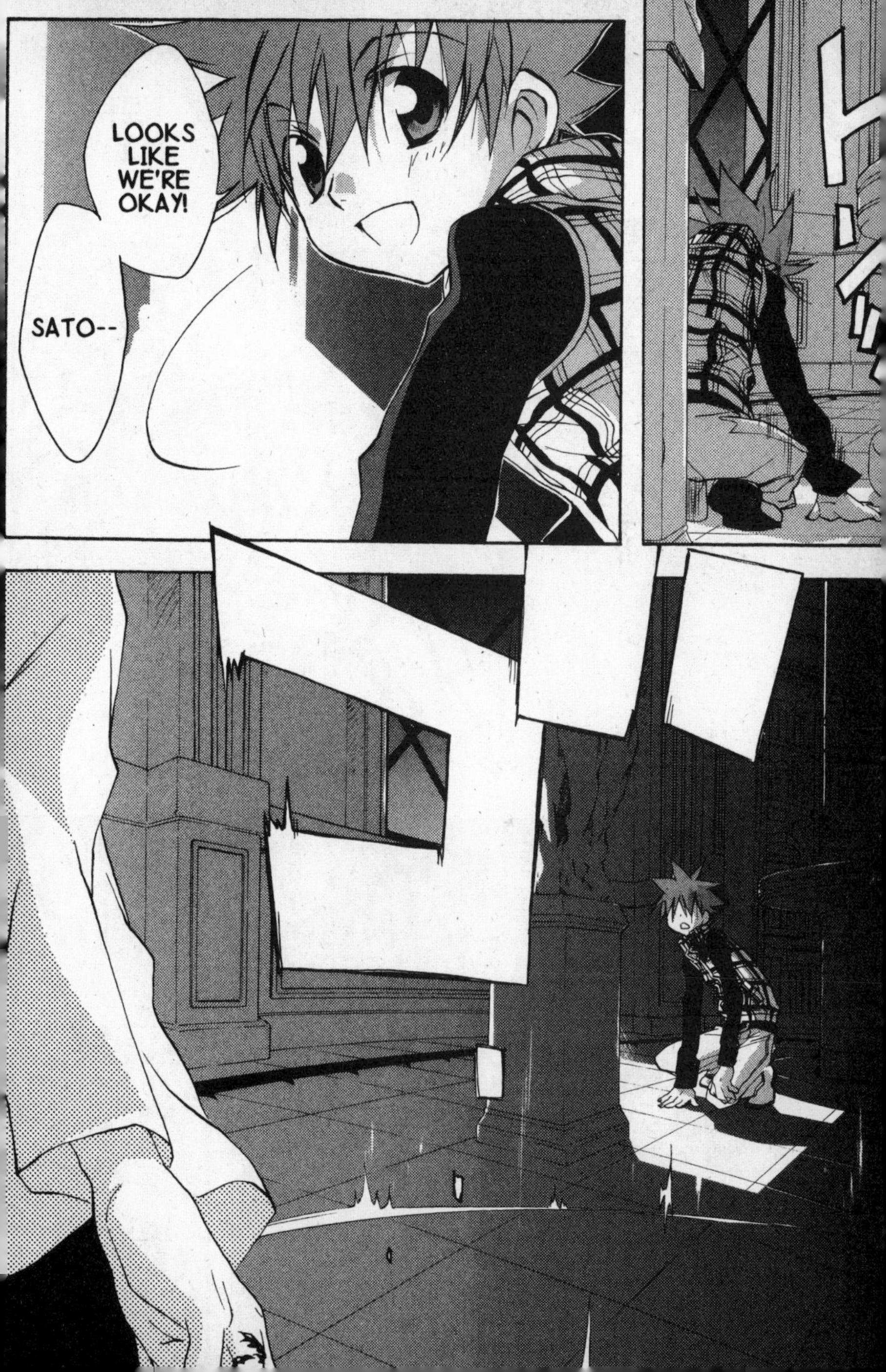
LOOKS LIKE WE'RE OKAY!
SATO--

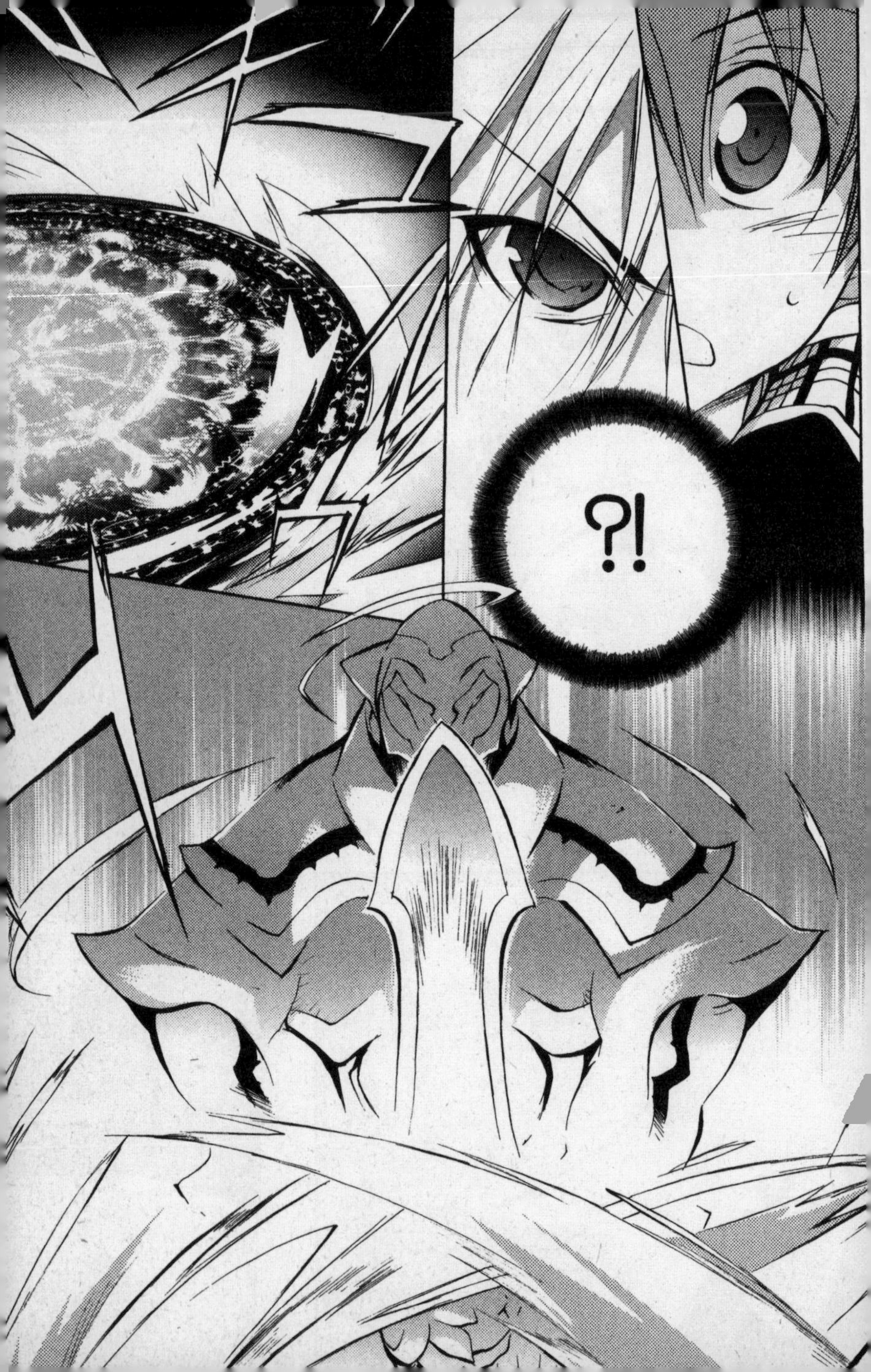
?!

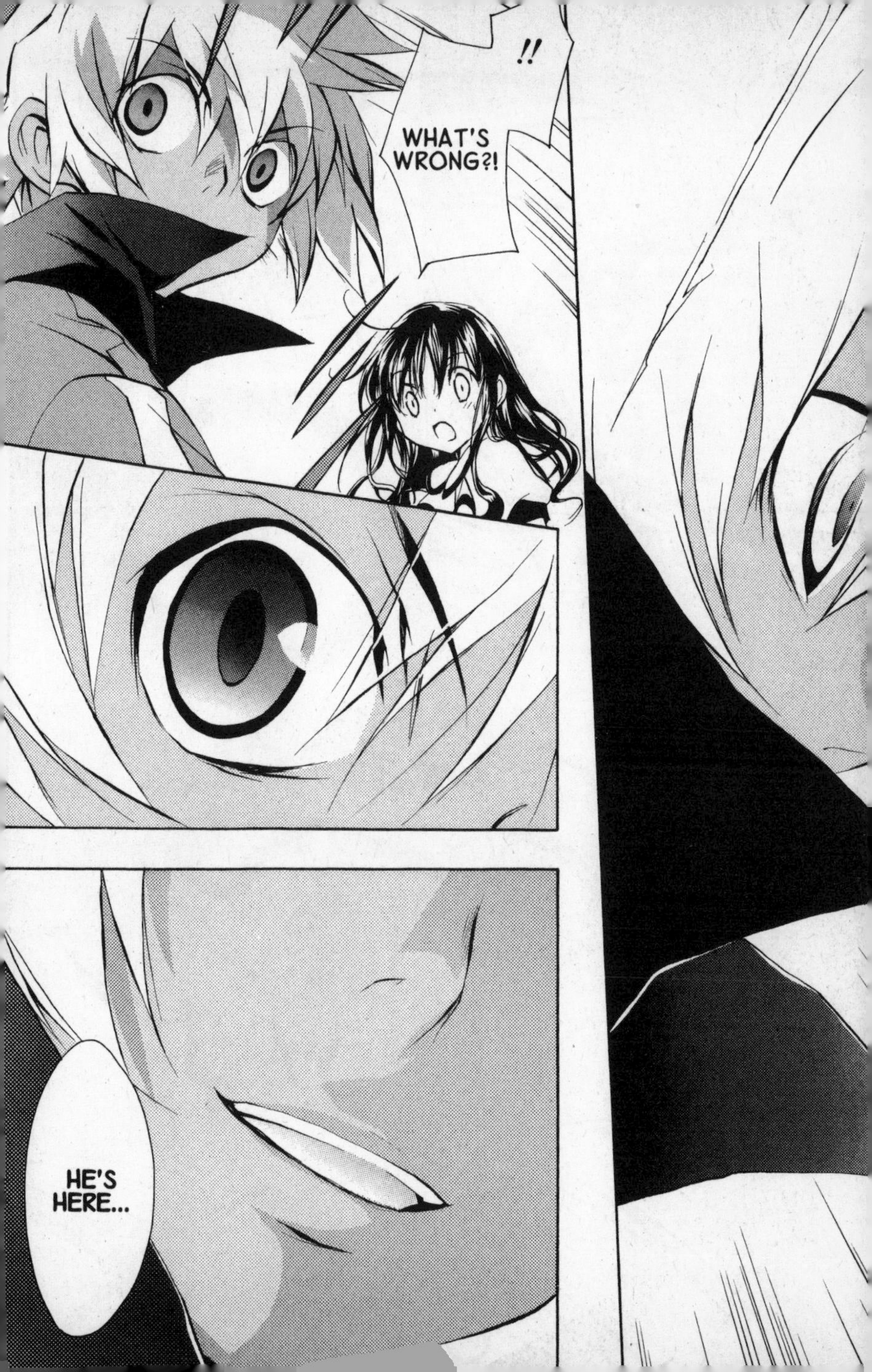
!!
WHAT'S WRONG?!
HE'S HERE...

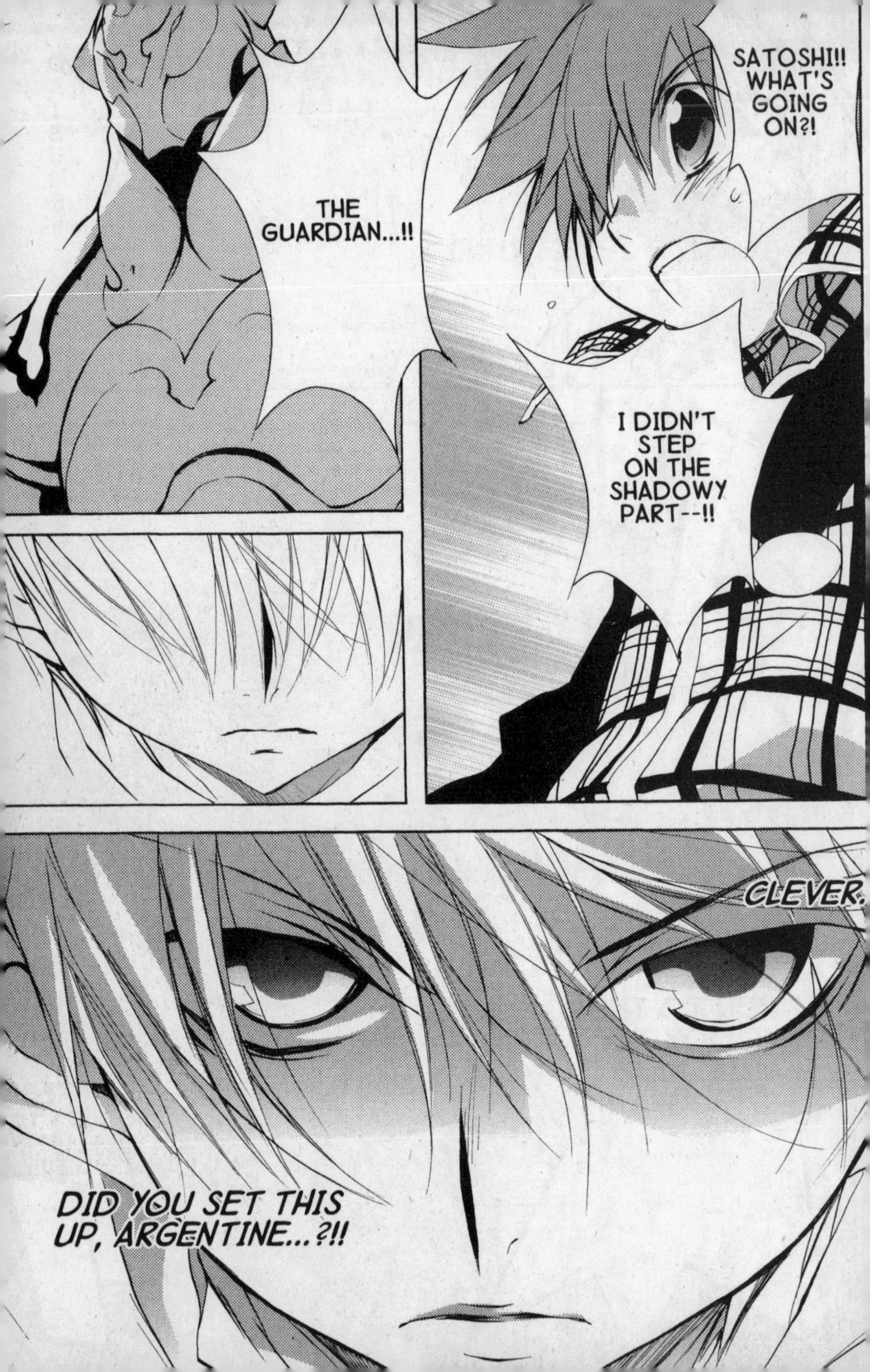
SATOSHI!! WHAT'S GOING ON?!
I DIDN'T STEP ON THE SHADOWY PART--!!
THE GUARDIAN...!!
CLEVER.
DID YOU SET THIS UP, ARGENTINE...?!!

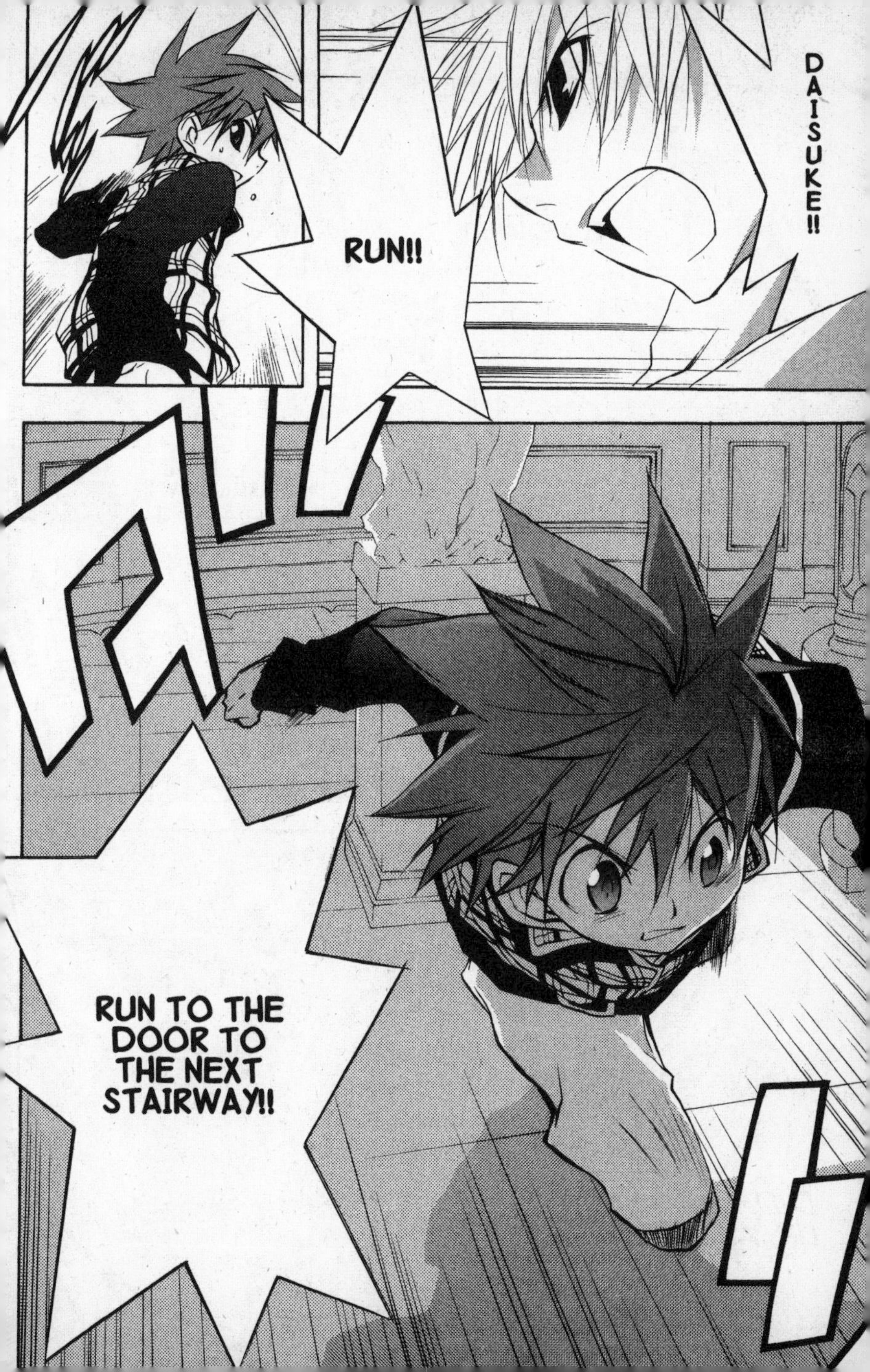
DAISUKE!!
RUN!!
RUN TO THE DOOR TO THE NEXT STAIRWAY!!

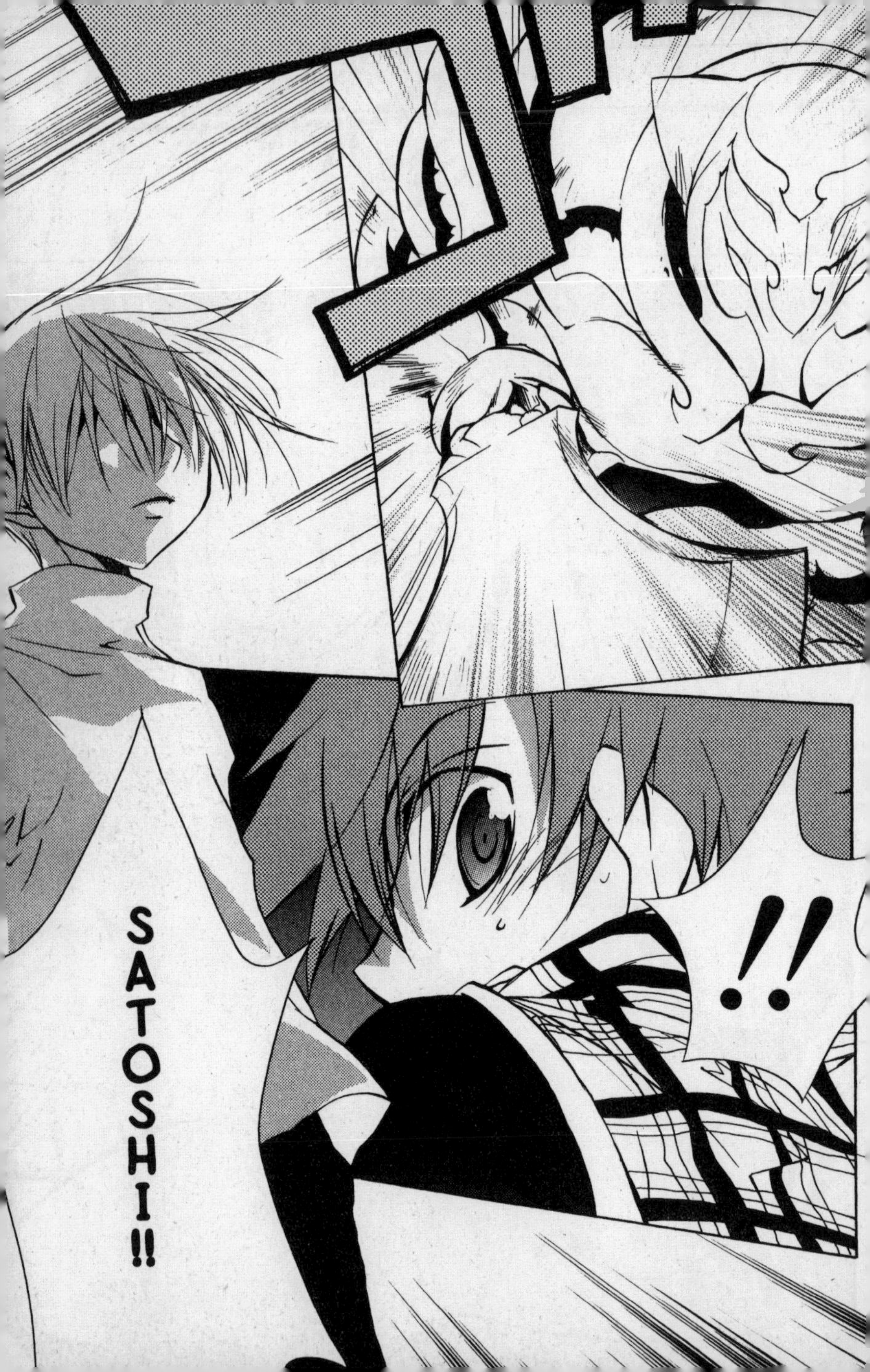
!!
SATOSHI!!

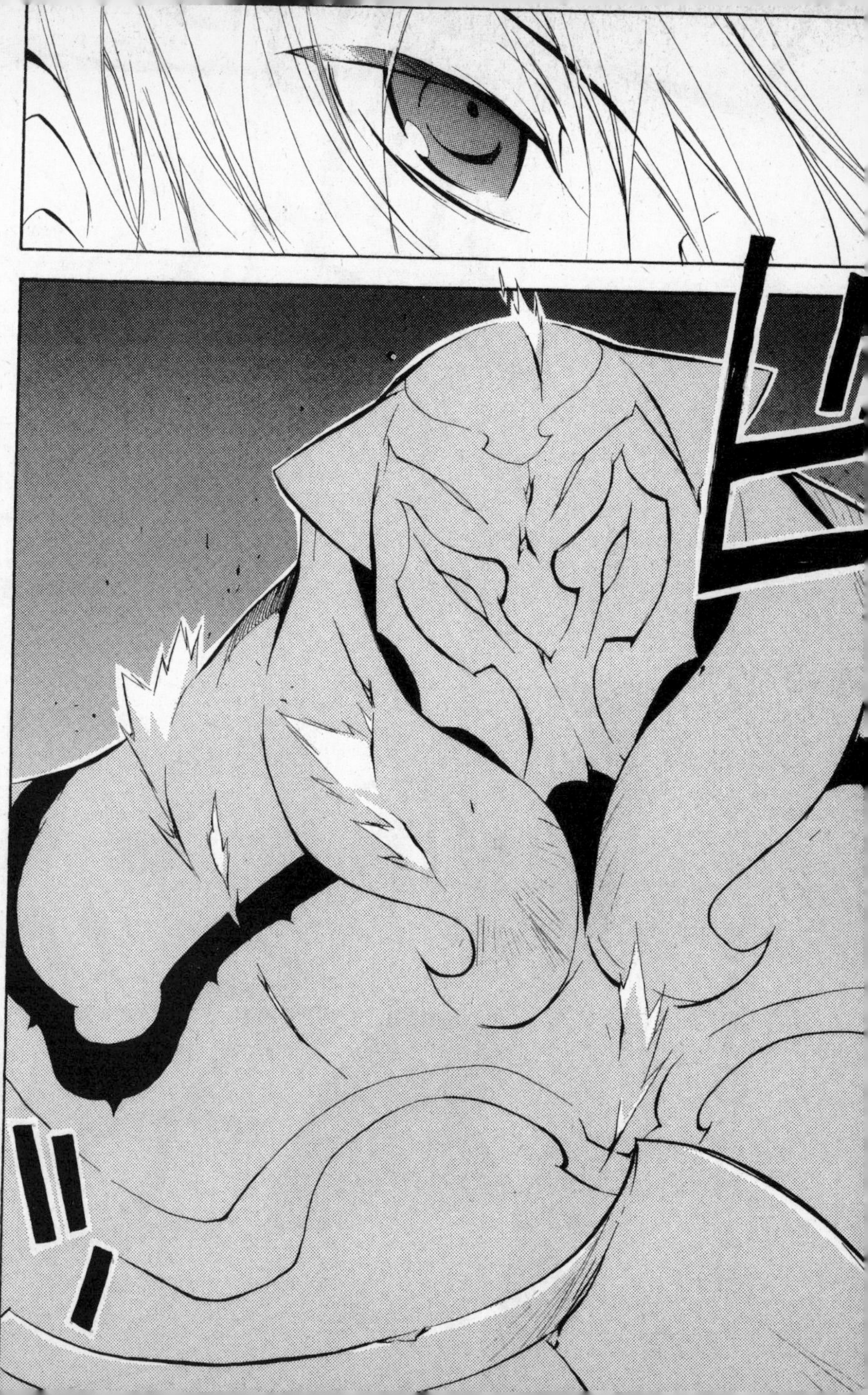

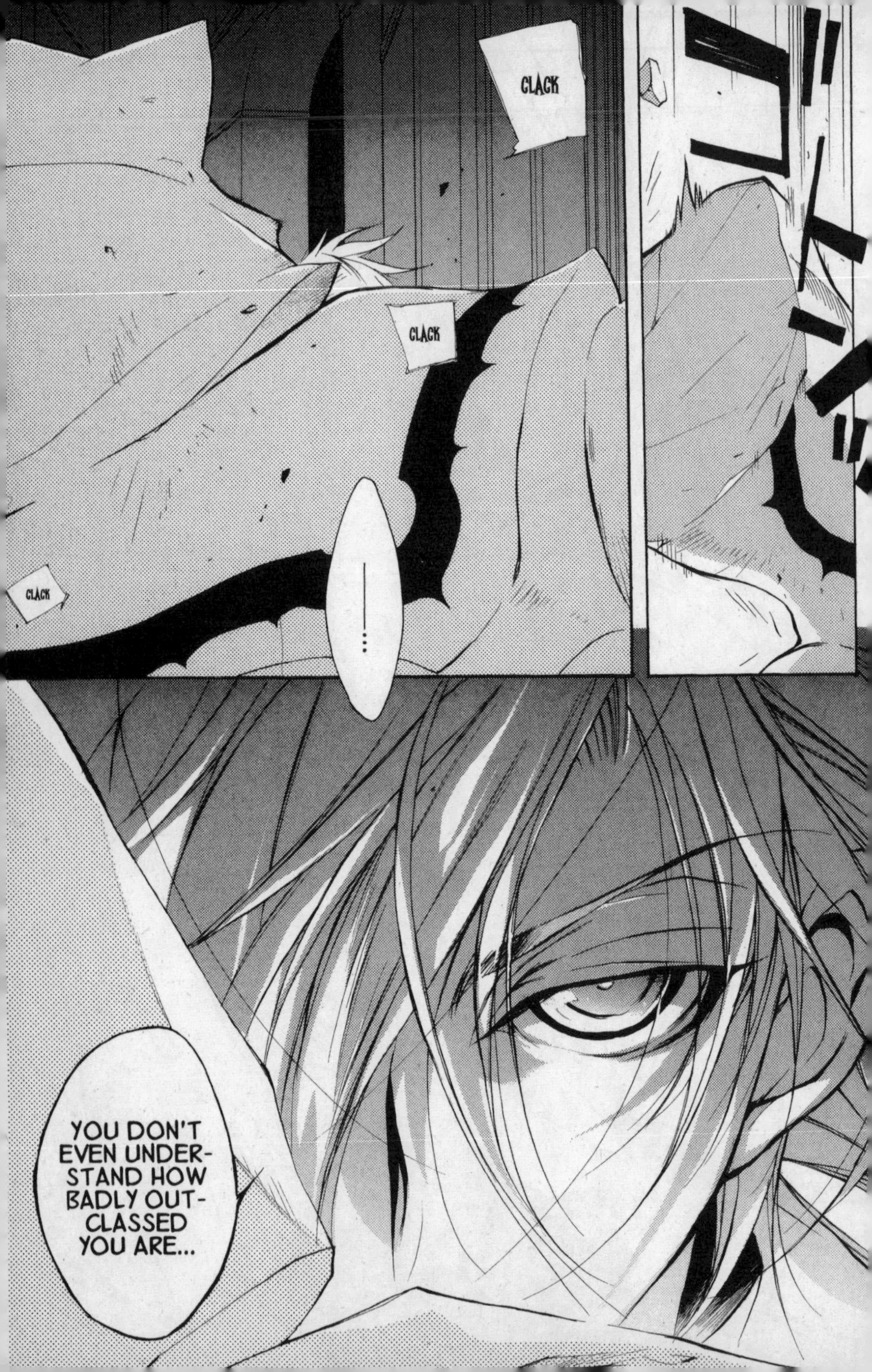
CLACK
CLACK
—...
CLACK
YOU DON'T EVEN UNDER-STAND HOW BADLY OUT-CLASSED YOU ARE...

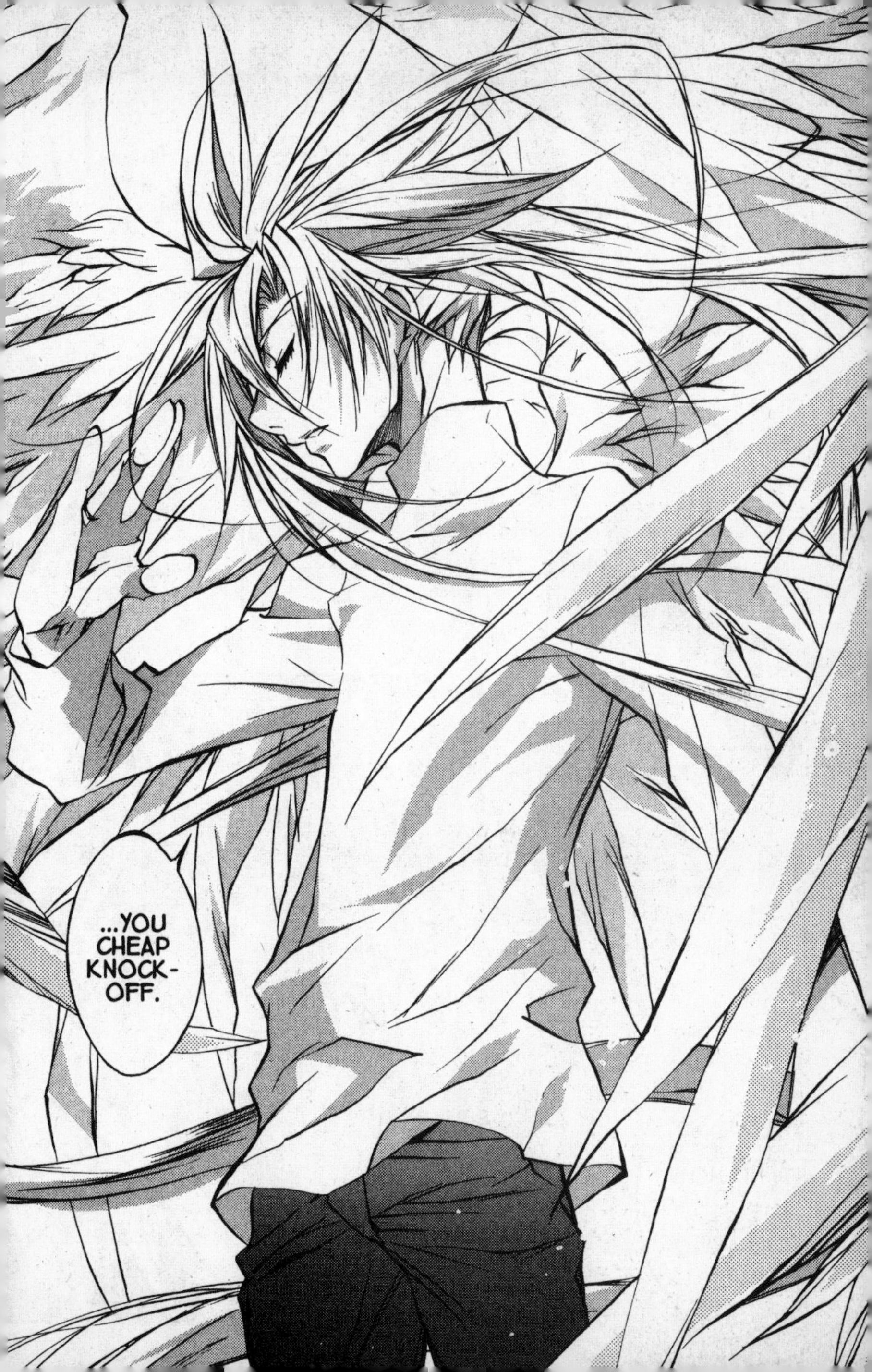
...YOU CHEAP KNOCK-OFF.

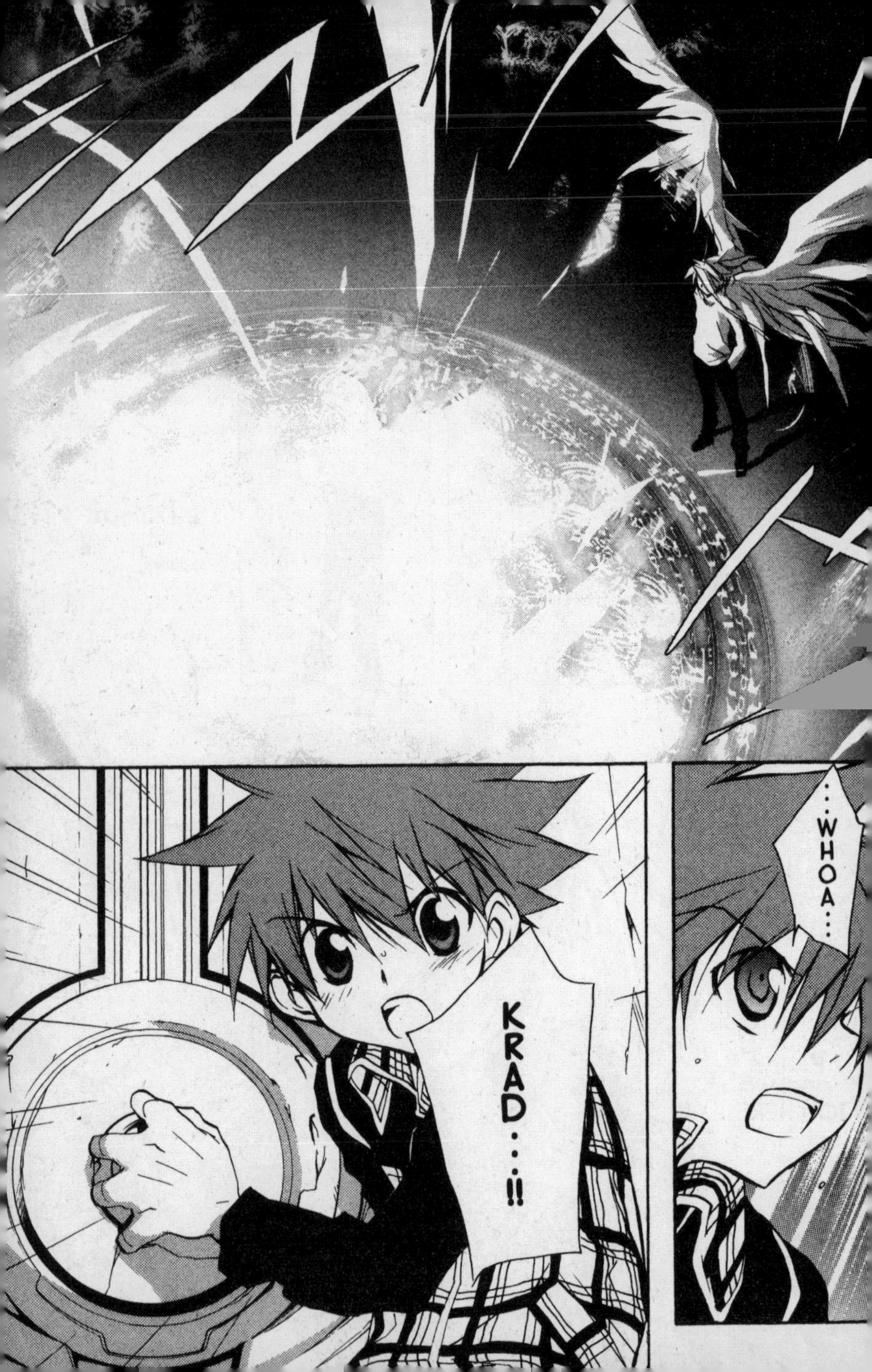
...WHOA...
KRAD...!!

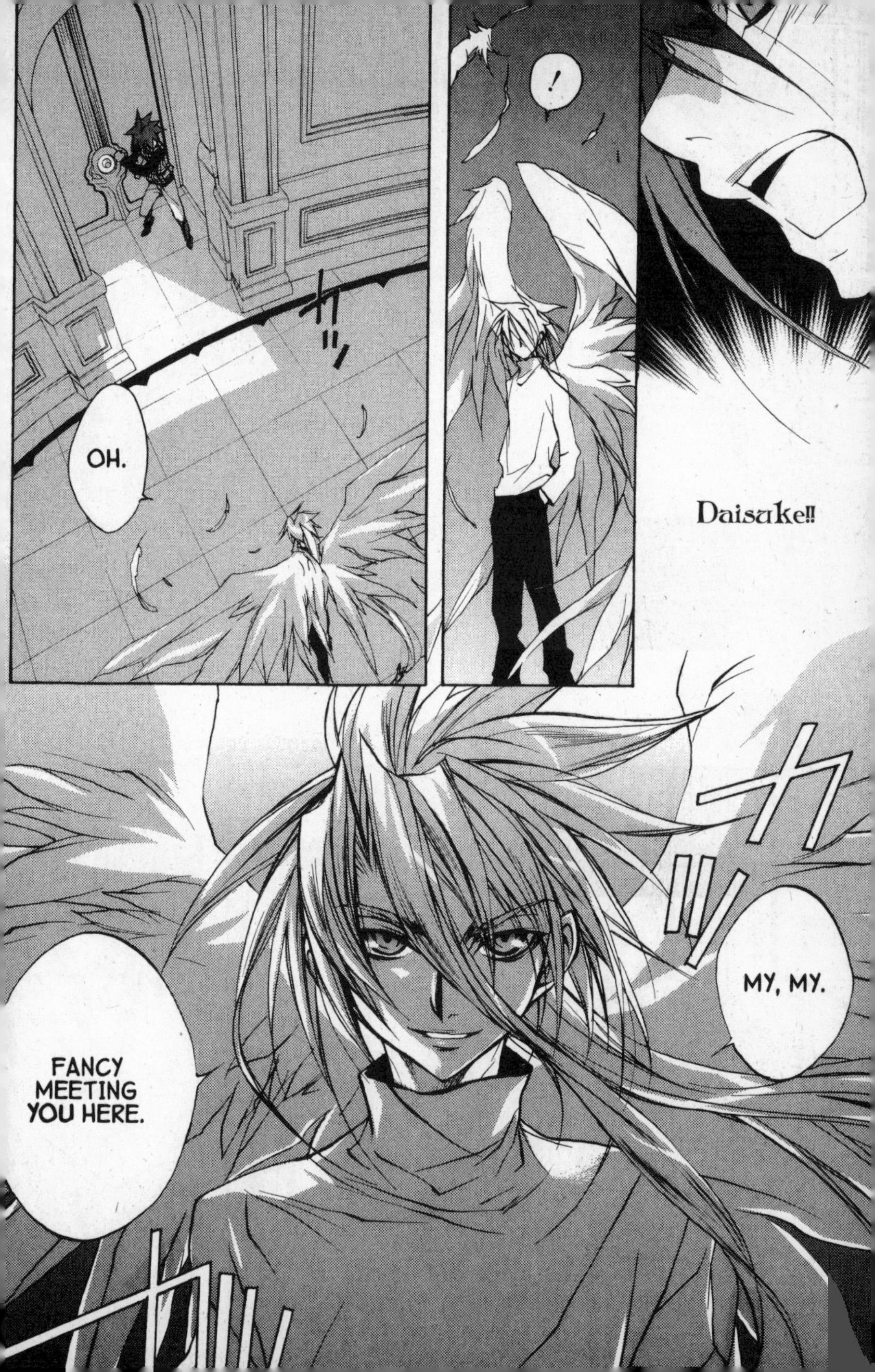
Daisuke!!
!
OH.
MY, MY.
FANCY MEETING YOU HERE.

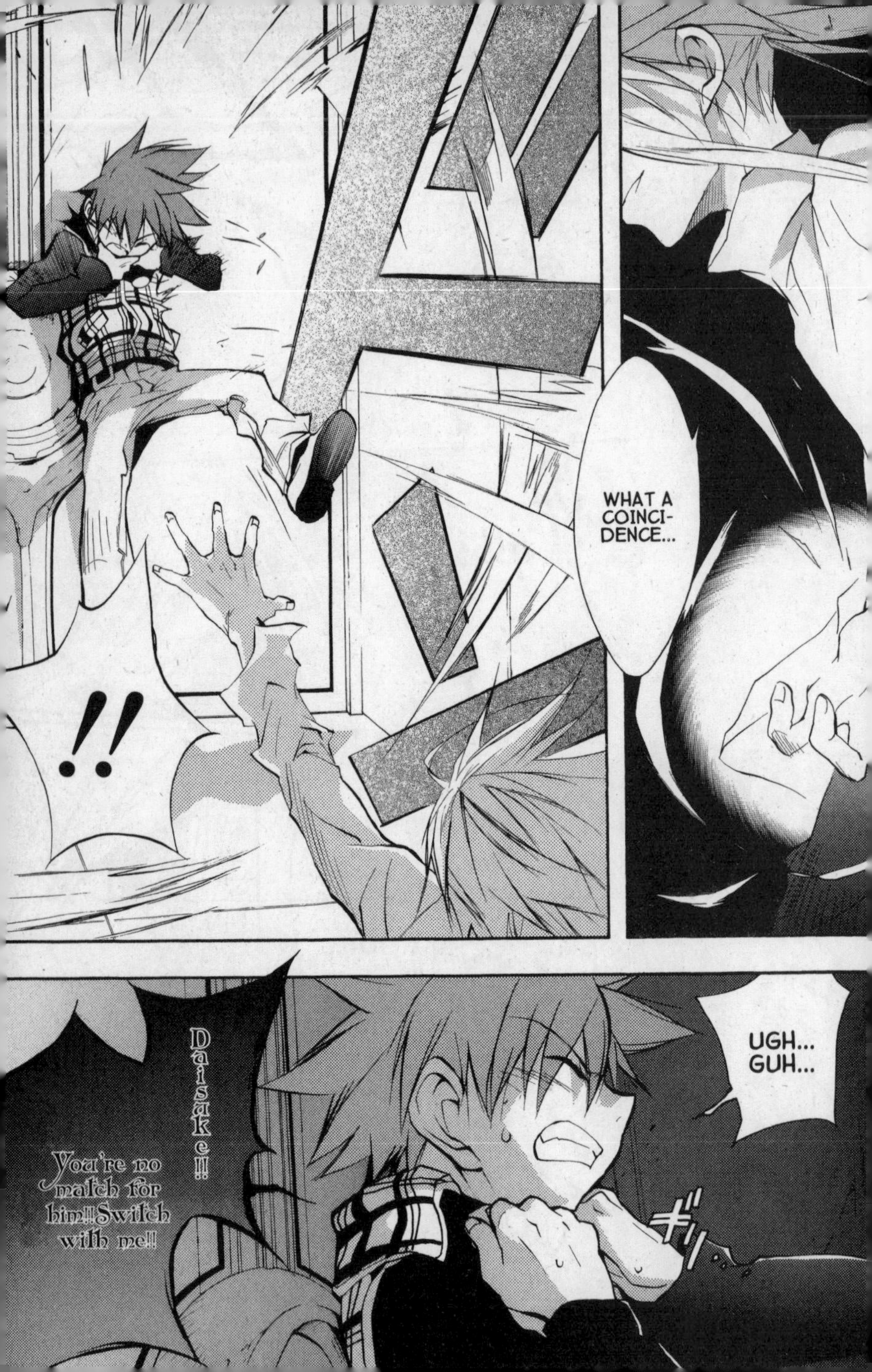
WHAT A COINCI-DENCE...
!!
UGH... GUH...
ギリ
Daisuke!!
You're no match for him!! Switch with me!!

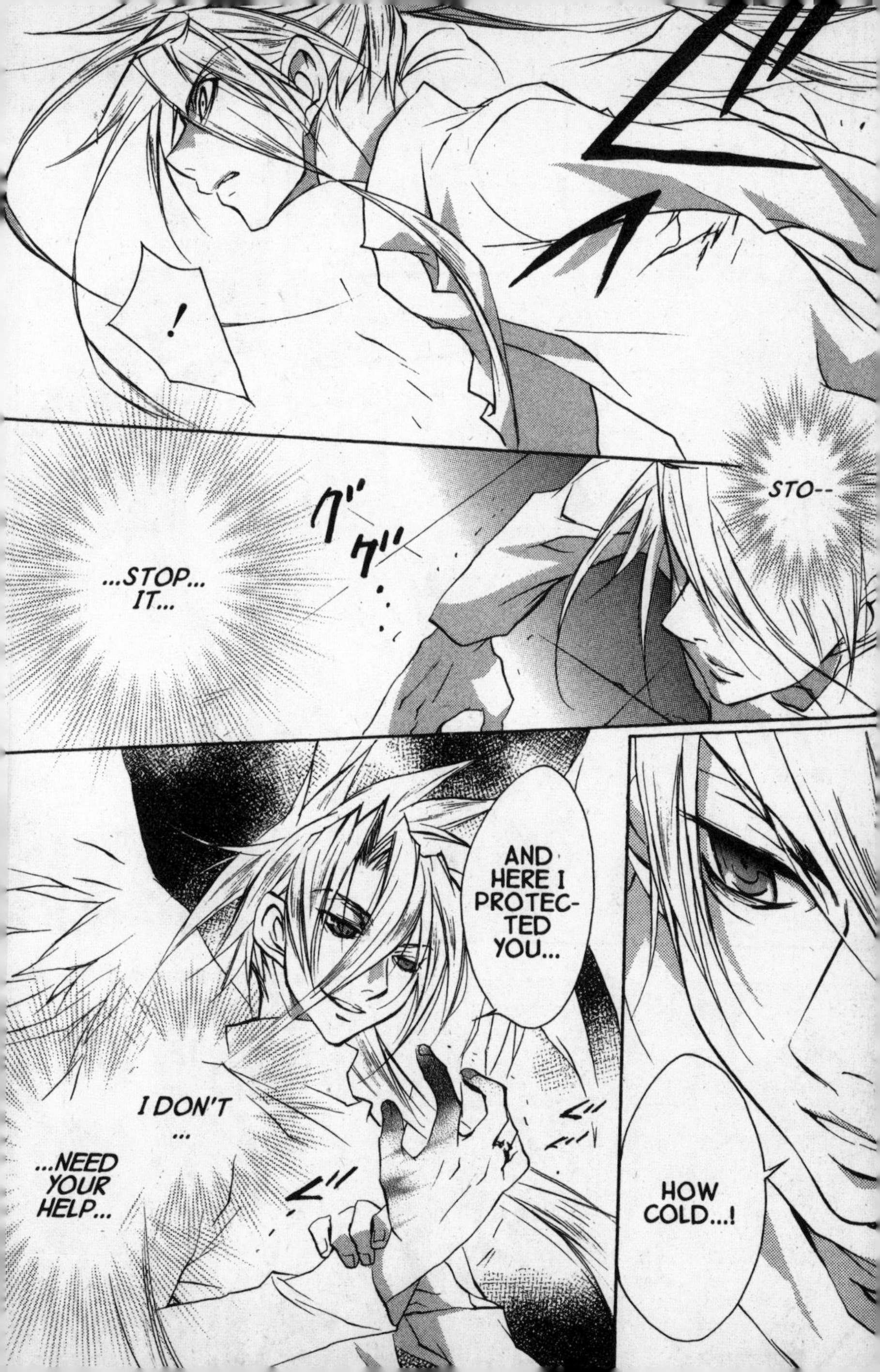
!
STO--
ググ
...STOP... IT...
HOW COLD...!
AND HERE I PROTECTED YOU...
I DON'T ...
...NEED YOUR HELP...

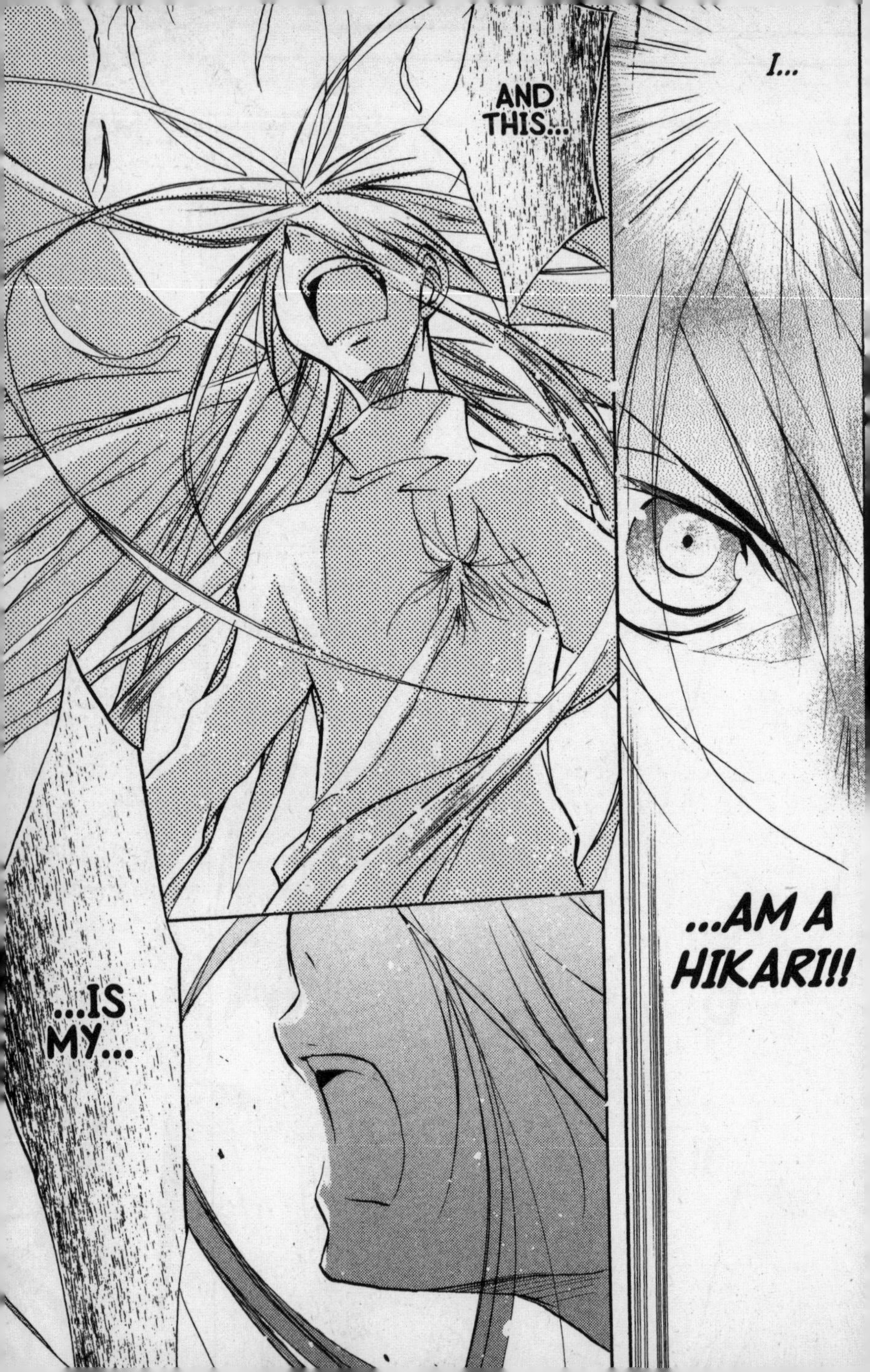
I...
...AM A HIKARI!!
AND THIS...
...IS MY...

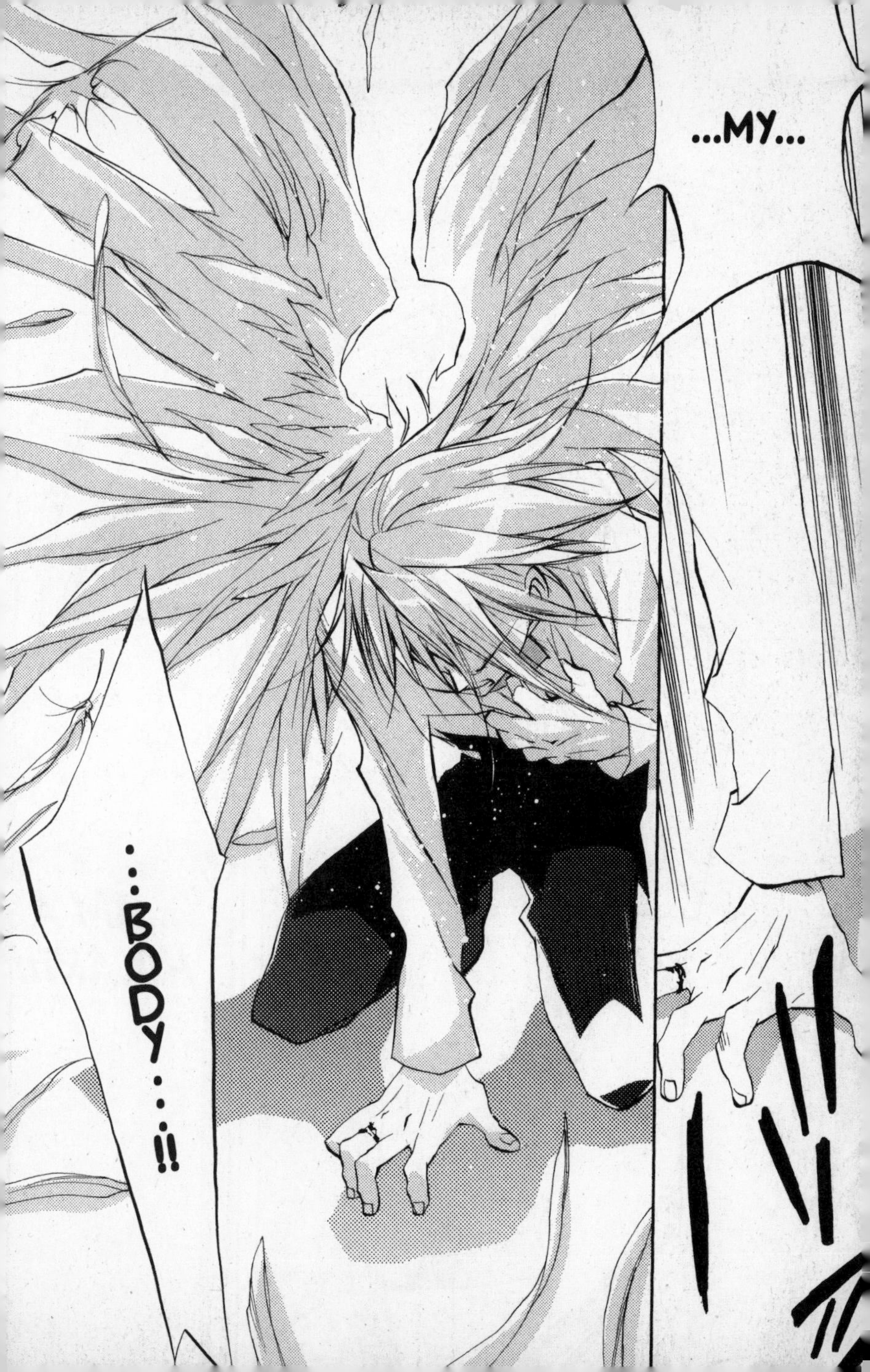
...MY...
...BODY...!!

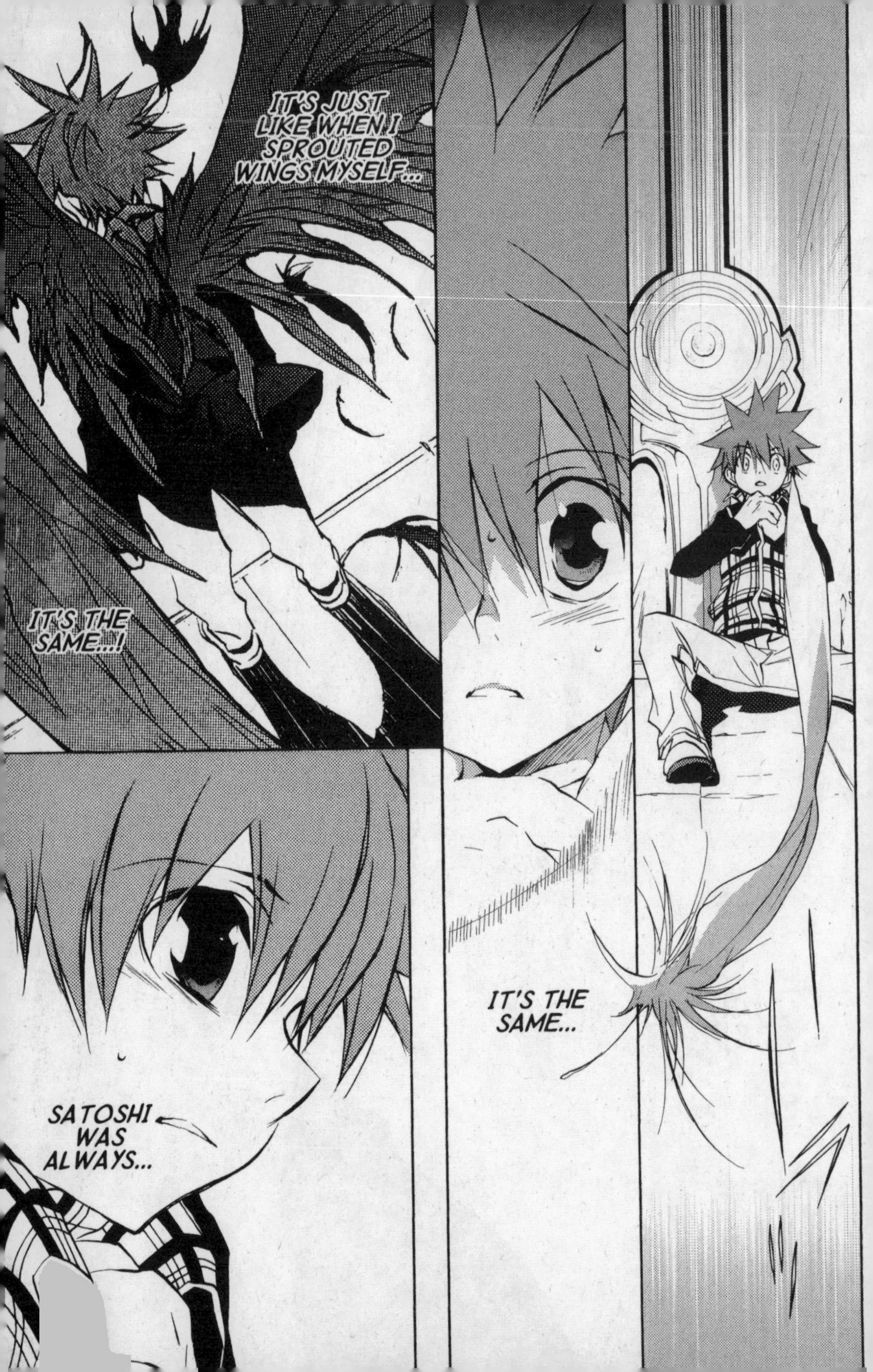
IT'S THE SAME...
IT'S JUST LIKE WHEN I SPROUTED WINGS MYSELF...
IT'S THE SAME...!
SATOSHI WAS ALWAYS...

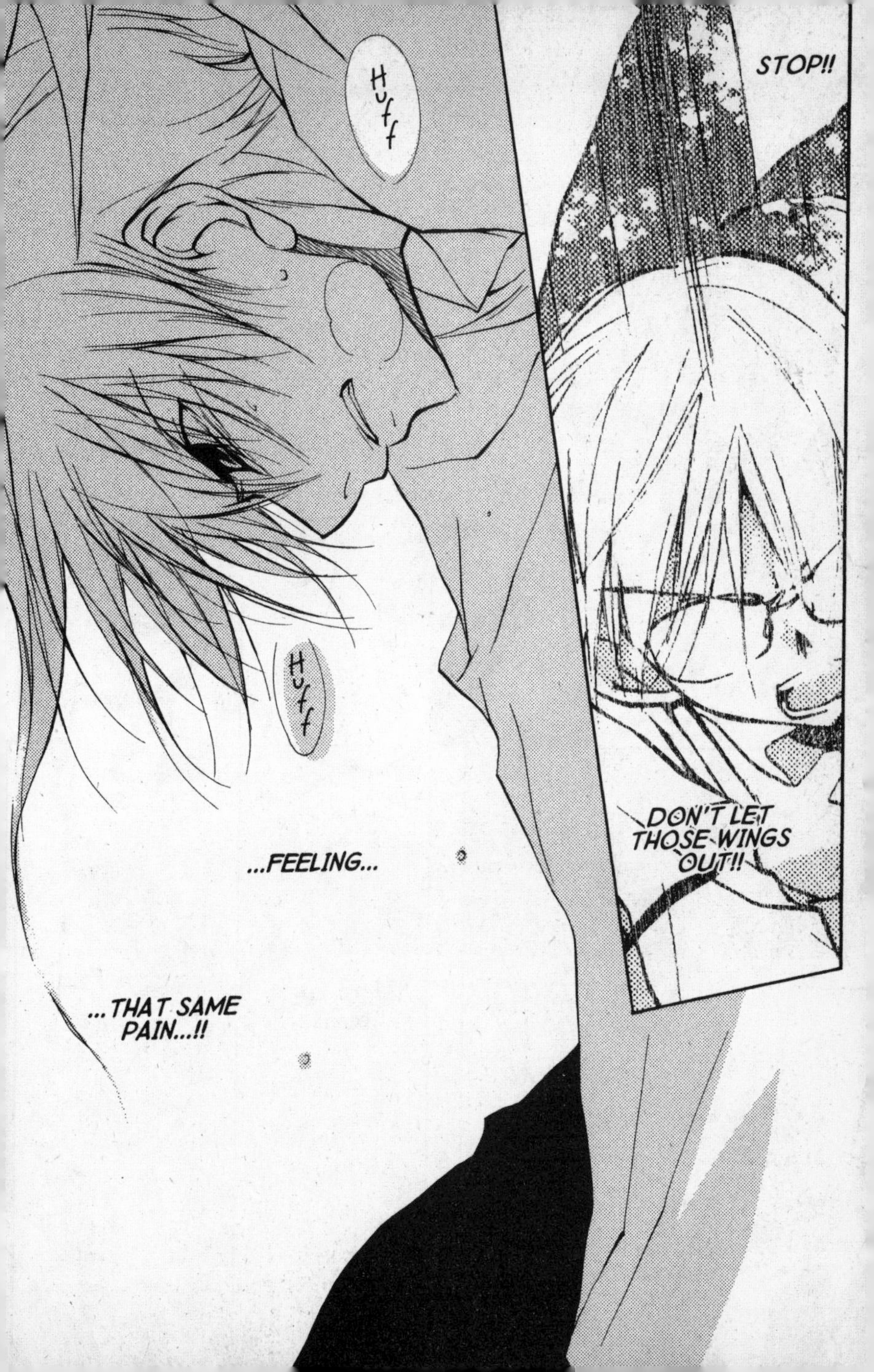
STOP!!
DON'T LET THOSE WINGS OUT!!
Huff
Huff
...FEELING...
...THAT SAME PAIN...!!

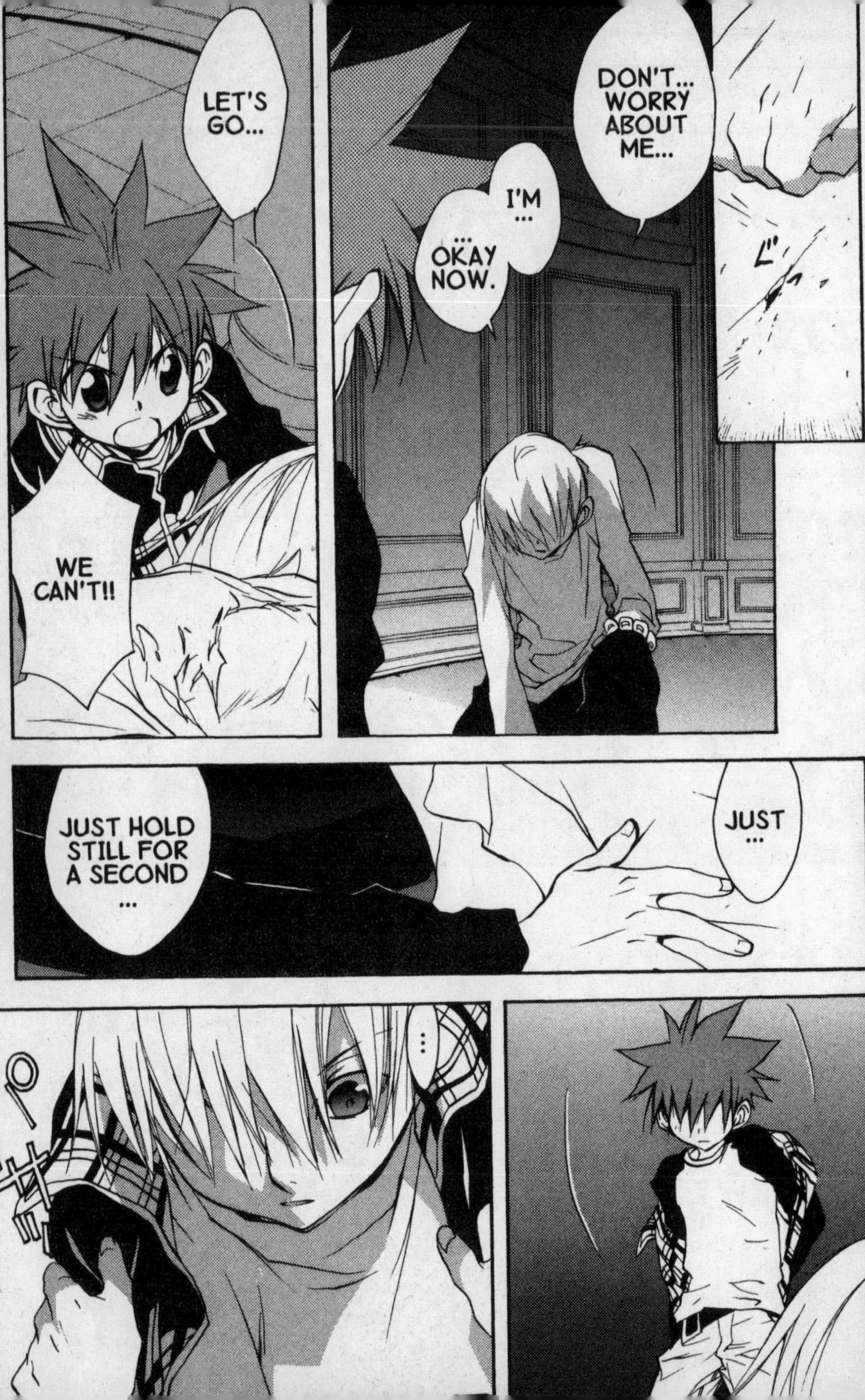
DON'T... WORRY ABOUT ME...
I'M ...
... OKAY NOW.
LET'S GO...
WE CAN'T!!
JUST ...
JUST HOLD STILL FOR A SECOND ...
...

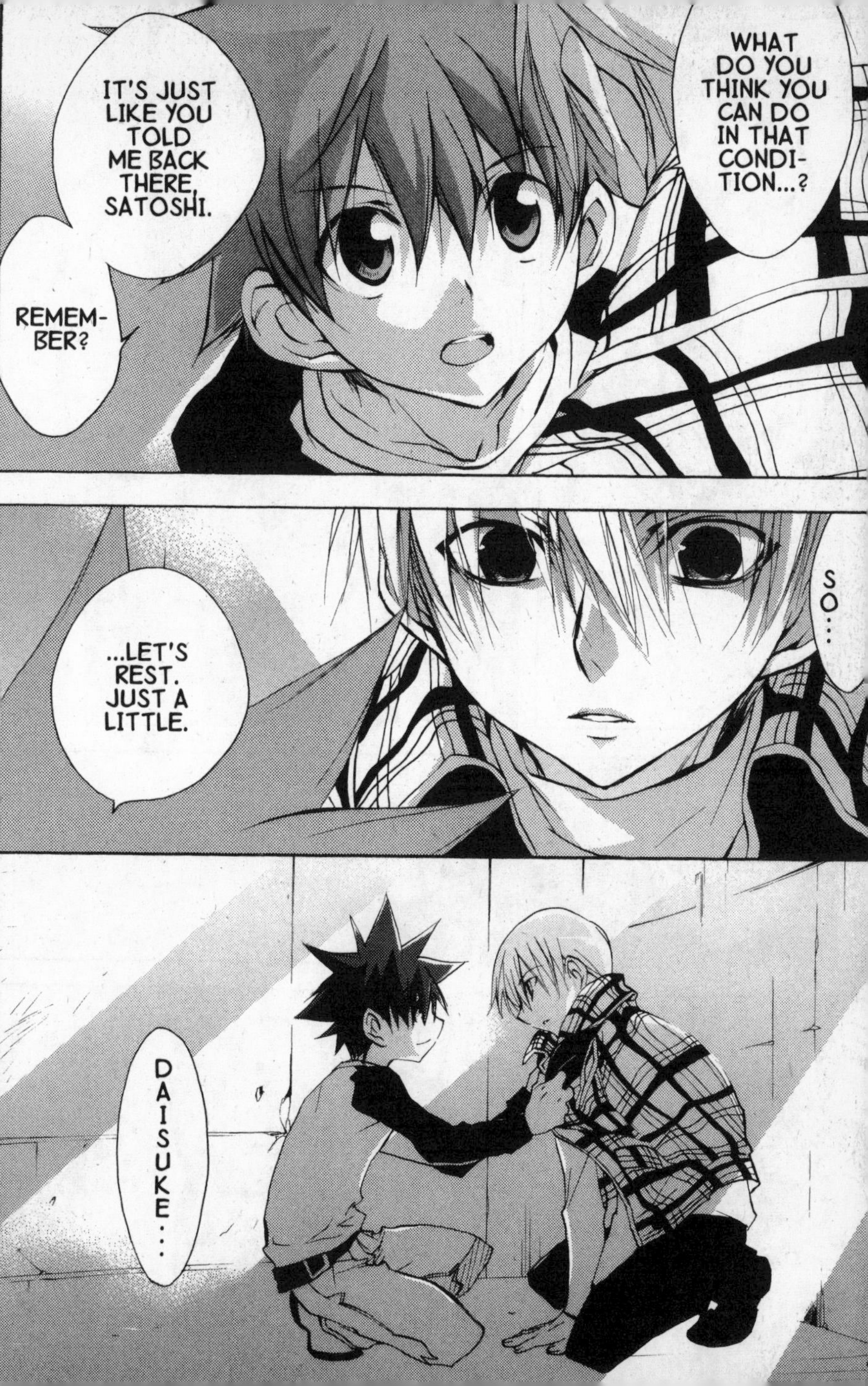
WHAT DO YOU THINK YOU CAN DO IN THAT CONDITION...?
IT'S JUST LIKE YOU TOLD ME BACK THERE, SATOSHI.
REMEMBER?
SO...
...LET'S REST. JUST A LITTLE.
DAISUKE...

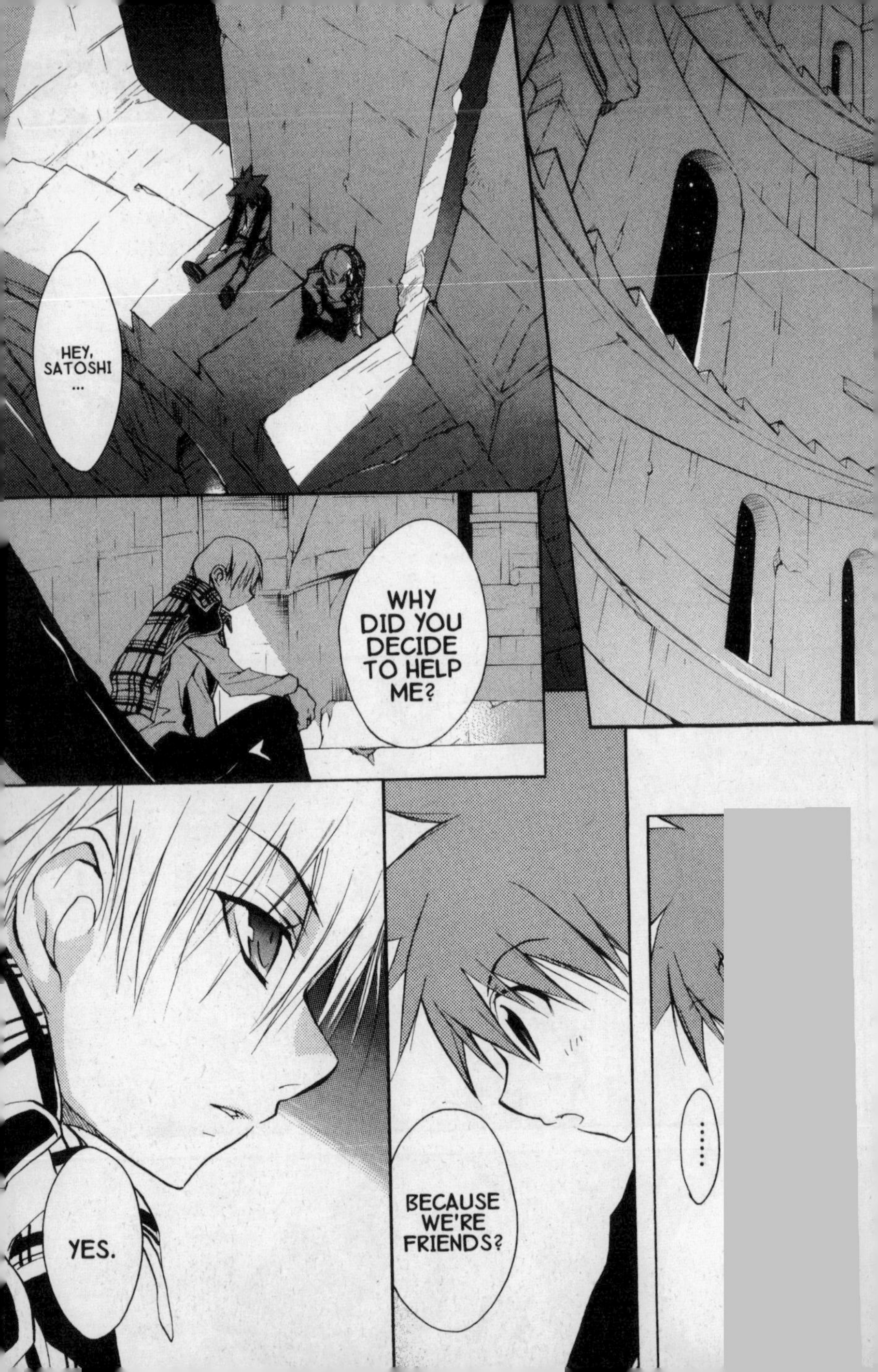
HEY, SATOSHI ...
WHY DID YOU DECIDE TO HELP ME?
......
BECAUSE WE'RE FRIENDS?
YES.

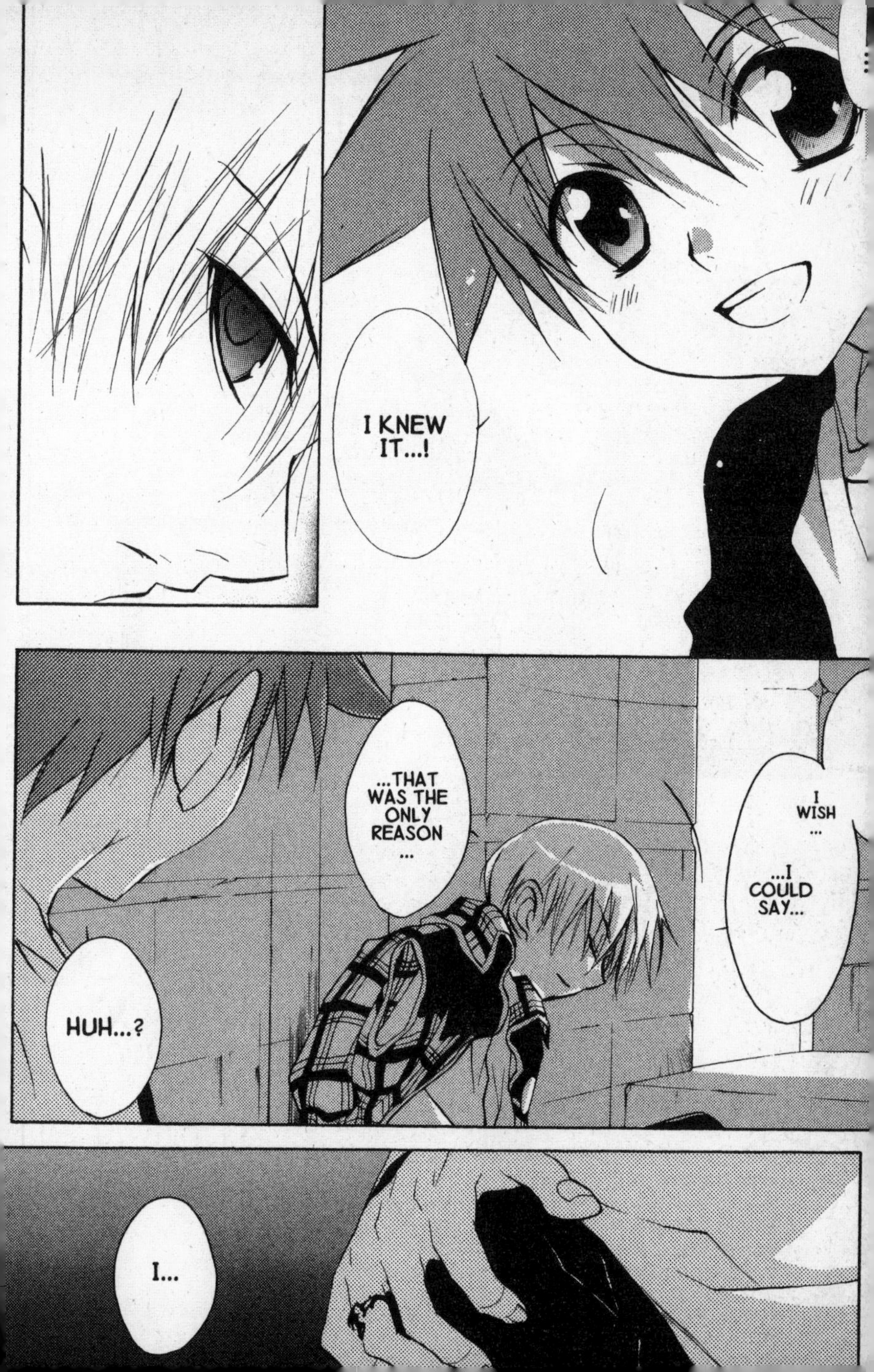
I KNEW IT...!
I WISH ...
...I COULD SAY...
...THAT WAS THE ONLY REASON ...
HUH...?
I...

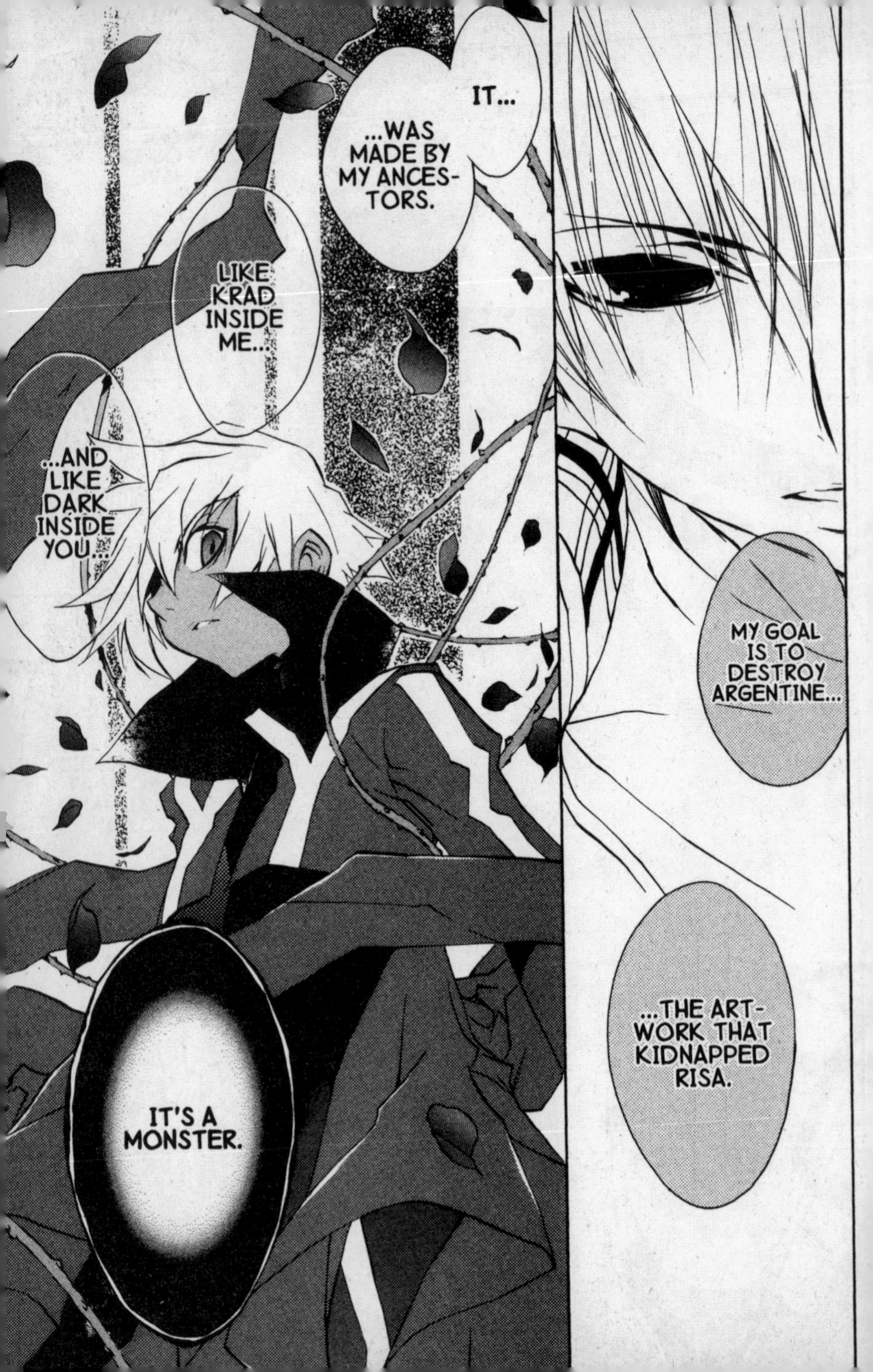
MY GOAL IS TO DESTROY ARGENTINE...
...THE ART-WORK THAT KIDNAPPED RISA.
IT...
...WAS MADE BY MY ANCES-TORS.
LIKE KRAD INSIDE ME...
...AND LIKE DARK INSIDE YOU...
IT'S A MONSTER.

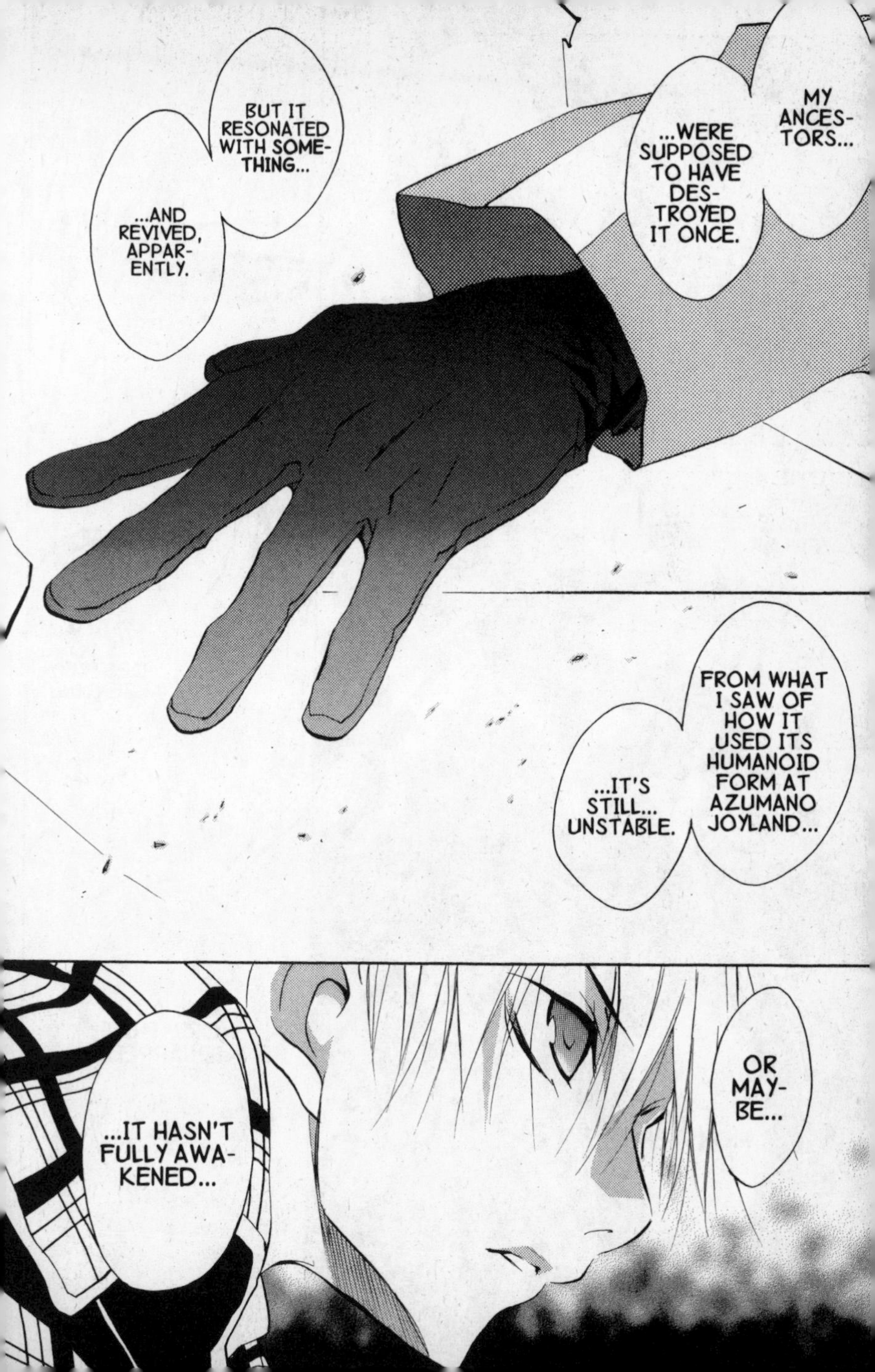
MY ANCESTORS...
...WERE SUPPOSED TO HAVE DESTROYED IT ONCE.
BUT IT RESONATED WITH SOMETHING...
...AND REVIVED, APPARENTLY.
FROM WHAT I SAW OF HOW IT USED ITS HUMANOID FORM AT AZUMANO JOYLAND...
...IT'S STILL... UNSTABLE.
OR MAYBE...
...IT HASN'T FULLY AWAKENED...

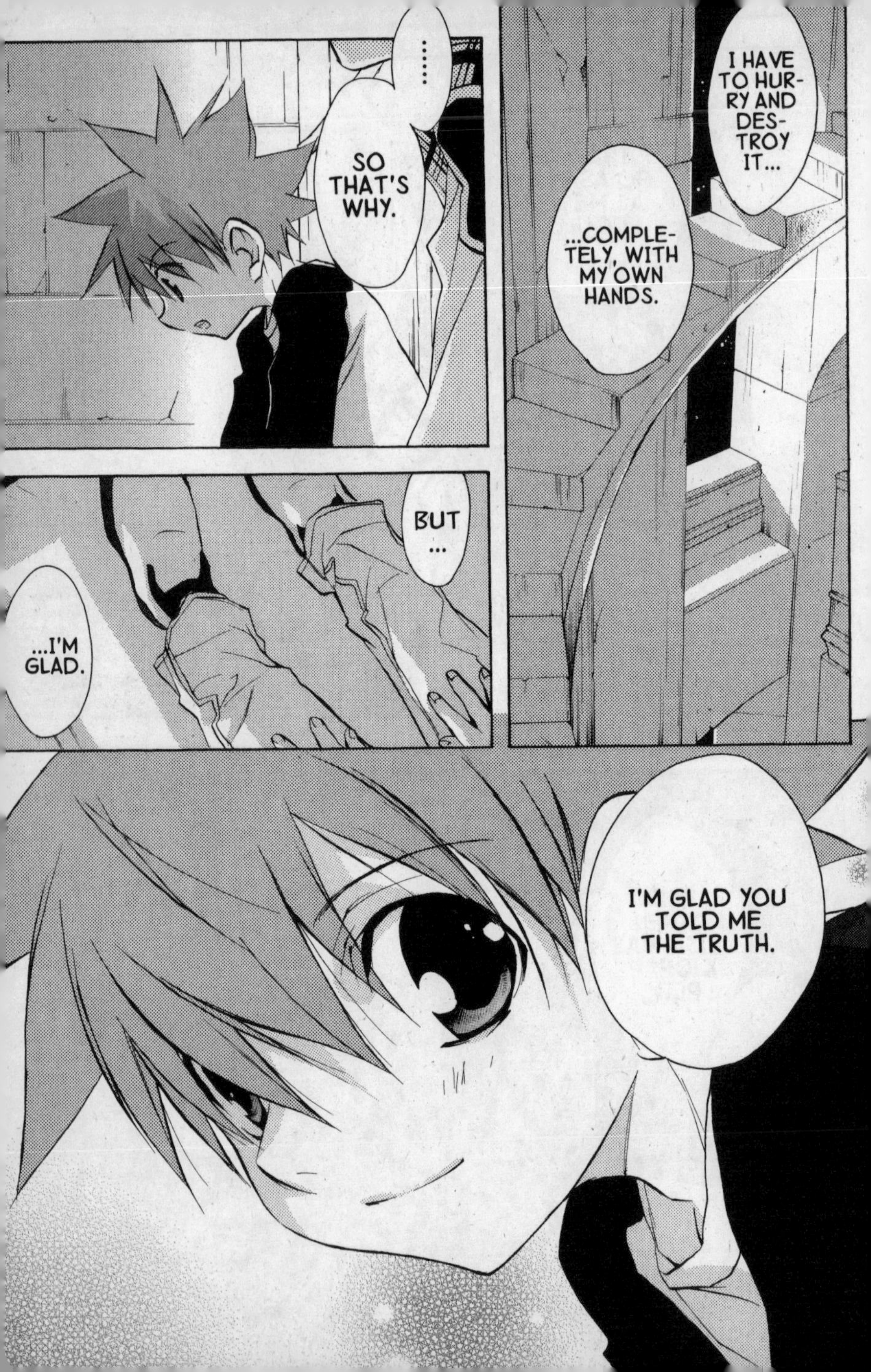
I HAVE TO HURRY AND DESTROY IT...
...COMPLETELY, WITH MY OWN HANDS.
......
SO THAT'S WHY.
BUT ...
...I'M GLAD.
I'M GLAD YOU TOLD ME THE TRUTH.

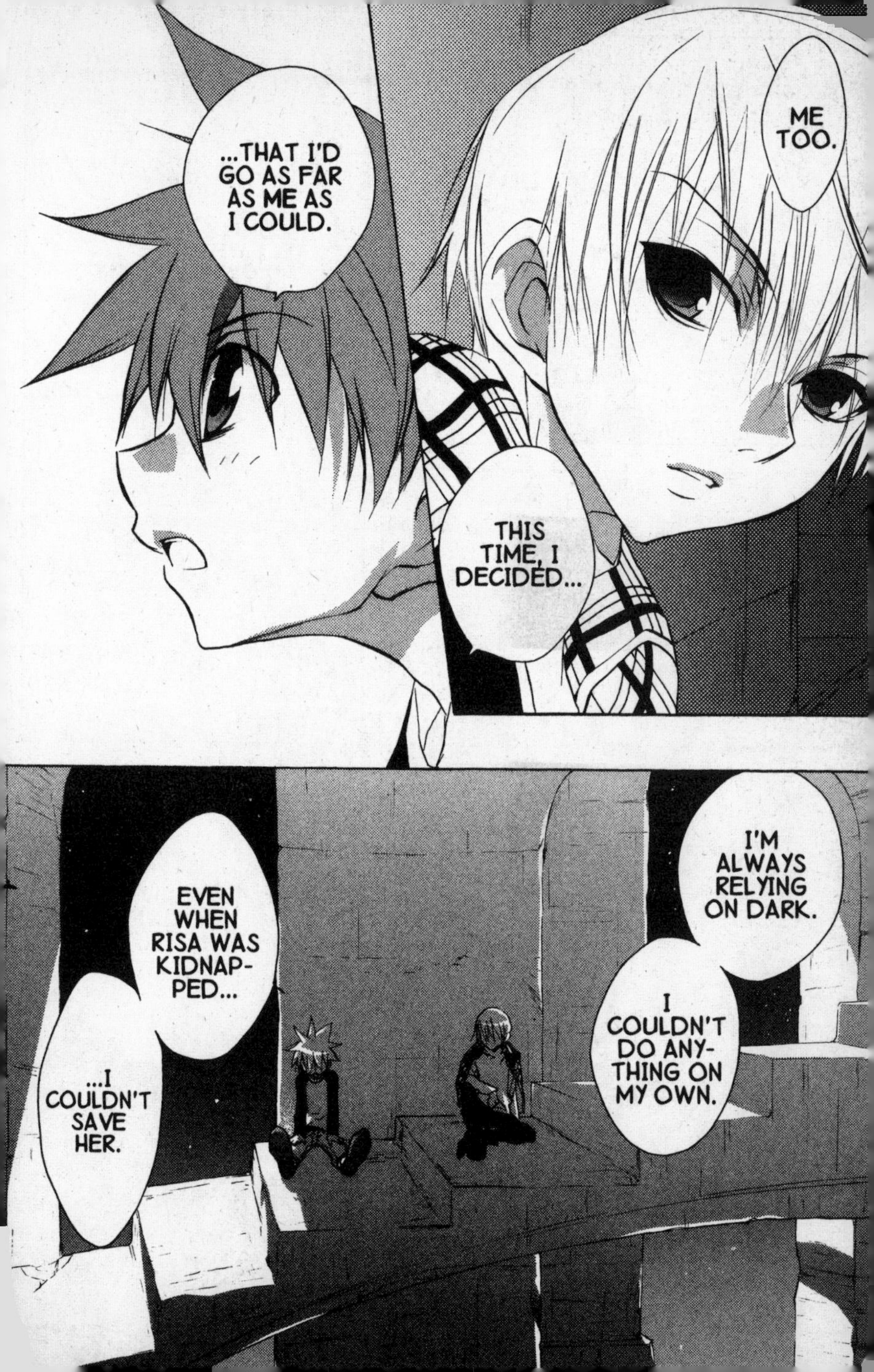
THIS TIME, I DECIDED...
...THAT I'D GO AS FAR AS ME AS I COULD.
ME TOO.
I'M ALWAYS RELYING ON DARK.
I COULDN'T DO ANY-THING ON MY OWN.
EVEN WHEN RISA WAS KIDNAP-PED...
...I COULDN'T SAVE HER.

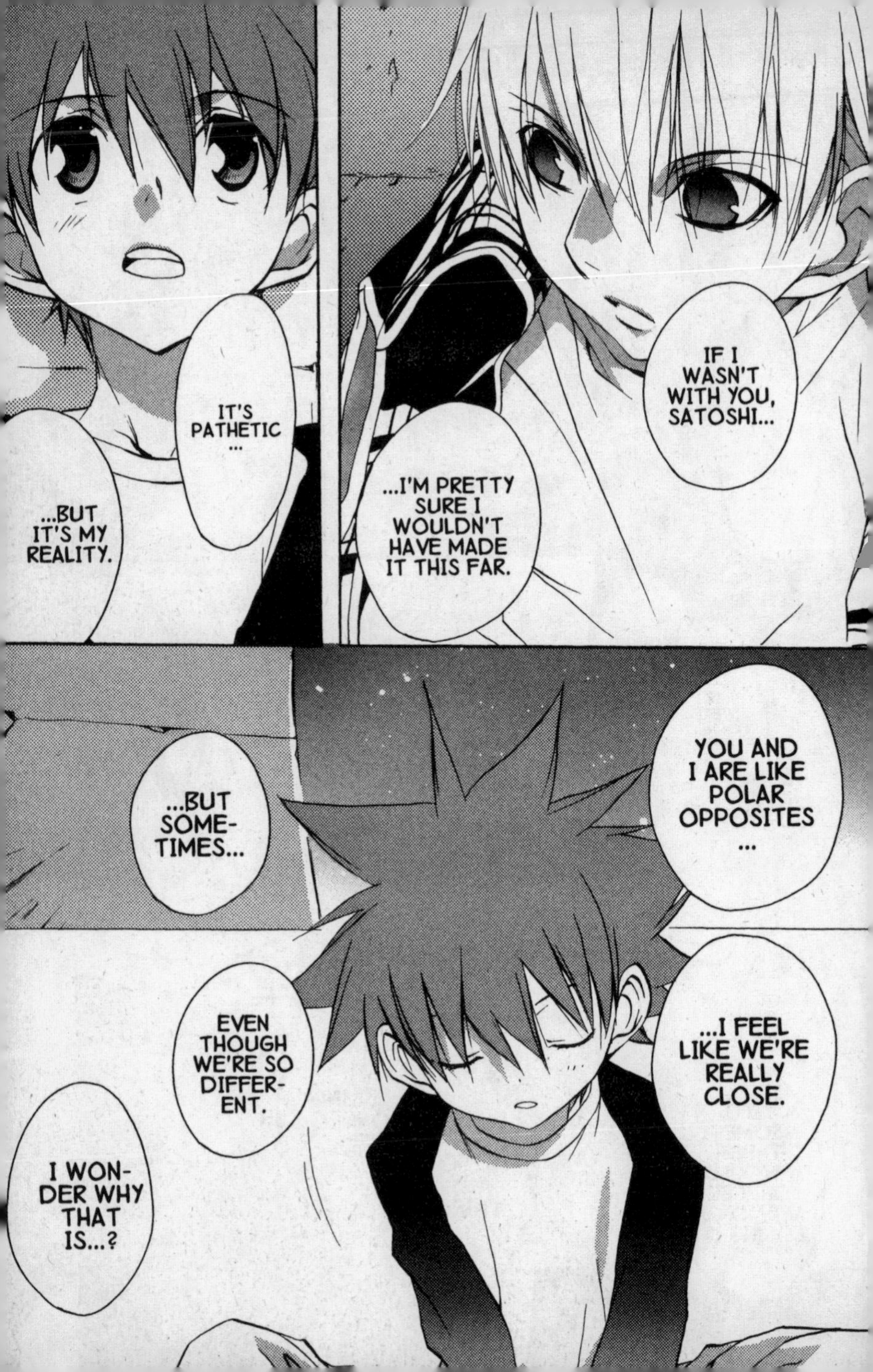
IF I WASN'T WITH YOU, SATOSHI...
...I'M PRETTY SURE I WOULDN'T HAVE MADE IT THIS FAR.
IT'S PATHETIC...
...BUT IT'S MY REALITY.
YOU AND I ARE LIKE POLAR OPPOSITES...
...BUT SOMETIMES...
...I FEEL LIKE WE'RE REALLY CLOSE.
EVEN THOUGH WE'RE SO DIFFERENT.
I WONDER WHY THAT IS...?

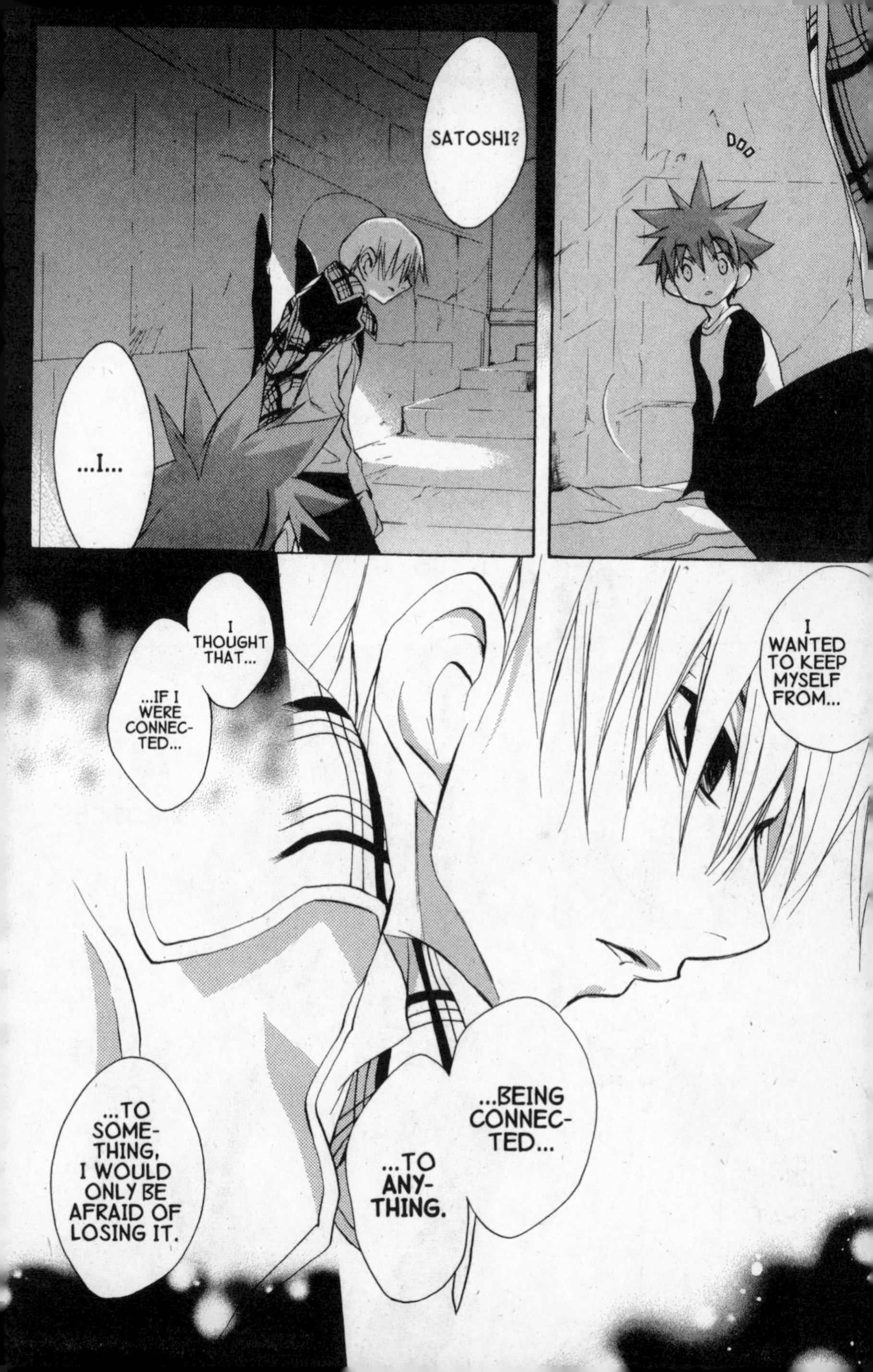
DOO
SATOSHI?
...I...
I WANTED TO KEEP MYSELF FROM...
...BEING CONNEC-TED...
...TO ANY-THING.
I THOUGHT THAT...
...IF I WERE CONNEC-TED...
...TO SOME-THING, I WOULD ONLY BE AFRAID OF LOSING IT.

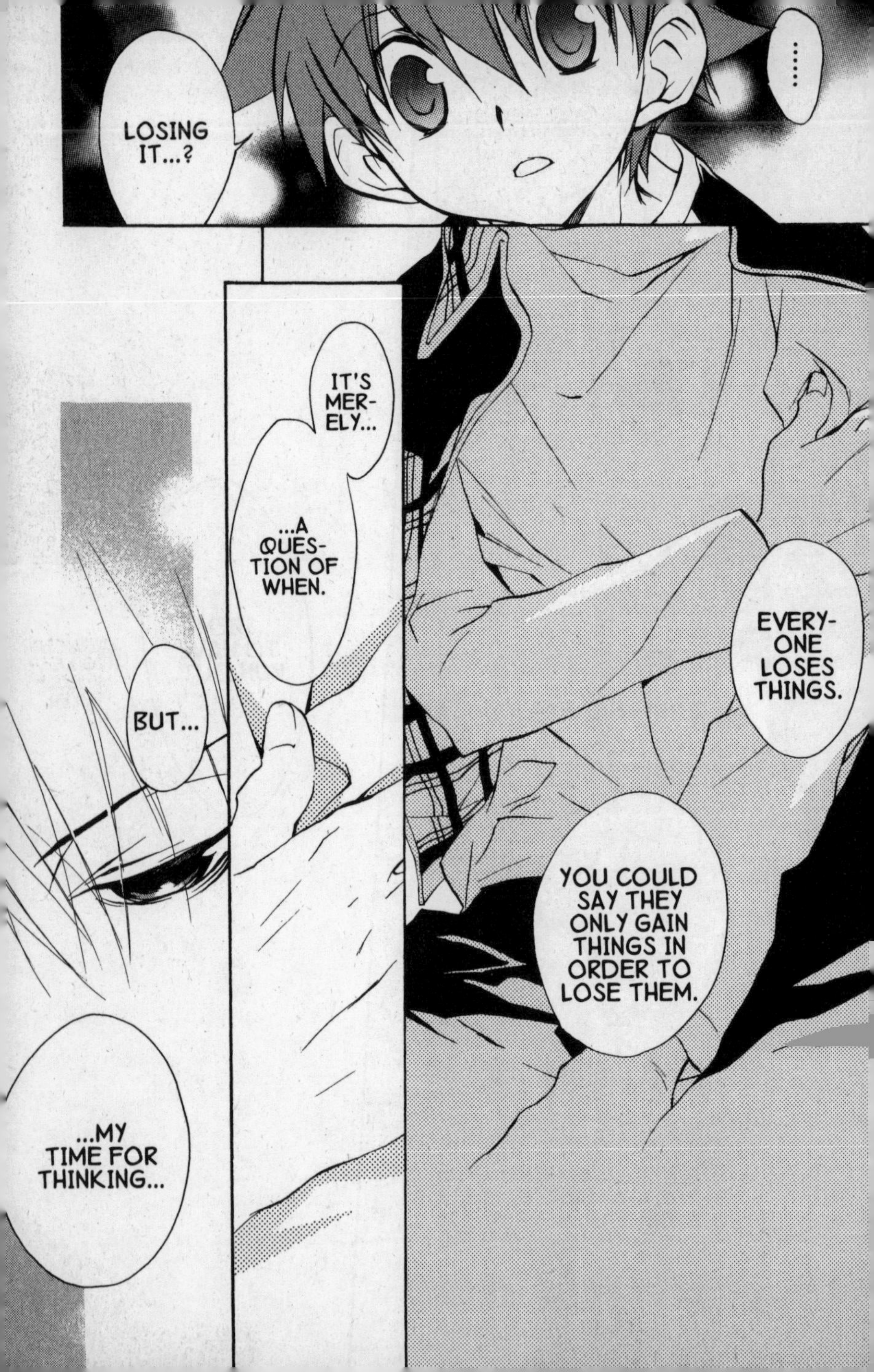
......
LOSING IT...?
EVERYONE LOSES THINGS.
YOU COULD SAY THEY ONLY GAIN THINGS IN ORDER TO LOSE THEM.
IT'S MERELY...
...A QUESTION OF WHEN.
BUT...
...MY TIME FOR THINKING...

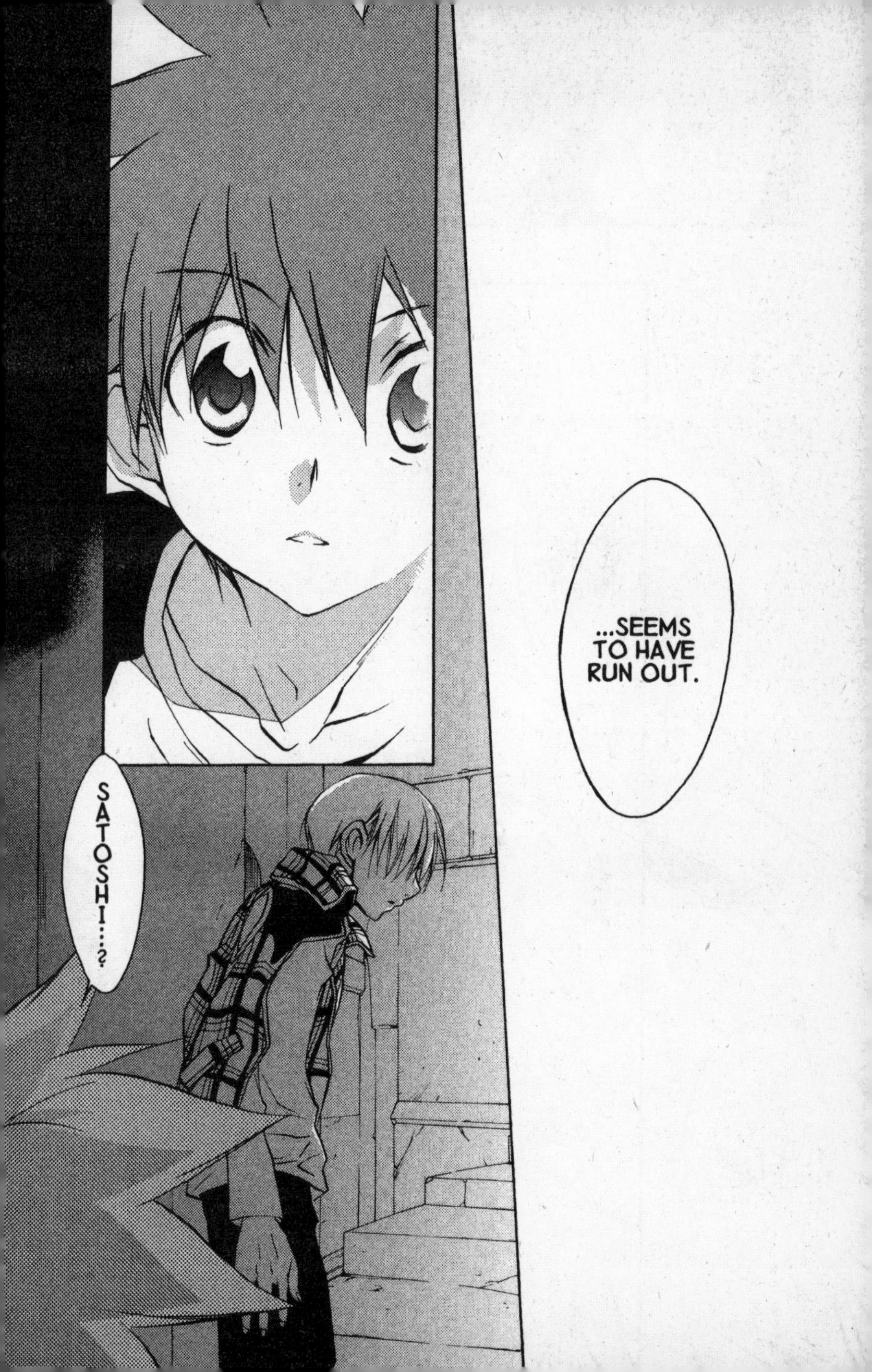
...SEEMS TO HAVE RUN OUT.
SATOSHI...?

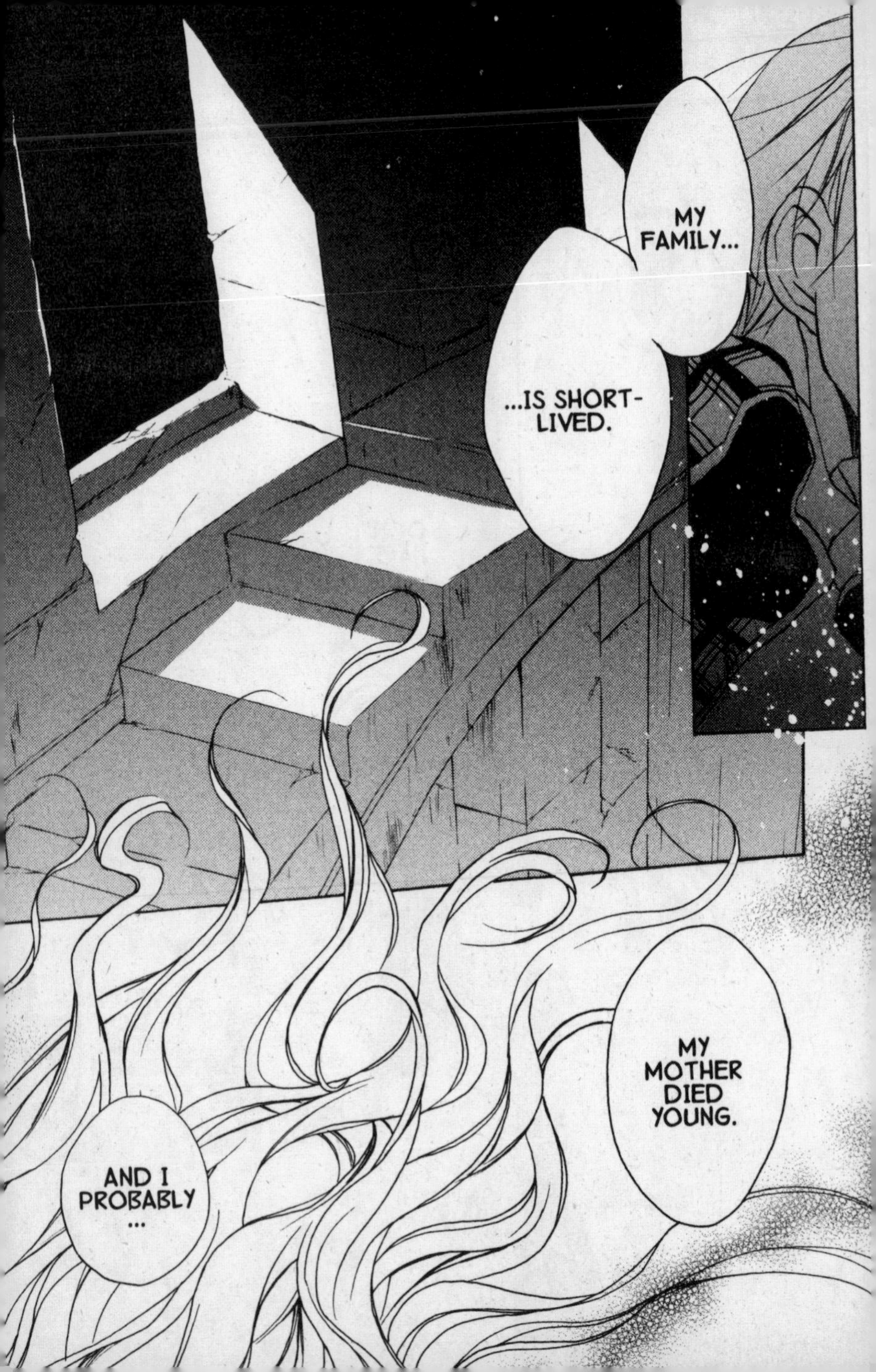
MY FAMILY...
...IS SHORT-LIVED.
MY MOTHER DIED YOUNG.
AND I PROBABLY ...

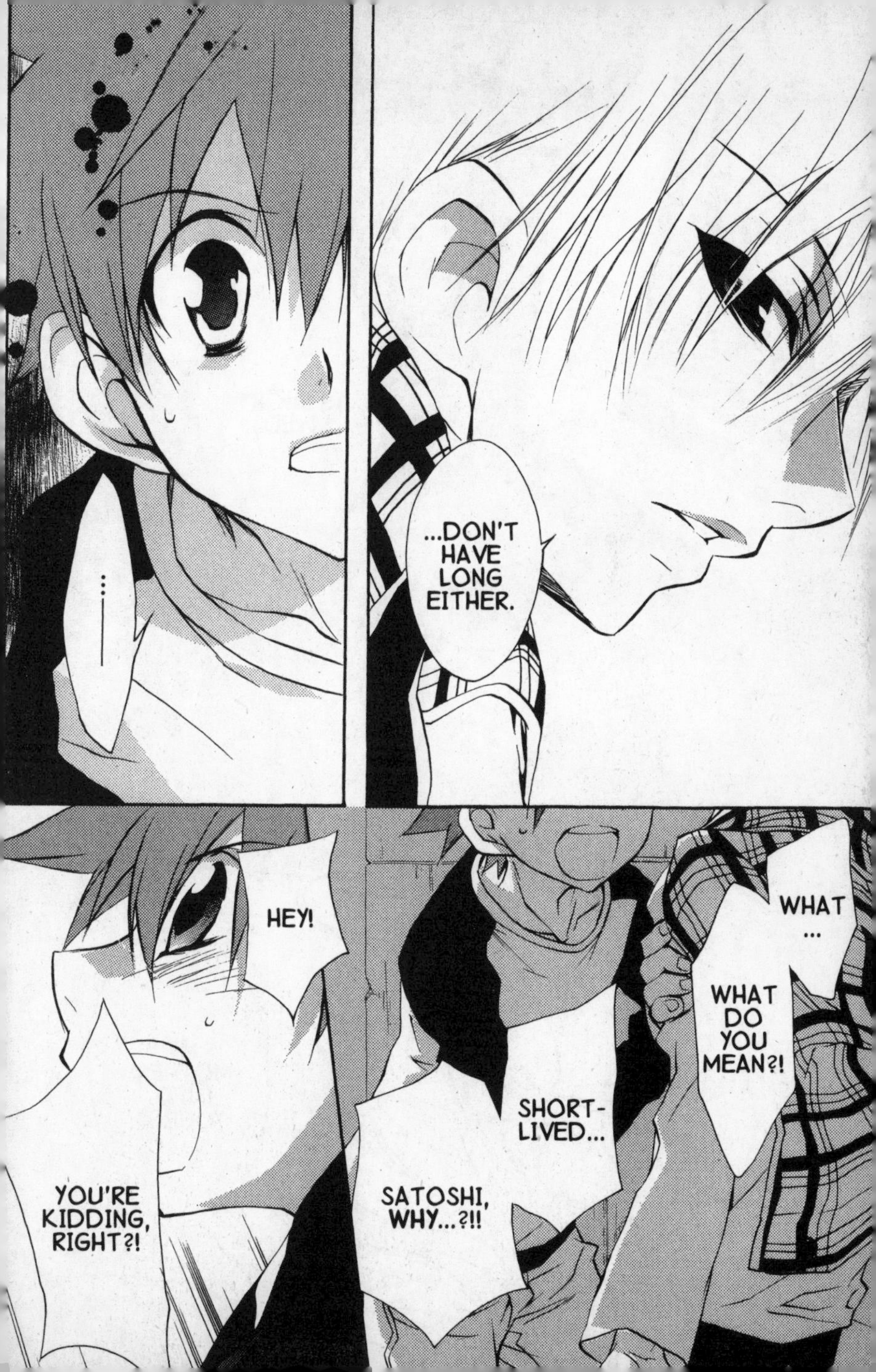
...DON'T HAVE LONG EITHER.
WHAT ...
WHAT DO YOU MEAN?!
SHORT-LIVED...
SATOSHI, WHY...?!!
HEY!
YOU'RE KIDDING, RIGHT?!

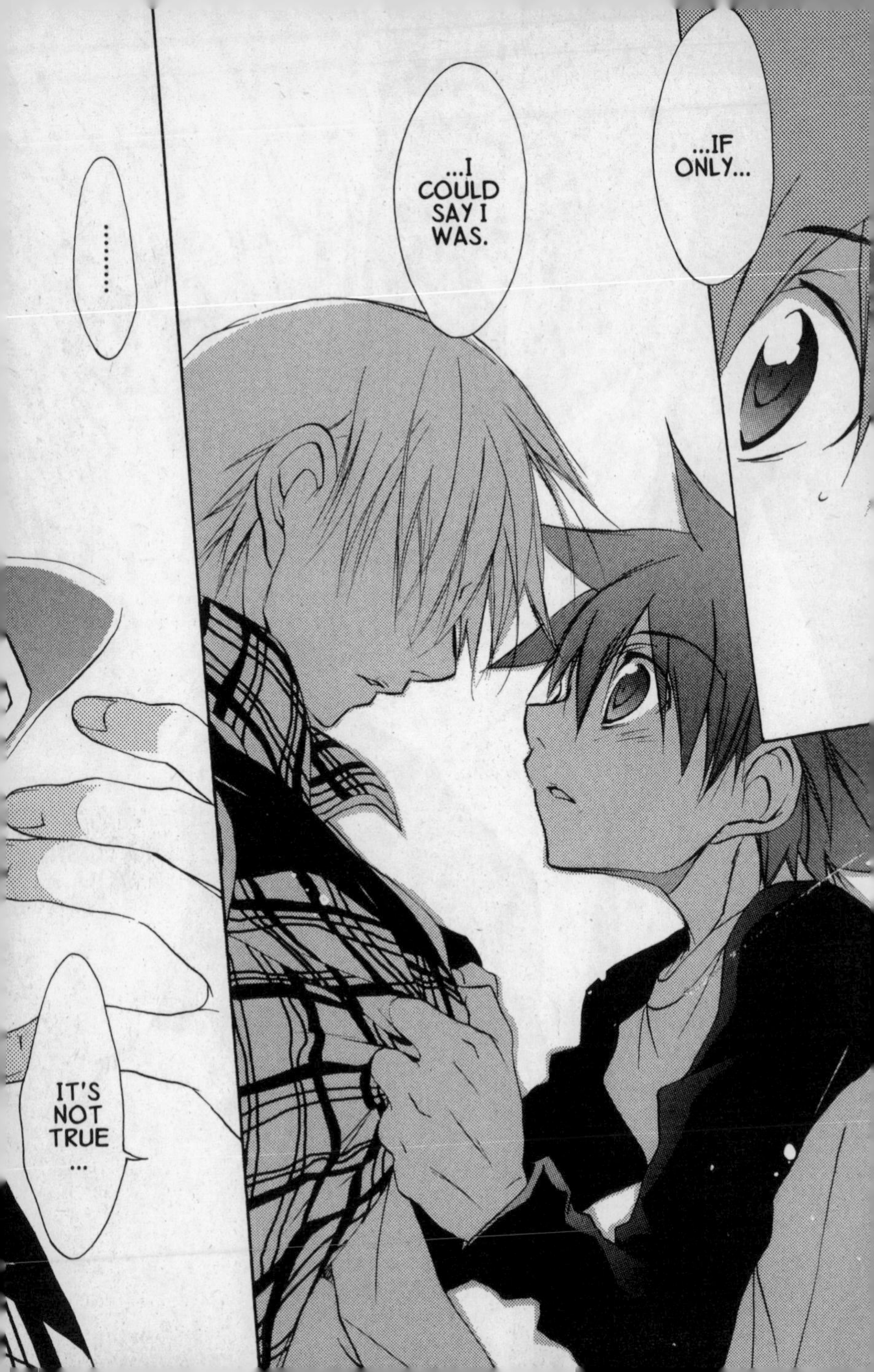
...IF ONLY...
...I COULD SAY I WAS.
......
IT'S NOT TRUE ...

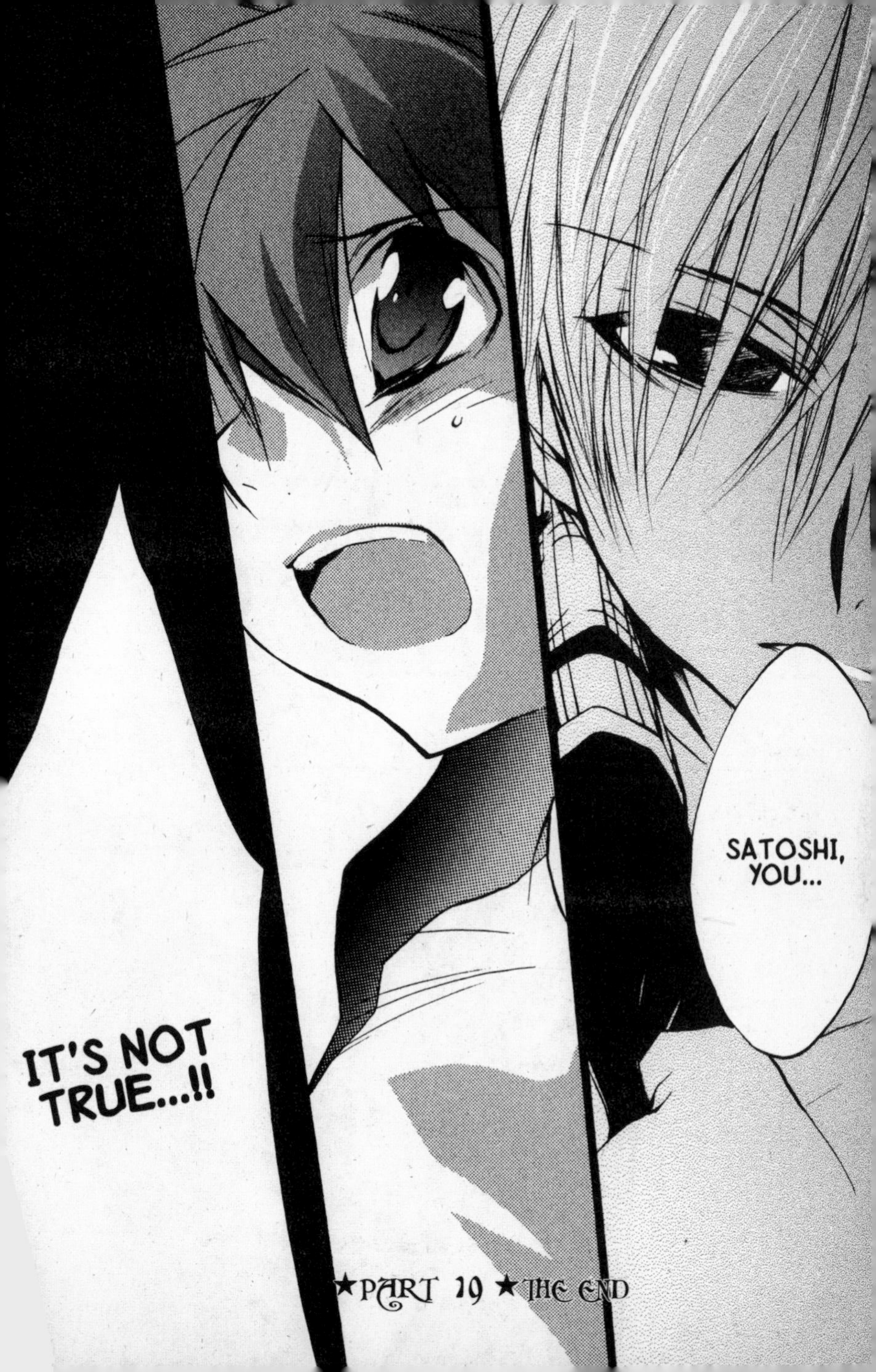
SATOSHI, YOU...
IT'S NOT TRUE...!!
★PART 19★THE END

D·N·ANGEL·
YUKIRU SUGISAKI

MAMORU SUGISAKI

A.NAKAMURA

S.SHIMOZATO

Y.HONZAWA

J.OKU

R.IZUMI

M.NAKAMURA

Y.HISHINUMA

A.KASUGA

D•N•ANGEL
THINGS TO COME...

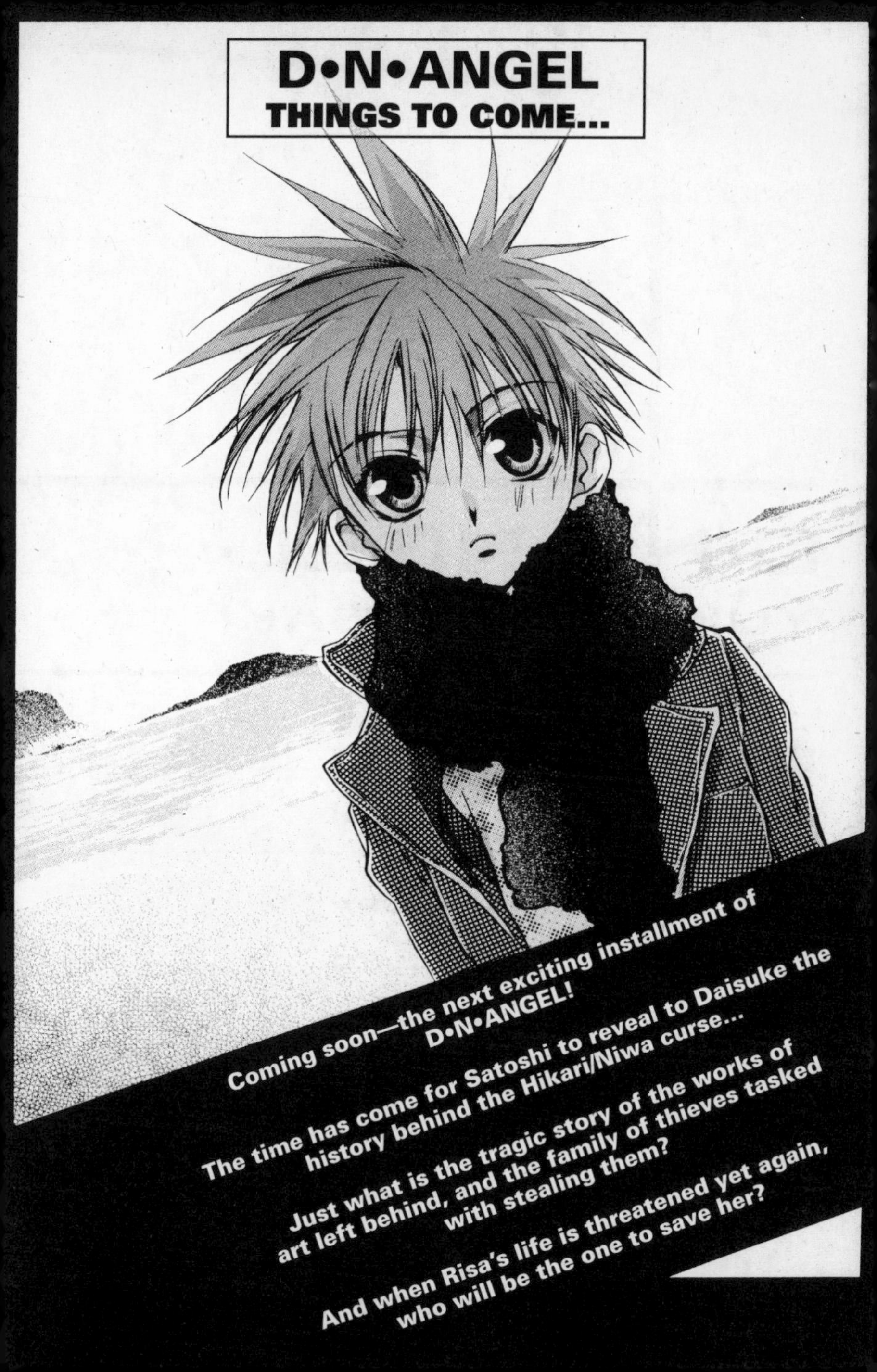

Coming soon—the next exciting installment of D•N•ANGEL!

The time has come for Satoshi to reveal to Daisuke the history behind the Hikari/Niwa curse...

Just what is the tragic story of the works of art left behind, and the family of thieves tasked with stealing them?

And when Risa's life is threatened yet again, who will be the one to save her?

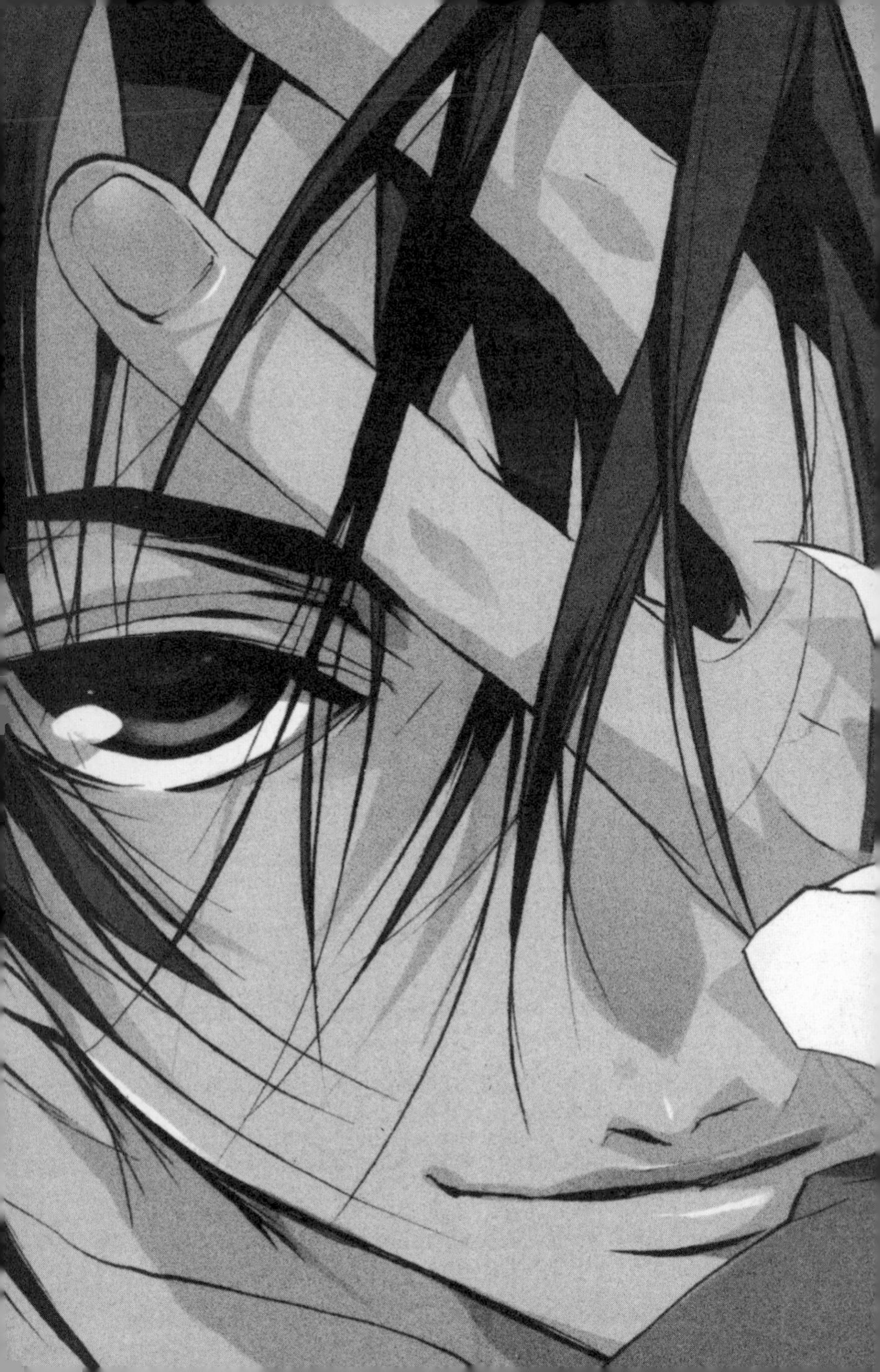

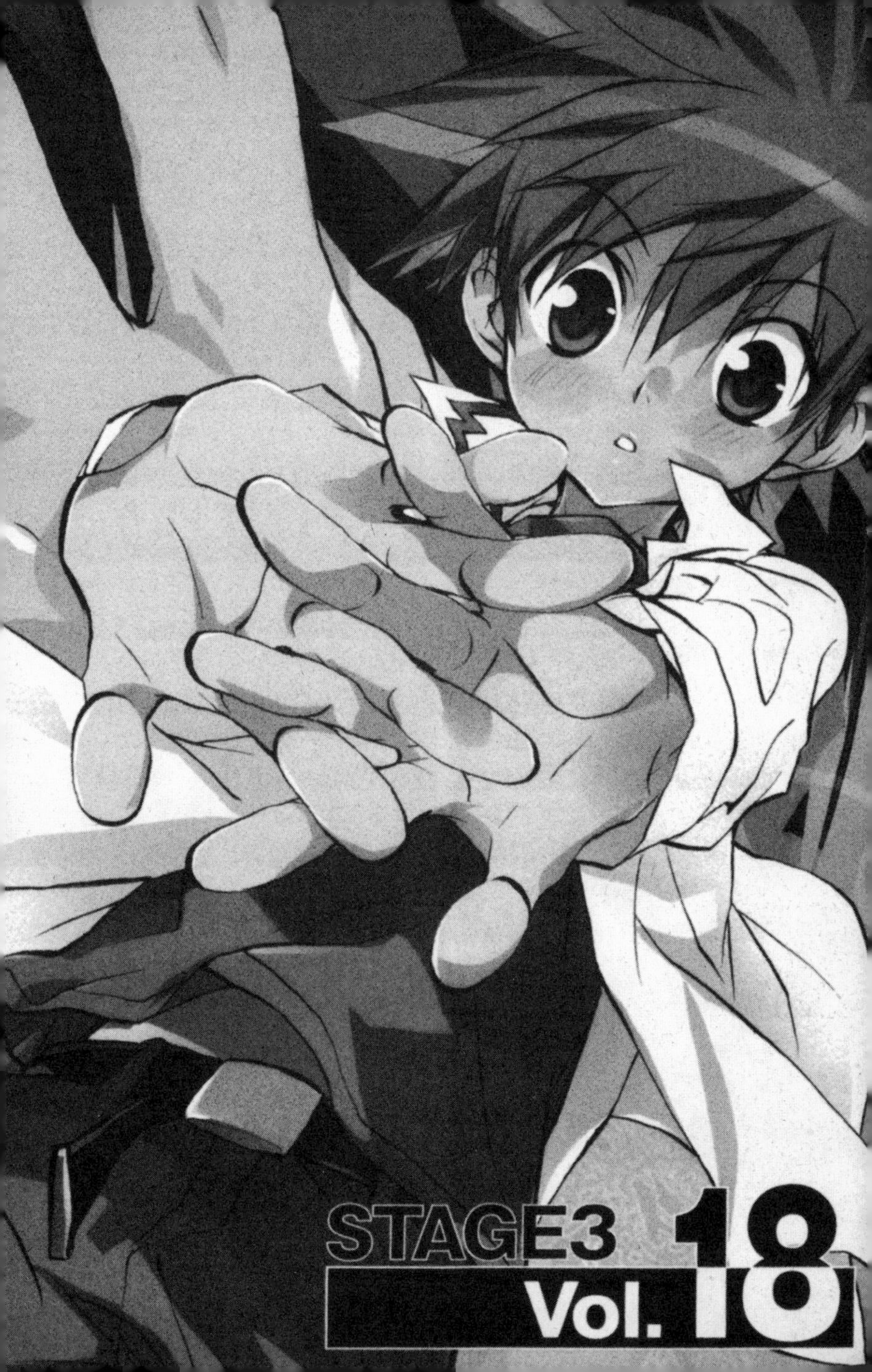
STAGE3 18
Vol. 18

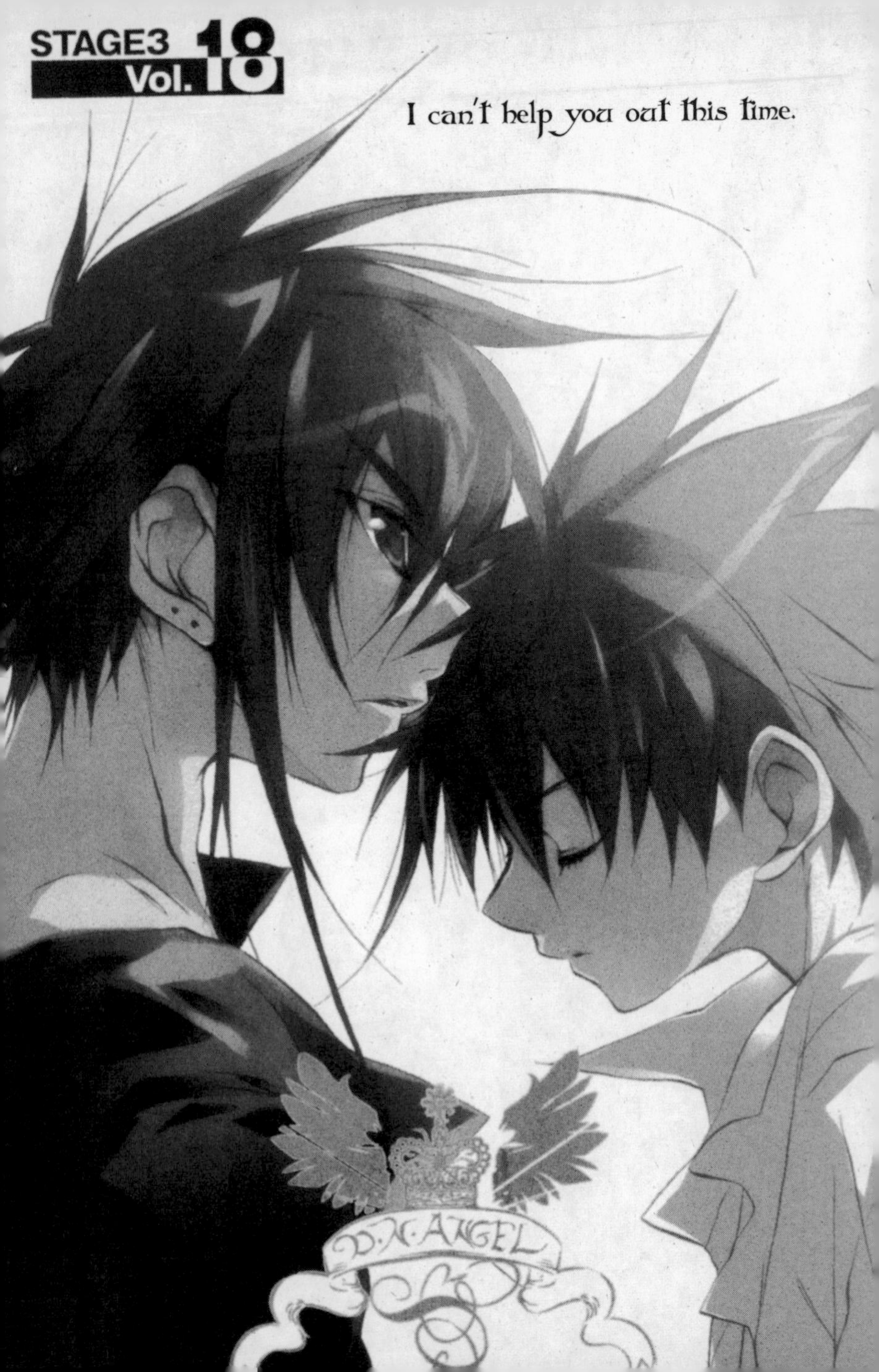
STAGE3 10
Vol. 10
I can't help you out this time.
D.N.ANGEL

CONTENTS

CHARACTERS & STORY

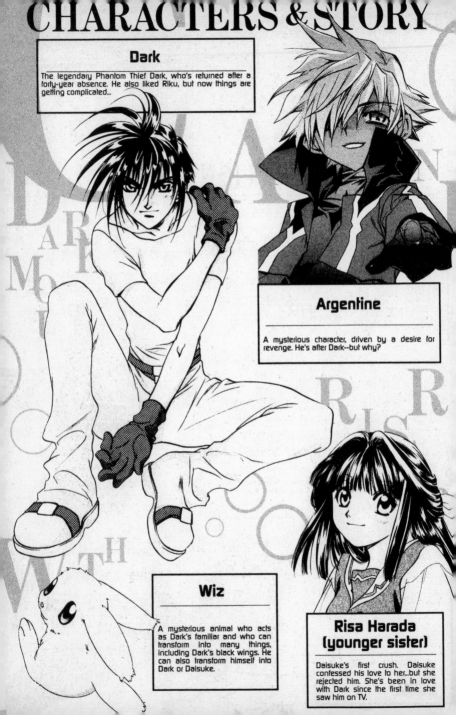

Dark

The legendary Phantom Thief Dark, who's returned after a forty-year absence. He also liked Riku, but now things are getting complicated...

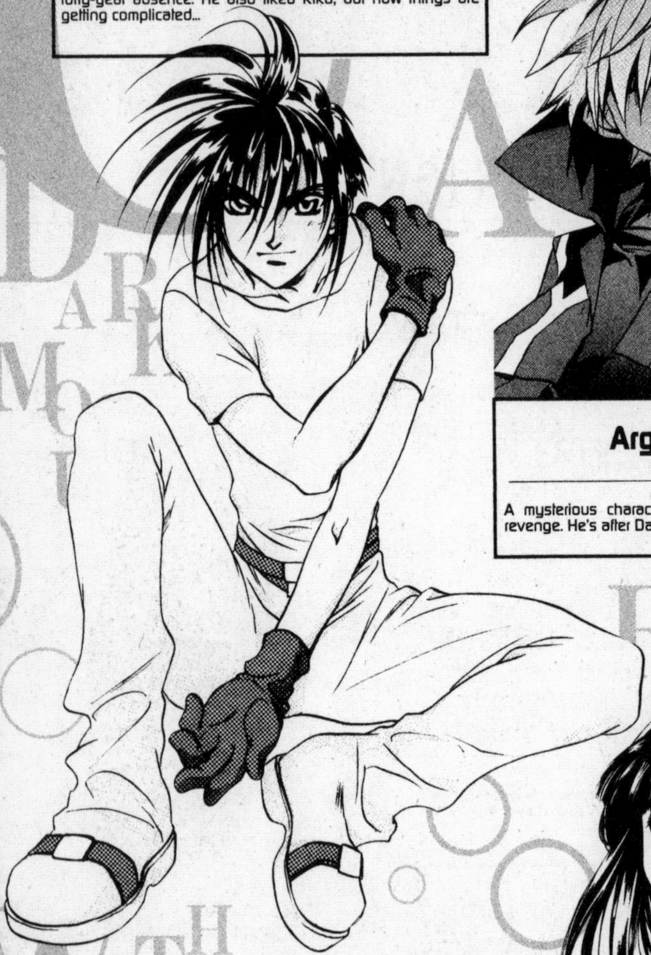

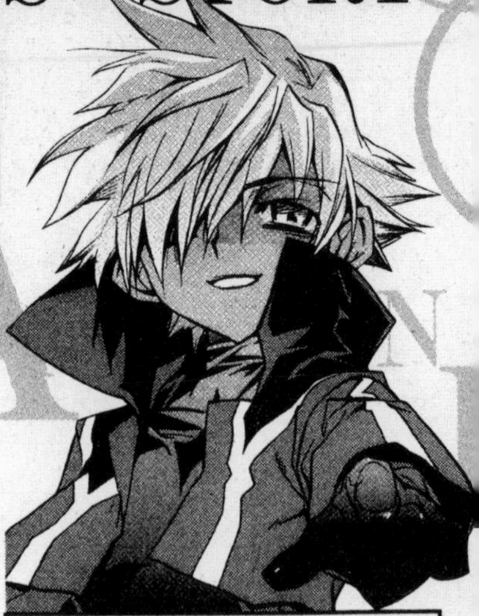

Argentine

A mysterious character, driven by a desire for revenge. He's after Dark--but why?

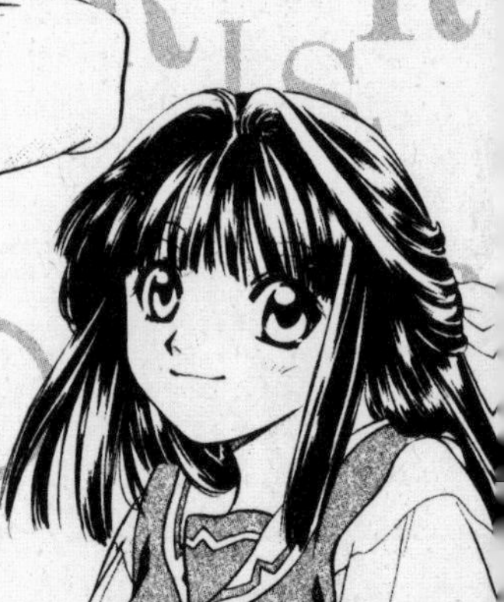

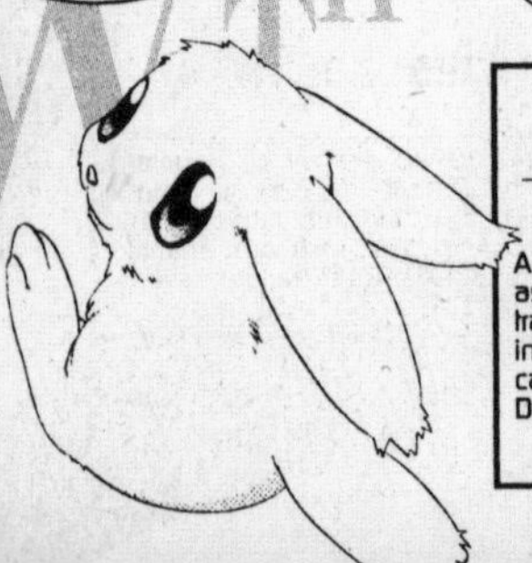

Wiz

A mysterious animal who acts as Dark's familiar and who can transform into many things, including Dark's black wings. He can also transform himself into Dark or Daisuke.

Risa Harada (younger sister)

Daisuke's first crush. Daisuke confessed his love to her...but she rejected him. She's been in love with Dark since the first time she saw him on TV.

Story so far!

Daisuke once had a crush on his classmate Risa, but he finally realized it was her twin sister, Riku, that he had feelings for. The two of them have now resolved their relationship and are happily in love. But when Daisuke and Dark are on a double date with Risa and Riku at an amusement park, Risa is kidnapped by Argentine! Daisuke feels responsible for Risa being placed in danger and falls into a depression...and then Satoshi Hiwatari offers a helping hand.

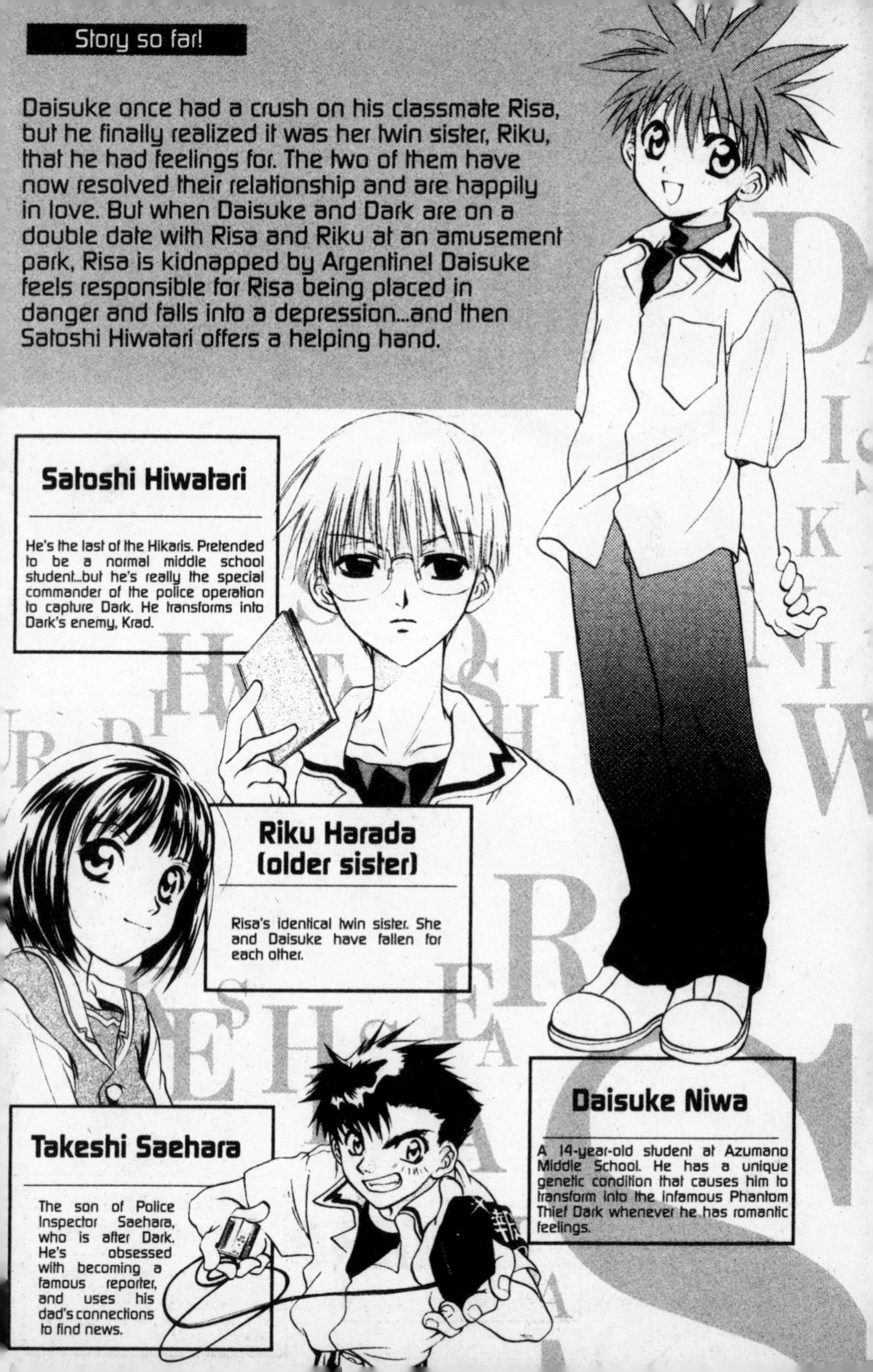

Satoshi Hiwatari

He's the last of the Hikaris. Pretended to be a normal middle school student...but he's really the special commander of the police operation to capture Dark. He transforms into Dark's enemy, Krad.

Riku Harada (older sister)

Risa's identical twin sister. She and Daisuke have fallen for each other.

Daisuke Niwa

A 14-year-old student at Azumano Middle School. He has a unique genetic condition that causes him to transform into the infamous Phantom Thief Dark whenever he has romantic feelings.

Takeshi Saehara

The son of Police Inspector Saehara, who is after Dark. He's obsessed with becoming a famous reporter, and uses his dad's connections to find news.

Volume 12

By

Yukiru Sugisaki

HAMBURG // LONDON // LOS ANGELES // TOKYO

Goldsworthy and Mort Blast Off

Written by Marcia Vaughan
Illustrated by Linda Hendry

W9-BNT-379

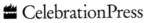
CelebrationPress

An Imprint of ScottForesman
A Division of HarperCollinsPublishers

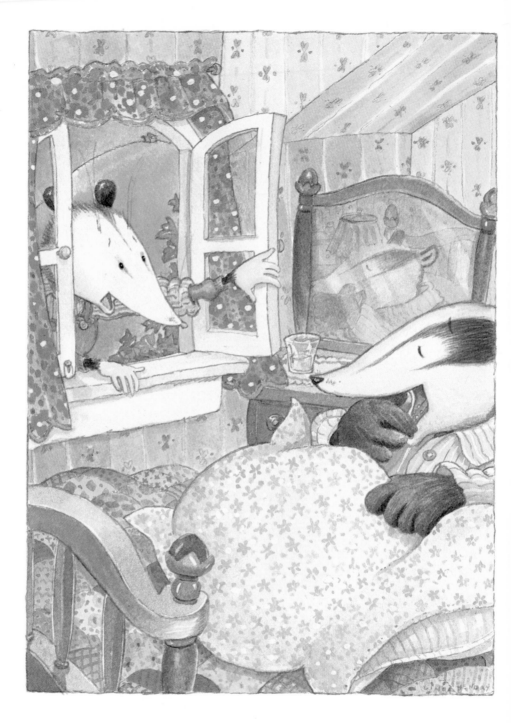

Mort rushed up the path to Goldsworthy's house. He poked his head through the bedroom window and shouted, "Goldsworthy, wake up. Wake up, quick!"

Goldsworthy pulled the pillow off his face. "What's going on, Mort?" he blinked. "I was having my beauty sleep. Come back later," he yawned.

"It might be gone," Mort panted.

"What might be gone?" said Goldsworthy.

"The big brown Thingamajig at the top of Hazelnut Hill," said Mort.

"Great galloping gumballs. I've never seen a big brown Thingamajig," Goldsworthy said.

Goldsworthy leaped out of bed. He jumped into his jacket and jeans. He slipped on his sneakers and dashed out the door.

"Follow me, good buddy," Mort cried.

They raced into the woods, over the bridge, through the gravel pit, around the swamp, and all the way to the top of Hazelnut Hill.

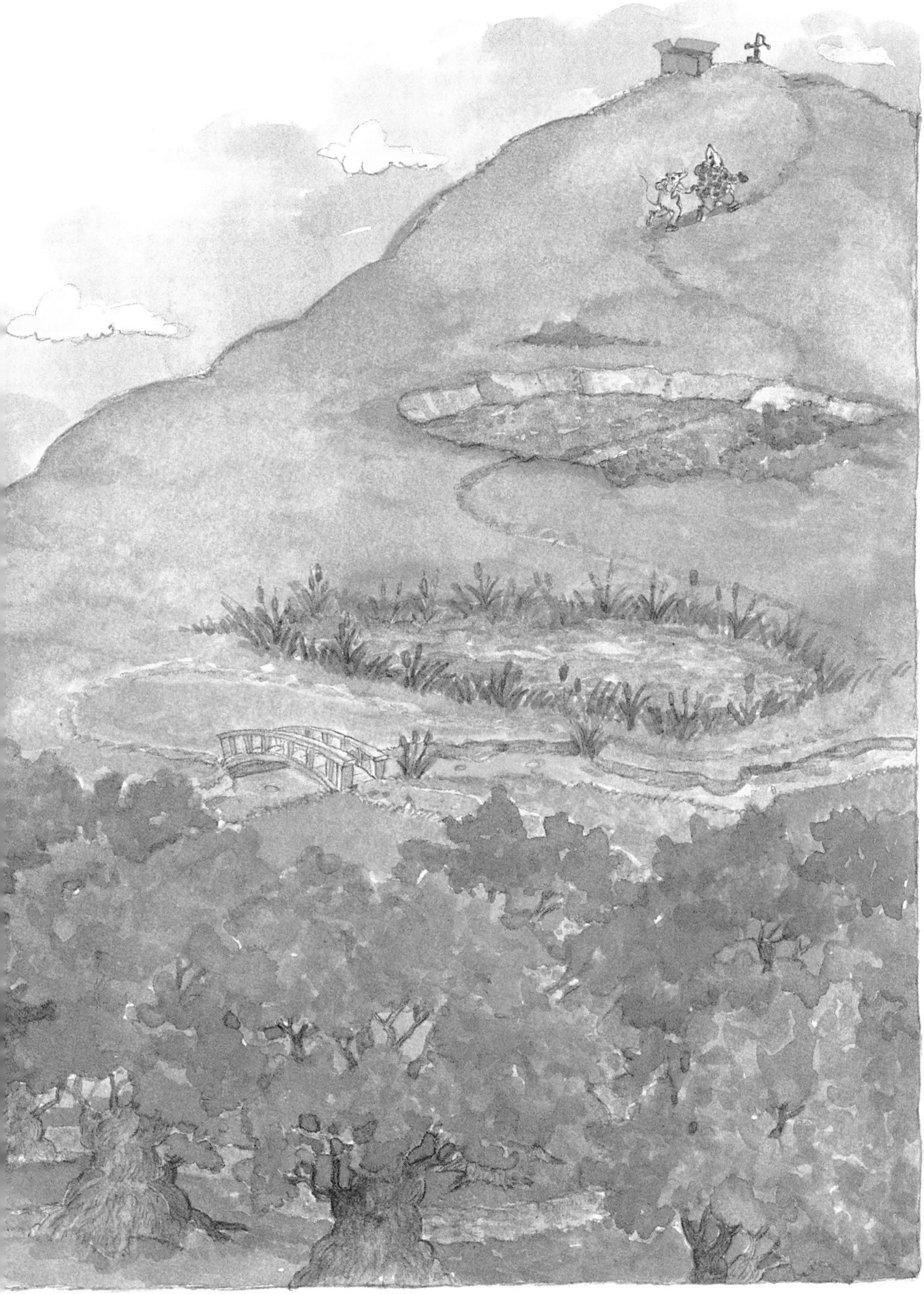

"There it is," pointed Mort, "a real Thingamajig!"

Goldsworthy walked all around the big brown Thingamajig. "Sorry, Mort, but this is no Thingamajig."

Mort scratched his head. "Are you sure?"

"Yes," Goldsworthy began. "This is a Gizmo. A real, honest-to-goodness, space-soaring, go-go Gizmo!"

"Wow!" Mort shouted. He ran his paw over the smooth, brown surface.

"Be careful, Mort," Goldsworthy warned. "It might blast off at any moment."

"Blast off?" said Mort, pulling back his paw. "You mean out into space?"

"All the way to Planet X. All the way to Planet Zlammo," Goldsworthy said.

Mort stared at the space-soaring, go-go Gizmo.
"Goldsworthy, do you think it would be all right if
we sat in it?"

"Of course we can sit in it," Goldsworthy said.
"We're very brave after all."

Goldsworthy and Mort popped on their helmets
and climbed aboard the Gizmo.

"Let's pretend to be astronauts," Mort said.

"Let's pretend we're taking a trip to Planet X,"
Goldsworthy added.

"Countdown! Five," said Goldsworthy.

"Four," said Mort.

"Three," said Goldsworthy.

"Two," said Mort.

"One," said Goldsworthy.

"Blast off!" they yelled as loudly as they could.

With a rumble and tumble, Goldsworthy and Mort felt the Gizmo take off.

"Aghhh!" cried Goldsworthy.

"Aghhh!" cried Mort, as they went racing into outer space.

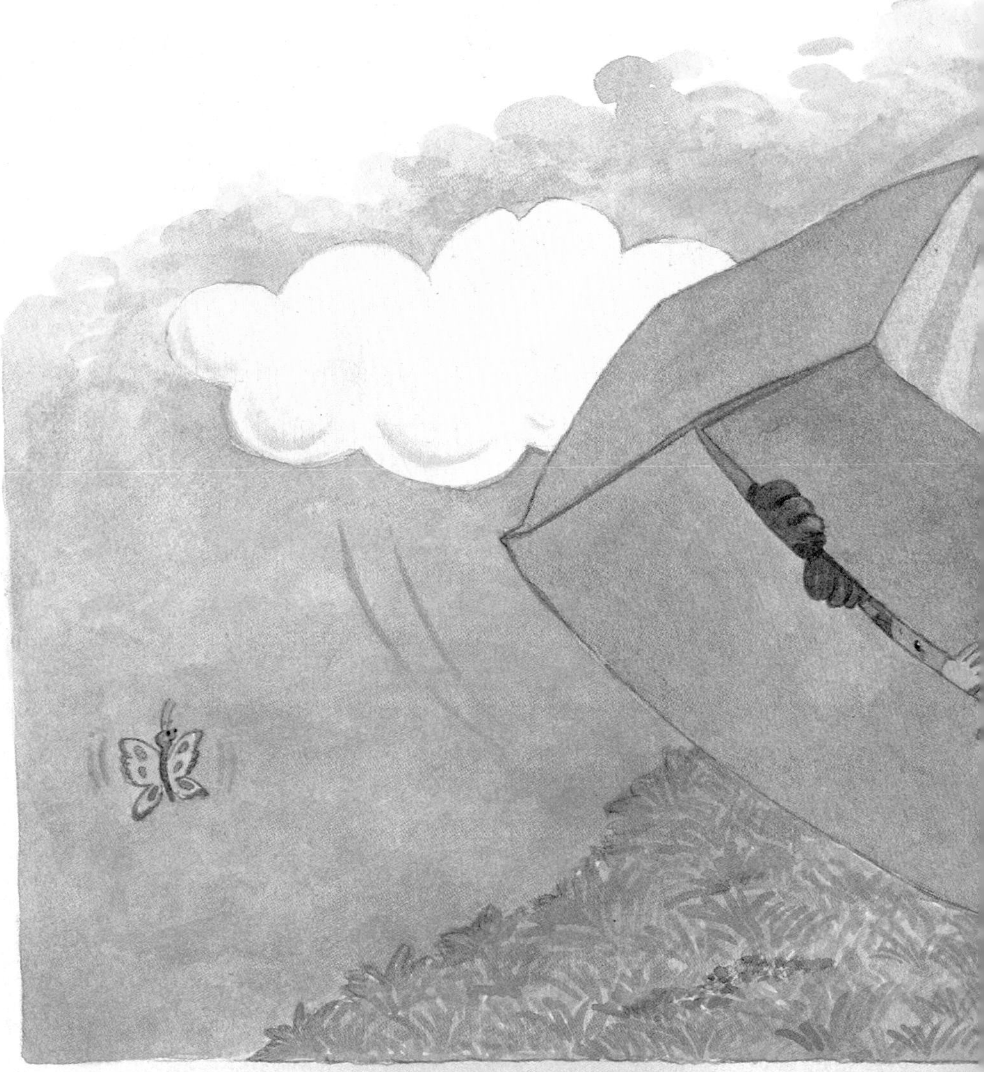

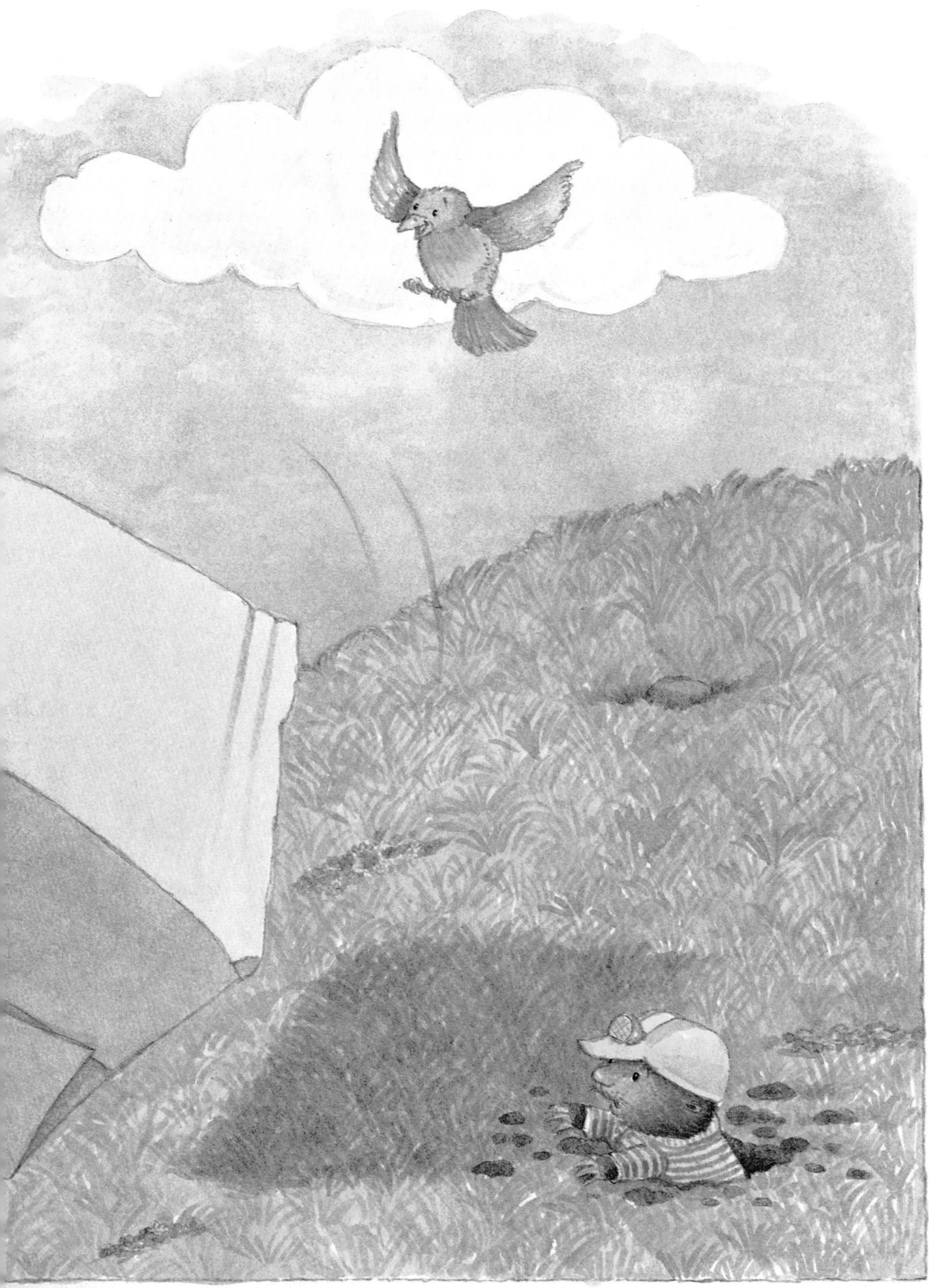

In no time they landed. Goldsworthy and Mort crawled out of the Gizmo.

"Where are we?" whispered Mort.

"On Planet X, millions of miles from Earth," Goldsworthy answered.

"This planet is spooky," said Mort.

"Ooh whooo," called a voice from the shadows.

"That sounded like a space creature. A hungry space creature," gasped Goldsworthy.

"What do you think hungry space creatures like to eat on Planet X?" said Mort. "Rocks? Dust? Dirt?"

Goldsworthy frowned. "Or big brave astronauts, like us?"

"Let's get out of here," cried Mort.

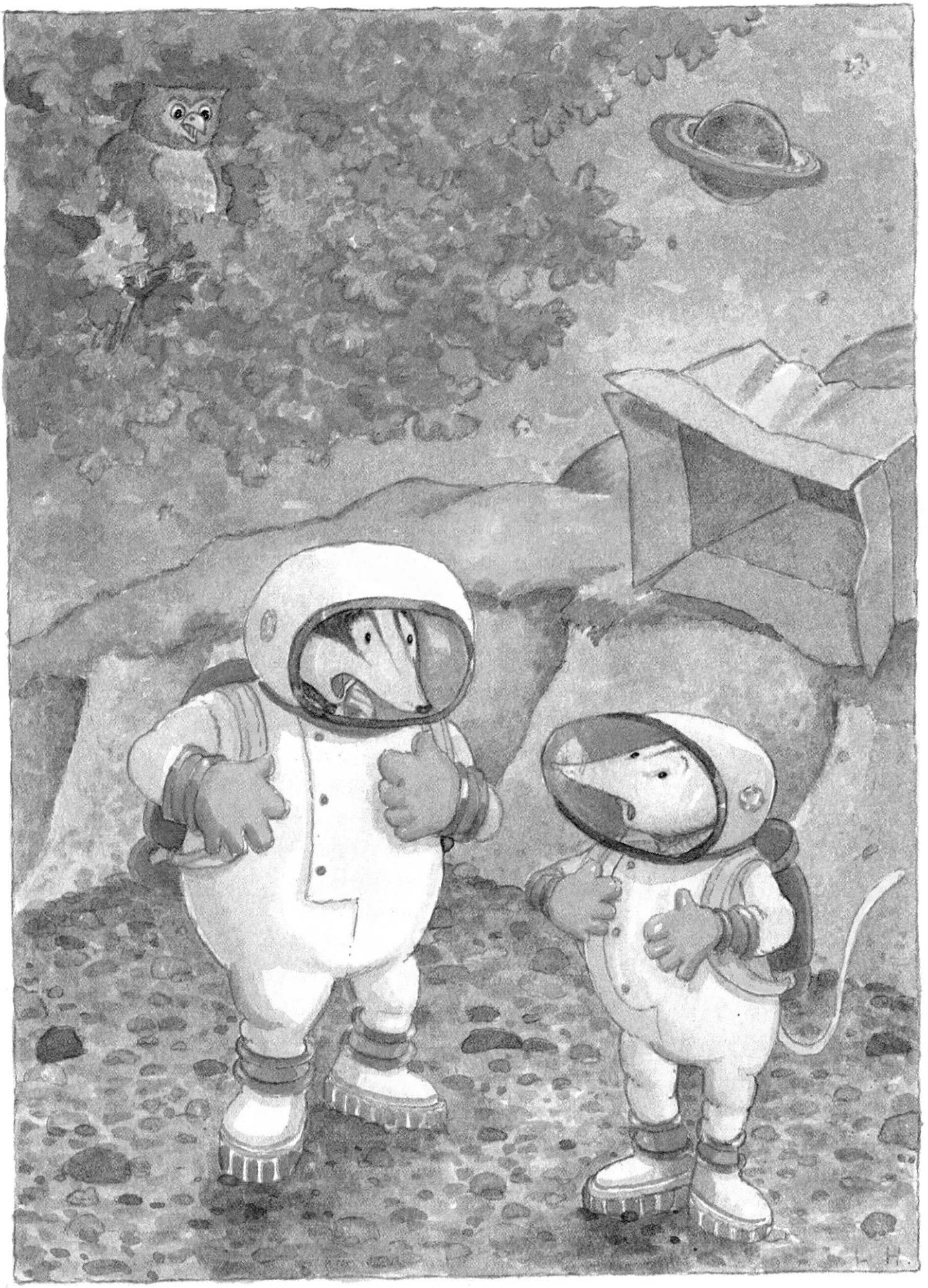

"Five," said Goldsworthy.

"Four," said Mort.

"Three," said Goldsworthy.

"Two," said Mort.

"One," said Goldsworthy.

"Blast off!" they yelled as loudly as they could.

With a shake and a quake, Goldsworthy and Mort felt the Gizmo go racing through space.

A shower of meteors spattered the spaceship as it sped along.

"Aghhh!" cried Goldsworthy.

"Aghhh!" cried Mort.

In no time they landed. Goldsworthy and Mort poked their heads out of the Gizmo.

"Where are we?" asked Mort.

"We're on Planet Zlammo," Goldsworthy said.

"This is a mooshy planet," said Mort.

"This is a gooshy planet," added Goldsworthy.

"Katydid. Katydid," called a voice from the shadows.

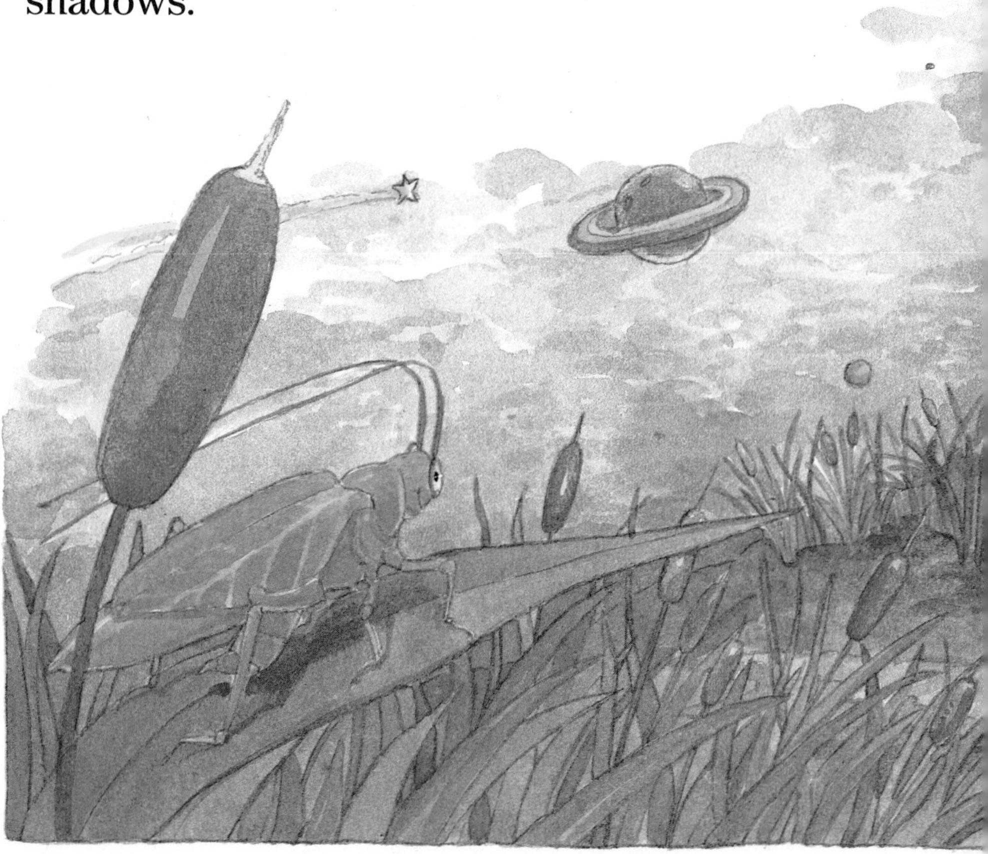

"That sounded like a space creature. A hungry space creature," gasped Goldsworthy.

"What do you think hungry space creatures eat on Planet Zlammo?" asked Mort. "Mushy mud? Gooshy goo? Sloppy slime?"

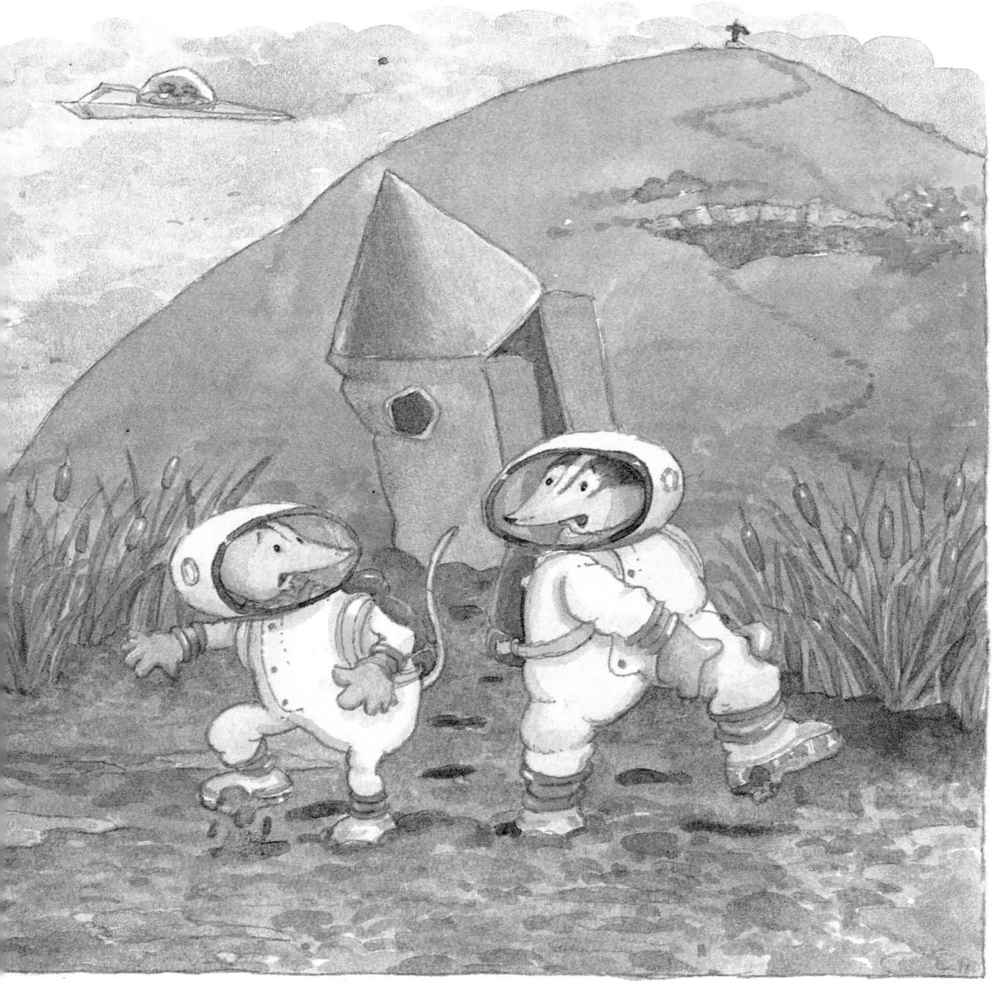

Goldsworthy frowned. “Or big brave astronauts like us?”

“I don’t want to stay and find out,” cried Mort. “I want to go home.”

“Me, too,” said Goldsworthy.

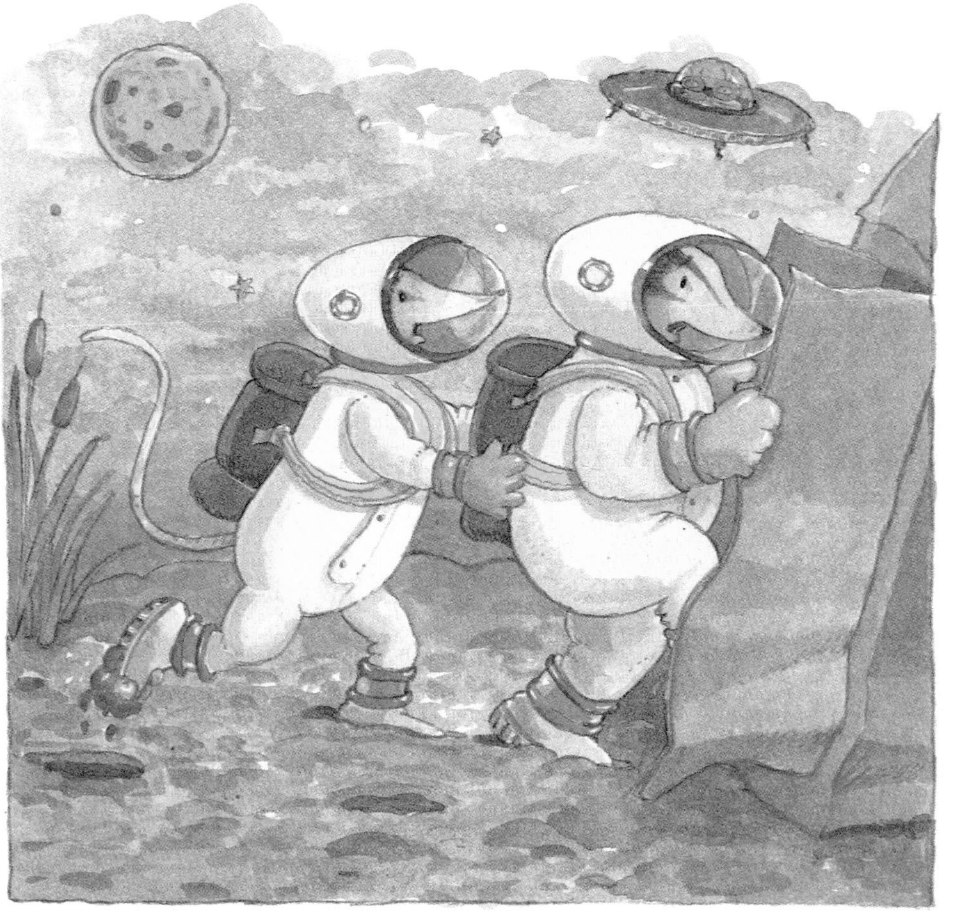

"Five," said Goldsworthy.

"Four," said Mort.

"Three," said Goldsworthy.

"Two," said Mort.

"One," said Goldsworthy.

"Blast off!" they yelled as loudly as they could.

With a thump and a bump, Goldsworthy and Mort felt the Gizmo go racing through space. In no time they landed. Goldsworthy poked his head out of the Gizmo and looked around.

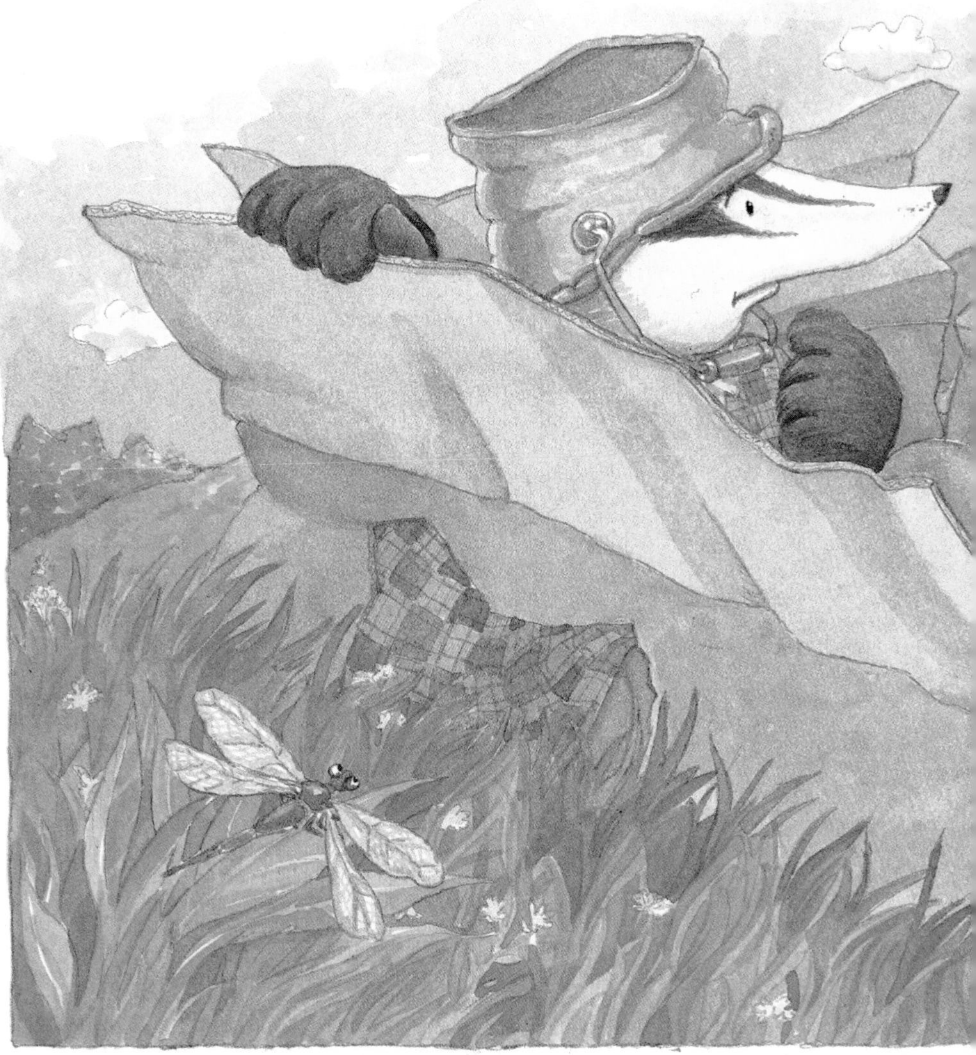

"Where are we?" whimpered Mort, with his eyes shut tight.

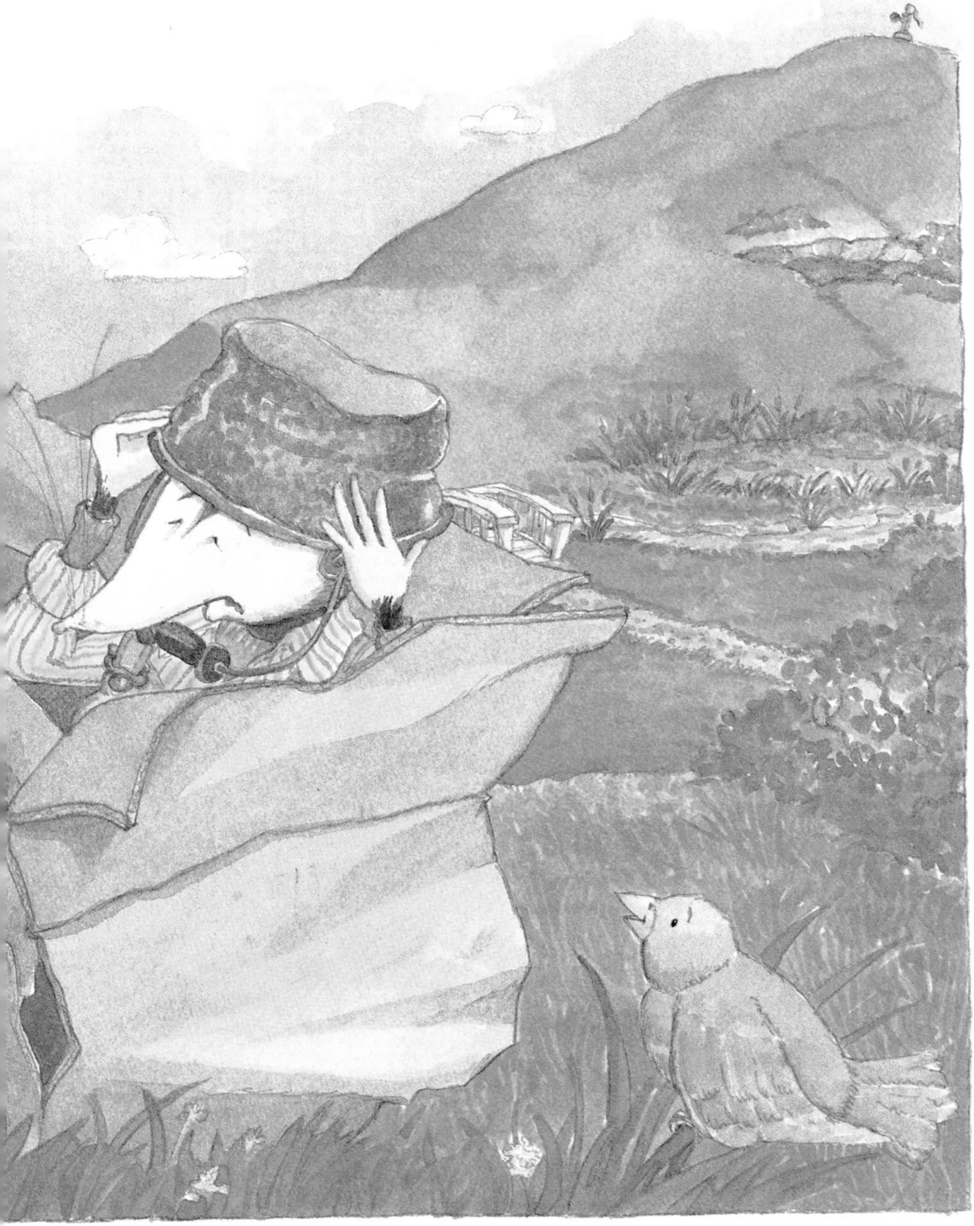

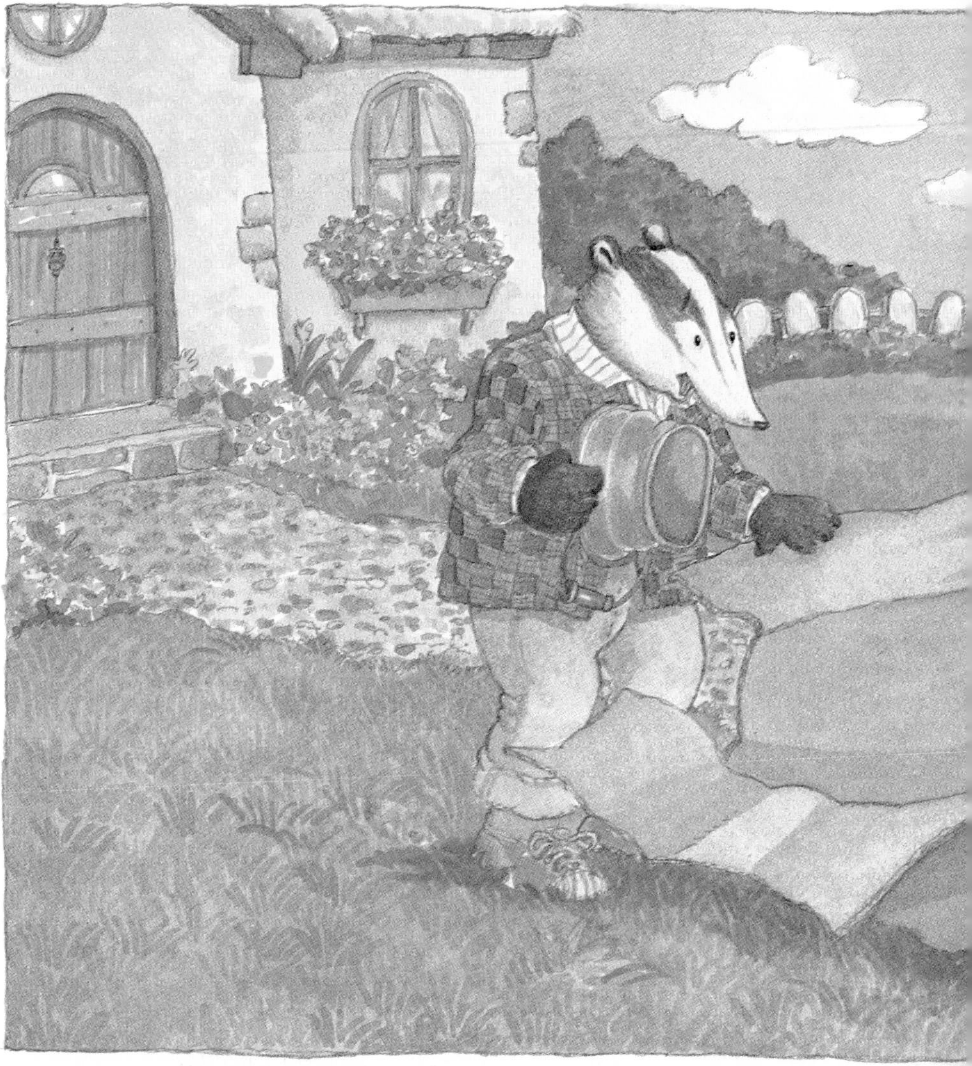

Goldsworthy grinned. “We’re home.”

Mort opened one eye. He opened the other eye. “Oh, Goldsworthy,” he cheered, “we’ve landed right at the bottom of Hazelnut Hill. Hurrah!”

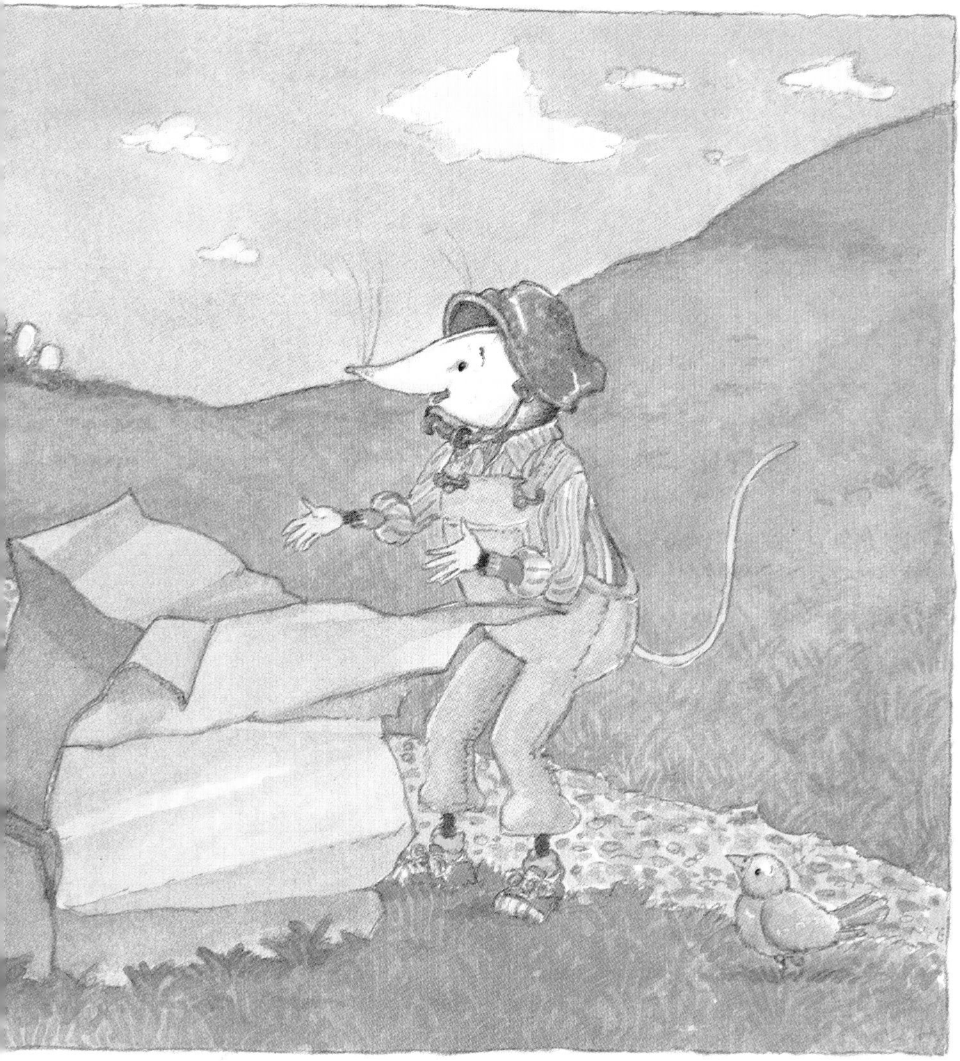

“What shall we do with our space-soaring, go-go Gizmo?” Goldsworthy wondered. “It will never fly again.”

“I know just the thing,” Mort answered.

And the two friends spent all afternoon painting a big brown sign that said:

HOME SWEET HOME.

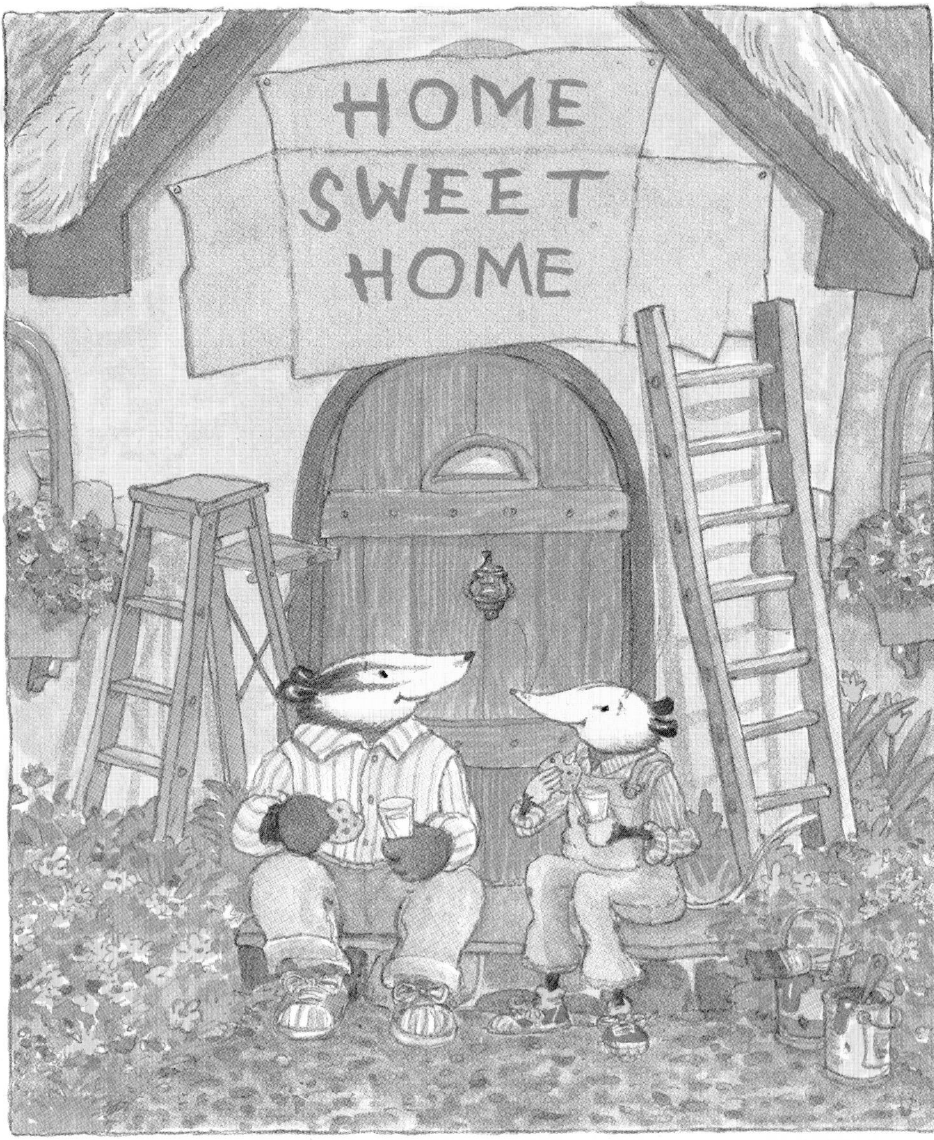
HOME
SWEET
HOME